Scenic Design
on
BROADWAY

Recent Titles in
Bibliographies and Indexes in the Performing Arts

Memorable Film Characters: An Index to Roles and Performers, 1915-1983
Susan Lieberman and Frances Cable, compilers

Stage Lives: A Bibliography and Index to Theatrical Biographies in English
George B. Bryan, compiler

The Federal Theatre Project: A Catalog-Calendar of Productions
The Staff of the Fenwick Library, George Mason University, compilers

Victorian Plays: A Record of Significant Productions on the London Stage,
1837-1901
Donald Mullin, compiler

Costume Design on Broadway: Designers and Their Credits, 1915-1985
Bobbi Owen

Eighteenth Century British and Irish Promptbooks: A Descriptive
Bibliography
Edward A. Langhans

The German Stage: A Directory of Playwrights and Plays
Veronica C. Richel, compiler

Stage Deaths: A Bibliographical Guide to International Theatrical Obituaries,
1850 to 1990
George B. Bryan, compiler

The Stratford Festival Story: A Catalogue-Index to the Stratford, Ontario,
Festival, 1953-1990
J. Alan B. Somerset

Scenic Design
on
BROADWAY

Designers and Their Credits, 1915-1990

Bobbi Owen

Bibliographies and Indexes in the Performing Arts, Number 10

Greenwood Press
New York • Westport, Connecticut • London

Library of Congress Cataloging-in-Publication Data

Owen, Bobbi.
    Scenic design on Broadway : designers and their credits, 1915-1990
/ Bobbi Owen.
        p.   cm.—(Bibliographies and indexes in the performing arts,
    ISSN 0742-6933 ; no. 10)
    Includes bibliographical references and index.
    ISBN 0-313-26534-8 (alk. paper)
    1. Set designers—New York (N.Y.)—Biography—Dictionaries.
I. Title.   II. Series.
PN2096.A1094   1991
792'.025'09227471—dc20   91-25254
    [B]

British Library Cataloguing in Publication Data is available.

Library of Congress Catalog Card Number: 91-25254
ISBN: 0-313-26534-8
ISSN: 0742-6933

First published in 1991

Greenwood Press, 88 Post Road West, Westport, CT 06881
An imprint of Greenwood Publishing Group, Inc.

Printed in the United States of America

The paper used in this book complies with the
Permanent Paper Standard issued by the National
Information Standards Organization (Z39.48-1984).

10 9 8 7 6 5 4 3 2 1

Contents

Illustrations

Illustrations appear following page 210.

Preface

I recently listened to Desmond Heeley give a pep talk to a group of undergraduate students who were working very long hours for very little immediate reward. The distinguished scenic designer recounted going to see a play at the request of a friend who had designed the set. Upon seeing the friend later, he was asked for criticism of the set and realized that he had not noticed it – not consciously noticed it, that is. He had become so involved in the performance that he had not separated the set, designed by a friend and the reason he went to see the play in the first place, from the entire performance.

I have become increasingly interested in the people who design and work in an art that is essentially collaborative. As was true in writing *Costume Design on Broadway* prior to its publication in 1987, my greatest pleasure in compiling this book has been meeting designers and having the opportunity to talk with them and see their creative work and environments. I have been especially delighted to track down designers who no longer live in New York City or who are no longer actively designing and have left only a faint trail to their current location. Every designer I reached was generous with his or her time and willingly supplied missing biographical information. I have not attempted to catalog the history of design in this book, but rather to provide information about designers, those with names we recognize and those who are not remembered but who have nonetheless made a contribution to the current trends and innovations in design.

My success in tracking down elusive information and individuals has been due in great part to the resourcefulness of my research assistant, Lynn Roundtree. Lynn and I have spent the better part of the last two years working closely together, and I quickly realized that I was fortunate to have found an assistant who had extensive experience with biographical research and in reference collections. The extent of his abilities has been amazing. The completeness and accuracy of the biographies are due to his diligence. I am also grateful to Becket Royce, who worked with me also on *Costume Design on Broadway*. She has since relocated to New York City from Chapel Hill, North Carolina and has again been helpful. Cindy Stewart joined me in New York for several weeks of painstaking searches through playbills for designers' names and she provided both good moral support during a seemingly endless task and excellent help. In Chapel Hill, I was assisted by Sheketha Hauser, Aaron Carlos, Joel Reider and Shelle Wheless, all of whom photocopied, filed and collated information for my easy access. Also in Chapel Hill, the Academic Affairs Library at the University of North Carolina, especially the Humanities Reference staff, was supportive and patient. Ann Parker and Tom Morris both assisted me, providing computer access and assistance.

The Billy Rose Theatre Collection of the New York Public Library at Lincoln Center was a valuable resource, and the pages, Louis Paul, Evelyn Lyman, Scherece Williams and Adeline Maxineau were especially helpful. I would not have been able to use the library collection without the support provided by Judy and David Adamson, who assure me I have not worn out my welcome in their home.

Ann Oldham, my secretary, not only helped me meet my other obligations in Chapel Hill and stay on schedule, but also tirelessly entered data. I received support from many individuals and places, including the scholarly publications committee of the College of Arts and Sciences, which provided financial support for illustrations, and The Institute for the Arts and Humanities, where I was a fellow in Summer 1990 and where my attention was focused on completing the task at hand. I am especially grateful to my husband (and expert computer resource), Gordon Ferguson.

Numerous designers with whom I spoke acknowledged individuals who had been mentors or special influences, often helping when careers were starting or stalling. These individuals are often teachers, family members, or colleagues who allow us to learn, grow, and make mistakes without penalty. And so, to all those mentors, and to my own mentor and friend, Tom Haas – who helped me understand that theatrical design was more than technique and history – I dedicate this book.

Introduction

"We must have a wall in the great chamber."
A Midsummer Night's Dream

Theatrical design is an applied art. Unlike painting or sculpture, it is not practiced as an end in itself but rather as part of a process. Therefore, design represents only a small portion of the product. It is an art form that borrows heavily from many and varied sources as it seeks to evoke an image, provide a frame for the world of the play, and reveal just the right amount of information (but not tell too much). Many plays that move from one location to another must be redesigned in part or altogether as the context in which the audience sees the work changes.

The general public that attends the performances, the director, and even the playwright may not always be acutely aware of the contribution of the designers. Audience members certainly appreciate spectacle even if they are not consciously aware of its function. Certainly designers have egos and like their work to be noticed and favorably reviewed, but the best designs and the best designers contribute their individual work to that of the whole – team work of the best possible kind.

Theatrical design has yet another aspect because it is created within a cycle. Once technical and dress rehearsals are completed, the designer's role is virtually ended. Yet the actors are only beginning the transition from rehearsal into performance and a play in production takes on its own life. Whatever "art" has been created, and however perfect an individual element might be – the proportions, colors, lines – any isolated object takes on a different life within the whole of a production.

It is often very difficult to understand a design when taken out of its context. Donald Oenslager wrote that:

> The life of a setting in the theatre is only as long as stage hands will wrestle with it, actors will grace it and an audience is willing to behold it. When the production of a play ultimately closes, it belongs overnight, unfortunately, to the tarnished ages; for it is either forgotten in a dusty warehouse or it is reduced to sacred ashes on a pyre on the Jersey flats. A few thumbed and spattered sketches of the scenic designer are all that remain as permanent records of the ephemeral world they have nightly served. (*Theatre Then and Now*, New York: Russell and Russell, 1966)

During the early years of the twentieth century, as the number of theatres in New York City and the plays produced in them multiplied, several developments led to the growing recognition of the contribution that specialists in design might make to a production. The factors that contributed to the specializations in scenery, costume, and lighting design include an increasd focus on visual elements, an effort by a group of active and influential designers to specialize in a particular area, the incorporation of designers into unions, and the salary structure of the Federal Theatre Project.

In 1915, Robert Edmond Jones designed *The Man Who Married a Dumb Wife*, which is generally regarded as the design that introduced "the new American stagecraft." This movement followed the European model of unity in design refined by scenic designers Adolphe Appia and Edward Gordon Craig and influenced by director Max Reinhardt among others. The years preceding World War I, both in the United States and Europe, were ones of remarkable innovation in stage design. The course of modern design remains indebted to the innovations of Inigo Jones (1573-1652), the English architect and artist who introduced the proscenium arch to England, added color to stage light, and introduced a model for unified design by assuming responsibility for all the elements of the Court Masques he created. However, the twentieth century Broadway stage owes much to the scenic innovations brought to New York by Robert Edmond Jones in the second decade of this century. Along with Robert Edmond Jones and Norman Bel Geddes, the following generation of designers – among them Lee Simonson, Jo Mielziner and Donald Oenslager – inserted their own ideas and were part of an influential generation of designers who continued to alter the kind of design (scenery, costumes and lights) created during the first fifty years of this century. Changes in design style and approach, however, have not stopped. Design continues to evolve and new generations of designers continue to emerge. Ming Cho Lee, Santo Loquasto, Tony Walton, Robin Wagner, and other current innovators will be followed in turn by another generation whose individual design instincts will evolve and continue to reflect the spirit of the time.

Several factors influenced the change from one designer controlling all the visual elements of a theatrical production to a group of designers collaborating on the design and specializing not simply in theatrical design, but on scenery, costumes or lights. In the early 1920s, an increasing focus was placed on all the visual arts. This movement toward a strong visual format also had an impact on theatrical design. At the time it was standard practice for a single designer to control all of the visual elements of a production, including scenery and costumes, and to have assistants follow the various elements through the building process. The process was especially complex when the same designers were involved with many productions at the same time. Aline Bernstein, for instance,

regularly used Emeline Clarke Roche as her assistant for scenery and Irene Sharaff as her assistant for costumes. Gradually, designers such as Aline Bernstein, Jo Mielziner, and Robert Edmond Jones admitted the difficulty of maintaining control over such a wide range of activities, and initiated a trend toward specialization. They began by using assistants in the areas of scenery, costumes, and lights and gradually these assistants assumed more responsibility for the various elements. The movement from having a designer for scenery, costumes, and lights to having one for scenery, one for costumes, and eventually one for lights was gradual. Even in the 1990s, however, many designers remain active in more than one facet of design.

The costume design specialization was aided by the Actors' Strike for better wages and working conditions in 1919. The star system has long been an important part of the Broadway scene, and a star who could keep the seats filled was a performer to be treated with every courtesy, including costumes specially designed and constructed by knowledgable individuals. As a result of this strike, producers were required to provide costumes, wigs, shoes, and stockings for all women in principal roles and in the chorus. If the producers were going to foot the bill for costumes, it quickly became apparent that a costume design specialist should make the decisions about costume selections.

The general availability of electricity certainly aided in the transformation of illuminating engineers into lighting designers. As it became possible to insure the visibility of actors and vary the quantity of light on stage, it also became possible to affect the quality of light reaching the stage. Individuals who could do this effectively were readily employed, although in the earlier decades of the century designers who specialized in lighting joined United Scenic Artists through other categories.

In the early 1920s scenic designers joined United Scenic Artists, which until that time was called as the United Scenic Artists Association, and known primarily as a union for stage painters. Affiliated with the Brotherhood of Painters, Decorators and Paperhangers as Local Union 829 beginning in 1918, they helped stabilize the role of design in a production. This helped to convince producers and directors that design elements were as necessary to the success of a production as the script and the actors. Accompanied by an ever-expanding desire for authenticity and historical accuracy, increased attention was focused on individuals capable of creating appropriate scenery, properties, and costumes. By 1936 the union had a special section for costume designers, although they were not given voting rights until 1966. In the 1960s lighting designers received their own category and entrance requirements specific to their art.

The creation of the Federal Theatre Project during the early days of the Depression era, founded to provide employment for all varieties of theatre professionals, proved to be another powerful agent of change. Having many different people doing specialized jobs meant that more individuals were paid, however little, for their work. Once the specializations of costume and lighting design were developed, there was little possibility of returning to the format used in the past. What began as a New Deal full employment program had a lasting impact on theatrical design.

Theatre playbills from 1915, which is generally recognized as the beginning of the modern era of Broadway, until the present reveal a history of the profession of theatrical designers. The references to designers that do exist in early playbills are difficult to find, generally being buried in the back along with acknowledgments to piano tuners and vegetable market. Even when credited, a designers' contribution is often difficult to decipher. The distinctions between credits for decor or production design (especially when accompanied by a costume design credit), and those that identify two designers, one responsible for interior decoration and one for exterior decoration, are difficult to discern even for those knowledgable about scenic design.

Gradually, very gradually, more recognition was given to the contribution of the designer. As this happened, the personalities of designers emerged and the work of certain individuals became recognizable. Today designers even have their own following and are often acknowledged for bringing audiences into the theatre.

With the passing of each year since 1915, more designers have received credit for their designs in Broadway plays. At the turn of the century approximately two costume designers are mentioned for every one hundred productions, only one lighting designer (usually "electrical effects"), and perhaps ten scenic designers. By the 1943-44 season, almost half of the shows listed costume designers, one-fourth listed lighting designers, three-fourths listed scenic designers. At present it is extremely rare for a program not to list the full slate of designers. For the approximately 7,500 hundred plays produced on Broadway between 1915 and 1990, there were approximately 1,100 costume designers, just under 1,000 scenic designers and over 400 lighting designers.

The individuals who work as designers come from many different backgrounds. Many are drawn to design for a specific production given their particular background or talent, such as the graphic artist, Edward Gorey, for a recent Broadway production of *Dracula*. Some are artists in fields such as sculpting, painting, and fibre arts. Some begin as performers or as construction specialists. Some are fashion designers or architects or employees in related trades. Some are married to producers and assist their spouses by utilizing their knowledge of contemporary fashions or furnishings. Many are historians or playwrights lending their expertise to a particular production with which they are involved. One designer worth noting was the governor of a province in Spain who lent his considerable knowledge of the folklore of his region to create costumes and sets for a 1930s Broadway production. When Florine Stettheimer designed *Four Saints in Three Acts* on Broadway in 1934, she was the first mainstream, established artist to do so. Since then, this practice has become so common it is hardly a matter for comment. More frequently, however, many are specialists in design who are trained through an apprenticeship with another designer, with a theatre, or in one of the growing number of graduate programs offering degrees in design.

The focus of this book is on the individuals who design scenery. Short biographies summarize backgrounds, education, and representative credits, along with career influences. Broadway credits for scenery are listed in chronological order and are followed by costume and lighting designs also on Broadway. A section of illustrations offers a brief sampling of various styles and productions, and the appendixes list recipients of design awards related to Broadway activity: the Tony Awards, Maharam Awards, Donaldson Awards, and the American Theatre Wing Awards. The index lists the approximately 7,500 plays produced on Broadway together with the designer's name. These play titles can also be found under the scenic designer's name in the main portion of the text. "Ack Only" appears in those instances where the playbill listed no designer but did acknowledge a source for furnishings or properties, and "None" indicates that the playbill provided no information at all about scenery. Entries for "Acknowledgements" and "None" also appear in the main section of this volume among the "Designers and Their Credits."

Many effective and illuminating books have chronicled the development of scenic design in the United States. A brief bibliography of recommended sources is included following the illustrations and preceding the index.

Scenic Design
on
BROADWAY

Designers and Their Credits

Franklin Abbott

Franklin Abbott designed the settings for one production on Broadway in 1924. An architect, he was associated with Peabody, Wilson and Brown at 389 Fifth Avenue, New York City in 1918 and resided in Philadelphia, Pennsylvania. In the early 1930s, he established his own firm at 420 Lexington Avenue.

Scenic Designs:
1924: *Way Things Happen, The*

Harry L. Abbott

Harry L. Abbott was set designer for a single Broadway production in 1938. As early as 1918 he was president and treasurer of Abbott Scrim Profile Company, remaining in that position through the early 1930s. The company was located at 539 West 46th Street in 1918 and at 266 West 44th Street, New York City in 1932.

Scenic Designs:
1938: *Wild Duck, The*

P. Dodd Ackerman

Philip Dodd Ackerman (a.k.a. Ackermann) initially received credit for the scene designs of a Broadway show in 1916, after which his name appeared in numerous playbills during the 1920s and 1930s. His design expertise was generally used for scenery, although he contributed lighting designs to two productions in the late 1920s. He was also the principal designer of P. Dodd Ackerman Scenic Studio.

Scenic Designs:
1916: *Any House; Her Soldier Boy; Passing Show of 1916, The; Pay-Day; Robinson Crusoe, Jr.* 1917: *De Luxe Annie; Furs and Frills; Grass Widow, The* 1918: *Passing Show of 1918, The* 1919: *Carnival; Lonely Romeo, A; Take It from Me* 1920: *Broken Wing, The; Guest of Honor, The; Her Family Tree; Little Miss Charity; Passion Flower, The; Three Live Ghosts* 1921: *Danger; Ghost Between, The; Nightcap, The; Nobody's Money; Skirt, The; Title, The* 1922: *Advertising of Kate, The; For Goodness Sake; Frank Fay's Fables; Go Easy, Mabel; Kempy; Rotters, The* 1923: *Chicken Feed; Ginger; Little Jessie James; Magnolia; Polly Preferred; Stepping Stones; Thumbs Down; Wasp, The* 1924: *Alloy; Betty Lee; Conscience; Lady Killer, The; My Girl; Pigs; Sitting Pretty; Stepping Stones* 1925: *Alias the Deacon; All Dressed Up; Green Hat, The; Kiss in a Taxi, A; Merry, Merry; No, No Nanette; Pelican, The; Piker, The* 1926: *2 Girls Wanted; Castles in the Air; Climax, The; Ghost Train, The; Girl Friend, The; Twinkle, Twinkle; Up the Line; Weak Woman, A; What's the Big Idea; Woman Disputed, The* 1927: *Barker, The; Crime; Excess Baggage; Half a Widow; Honor Be Damned; It Is to Laugh; Just Fancy; Kempy; Lady Alone; Lost; Madame X; My Princess; Sinner; Spring Board, The; Trial of Mary Dugan; Window Panes* 1928: *Caravan; Crashing Through; Cross My Heart; Father, The; Hello, Yourself; Jealousy; Just a Minute; La Gringa; Lady of the Orchids, The; Marriage on Approval; Relations* 1929: *Conflict; Freddy; Headquarters; Humbug, The; Mountain Fury; Murder on the Second Floor*

1930: *Challenge of Youth, The; Courtesan; Dear Old England; Farewell to Arms, A; Five Star Final; Frankie and Johnnie; I Want My Wife; Long Road, The; Ninth Guest, The; Phantoms; Recapture; Tyrant, The* **1931:** *Cold in Sables; Divorce Me, Dear; It Never Rains; Nikki; Steel* **1932:** *Budget, The; Devil Passes, The; East of Broadway; Girl Outside, The; Inside Story, The; Life Begins; Nona* **1933:** *Marathon; Move On, Sister; Sailor, Beware; Strange Gods; Undesirable Lady, An* **1934:** *Birthday; Brittle Heaven; Divine Moment, A; Hotel Alimony; No Questions Asked; Picnic; Queer People; Red Cat, The; Richard of Bordeaux; Strangers At Home; Yesterday's Orchids* **1935:** *Abide with Me; How Beautiful with Shoes; Lady Detained, A; Little Shop; Macbeth; Othello; Sailor, Beware; Stick-in-the-Mud; Touch of Brimstone, A* **1936:** *Among Those Sailing; In the Bag* **1937:** *House in the Country, A* **1938:** *Happiest Days, The; Time and the Conways*

Lighting Designs:
1927: *Honor Be Damned* **1929:** *Hot Chocolates*

P. Dodd Ackerman Studio

P. Dodd Ackerman was the principal designer at the P. Dodd Ackerman Scenic Studio, located at 140 West 39th Street, New York City. Ackerman worked in creative association with Ben Glick and D. Frank Dodge. Members of the Board of Directors were Charles Chapman, Vice-President and Louis Ehrenberg, Secretary. The scenic studio produced designs for many productions between 1915 and 1934 and also painted productions for other designers. For additional information, see "P. Dodd Ackerman".

Scenic Designs:
1915: *World of Pleasure, A* **1916:** *If I Were King* **1917:** *Barbara* **1918:** *Riddle: Woman, The* **1919:** *Our Pleasant Sins* **1920:** *Betty Be Good* **1921:** *Six-Fifty, The* **1923:** *Aren't We All?; If Winter Comes; Not So Fast; What's Your Wife Doing* **1924:** *Shipwrecked; Sweet Seventeen* **1925:** *Aren't We All?; Patsy* **1926:** *Head Or Tail; Noose, The; Treat 'Em Rough* **1927:** *Blood Money; Merry-Go-Round; Yes, Yes, Yevette* **1929:** *Be Your Age; Her Friend, the King* **1932:** *Troilus and Cressida* **1934:** *Every Thursday*

"Acknowledgements"

Scenic designers were the first designers to receive credit for their contributions to theatre. However, until the mid-1920s playbills did not consistently list designers names on the title page, and even when the practice became more common some productions omitted the credit. The index of this book uses the citation "Ack Only" when no designer is listed, but acknowledgements exist for scenic elements or properties. Quite often there are references to scenic studios, some of which remain active. Scenic studios have been part of theatre production since the nineteenth century, when firms such as Joseph and Phil Harker in London and Cirker and Robbins in the United States supplied standard settings for plays in the repertoire of a company and those requiring contemporary furniture. Collaborations between designers, studios, interior decorators, and properties were often acknowledged at the end of playbills even as the profession of scenic designer developed. Literally thousands of productions in the twentieth century on Broadway list only suppliers and studios.

Prior to the time when designers consistently received credit in playbills, the following studios were often cited:

Arden Studios, Elizabeth A. Rogerson, President, Eta Pitman, Secretary, located at 599 5th Avenue, in 1916;

P. Dodd Ackerman Scenic Studios, 140 W. 39th Street;

Beaux Arts Studios, George W. Korb and E. Van Ackerman, located in Newark, New Jersey in the 1920s;

William Birns, a specialist in furniture and properties;

Carlos Studios, located at 503 W. 3rd, New York City in 1931 and operated by Joseph Errico, Frank W. Koetzner and L. J. Peltin;

Cleveland & Randall, Inc., Grover Cleveland, President, Herbert A. May, Vice-President, John Randall, Secretary-Treasurer, operated at 17 E. 45th Street in 1937, including a team of interior decorators;

Cirker and Robbins Studio, Inc., run by Mitchell Cirker and Robert N. Robbins, active from 1919 to 1934;

Fantana & Hartmann, managed by Martin Fantana and John Hartmann supplying theatrical properties; from 518 W. 30th Street, New York City in 1931;

Golding Scenic Studios, Inc., located at 1493 Broadway in 1919 with Stephen Golding, President, William Golding, Vice-President and Bert LaMont, Secretary;

Gordon Studios, located at 850 Broadway in 1927;

Lee Lash Studios, formed by scenic artist Lee Lash in Mt. Vernon, New York but moved to New York City by his son, Samuel Lash in the early 1920s;

Manhattan Scenic Studios, operated in the early 1920s by James Van Sickler and Walter Lewis;

Neppell and Brousseau Scenic Construction Company, operated at 428 11th Avenue in New York City in 1927 by Hermann Neppell and James Brousseau;

Novelty Scenic Studios, 340 West 41st Street, New York City, with Abraham T. Kessler and Morris Golden;

Premier Scenic Studios, active from 1927 to 1931 with Abraham I. Kessler and Maurice Bolder;

Savoy Studios, operated at 510 5th Avenue in 1919 by Mrs. Steward A. Colby;

Stagecraft Studios, located at 17 East 39th Street, New York City, operated by Elmer Johnson, Ashmead Scott and Cecil Owen in 1922;

Studio Alliance specialized in scenic construction after World War II, formed by Arthur Segal with G. Bradford Ashworth and Robert Barnhardt;

Theatrical Scenic Studios, 501 W. 44th Street in 1931, William F. Harrover and Robert A. Reamer;

Vail Scenic Construction Company, founded in 1910 by George M. Vail, became Chester Rakeman Scenic Studios in 1950;

Ward and Harvey Studios, Inc., with Walter Harvey, Secretary and Treasurer, active in the 1930s.

These studios represent only a small proportion of the studios which have contributed to New York theatrical activity. Additional scenic studios included Belmont Studios, John Brunton Studios, Continer and Golding, Fisher and Bray, Steven Gordon Scenic Studio, Holak Studios, Jensen Studios, Metropolitan Studios, Turner Scenic Construction Company, United Studios, Vitolo Willoughby Studios and Vitolo Pearson Studios among many others. In the latter part of this century, scenic studios have tended to move out of mid-town Manhattan and proximity to the theatre district to locations where large spaces are more reasonably available. Nolan Scenic Studio, Scenic Central, Showtech, National Scenery, Roma, Acadia, Showman Fabricators, Inc., Metro Scenic, Feller Precision, Adirondack, Atlas, and Half Moon, are only a few of those currently turning designs into reality.

John Wolcott Adams

John Wolcott Adams, who died in New York City on June 23, 1925, was born in Worcester, Massachusetts in 1874, the descendant of two presidents of the United States. He was a popular magazine illustrator and artist whose choice of favorite subject matter and style was influenced by his teacher, Howard Pyle. His theatrical experience was mainly as an actor. In addition to designing a set on Broadway for Walter Hampden he appeared in the 1913 film, *Saved by Parcel Post.*

Scenic Designs:
1923: *Jolly Roger, The*

Eric Adeney

Eric Adeney (a.k.a. Eric Ardenay) was an artist and actor who collaborated with Donald Wolfit on the designs for the 1947 production of *Hamlet* on Broadway. He appeared in the silent film version of *Hamlet* as Francisco and Reynoldo. In 1950 his studio was located on Albert Street in London.

Scenic Designs:
1947: *Hamlet*

Costume Designs:
1947: *Hamlet*

D.M. Akin

D.M. Akin created settings for a Broadway production in 1917.

Scenic Designs:
1917: *Oh Boy!*

Ernest Albert

Known primarily as a landscape artist, Ernest Albert died at the age of 88 in New Canaan, Connecticut on March 26, 1946. He was born in Brooklyn, New York, studied in New York City, and in 1880 became art and scenic director at Pope's Theatre in St. Louis, Missouri. He helped design color schemes for buildings at the 1893 World's Fair in Chicago. In 1894 he moved to New York where he specialized in settings for Shakespearean plays and painted. He began to exhibit oils and watercolors at the turn of the century. In 1919 he was elected president of the Allied Artists of America.

Scenic Designs:
1917: *Jack O'Lantern* 1918: *Better 'Ole, The*

Kurd Albrecht

Kurd (or Kurt) Albrecht, the German painter and scenic designer, lived in Berlin. In 1909 and 1910 his paintings, "Dans le Port" and "La Premiere Neige" were shown in a major exhibition in Berlin. In November 1930 he arrived in New York to make preparations for the German Opera Company 1931 tour of the United States. He was stage manager of the company at that time.

Scenic Designs:
1929: *Freiburg Passion Play, The*

Elizabeth Alexander

Elizabeth Alexander (a.k.a. Mrs. John Alexander) is most often remembered as the creator of costumes for *Peter Pan* for Maude Adams. A native of New York City, she was born in 1867 and married John W. Alexander in 1887 (no relation though they shared the same last name). Mrs. Alexander received no formal training in the arts or theatre prior to her successful career designing sets and costumes, and the majority of her credits are before 1915. Shortly after the death of her husband in 1915, she retired from theatrical design and helped establish the Arden Galleries in New York. Until her death at the age of 80 in 1947 she was an active and enthusiastic patron of the arts. She served at various times with the School Art League and the Arts Council of New York. She was on the executive committee in the United States

which helped raise funds for the construction of the Shakespeare Memorial Theatre in Stratford-upon-Avon. Mr. and Mrs. Alexander had one son, James W. Alexander, named for her father.

Scenic Designs:
1916: *Kiss for Cinderella, A*

Costume Designs:
1916: *Kiss for Cinderella, A* 1917: *Imaginary Invalid, The*

Leigh Allen

Leigh Allen designed settings for a production in 1934 on Broadway.

Scenic Designs:
1934: *Mother Lode*

Paul Allen

In 1923 Paul N. Allen designed settings for a Broadway play. He was associated with Harry Greene in Allen & Greene, a theatrical business at 1493 Broadway in the late teens and resided at 501 West 15th Street, New York City.

Scenic Designs:
1923: *Alarm Clock, The*

George Allgier

The settings for a Broadway play in 1933 were designed by George J. Allgier. A teacher at Textile High School, he resided at 301 West 24th Street in New York City in the 1930s.

Scenic Designs:
1933: *Church Mouse, A*

Ralph Alswang

Ralph Alswang made his debut on Broadway as a set designer for *Comes the Revelation* in 1942, as a lighting designer for *Home of the Brave* in 1945, and as a costume designer for *Beggars Are Coming to Town* in 1945. He was born in 1916 and raised in Chicago where he attended classes at the Chicago Art Institute and the Goodman Theatre. He also studied with Robert Edmond Jones. For the majority of his distinguished career Mr. Alswang concentrated on scenery and lighting, but he also designed costumes for twelve shows between 1945 and 1966. In addition he designed theatres (including the Uris in New York City), guided restorations of theatres (including the Palace Theatre in New York City), directed and produced. He developed a theatre technique called "Living Screen" which integrated live action and motion pictures, and produced *Is There Intelligent Life on Earth?* using the method, for which he held three patents. Ralph Alswang was married in 1944 to Betty Taylor, an interior designer, and had three children. He died in New York City on February 15, 1979 at age 62.

Scenic Designs:

1942: *Comes the Revelation* **1945:** *Home of the Brave* **1946:** *I Like It Here; Lysistrata; Swan Song* **1947:** *Gentlemen from Athens, The; Our Lan'; Whole World Over, The; Young Man's Fancy, A* **1948:** *Jenny Kissed Me; Last Dance, The; Seeds in the Wind; Set My People Free; Small Wonder; Story for Strangers, A; Strange Bedfellows; Trial By Jury* **1949:** *How Long Till Summer; Mikado, The; Pirates of Penzance, The; Trial By Jury* **1950:** *Julius Caesar; Katherine Dunham and Her Company; King Lear; Legend of Sarah; Let's Make An Opera; Peter Pan; Pride's Crossing; Tickets, Please* **1951:** *Courtin' Time; Love and Let Love; Number, The; Out West of Eighth* **1952:** *Conscience; Iolanthe; Mikado, The; Pirates of Penzance, The; Trial By Jury/ H.M.S. Pinafore; Two's Company* **1953:** *Bat, The; Be Your Age; Ladies of the Corridor, The; Pink Elephant, The; Sing Till Tommorrow* **1954:** *Fragile Fox; Magic and the Loss, The;* **1955:** *Catch a Star; Deadfall; Southwest Corner, The* **1956:** *Affair of Honor; Best House in Naples, The; Hot Corner, The; Time Limit; Uncle Willie* **1957:** *First Gentleman, The; Hide and Seek; Tunnel of Love, The* **1958:** *Love Me Little; Sunrise At Campobello* **1959:** *Girls Against the Boys, The; Hostile Witness; Raisin in the Sun, A* **1961:** *Come Blow Your Horn* **1963:** *Advocate, The* **1964:** *Comedy in Music Opus 2; Fair Games for Lovers* **1965:** *Ken Murray's Hollywood; World of Charles Aznavour* **1966:** *At the Drop of Another Hat; Committee, The* **1967:** *Halfway Up the Tree* **1972:** *Fun City*

Lighting Designs:

1945: *Home of the Brave* **1946:** *Lysistrata; Swan Song* **1947:** *Gentlemen from Athens, The; Our Lan'; Young Man's Fancy, A* **1948:**

Play's the Thing, The; Small Wonder; Story for Strangers, A; Strange Bedfellows; Trial By Jury **1949:** *How Long Till Summer; Mikado, The; Pirates of Penzance, The; Trial By Jury* **1950:** *Daphne Laureola; Julius Caesar; King Lear; Let's Make An Opera; Peter Pan; Pride's Crossing* **1953:** *Anna Russell and Her Little Show; Bat, The; Ladies of the Corridor, The; Pink Elephant, The; Sing Till Tommorrow* **1955:** *Fragile Fox; Rainmaker, The* **1955:** *Deadfall; Southwest Corner, The* **1956:** *Affair of Honor; Best House in Naples, The; Hot Corner, The; Time Limit; Uncle Willie* **1957:** *First Gentleman, The; Hide and Seek; Tunnel of Love, The* **1958:** *Epitaph for George Dillon; Sunrise At Campobello* **1959:** *At the Drop of a Hat; Girls Against the Boys, The; Hostile Witness; Raisin in the Sun, A* **1961:** *Come Blow Your Horn* **1963:** *Advocate, The; School for Scandal, The* **1964:** *Comedy in Music Opus 2; Fair Games for Lovers* **1965:** *Beyond the Fringe; Ken Murray's Hollywood; World of Charles Aznavour* **1966:** *At the Drop of Another Hat; Committee, The* **1967:** *Halfway Up the Tree*

Costume Designs:

1945: *Beggars Are Coming to Town; Home of the Brave* **1947:** *Whole World Over, The* **1948:** *Happy Journey, The/ Respectful Prostitute, The; Last Dance, The* **1955:** *Deadfall* **1964:** *Comedy in Music Opus 2; Fair Games for Lovers* **1965:** *Ken Murray's Hollywood* **1966:** *At the Drop of Another Hat*

Nathan Altman

Nathan Altman was a Russian painter, book, scenic and graphic designer, and member of the Russian avant-garde art community. He was born on December 10, 1889 and died on December 12, 1970 in Leningrad where he resided most of his life. He lived in Paris during the 1920s and 1930s and while there received a gold medal for scene design in the 1925 International Exhibit for the Decorative Arts and Industry. Marc Chagall and Nathan Altman were the principal designers for the Moscow State Jewish Theatre, which opened in 1919 and was closed by an edict of Stalin in 1948.

Scenic Designs:

1926: *Dybbuck, The* **1948:** *Dybbuck, The*

Franklyn Ambrose

Franklyn Geramia Ambrose designed settings for Broadway plays during the 1930s. In 1920 he worked as a clerk and resided at 246 East 120th Street, New York City.

Scenic Designs:
1934: *Drunkard, The* 1935: *Mulatto* 1936: *Pirates of Penzance, The*

Karle O. Amend

Karle Otto Amend was born in Columbus, Ohio on January 15, 1889. Although his first job in the theatre was as a paint boy for Schell Scenic Studios in Columbus, he initially intended to be an actor and performed with both vaudeville and stock companies. His first credit as a scenic artist was for a 1912 production of *East Lynne* in Ohio, after which he devoted his talents to creating and painting scenery. He became a member of United Scenic Artists in 1918 and established the Karle O. Amend Scenic Studio in the early 1920s. He designed settings for numerous productions under his own name and others for which his studio received design credit. Karle O. Amend died on January 2, 1944 at the age of 54.

Scenic Designs:
1925: *Dagger, The; Earl Carroll's Vanities; Florida Girl; Mercenary Mary* 1926: *Potash and Perlmutter, Detectives* 1927: *Tommy* 1928: *Keep Shufflin'; Sh! The Octopus; We Never Learn* 1929: *Town Boy* 1931: *Coastwise; Devil's Host, The; Nikki; School for Virtue* 1932: *Angeline Moves in; Border Land; Broadway Boy; Few Wild Oats, A; Shuffle Along of 1933* 1933: *Before Morning; Locked Room, The; Under Glass* 1934: *Broadway Interlude; Gypsy Blonde; Her Majesty, the Widow; Slightly Delirious; Too Much Party* 1935: *Nowhere Bound; One Good Year; Potash and Perlmutter; Smile At Me; Them's the Reporters* 1936: *Devil of Pei-Ling, The; Sap Runs High, The* 1937: *Cross-Town; Howdy Stranger* 1939: *I Must Love Someone; When We Are Married* 1942: *Time, the Place, and the Girl, The* 1944: *Right Next to Broadway*

Karle O. Amend Studio

Karle O. Amend established the Karle O. Amend Scenic Studio in the early 1920s, an enterprise which remained in operation until the early 1940s in various New Jersey locations. Unlike many other scene shops the studio stayed open during the Depression, due mainly to Amend's persistence. The Karle O. Amend Scenic Studios also produced and painted scenery for other designers including Albert R. Johnson and Hugh Willoughby.

Scenic Designs:
1923: *Newcomers, The* 1926: *Love City, The* 1929: *Nice Women* 1930: *Spook House* 1931: *Ebb Tide; Wooden Soldier, The* 1932: *Man Who Changed His Name, The* 1933: *Crucible; Tommy* 1934: *One More Honeymoon* 1937: *Work Is for Horses*

Michael Anania

Michael Anania is a native of Brockton, Massachusetts where he was born on October 1, 1951. After receiving a B.F.A. at Boston University, he became designer in residence at Tufts University, subsequently spending ten years on the faculty of Emerson College. He has been resident scenic designer at the Paper Mill Playhouse since 1985 where he has designed numerous productions. He has many opera designs to his credit, including *Pajama Game* at the New York City Opera in 1989, *Desire under the Elms* at the New York Opera Repertory Theatre at City Center Theatre, and several productions for the Lake George Opera Festival.

Scenic Designs:
1980: *Canterbury Tales* 1989: *Run For Your Wife* 1990: *Change in the Heir*

John Murray Anderson

John Murray Anderson, a native of St. John's, Newfoundland, was born on September 20, 1886 and died at the age of 67 on January 30, 1954. He came to the United States in 1910 after studying in Lausanne, Switzerland and Edinburgh. He served the theatre in a variety of functions: dancer, producer, writer, director, and lyricist. He devised six *Greenwich Village Follies*, also serving as a costume designer on one of the productions and a set designer on another. In fact in all of the productions for which he received credit as a designer he had an additional role, often as director. "Murray" also worked as a producer for Radio City Music Hall, the New York Hippodrome, and Metro-Goldwyn-Mayer as well as on Broadway, and encouraged the talents of young theatre aspirants, including E. Carleton Winckler.

Scenic Designs:
1923: *Greenwich Village Follies*

Lighting Designs:
1939: *One for the Money* 1940: *Two for the Show* 1948: *Heaven on Earth*

Costume Designs:
1924: *Greenwich Village Follies*

Keith Anderson

Keith Anderson lives in Siesta Key, Florida and designed the 1990/91 edition of Ringling Brothers and Barnum & Bailey Circus. A production designer, he designed both sets and costumes for a production on Broadway in 1989. He is also a writer and teaches trapeze.

Scenic Designs:
1989: *Meet Me in Saint Louis*

Costume Designs:
1989: *Meet Me in Saint Louis*

Percy Anderson

Percy Anderson died in London on October 10, 1928 at the age of 77 after a long and distinguished career designing costumes (and occasionally sets) in the United States and Great Britain. At a period in theatrical history when little credit was extended to costume designers, Mr. Anderson's name appeared in playbills and his contribution was acknowledged in reviews. He was instrumental in laying the groundwork for the costume designers working as professionals today, blending theatrical necessity with historical period without following the pedantic modes common at the end of the nineteenth century. He was both well known and respected by the public and his contemporaries. In England Mr. Anderson was known for his work with the producer Sir Herbert Beerbohm Tree and for the original productions of the Gilbert and Sullivan operettas. Beginning with *The Yeoman of the Guard*, he was responsible for all the D'Oyly Carte productions at the Savoy. The majority of his design assignments on Broadway occurred prior to 1915 and included: 1894: *The*

Devil's Advocate; 1895: *His Excellency*; 1896: *The Geisha, Half A King*; 1897: *The Tempest*; 1898: *Trelawny of the 'Wells*; 1899 *Becky Sharp*; 1901 *Captain Jinks of the Horse Marines*; 1902 *Mary of Magdala*; 1905: *Adrea*; 1907: *Sappho and Pharon*; and 1910: *Kismet*. Mr. Anderson also painted watercolor portraits of many distinguished people, and exhibited with the New Water Colour Society in London.

Scenic Designs:
1916: *Macbeth*; *Merry Wives of Windsor, The*

Costume Designs:
1916: *Macbeth*; *Merry Wives of Windsor, The* 1917: *Chu Chin Chow* 1919: *Aphrodite*; *Monsieur Beaucaire* 1920: *Mecca* 1924: *Macbeth* 1936: *Princess Ida*

Mariano Andreu

Mariano Andreu was a Catalan artist and illustrator, born in Barcelona in 1888. His graphic talent led him from illustrating books to sketching sets and costumes. He spent much of his life in London, where he designed often for Michel Fokine, including the world premier of *Don Juan* at the Alhambra. His work was also seen in New York for the Ballet Russe de Monte Carlo in their appearances at the Metropolitan Opera. The production he designed on Broadway, *Much Ado About Nothing*, starred John Gielgud and Margaret Leighton and was originally produced in London.

Scenic Designs:
1959: *Much Ado About Nothing*

Costume Designs:
1959: *Much Ado About Nothing*

Herbert Andrews

Herbert Garnet Andrews, born in New York City in 1909, studied at the Pratt Institute and the Berkshire School of Design. Mr. Andrews was well known as a scenic designer for the theatre and for NBC-TV where he designed over ten thousand sets in the past thirty years. Mr. Andrews began his career as a designer in summer stock and with the Group Theatre. After that time he designed extensively for stage, television, and motion pictures. In addition to his credits on Broadway for costume design, he created clothes for many television productions, including twenty *Miss America Pageants*. He became a member of United Scenic Artists in 1934 and a life member in 1985. Mr. Andrews died in September 1990.

Scenic Designs:
1938: *My Heart's in the Highlands; Sing for Your Supper* **1939:** *Swingin' the Dream* **1940:** *Cue for Passion* **1942:** *Let Freedom Sing; Porgy and Bess* **1943:** *Porgy and Bess* **1944:** *Porgy and Bess*

Costume Designs:
1936: *Battle Hymn* **1938:** *My Heart's in the Highlands* **1939:** *Swingin' the Dream*

Boris Anisfield

Boris Anisfield (a.k.a. Boris (Ber) Izrailevich Anisfeldt), a painter whose works are in the permanent collections of the Hermitage, Chicago Art Institute and the Brooklyn Museum was born in Beltsy, Bessarabia, Russia on October 2, 1890. His works have been widely exhibited. He came to the United States in 1918 and became a naturalized citizen in 1924. He spent several years in New York painting scenery and designing costumes and scenery for opera, ballet and one Broadway production. In 1928, he was appointed Professor of Advanced Drawing and Painting at the Chicago Art Institute and held that position until retirement in 1968. He died in Waterford, Connecticut on December 4, 1973 at age 94. Mr. Anisfield, who married in 1904, had one daughter.

Scenic Designs:
1926: *Schweiger*

Costume Designs:
1926: *Schweiger*

Kathleen Ankers

Kathleen Ankers is known as an art director on television, with credits including *Late Night with David Letterman* and *F.Y.I.* on ABC-TV, and numerous specials and series. Born in London, she has designed for the Old Vic in Bristol, London and Liverpool, the Citizen's Theatre in Glasgow and in London's West End among other theatres. Kathleen Ankers began her career in the theatre in her teens with a repertory

company in Farnham, where she went hoping to work on scenery and costumes, but was hired to work in the box office. When the designer came down with the mumps, she got her start creating sets and costumes. In addition to her designs on Broadway, she has designed sets and costumes off-Broadway and for regional theatres, including the Hartford Stage.

Scenic Designs:
1952: *Mr. Pickwick*

Lighting Designs:
1952: *Mr. Pickwick*

Costume Designs:
1952: *Fancy Meeting You Again; Mr. Pickwick*
1974: *My Sister, My Sister*

Michael Annals

Michael Annals, a British designer, was born on April 21, 1938 and attended the Hornsey College of Art. He designed sets and costumes for many companies around the world, including the Royal Shakespeare Company, the Stratford (Ontario) Festival, The National Theatre, Covent Garden, American Ballet Theatre, and the Royal Ballet. His career began at the Old Vic in 1961 when he designed *Macbeth*. Designs in London's West End included sets and costumes for *Design for Living, Privates on Parade*, and *Noises Off*. He also designed for film, notably *Joseph Andrews*. During the 1966-67 academic year he was an Associate Professor of Scenic Design at Yale University. Mr. Annals always preferred to design both sets and costumes for a production, as was the case with most of his credits on Broadway. Michael Annals died in London on June 1, 1990.

Scenic Designs:
1965: *Royal Hunt of the Sun* **1966:** *Those That Play the Clowns* **1968:** *Her First Roman; Morning Noon and Night; Staircase* **1972:** *Captain Brassbound's Conversion* **1983:** *Noises Off* **1985:** *Benefactors*

Costume Designs:
1965: *Royal Hunt of the Sun* **1966:** *Those That Play the Clowns* **1968:** *Her First Roman; Morning Noon and Night; Staircase* **1983:** *Noises Off*

Yuri Annenkov

Yuri Pavlovich Annenkov (a.k.a. Jurij Annyenkoff, Georges Annenkopf, George Annet,

George Annenkov etc.), the Russian designer, artist and art critic was born in Petropavlosk, Russia on June 1, 1889. He studied at St. Petersburg University and with Savelii Zeidenberg. His creative and innovative designs were seen in St. Petersburg at the Bat and Kholmskaya's Crooked Mirror Theatre and in Petrograd for Tolstoi's *The First Distiller* among many theatres. He emigrated to Germany in 1924 and then to France, continuing to design for theatre and films. He also painted portraits which are collected in museums around the world, and wrote essays on art. In 1965, he published his memoirs, *Diary of My Acquaintances.* Yuri Annenkov died on July 18, 1974 in Paris.

Scenic Designs:
1931: *New Chauve-Souris* 1935: *Revisor*

Costume Designs:
1931: *New Chauve-Souris*

Robert Anton

Robert Anton (a.k.a. Robbie Anton), a native of Fort Worth, Texas studied set design at Carnegie Tech and Lester Polakov's Studio and Forum of Stage Design. Known primarily as a puppet designer, his Anton Theatre toured throughout the United States and Europe. He died a suicide on August 29, 1984 in Los Angeles at age 35.

Scenic Designs:
1972: *Elizabeth I*

Loy Arcenas

Loy Arcenas was born on March 3, 1953 in the Philippines and was a pre-med student at the University of the Philippines prior to taking a design course at the English National Opera. His first scenic designs were for *Antigone* in the Philippines. He has extensive credits in regional theatres, off-Broadway and in his native land. Recent productions include *The Pinter Plays* at CSC, *Nebraska* at La Jolla Playhouse, *The Glass Menagerie* at Arena Stage and *Life is a Dream* at American Repertory Theatre. He has designed for many theatres on the West Coast and in 1987 received the Los Angeles Critics Circle Award for *Three Postcards* at South Coast Repertory Theatre. His designs for *Once on This Island*, which moved from the off-Broadway

Playwrights Horizons to the Booth Theatre on Broadway in October 1990, received excellent notices for the hand-painted impastoed background of the Caribbean setting. He recently designed *Caucasian Chalk Circle* for the New York Shakespeare Festival, directed by George C. White.

Scenic Designs:
1990: *Prelude to a Kiss*

Horace Armistead

Horace Armistead was born in 1898 in England where he got his start in theatre as a studio paint boy. He moved to the United States in 1924 and worked initially as a charge man for Cleon Throckmorton, the designer and producer. He later opened his own shop. He designed many sets on Broadway and won the Tony Award in 1948 for the sets for Gian Carlo Menotti's opera, *The Medium,* for which he also created the costumes. He also designed sets and costumes for the Metropolitan Opera and the New York City Ballet. Mr. Armistead died in 1980 at the age of 82.

Scenic Designs:
1936: *Fields Beyond, The* 1942: *What Big Ears* 1947: *Telephone, The and The Medium* 1949: *Regina* 1950: *Arms and the Girl; Consul, The*

Costume Designs:
1947: *Telephone, The and The Medium*

Dorothy Armstrong

As a child, Dorothy Armstrong performed in vaudeville with her brother, Ellis Armstrong. They toured in *The Man from Mexico* and Rutan's *Song Birds.* She collaborated on the designs for two Broadway shows, the sets for one and costumes for another.

Scenic Designs:
1922: *Greenwich Village Follies*

Costume Designs:
1921: *Tangerine*

Will Steven Armstrong

Will Steven Armstrong specialized in scenic design during his career in theatre although he also designed lights and costumes. He was awarded the Tony for outstanding scene design in 1962 for *Carnival*. Mr. Armstrong was born in New Orleans in 1930 and died August 12, 1969. He studied both at Louisiana State and Yale Universities. Mr. Armstrong designed the stage of the American Shakespeare Festival in Stratford, Connecticut as well as sets, lights and costumes for that company.

Scenic Designs:
1959: *Andersonville Trial, The* 1960: *Caligula* 1961: *Carnival; Cook for Mr. General, A; I Can Get It for You Wholesale; Kwamina; Subways Are for Sleeping* 1962: *Tchin-Tchin* 1963: *Dear Me, the Sky Is Falling; Nobody Loves An Albatross; One Flew Over the Cuckoo's Nest* 1964: *I Had a Ball; Passion of Joseph D, The; Ready When You Are; Three Sisters, The* 1966: *Lion in Winter, The; Pousse-Cafe; Three Bags Full; Wayward Stork* 1967: *Imaginary Invalid, The; Something Different; Tonight At 8:30; Touch of the Poet, A* 1968: *Forty Carats* 1969: *Front Page, The; Zelda*

Lighting Designs:
1959: *Andersonville Trial, The* 1961: *Carnival; Cook for Mr. General, A; I Can Get It for You Wholesale; Kwamina; Subways Are for Sleeping* 1962: *Tchin-Tchin* 1963: *Dear Me, the Sky Is Falling; Nobody Loves An Albatross; One Flew Over the Cuckoo's Nest; Rehearsal, The; Semi-Detached* 1964: *I Had a Ball; Passion of Joseph D, The; Ready When You Are* 1966: *Three Bags Full* 1967: *Something Different* 1969: *Front Page, The; Zelda*

Costume Designs:
1959: *Andersonville Trial, The* 1960: *Caligula* 1964: *Girl Could Get Lucky, A* 1966: *Lion in Winter, The*

Peter Arno

Born on January 8, 1904, Curtis Arnoux Peters was known through his professional life as Peter Arno. He launched his career as a cartoonist with a sale to *The New Yorker* in 1925, where he became a regular contributor. His cartoons, featuring bold lines and satirizing society, were collected in several books. Mr. Arno wrote revues to which he also contributed costume and scenic designs. He also wrote one-man shows in which he performed. Peter Arno died in 1968.

Scenic Designs:
1930: *New Yorkers, The* 1931: *Here Goes the Bride*

Costume Designs:
1927: *New Yorkers, The* 1929: *Murray Anderson's Almanac* 1930: *New Yorkers, The*

Barry Arnold

Barry Arnold, a native of New York City, was production designer for one show in 1970. He started designing in summer stock at Eagles Mere Playhouse and first worked in New York at the Equity Library Theatre. Off-Broadway designs include *Curley McDimple, The Millionairess*, and *Love and Maple Syrup*.

Scenic Designs:
1970: *President's Daughter, The*

Lighting Designs:
1970: *President's Daughter, The* 1976: *Bubbling Brown Sugar* 1982: *Joseph and the Amazing Technicolor Dreamcoat*

Costume Designs:
1970: *President's Daughter, The*

Boris Aronson

Boris Aronson, painter, scenic designer and occasionally a costume and lighting designer, was born in Kiev, Russia in 1900 and studied at the State Art School, the School of Modern Painting, and with Alexandra Exter at the School of Theatre. He created sets and costumes in the United States for the first time at the New York City Yiddish Theatre in 1924, beginning five decades of outstanding design. Among the many prizes won by Mr. Aronson were several Tony Awards for outstanding scenic design for *The Rose Tattoo, Follies, Company, Zorba, Cabaret* and *Pacific Overtures*. He designed extensively for the theatre, ballet and film. The breadth and creativity of his work has received belated recognition since his death on November 16, 1980. The lavishly illustrated *The Theatre Art of Boris Aronson* by Frank Rich was published by Knopf in 1987, and his designs continue to be collected and featured in exhibitions.

Scenic Designs:
1927: *2x2=5* 1930: *Josef Suss* 1932: *Walk a Little Faster* 1934: *Ladies' Money; Small Miracle* 1935: *Awake and Sing; Battleship Gertie; Body Beautiful, The; Paradise Lost; Three*

Men on a Horse; Weep for the Virgins **1937:**
Western Waters **1938:** *Merchant of Yonkers,
The* **1939:** *Awake and Sing; Gentle People,
The; Ladies and Gentlemen* **1940:** *Cabin in
the Sky; Heavenly Express; Unconquered, The*
1941: *Clash By Night; Night Before Christmas, The* **1942:** *Cafe Crown; R.U.R.; Russian People, The* **1943:** *Family, The; South Pacific by Rigsby; What's Up* **1944:** *Sadie Thompson* **1945:** *Assassin, The; Stranger, The* **1946:**
Gypsy Lady; Truckline Cafe **1948:** *Love Life;
Skipper Next to God; Survivors, The* **1949:** *Detective Story* **1950:** *Bird Cage, The; Country
Girl, The; Season in the Sun* **1951:** *Barefoot
in Athens; I Am a Camera; Rose Tattoo, The*
1952: *I've Got Sixpence* **1953:** *Crucible, The;
Frogs of Spring, The; My Three Angels* **1954:**
Mademoiselle Colombe **1955:** *Bus Stop; Diary
of Anne Frank, The; Once Upon a Tailor; View
from the Bridge, A* **1956:** *Girls of Summer*
1957: *Hole in the Head, A; Orpheus Descending; Rope Dancers, The; Small War on Murray Hill* **1958:** *Cold Wind and the Warm, The;
Firstborn, The; J.B.* **1959:** *Flowering Cherry;
Loss of Roses, A* **1960:** *Do Re Mi; Semi-
Detached* **1961:** *Garden of Secrets, The; Gift of
Time, A* **1963:** *Andorra* **1964:** *Fiddler on the
Roof* **1966:** *Cabaret* **1968:** *Price, The; Zorba*
1970: *Company* **1971:** *Follies* **1972:** *Creation
of the World and Other Business,; Great God
Brown, The* **1973:** *Little Night Music, A* **1976:**
Fiddler on the Roof; Pacific Overtures **1981:**
Fiddler on the Roof

Lighting Designs:
1945: *Stranger, The* **1948:** *Survivors, The*
1950: *Country Girl, The; Season in the Sun*
1952: *I've Got Sixpence* **1953:** *Frogs of Spring,
The* **1957:** *Rope Dancers, The; Small War on
Murray Hill*

Costume Designs:
1927: *2x2=5* **1937:** *Western Waters* **1938:**
Merchant of Yonkers, The **1940:** *Cabin in the
Sky; Heavenly Express* **1968:** *Price, The*

Don Ashton

Don Ashton designed sets for one show on
Broadway in 1963.

Scenic Designs:
1963: *Photo Finish*

G. Bradford Ashworth

G. Bradford Ashworth founded Studio Alliance
in 1936 with Arthur Segal and Robert Barnhart
in an effort to supply all details to a production.
The first production mounted by Studio Alliance
was *Dead End* in 1936, designed by Norman Bel
Geddes. In addition he also designed sets for
plays. Studio Alliance was closed in 1953 by
Arthur Segal, who had become president of the
organization.

Scenic Designs:
1934: *Lost Horizons; Tight Britches* **1935:** *On
Stage; Whatever Goes Up*

Nils Asther

Nils Asther, a star of silent films in his native
Sweden, made a successful transition to talkies
in Hollywood after taking a two year hiatus from
movies to study voice and diction in England.
He starred in many movies, including *The Sin-
gle Standard* with Greta Garbo and *The Bitter
Tea of General Yen* with Barbara Stanwyck. His
infrequent appearances on Broadway included
Flight into Egypt directed by Elia Kazan and
The Strong and Lonely directed by Margaret
Webster. Born in Hellerup, Denmark to Swedish
parents on January 17, 1897, he was raised in
Malmö, Sweden and attended the Royal Danish
Theatre School. He died at age 84 in 1981.

Scenic Designs:
1936: *Lights O'London, The*

Laura Sawyer Atkinson

Laura Sawyer Atkinson was an actress who appeared as Laura Sawyer in early movies, with
Otis Skinner's Stage Company, and as leading
lady of the Edison Company. She was born in
1885 and died at age 85 on September 7, 1970
in Matawan, New Jersey, the widow of Charles
Frederick Wolff. She appeared in the 1912 film
The Lighthouse Keeper's Daughter and the 1913
films *The Daughter of the Hills, Three of a Kind,
Leaves of a Romance* and *The Battle of Trafal-
gar.*

Scenic Designs:
1921: *Survival of the Fittest, The*

Charles J. Auburn

Charles J. Auburn designed settings on Broadway in the 1920s. In addition, the Charles J. Auburn Scenic Studio received credit for additional productions between 1925 and 1932. In 1932 he worked as an electrician and resided at 242 East 19th Street in New York City.

Scenic Designs:
1923: *For Value Received; Go West, Young Man; Love Set, The; My Aunt from Yipsilanti* **1924:** *Shooting Shadows; Strong, The* **1925:** *Gorilla, The*

Charles J. Auburn Scenic Studio

Scenic designer Charles J. Auburn operated a scenic studio in New York between 1925 and 1932. For additional information, see "Charles J. Auburn".

Scenic Designs:
1925: *Four Flusher, The; Two By Two* **1930:** *Traitor, The* **1932:** *Air Minded*

Adrian Awan

Adrian Awan spent the majority of his professional life on the West Coast. At the time of his death on June 10, 1968, he had recently retired from 20th Century Fox where he had been employed as exploitation manager. He also supervised the technical aspects of productions for the Hollywood Bowl and musicals for the Los Angeles and San Francisco Civic Light Opera Associations.

Scenic Designs:
1945: *Red Mill, The*

Lighting Designs:
1945: *Red Mill, The* **1946:** *Gypsy Lady*

Elizabeth Axtman

Elizabeth Axtman was active on Broadway from 1915 to 1917 during which time she designed costumes for seven productions. For one production, *The Claim*, she also designed the set. In 1915 she worked primarily as a dressmaker and resided at 55 East 55th Street in New York City.

Scenic Designs:
1917: *Claim, The*

Costume Designs:
1915: *Earth, The; Liars, The; Major Barbara; Captain Brassbound's Conversion; New York Idea, The* **1917:** *Claim, The; L'Elevation*

Lemuel Ayers

Lemuel Ayers was both a designer of sets and costumes and a theatrical producer. He was born in New York City on January 22, 1915. He received a degree in architecture from Princeton University and one in drama from the University of Iowa. Mr. Ayers received the Donaldson Award for both sets and costumes for *Kiss Me Kate* in 1943, and for *Camino Real* in 1952. He also received the Donaldson Award for *My Darlin' Aida* in 1952 and *Kismet* in 1953. He was married in 1939 and had two children. Mr. Ayers died in 1955 after a brief but brilliant career. His credits on Broadway as a set designer were extensive, and include *High Button Shoes* and *Oklahoma!*. He served as art director for the film *Meet Me in St. Louis*.

Scenic Designs:
1939: *Journey's End; They Knew What They Wanted* **1941:** *Angel Street; As You Like It; Eight O'Clock Tuesday; They Walk Alone* **1942:** *Autumn Hill; Pirate, The; Plan M; Willow and I, The* **1943:** *Harriet; Oklahoma!* **1944:** *Bloomer Girl; Peepshow; Song of Norway* **1946:** *Cyrano De Bergerac; St. Louis Woman* **1948:** *Inside U.S.A.; Kiss Me Kate* **1950:** *Out of This World* **1951:** *Music in the Air; Oklahoma!* **1952:** *Kiss Me Kate; My Darlin' Aida; See the Jaguar* **1953:** *Camino Real; Kismet* **1954:** *Pajama Game, The*

Lighting Designs:
1944: *Bloomer Girl* **1951:** *Music in the Air* **1952:** *My Darlin' Aida* **1953:** *Camino Real*

Costume Designs:
1941: *Angel Street; As You Like It; Macbeth* **1946:** *Cyrano De Bergerac; St. Louis Woman* **1948:** *Kiss Me Kate* **1950:** *Out of This World* **1951:** *Music in the Air* **1952:** *Kiss Me Kate; My Darlin' Aida; See the Jaguar* **1953:** *Camino Real; Kismet* **1954:** *Pajama Game, The*

James Bailey

James Bailey was a British designer and painter. He designed a production in 1949 of *A Midsummer Night's Dream* at Stratford-upon-Avon, ballets including *Giselle* and the operas *Mannon Lescault* and *Rigoletto* at Covent Garden. He was also associated with Sadler's Wells ballet. James Bailey lived from 1922 until 1980.

Scenic Designs:

1950: *As You Like It* 1952: *Millionairess, The*

Costume Designs:

1950: *As You Like It*

Léon Bakst

Léon Bakst, after a fortunate meeting with Diaghilev, designed many works for the Ballets Russe. He was a major influence on both fashion and costume during his lifetime. Bakst was born in Grodno, Russia in 1866 and studied in St. Petersburg but spent most of his life in Paris where he died in 1924. In addition to his designs for the stage he created clothes for couture houses, including Worth and Pacquin. An artist of great originality, Léon Bakst used strong colors and bold geometric forms. His designs graced the Broadway stage during the late teens and early twenties.

Scenic Designs:

1916: *Big Show, The* 1922: *Revue Russe*

Costume Designs:

1916: *Big Show, The* 1919: *Aphrodite* 1920: *Mecca* 1922: *Revue Russe*

Frances H. Ball

Frances H. Ball designed scenery for one play on Broadway in 1927. She resided at 147 West 74th Street in New York City in the 1920s.

Scenic Designs:

1927: *Wandering Jew, The*

Lucinda Ballard

Lucinda Ballard was born in New Orleans on April 3, 1908. Her father was a lawyer and her mother the political cartoonist Doré. Trained as an artist in New York City and Paris, she married William F. R. Ballard in 1930. That marriage ended in 1938 and in 1951 she married lyricist Howard Dietz. Miss Ballard began her active career in theatre as an assistant to the scenic designers Norman Bel Geddes and Claude Bragdon. In 1947 she received the first Antoinette Perry Award for Costume Design for five plays: *Happy Birthday*, *Another Part of the Forest*, *Street Scene*, *John Loves Mary* and *The Chocolate Soldier*. She won a second Tony Award in 1961 for *The Gay Life* and received the Donaldson Award for *The Glass Menagerie* in 1945. Her career designing costumes encompassed theatre, film and ballet. In recent years she has supervised revivals of productions which she originally designed.

Scenic Designs:

1943: *Moon Vine, The* 1948: *Make Way for Lucia*

Costume Designs:

1937: *As You Like It* 1938: *Great Lady* 1939: *Mornings At Seven; Three Sisters, The* 1940: *Higher and Higher* 1942: *Solitaire; Stars on Ice* 1943: *Moon Vine, The; My Dear Public* 1944: *I Remember Mama; Listen Professor; Sing Out, Sweet Land* 1945: *Memphis Bound; Place of Our Own, A* 1946: *Annie Get Your Gun; Another Part of the Forest; Happy Birthday; Show Boat* 1947: *Allegro; Chocolate Soldier, The; John Loves Mary; Street Scene; Streetcar Named Desire, A* 1948: *Love Life; Make Way for Lucia* 1949: *Rat Race, The* 1950: *Wisteria Trees, The* 1951: *Fourposter, The* 1952: *Mrs. McThing* 1953: *Carnival in Flanders; My Three Angels* 1955: *Cat on a Hot Tin Roof; Silk Stockings* 1957: *Clearing in the Woods, A; Dark At the Top of the Stairs, The; Orpheus Descending* 1958: *Girls in 509, The; Handful of Fire; J.B.* 1959: *Loss of Roses, A; Sound of Music, The* 1960: *Invitation to a March* 1961: *Gay Life, The* 1962: *Lord Pengo; Romulus; Tiger Tiger Burning Bright*

Ariel Ballif

Ariel Ballif was born in Rexburg, Idaho on May 29, 1926 and received a B.A. in art and theatre from Brigham Young University in 1947. After a brief stay in New York City taking theatre design courses at the New School for Social Research and creating displays for Macy's, he studied with Donald Oenslager and Frank Poole Bevan at Yale, receiving an M.F.A. His New York and Broadway debut occurred in 1953, shortly after completing graduate school. Throughout his subsequent career he has designed and taught at Brandeis University, Yale and the University of Utah, where he currently serves on the faculty. He was resident designer for the Virginia Museum Theatre when it opened and subsequently founded The Renaissance, a dinner theatre in Virginia. He also founded Theatre 138 in 1962 in Salt Lake City, Utah which remained active for twenty years. Recent credits include scenery for *Big River, The Miser, Driving Miss Daisy* and *The Three Musketeers* for the Pioneer Memorial Theatre at the University of Utah and a new production of *The Nutcracker* for the 1991/92 season at BalletWest.

Scenic Designs:
1953: *Pin to See the Peepshow, A*

Ballou

David R. (Tex) Ballou was born in Manila, The Philippines in 1925, the son of Charles Nicholas Senn Ballou and Emily Barnes Smith Ballou. His family includes a portrait artist, Bertha Ballou. Ballou received an M.F.A. at the Goodman Art Institute where he later spent six years as head of the costume program, teaching among others Theoni V. Aldredge. Ballou credits Mordecai Gorelik as a major influence on his career along with Richard Whorf and his other teachers while studying at Biarritz. His debut was for *Bachelor Born* for the Lynchburg (Virginia) Little Theatre. Ballou, who designs both scenery and costumes, has been awarded almost every professional prize in the New York theatre, including a Tony nomination for the scenic design for *The Legend of Lizzie* in 1959, the Vernon Rice award for *Machinal*, and Obie awards for *Machinal, A Doll's House* and the design of the off-Broadway Theatre Four. He is also an active industrial designer and has over three hundred credits for productions for Coca-Cola, I.B.M., Chevrolet, McDonald's, Charles of the Ritz and many others.

Scenic Designs:
1956: *Wake Up, Darling* **1959:** *Legend of Lizzie*

Lighting Designs:
1956: *Wake Up, Darling*

Costume Designs:
1954: *Flowering Peach, The* **1955:** *Red Roses for Me* **1959:** *Legend of Lizzie*

Bill Ballou

Bill Ballou has designed sets, sound, and lights and worked as a technician throughout New England, beginning with musicals in high school and followed by productions at the Rockland County Community Theatre. His credits include productions at Hartford Stage Company, American Place Theatre, Smith College, StageWest and Shakespeare and Company. His credits also include sound design off-Broadway and in regional theatres. He was born in Manhattan on April 26, 1950 and received a B.A. in theatre from Hampshire College in 1978. His mother, Billie Ballou, is a storyteller. He maintains a shop specializing in metal work and woodwork for theatres and also consults on the conception and coordination of feature films.

Scenic Designs:
1981: *Heartland*

Lighting Designs:
1981: *Heartland*

Leslie Banks

Leslie Banks was an actor in movies and the theatre in both New York and England who also directed and produced during a career lasting forty years. He was born in Liverpool, England on June 8, 1890 and died in London on April 21, 1952. As a young man he considered the priesthood, then painting, before appearing on stage at the Town Hall, Brechin as Old Gobbo in *The Merchant of Venice*. His New York debut on stage was in 1914 in *Eliza Comes to Stay*. In 1930 he not only designed the set, but also directed and starred in *The Infinite Shoeblack*. He was honored as a Commander of the British Empire in 1950.

Scenic Designs:
1930: *Infinite Shoeblack, The*

Vicki Baral

Vicki Baral works primarily with her husband Gerry Hariton creating sets and lights for plays and television on the East and West Coasts. Designs for television include the setting for Joan Rivers' *The Late Show*. She was born in Baltimore and graduated from Brandeis University. Baral and Hariton work extensively in California on set and lighting designs and as art directors/production designers. From 1974 to 1978 they were resident designers at the University of California at Riverside and have also served as resident designers for the Matrix Theatre. Their designs for the setting and lighting of *Betrayal* for the Matrix Theatre won two Los Angeles Critics Awards in 1982. Vicki Baral has also designed many productions at the Pasedena Playhouse.

Scenic Designs:
1986: *Raggedy Ann*

George Barbier

George Barbier is most often remembered as an illustrator who contributed to *Gazette du Bon Ton, Femina, Journal des Dames et des Modes, Vogue* and many others. He spent his life painting, illustrating and designing after studying at the Academie des Beaux-Arts in Paris. George Barbier, a disciple of Léon Bakst and Paul Poiret, was born in Nantes, France in 1882 and died in Paris in 1932. He received credits for many individual costumes or gowns for productions and only once in his career also contributed scenic designs to a Broadway show.

Scenic Designs:
1923: *Casanova*

Costume Designs:
1922: *Bunch and Judy, The* **1923:** *Casanova* **1928:** *Age of Innocence, The*; *Angela*; *Red Robe, The*; *White Lilacs* **1929:** *Boom Boom*; *Broadway Nights*; *Pleasure Bound* **1947:** *Street Scene*

Alan Barlow

Alan Barlow, a native of England, began designing for the Old Vic when he was 19 years old. Since that time he has designed numerous productions for the Stratford (Ontario) Festival, Dublin's Abbey Theatre, Covent Garden, and the Old Vic. Specializing in theatre and opera, Mr. Barlow has also taught at the National Theatre School in London.

Scenic Designs:
1972: *There's One in Every Marriage*
Costume Designs:
1972: *There's One in Every Marriage*

Robert Barnhart

Robert Barnhart both created sets and acted in Broadway shows. He was a partner with G. Bradford Ashworth and Arthur Segal in Studio Alliance, a scenery construction business, when it was founded in 1936. He also designed the set for a 1938 production of *The Two Bouquets*. He joined the Broadway cast of *Tobacco Road* in 1940, replacing Del Hughes in a role he had played previously with the Boston Company.

Scenic Designs:
1934: *Invitation to Murder*; *Too Many Boats*; *While Parents Sleep* **1935:** *Petticoat Fever* **1944:** *Good Morning Corporal*

Watson Barratt

Watson Barratt was a prolific scenic designer who occasionally also designed costumes and lights. He was born in Salt Lake City, Utah, on June 27, 1884 and studied in New York and Wilmington, Delaware. He began professional life as an illustrator, specializing in magazine covers. He entered the theatre as a scenic artist, later becoming the chief scenic designer for the Shuberts. His first scene designs on Broadway were seen in 1917 and he debuted as a costume designer on Broadway in 1926, after which he did numerous productions, including lighting for one in 1950. Mr. Barratt, who also served as director of the St. Louis Municipal Opera for several years, died in 1962.

Scenic Designs:
1917: *Night in Spain, A* **1918:** *Girl O' Mine*; *Ideal Husband, An*; *Little Journey, A*; *Little Simplicity*; *Melting of Molly, The*; *Passing Show of 1918, The*; *Sinbad*; *Sleeping Partners* **1919:** *Dancer, The*; *Monte Cristo, Jr*; *Oh, What a Girl*; *Passing Show of 1919, The*; *Shubert Gaieties of 1919*; *Sleepless Night, A* **1920:** *Cinderella on Broadway*; *Floradora*; *Outrageous Mrs. Palmer, The*; *Tick-Tack-Toe* **1921:** *Blossom Time*; *Bombo*; *In the Night Watch*; *Last Waltz, The*; *Mimic World, The*; *Silver Fox, The*; *Whirl of New York, The* **1922:** *Goldfish, The*;

Hotel Mouse, The; Lady in Ermine, The; Make It Snappy; Passing Show of 1922, The; Rose of Stamboul, The; Springtime of Youth; Thin Ice **1923:** *Artists and Models; Caroline; Dancing Girl, The; Dew Drop Inn; For All of Us; Passing Show of 1923, The; Topics of 1923* **1924:** *Artists and Models; Blossom Time; Dream Girl, The; Farmer's Wife, The; Innocent Eyes; Passing Show of 1924, The; Student Prince, The; Vogues of 1924; Werewolf, The* **1925:** *Artists and Models; Big Boy; Gay Paree; June Days; Lady's Virtue, A; Love Song, The; Mayflowers; Princess Flavia; Virgin of Bethulia, The* **1926:** *Blossom Time; Countess Maritza; First Love; Gay Paree; Great Temptations; Katja; Merry World, The; Night in Paris, A; Padre, The; Pearl of Great Price, The* **1927:** *Artists and Models; Cherry Blossoms; Circus Princess, The; Crown Prince, The; Immortal Isabella?; Love Call, The; Mixed Doubles; My Maryland; Night in Spain, A; Nightingale, The; Scarlet Lily, The* **1928:** *12,000; Angela; Countess Maritza; Greenwich Village Follies; Kingdom of God, The; Luckee Girl; Red Robe, The; Silent House, The; Sunny Days; Young Love* **1929:** *Boom Boom; Broadway Nights; Lady from the Sea, The; Love Duel, The; Music in May; Night in Venice, A; Pleasure Bound; Street Singer; Wonderful Night, A* **1930:** *Artists and Models; Lost Sheep; Meet My Sister; Nina Rosa; Royal Virgin, The; Scarlet Sister Mary; Three Little Girls* **1931:** *As You Desire Me; Blossom Time; Cynara; Experience Unnecessary; If I Were You; Peter Ibbetson; School for Scandal, The; Student Prince, The; Wonder Bar, The* **1932:** *Little Rocketeer, A; Marching By; Smiling Faces* **1933:** *Mikado, The; Ten Minute Alibi* **1934:** *Music Hath Charms; No More Ladies; Perfumed Lady, The; Roman Servant, A; Shatter'd Lamp, The; So Many Paths; Ziegfeld Follies: 1934* **1935:** *Knock on Wood; Laburnum Grove; Living Dangerously* **1936:** *Black Limelight; Case of Clyde Griffiths, The; Come Angel Band; Golden Journey, The; Green Waters; Lady Precious Stream; Laughing Woman, The; Mid-West* **1937:** *Frederika; Hitch Your Wagon; Lady Has a Heart, The; Merely Murder; Tell Me, Pretty Maiden; Three Waltzes; Wise Tomorrow* **1938:** *Bachelor Born; Blossom Time; Come Across; Madame Capet; Outward Bound; You Never Know* **1939:** *Billy Draws a Horse; Clean Beds; Close Quarters; Foreigners; Importance of Being Earnest,*

The; Time of Your Life, The; White Steed, The **1940:** *Kind Lady; Leave Her to Heaven; Love's Old Sweet Song; Romantic Mr. Dickens; Time of Your Life, The; Walk with Music* **1941:** *Ah, Wilderness; Golden Wings; Hope for a Harvest; My Fair Ladies; Night of Love* **1942:** *Little Darling; Magic/ Hello, Out There; Rivals, The; Yesterday's Magic* **1943:** *Artists and Models; Ask My Friend Sandy; Blossom Time; Student Prince, The; This Rock; Ziegfeld Follies: 1943* **1944:** *Bright Boy; Pick-Up Girl; Sheppy* **1945:** *Happily Ever After; Lady Says Yes, A; Rebecca* **1946:** *Flamingo Road; January Thaw* **1947:** *Heads Or Tails; Little A; Lousianna Lady* **1948:** *Ghosts; Hedda Gabler; My Romance* **1950:** *With a Silk Thread* **1954:** *Starcross Story, The* **1955:** *Righteous Are Bold, The*

Lighting Designs:
1950: *With a Silk Thread*

Costume Designs:
1926: *Pearl of Great Price, The* **1930:** *Hello, Paris* **1935:** *Living Dangerously* **1939:** *Importance of Being Earnest, The* **1942:** *Magic/ Hello, Out There; Rivals, The* **1950:** *With a Silk Thread*

Lewis Barrington

Lewis Barrington designed sets on Broadway in the mid-1920s. An artist, his studios were located at 220 West 14th Street in New York City in 1925.

Scenic Designs:
1925: *Book of Charm, The* **1927:** *Big Lake*

John Barrymore

John Barrymore, a member of one of the most respected American theatrical families, was interested in painting early in his life and studied art in Europe. A position as a cartoonist for the *New York Journal* ended soon after it began and he turned to acting at age twenty-one, finding enormous success on stage and in movies. Known as "The Great Profile," he had a flair for comedy and was known as a great lover on stage and off. John Barrymore, who used his artistic training to occasionally offer designs for settings, died on May 29, 1942 at age 60.

Scenic Designs:
1921: *Clair De Lune*

Ralph Barton

Ralph Barton was born in Kansas City, Missouri on August 14, 1891 and studied in Paris. He was a skilled cartoonist and caricaturist whose work appeared in *Vanity Fair, Judge, Life* and *Smart Set*. He illustrated books, designed the theatre curtain of caricatures for the 1922 *Chauve Souris*, and created sets for one Broadway show. Ralph Barton died a suicide on May 20, 1931.

Scenic Designs:
1923: *Poppy*

Charles Basing

Charles Basing, an American painter of murals, was born on July 23, 1865 in Victoria, Australia. He painted, among other projects, the ceiling in Grand Central Station and also designed museum interiors in New York City for Columbia University and in Pittsburgh for the Carnegie Institute. He died on February 3, 1933 in Marrakech, Morocco. He worked in collaboration with brothers Arthur T. and J. Monroe Hewlett on stage settings and murals. For credits and additional information see the entry "Hewlett and Basing".

Alfred Bauer

Alfred Bauer designed sets in 1935 on Broadway.

Scenic Designs:
1935: *Few Are Chosen*

Peter Bax

Peter Bax designed sets in the early 1930s on Broadway. He was the assistant stage manager for numerous productions in London directed by William Abingdon, including *The Forest, London Life, A Midsummer Night's Dream* and *The Claimant* in 1924, *Rose Marie* in 1925, *The Desert Song* and *The Wandering Jew* in 1927, *Show Boat* and *London Pride* in 1928, and *The New May* in 1929. As was the practice in the theatre of the time, he very likely contributed designs to these productions and others, particularly contemporary pieces or those in the standard repertory, in his capacity as assistant stage manager.

Scenic Designs:
1931: *Venetian, The*

John W. Baxter

John W. Baxter, a British director of plays and movies, lived and worked primarily in England. He directed Deborah Kerr in the film *Love on the Dole* and was active directing and producing films between 1933 and 1959, after which he was named managing director of a television studio. He died in February 1975.

Scenic Designs:
1925: *Fall of Eve, The*

Howard Bay

Howard Bay, well known as a scenery and lighting designer, was involved with nearly two hundred productions during his career. Originally from Centralia, Washington where he was born on May 3, 1912, he directed and taught as well as designed for the theatre after his professional debut in 1933 with *There's a Moon Tonight*. Mr. Bay also designed for television, film, and industrial shows. He lectured, wrote books about design and was active in professional associations, serving as President of United Scenic Artists. Occasionally during his long, prolific career Mr. Bay also contributed costume designs to a production in addition to the sets and lights, including *Man of La Mancha* which he designed with Patton Campbell, and with whom he shared a Tony nomination. He won a Tony Award for *Toys in the Attic*, a Maharam Award for *Man of La Mancha* and Donaldson Awards for *Carmen Jones* and *Up in Central Park*. Mr. Bay died on November 21, 1986 at age 74 while working on a production of *The Music Man* to be presented at the Peking Opera House.

Scenic Designs:
1936: *Battle Hymn; Chalk Dust* **1937:** *Marching Song; Native Ground; One Third of a Nation; Power* **1938:** *Life and Death of An American; Merry Wives of Windsor, The; Sunup to Sundown; Trojan Incident* **1939:** *Little Foxes, The* **1940:** *Corn Is Green, The; Fifth Column, The; Morning Star* **1941:** *Brooklyn, U.S.A.; Man with Blond Hair, The* **1942:** *Count Me in; Eve of Saint Mark, The; Great Big Doorstop, The; Johnny 2x4; Moon Is Down, The; Strings, My Lord, Are False, The; Uncle Harry* **1943:** *Carmen Jones; Corn Is Green, The; Merry Widow, The; New Life, A; One Touch of Venus; Patriots, The; Something for the Boys* **1944:**

Catherine Was Great; Chicken Every Sunday; Follow the Girls; Listen Professor; Men to the Sea; Searching Wind, The; Storm Operation; Ten Little Indians; Violet; Visitor,the **1945:** *Deep Are the Roots; Devil's Galore; Marinka; Polonaise; Up in Central Park* **1946:** *Show Boat; Woman Bites Dog; Would-Be Gentleman, The* **1948:** *As the Girls Go; Magdalena* **1949:** *Big Knife, The; Magnolia Alley; Montserrat* **1950:** *Come Back, Little Sheba; Hilda Crane; Michael Todd's Peep Show* **1951:** *Autumn Garden, The; Flahooey; Grand Tour, The; Two on the Aisle* **1952:** *Shrike, The* **1953:** *Children's Hour, The; Mid-summer* **1955:** *Desperate Hours, The; Red Roses for Me* **1956:** *Night of the Auk; Very Special Baby, A* **1957:** *Music Man, The* **1958:** *Interlock* **1959:** *Desert Incident, A* **1960:** *Cool World, The; Cut of the Axe; Toys in the Attic; Wall, The* **1961:** *Isle of Children; Milk and Honey* **1963:** *Bicycle Ride to Nevada; My Mother, My Father and Me* **1964:** *Never Live Over a Pretzel Factory* **1969:** *Fire!* **1970:** *Cry for Us All* **1976:** *Home Sweet Homer; Poor Murderer* **1977:** *Man of La Mancha* **1979:** *Utter Glory of Morrissey Hale, The*

Lighting Designs:

1944: *Chicken Every Sunday; Follow the Girls; Men to the Sea* **1945:** *Up in Central Park* **1948:** *Magdalena* **1949:** *Magnolia Alley* **1951:** *Autumn Garden, The; Flahooey* **1953:** *Midsummer* **1955:** *Desperate Hours, The; Red Roses for Me* **1956:** *Night of the Auk; Very Special Baby, A* **1957:** *Look Back in Anger; Music Man, The; Romanoff and Juliet* **1958:** *Interlock* **1959:** *Desert Incident, A; Fighting Cock, The* **1960:** *Cool World, The; Cut of the Axe; Toys in the Attic; Wall, The* **1961:** *Isle of Children; Milk and Honey* **1963:** *Bicycle Ride to Nevada; My Mother, My Father and Me* **1964:** *Never Live Over a Pretzel Factory* **1969:** *Fire!* **1970:** *Cry for Us All* **1976:** *Home Sweet Homer; Poor Murderer* **1977:** *Man of La Mancha* **1979:** *Utter Glory of Morrissey Hale, The*

Costume Designs:

1938: *Merry Wives of Windsor, The; Sunup to Sundown; Trojan Incident* **1950:** *Hilda Crane* **1957:** *Look Back in Anger* **1976:** *Home Sweet Homer* **1977:** *Man of La Mancha*

Cecil Beaton

Cecil Beaton designed many handsome costumes and sets during his lifetime and will always be identified with his contribution to both the stage and film versions of *My Fair Lady.* Cecil Walter Hardy Beaton was born in London in 1904 and began sketching costumes at a very young age, dressing himself and his family for playlets which he also staged. Cecil Beaton's designs for opera, stage and film were regularly seen in the United States and England. He specialized in settings and costumes and for one production on Broadway in 1946 also designed the lighting. Details of his life as a photographer and designer have been well documented through publications of his diaries, reminiscences, and photographs. He selected an official biographer, Hugo Vickers, shortly before his death in 1980 at the age of 76. The book, *Cecil Beaton, A Biography* was published in 1986. He was nominated for six Tony awards and received four: *Quadrille* in 1955, *My Fair Lady* in 1957, *Saratoga* in 1960, and *Coco* in 1970.

Scenic Designs:

1946: *Lady Windermere's Fan* **1950:** *Cry of the Peacock* **1952:** *Grass Harp, The* **1954:** *Quadrille* **1955:** *Chalk Garden, The; Little Glass Clock, The* **1956:** *Glass Clock, The* **1959:** *Look After Lulu; Saratoga* **1960:** *Tenderloin* **1969:** *Coco*

Lighting Designs:

1946: *Lady Windermere's Fan*

Costume Designs:

1946: *Lady Windermere's Fan* **1950:** *Cry of the Peacock* **1952:** *Grass Harp, The* **1954:** *Portrait of a Lady; Quadrille* **1955:** *Chalk Garden, The; Little Glass Clock, The* **1956:** *My Fair Lady* **1959:** *Look After Lulu; Saratoga* **1960:** *Dear Liar; Tenderloin* **1969:** *Coco* **1976:** *My Fair Lady* **1981:** *My Fair Lady*

John Lee Beatty

John Lee Beatty was born on April 14, 1948 in Palo Alto, California. He attended Brown University, graduating cum laude with a B.A. in English literature in 1970. He attended Yale and received an M.F.A. in design in 1973. His career has been influenced by Ming Cho Lee, Arnold Abramson, and Douglas W. Schmidt. His first designs were for *The Jenkins Red Carriage* in the fourth grade. He has received numerous awards including the Tony, Obie, Drama Desk, Outer Critics Circle, Maharam, Jefferson (Chicago), and Los Angeles Drama Critics Award.

Scenic Designs:
1976: *Innocents, The; Knock Knock* **1978:** *Ain't Misbehavin'; Water Engine, The/ Mr. Happiness* **1979:** *Faith Healer; Whoopee* **1980:** *Fifth of July; Hide and Seek; Talley's Folly* **1981:** *Crimes of the Heart; Duet for One; Five O'clock Girl, The; Fools* **1982:** *Alice in Wonderland; Curse of An Aching Heart, The; Is There Life After High School; Monday After the Miracle* **1983:** *Angels Fall; Baby; Passion* **1985:** *Octette Bridge Club, The* **1986:** *Loot* **1987:** *Burn This; Nerd, The; Penn & Teller* **1988:** *Ain't Misbehavin'*

Norman Bel Geddes

Norman Bel Geddes was both a designer of sets and costumes, a producer and an industrial designer. He was born in 1893 in Adrian, Michigan and died in 1958. He began designing in 1916 in California and in 1918 designed sets for a production at the Metropolitan Opera, marking his debut in New York City. Mr. Bel Geddes never created costumes without also designing the sets for a production. His career was remarkable, and although his list of credits on Broadway is not long, he was involved in well over two hundred productions during his lifetime, designing, writing about design and producing. His creativity was well used in the theatre where he designed such innovative productions as *The Miracle* for Max Reinhardt and was important in the development of the New American Stagecraft movement. He also designed and consulted on the design of theatres around the world. Norman Bel Geddes was married to the costume designer Edith Lutyens, and is the father of the actress Barbara Bel Geddes.

Scenic Designs:
1917: *I.O.U.* **1918:** *I.O.U.* **1921:** *Ermine* **1922:** *Orange Blossoms; Truth About Blayds, The* **1923:** *Will Shakespeare* **1924:** *Lady, Be Good; Miracle, The; Quarantine; She Stoops to Conquer* **1925:** *Arabesque* **1926:** *Devil in the Cheese* **1927:** *Creoles; Damn the Tears; Five O'Clock Girl; John; Julius Caesar; Spread Eagle* **1928:** *Patriot, The; She Stoops to Conquer* **1929:** *Fifty Million Frenchmen* **1930:** *Change*

Your Luck **1931:** *Hamlet* **1932:** *Flying Colors* **1935:** *Dead End* **1936:** *Iron Men* **1937:** *Eternal Road, The; Seige* **1940:** *It Happens on Ice* **1941:** *It Happens on Ice* **1943:** *Sons and Soldiers* **1944:** *Seven Lively Arts*

Lighting Designs:
1917: *I.O.U.* **1918:** *I.O.U.* **1924:** *Miracle, The* **1931:** *Hamlet* **1932:** *Flying Colors* **1937:** *Eternal Road, The* **1940:** *It Happens on Ice*

Costume Designs:
1921: *Ermine* **1923:** *Will Shakespeare* **1924:** *Miracle, The* **1925:** *Arabesque* **1926:** *Devil in the Cheese* **1930:** *Change Your Luck* **1931:** *Hamlet* **1935:** *Dead End* **1936:** *Iron Men* **1937:** *Eternal Road, The* **1940:** *It Happens on Ice* **1941:** *It Happens on Ice* **1943:** *Sons and Soldiers*

Ursula Belden

Born in Germany on September 27, 1947, Ursula Belden is the daughter of Edith and Ernest Mugdan. She attended the University of Michigan and was in the class of 1976 at the Yale University School of Drama where she studied with Ming Cho Lee. Her first professional design was *Sleuth* at the Indiana Repertory Theatre in 1978, directed by Ed Stern. She received the Village Award for outstanding scene design off-Broadway for Strindberg's *Dream Play*, directed by Susan Einhorn.

Scenic Designs:
1984: *Quilters*

Stanley Bell

Stanley Bell, a British director, producer and scenic designer, worked occasionally in New York in 1930 and 1931 designing plays for Gilbert Miller and the Charles Frohman Company. He was born in North Hingham, England on October 8, 1881 and studied at the Leeds School of Science for a career as an analytical chemist. In 1897 he began painting scenery and in 1900 began acting. As a member of Sir Herbert Tree's Company he performed, designed sets, and stage managed from 1906 to 1914, after which he entered military service. Throughout the 1920s and 1930s he produced and designed numerous plays and ice spectacles in the United States and Great Britain. During World War

II he organized Garrison Theatres and Station Theatres. He was honored with a Commander of the British Empire (C.B.E.) in 1946. Stanley Bell died on January 4, 1952 at age 70.

Scenic Designs:
1930: *Dishonored Lady; Marseilles; One, Two, Three/ The Violet; Petticoat Influence; Stepdaughters of War* **1931:** *Company's Coming*

Constance Bellamy

Constance Bellamy designed scenery on Broadway in the mid-1920s. In addition, she was associated with the McIlroy Studios and also worked as a decorator from an office on 57th Street. In 1932 she was a member of the decorating firm Frances White, at 821 Madison Avenue, New York City.

Scenic Designs:
1924: *Red Falcon, The*

Issac Benesch

Issac Benesch designed three sets on Broadway, one each in 1931, 1932 and 1933. He also lectured at the Neighborhood Playhouse on theatrical design.

Scenic Designs:
1931: *People on the Hill* **1932:** *Merry-Go-Round* **1933:** *Sophisticrats, The*

H. Gordon Bennett

Harry Gordon Bennett designed sets on Broadway between 1935 and 1946 as H. Gordon Bennett. He also designed plays for Theatre 4, including *Dracula* in 1943, and the setting for *Cap and Gown* in 1941 while on assignment from the Special Services Office during World War II .

Scenic Designs:
1935: *Mother Sings* **1942:** *All Comforts of Home; Oy Is Dus a Leben!* **1944:** *According to Law; Strange Play, A* **1945:** *Lady in Danger* **1946:** *Duchess of Malfi*

Benrimo

J. Harry Benrimo was an actor, playwright, and producer who was active in the theatre in California, London and New York. His acting career began in California, but he soon moved to

New York where he first appeared in *The First Born* in 1897, later performing the same role in London. He co-authored several plays, including *The Yellow Jacket* with George C. Hazelton, which he also designed. Born in San Francisco on June 21, 1874, he died on May 26, 1942.

Scenic Designs:
1917: *Willow Tree, The* **1928:** *Yellow Jacket, The*

Lighting Designs:
1928: *Yellow Jacket, The*

Costume Designs:
1917: *Willow Tree, The* **1928:** *Yellow Jacket, The*

Thomas D. Benrimo

Thomas D. Benrimo, a surrealist painter, was the brother of J. Harry Benrimo. Thomas Benrimo worked at one time for the scenic studio Gates and Morange. He was a member of the Taos (New Mexico) Art Colony, living and painting in residence for the twenty years prior to his death in May 1958. Prior to moving to Taos he taught at Brooklyn's Pratt Institute in the Department of Advertising and Design from 1936 to 1939.

Scenic Designs:
1916: *Tempest, The*

Costume Designs:
1916: *Tempest, The*

Susan Benson

Susan Benson was born on April 22, 1942 in Bexley Heath, Kent, England. She studied at the West of England College of Art in Bristol. She moved to Canada in 1966 and is widely known for her designs at the Stratford (Ontario) Festival where she first designed in 1974, continuing steadily until 1987. Other designs include productions for the Canadian Opera Company, National Ballet of Canada, and the National Arts Center. Her many awards include six Dora Mavor Moore Awards, one Jessie and one Ace. In addition to being a theatrical designer she is a portrait painter. Her solo painting exhibitions have featured portraits of the prominent Stratford (Ontario) Festival actors William Hutt and Nicholas Pennel. She was elected to the Royal Canadian Academy in 1988.

Scenic Designs:
1987: *Mikado, The*

Costume Designs:
1987: *Mikado, The*

Frederick Bentley

Frederick Bentley designed one set on Broadway in 1926. A British actor and singer, he was understudy to Robert Blythe in the role of Perigrine Smith in *Wild Geese* in London in the 1920s. He also performed with Mohawk Minstrels in London as a child. At the time of his death on November 12, 1939 in London, he was a music publisher, having been music editor for the Lawrence Wright Music Company.

Scenic Designs:
1926: *Great Adventure, The*

Christian Bérard

Christian-Jacques Bérard, born in France in 1902, died at the age of 47 in 1949. During his short but productive life he painted, illustrated books, sketched fashions, created advertisements, and designed costumes and scenery. He designed for the theatre, ballet, and film, mainly in France. His designs were marked by a love of fantasy and baroque decoration which he used with considerable style. Noteworthy designs include the Cocteau film *Beauty and the Beast* and a production of *Clock Symphony* by Massine at Sadlers Wells.

Scenic Designs:
1948: *Madwoman of Chaillot* 1952: *Amphitryon; Les Fourberies De Scapin*

Costume Designs:
1948: *Madwoman of Chaillot* 1952: *Amphitryon; Les Fourberies De Scapin*

Ouida Bergere

Ouida Bergere, a film actress, talent agent and playwright for stage and screen, made her Broadway debut in *The Stranger* in 1911. She wrote many plays including *Bella Donna, That Woman, The Vicious Circle, Surburbia Comes to Paradise* and *Kick In* and also wrote silent film scripts. She was the widow of Basil Rathbone and was a famous hostess in Hollywood.

At the time of her death in New York City on November 29, 1974 at age 88 she was working on her memoirs.

Scenic Designs:
1927: *Command to Love, The* 1928: *Wrecker, The*

Robert W. Bergman Studio

Robert W. Bergman was Vice President of the Art Students' League of New York in 1916 and worked as a scenic artist at Lee Lash Studios in 1918. "Berg" had a reputation as a perfectionist and painted scenery for the Washington Player's shops. He also painted for Robert Edmond Jones and Norman Bel Geddes, who subsequently arranged for him to set up his own studio. In 1922 he was President of Bergman, Nayan Studios, Inc. and resided in Jamaica, Queens. Robert W. Bergman Studio, Inc. was located at 142 West 49th Street in New York City in 1931, an address shared with designer Robert Edmond Jones.

Scenic Designs:
1922: *Charlatan, The* 1924: *Old English* 1927: *Spellbound*

Aline Bernstein

Aline Bernstein had a distinguished career as the first prominent female scenic and costume designer. She was born on December 22, 1882, the daughter of actor Joseph Frankau, and originally hoped to follow in his footsteps. However, she began designing dresses for the Neighborhood Playhouse and soon left behind all thoughts of performing. In addition to designing on Broadway for thirty-four years, she helped found the Museum of Costume Art at Rockefeller Center (now at the Metropolitan Museum of Art). In 1926 she became the first woman to attain membership as a scenic designer in the Brotherhood of Painters, Decorators and Paperhangers of the American Federation of Labor, the union which at that time represented designers. In 1950 she received a Tony Award for the costumes for *Regina*. Mrs. Bernstein, in addition to a busy career designing, also wrote two novels, *Three Blue Suits* and *The Journey Down*. Her relationship with novelist Thomas Wolfe was recorded by Wolfe in many of his books. Their correspondence was collected in *My Other Loneliness*, edited by Suzanne Stutman and published in 1983 by the University of North Carolina Press. Married to Theodore Bernstein and the mother of two children, Aline Frankau Bernstein died in 1955 at the age of 72.

Scenic Designs:
1924: *Little Clay Cart, The* **1925:** *Critic, The; Dybbuck, The; Legend of the Dance, The* **1926:** *Apothecary, The; Grand Street Follies; Lion Tamer, The; Little Clay Cart, The; Ned Mc Cobb's Daughter, Romantic Young Lady, The* **1927:** *Commedia del'Arte; Grand Street Follies; If; Love Nest, The; Lovers and Enemies; Tone Pictures/The White Peacock* **1928:** *Caprice; Cherry Orchard, The; First Stone, The; Grand Street Follies; Hedda Gabler; Improvisations in June; L'Invitation Au Voyage; Maya; Peter Pan; Would-Be Gentleman, The* **1929:** *Cherry Orchard, The; Game of Love and Death, The; Grand Street Follies; Katerina; Lady from Alfaqueque, The; Living Corpse, The; Mademoiselle Bourrat; On the High Road; Seagull, The* **1930:** *Alison's House; Grand Hotel; Green Cockatoo, The; Lady from Alfaqueque, The; Romeo and Juliet; Siegfried; Women Have Their Way/ The Open Door* **1931:** *Getting Married; Reunion in Vienna; Tommorrow and Tomorrow* **1932:** *Animal Kingdom, The; Clear All Wires; Firebird; Jewel Robbery; Late Christopher Bean, The; Lenin's Dowry; Liliom* **1933:** *Cherry Orchard, The; Good Woman, Poor Thing, A; Thunder on the Left; We, the People* **1934:** *Between Two Worlds; Children's Hour; Judgement Day; L'Aiglon; Mackerel Skies* **1935:** *Camille; Night in the House; Sunny Morning, A/ The Women Have Their Way/ etc.* **1936:** *And Stars Remain; Days to Come* **1937:** *Storm Over Patsy; To Quito and Back* **1938:** *American Landscape* **1940:** *Male Animal, The* **1950:** *Happy Time, The*

Lighting Designs:
1924: *Little Clay Cart, The*

Costume Designs:
1916: *Inca of Perusalem, The; Queen's Enemies, The* **1921:** *Great Broxopp, The* **1922:** *Fashions for Men* **1924:** *Little Clay Cart, The; She Stoops to Conquer* **1925:** *Caesar and Cleopatra; Dybbuck, The; Grand Street Follies; Hamlet; Legend of the Dance, The* **1926:** *Apothecary, The; Grand Street Follies; Lion Tamer, The; Little Clay Cart, The; Ned Mc*

Cobb's Daughter; Romantic Young Lady, The; White Wings **1927:** *Commedia del'Arte; Doctor's Dilemma, The; Grand Street Follies; If; Love Nest, The; Lovers and Enemies; Tone Pictures/The White Peacock* **1928:** *Cherry Orchard, The; First Stone, The; Grand Street Follies; Hedda Gabler; Improvisations in June; Maya; Peter Pan; Would-Be Gentleman, The* **1929:** *Game of Love and Death, The; Grand Street Follies; Lady from Alfaqueque, The; Living Corpse, The; On the High Road; Seagull, The* **1930:** *Alison's House; Grand Hotel; Green Cockatoo, The; Lady from Alfaqueque, The; Romeo and Juliet; Siegfried; Women Have Their Way/ The Open Door* **1932:** *Clear All Wires; Dark Hours, The; Liliom* **1933:** *Cherry Orchard, The* **1934:** *L'Aiglon* **1935:** *Camille; Night in the House; Sunny Morning, A/ The Women Have Their Way/ etc.* **1937:** *To Quito and Back* **1938:** *American Landscape* **1939:** *Little Foxes, The* **1942:** *Willow and I, The* **1943:** *Harriet; Innocent Voyage, The* **1944:** *Feathers in a Gale; Searching Wind, The* **1947:** *Eagle Has Two Heads, The* **1949:** *Regina* **1950:** *Burning Bright; Enemy of the People, An; Happy Time, The; Let's Make An Opera*

Melville Bernstein

Melville Bernstein designed two sets in 1939 on Broadway.

Scenic Designs:
1939: *Cure for Matrimony; Steel*

Emile Bertin

Emile Bertin, who designed under the name "Bertin," was a painter, illustrator and scenic designer. He was born on January 29, 1878 in Surenes (Seine), France and lived and worked in Paris. He received a diploma in 1915 from the School of Decorative Arts and studied with Eugène Carrière. He participated in exhibitions at Salon d'Automne, Artistes Indépendants, and the Salon des Humanistes. At one time, he served as president of the union of scenic designers and scenic painters in France. He designed occasionally for the Comédie Française, where he mainly painted scenery, and also for the Champs-Elysees Theatre, Theatre des Arts, and Theatre du Gymnase in Paris. In London he designed *Mozart* in 1926, (revived in 1929), and *Mariette* in 1929. Emile Bertin died in Paris in 1957.

Scenic Designs:
1939: *Folies Bergère* **1955:** *Arlequin Poli Par 'Amour; Le Barbier De Seville*

Andre Bicat

Andre Bicat designed one set on Broadway in 1938.

Scenic Designs:
1938: *Murder in the Cathedral*

Jean Bilibine

Jean Bilibine (a.k.a. Iwan-Jakowlewitsch Bilibine, Ivan Yakovlevich Bilibin), a painter and theatrical designer, was born in St. Petersburg, Russia on August 4, 1876. He studied with Repin and created illustrations for Russian stories, recorded the designs of Russian peasant costumes, and worked in a museum in Moscow. A member of the Academie des Beaux Arts in St. Petersburg, he also designed sets and costumes for *Tzar Saltan* for the Opera Prive de Paris in 1929 and productions at other locations, including Broadway. His designs in London included costumes for the 1923 ballet *An Old Russian Folk Lore*, and scenery and costumes for the 1925 ballet *The Romance of a Mummy* at Covent Garden. He died in Leningrad on February 7, 1942.

Scenic Designs:
1930: *Glass of Water, A*

Costume Designs:
1930: *Glass of Water, A*

William Birns

William Birns contributed interior designs in collaboration with other designers for his Broadway credits. For his initial credit, *Taking Chances* he provided "decorations and hangings" and for *One Glorious Hour* he provided "interior decoration". In 1928 he received prominent credit for properties for *That Ferguson Family* in the playbill, a rarity at that time. In 1931 he also contributed furniture, paintings and objects of art from the Galleries of William Birns to *Joy of Living* and again received billing in the playbill. An antique dealer who specialized in renting furniture and properties for plays and movies, his business was located in 1919 at 103 West 37th Street prior to moving to 307 West 37th Street in New York City. Born in Germany, he moved to New York City in 1888 and quickly established his business there. His business suffered when the movie industry left New York for the West Coast, and he relocated his shop to Third Avenue at 55th Street. William Birns died at age 77 on January 9, 1948.

Scenic Designs:
1915: *Taking Chances* **1927:** *One Glorious Hour* **1928:** *That Ferguson Family*

Maria Bjornson

Maria Bjornson received Tony nominations for both the scenery and costumes of *Phantom of the Opera* and received Drama Desk Awards for both. She designs regularly for the Royal Shakespeare Company, Glasgow Citizens (where her career began), and the English National Opera. Her opera designs are known throughout Europe and the United States and include *Die Meistersinger, Don Giovanni* and *Katya Kabanova* for the Scottish Opera, *Jenufa* in Houston, and *Ernani, From the House of the Dead, Toussaint L'Ouverture, Rigoletto* and Wagner's *Ring Cycle* for the English National Opera. She was born in Paris in 1949 of Norwegian and Rumanian parents, and reared in England.

Scenic Designs:
1988: *Phantom of the Opera, The* **1990:** *Aspects of Love*

Costume Designs:
1988: *Phantom of the Opera, The* **1990:** *Aspects of Love*

Jack Blackman

Jack Blackman studied at Columbia University and with Lester Polakov at the Studio and Forum of Stage Design. Mr. Blackman is known as a set and lighting designer who works in theatre, film and television, especially for ABC-TV. He designed the off-Broadway theatre Stage 73 and was art director for the 1985 film *The Ultimate Solution of Grace Quigley*.

Scenic Designs:
1964: *Sign in Sidney Brustein's Window, The* **1965:** *Postmark Zero*

Lighting Designs:

1965: *Postmark Zero*

Costume Designs:

1965: *Postmark Zero*

John E. Blankenchip

John E. Blankenchip was born in Independence, Kansas on November 14, 1919. He received a B.F.A. in Scene Design and Directing from the Carnegie Institute of Technology in 1941, where he studied with Lloyd Weninger and Bess Schraeder Kimberly. In 1943 he received an M.F.A. from Yale, after studying with Donald Oenslager, Frank Bevan, George Eisenhower and Stanley McCandless. Mr. Blankenchip worked as assistant designer under Harry Horner for shows including *Winged Victory.* He designs all elements for a production when possible, and in his debut on Broadway created both sets and costumes. Mr. Blankenchip, who teaches design and directing at the University of Southern California, continues to design occasionally, including sets, costumes and lights for a recent production of *Pal Joey* in La Jolla.

Scenic Designs:

1951: *Angel in the Pawnshop* **1952:** *Long Watch, The*

Lighting Designs:

1951: *Angel in the Pawnshop*

Costume Designs:

1951: *Angel in the Pawnshop* **1952:** *Long Watch, The*

Albert Bliss

Albert Bliss designed scenery for five plays on Broadway between 1925 and 1928.

Scenic Designs:

1925: *Little Poor Man, The* **1926:** *Easter; Kept* **1927:** *Ink* **1928:** *Meek Mouse*

Rose Bogdanoff

Rose Bogdanoff designed costumes on Broadway for fifteen years before becoming one of television's first costume designers. She only rarely designed scenery. At the time of her death in 1957 at the age of 53, she was the senior costume designer for NBC-TV which she joined in 1948.

Miss Bogdanoff was born in Philadelphia and studied at the Art Institute of Chicago and the San Francisco Art School. Rose Bogdanoff was considered to be an expert on color and often lectured at universities and for the Free Lecture Series at the New York Public Library.

Scenic Designs:

1944: *War President*

Costume Designs:

1940: *Man Who Killed Lincoln, The* **1941:** *Cream in the Well; Junior Miss* **1942:** *Moon Is Down, The; Nathan the Wise* **1943:** *I'll Take the High Road; Patriots, The* **1944:** *Chicken Every Sunday; Last Stop; Sophie; War President* **1945:** *It's a Gift; Stranger, The* **1946:** *Lysistrata* **1948:** *Bravo; Kathleen; Me and Molly; Summer and Smoke; Survivors, The* **1951:** *Rose Tattoo, The* **1953:** *Trip to Bountiful, The*

Edgar Bohlman

Edgar Bohlman was born in Cottage Grove, Oregon on January 1, 1902 and studied architecture at the University of Oregon. He designed sets and costumes in New York between 1928 and 1931, and also for the American Opera Company and the Theatre Assembly. He then turned his attention to painting and illustrating, often on ballet and theatre subjects. His paintings were exhibited in New York and Europe. Other projects included documenting clothing worn in the Moroccan Sahara and illustrating *Moroccan Marriage.*

Scenic Designs:

1929: *Ledge, A; Lolly; Novice and the Duke, The* **1930:** *Everything's Joke; They Never Grow Up* **1931:** *Venetian Glass Nephew, The*

Costume Designs:

1929: *Lolly* **1930:** *They Never Grow Up*

Bill Bohnert

Bill Bohnert, son of the professional artists Herbert and Margaret Bohnert, was born on March 3, 1932. He received a B.A. in Architecture at the Massachusetts Institute of Technology and an M.F.A. in Stage Design at Yale, where he was influenced by Donald Oenslager. He is primarily an art director for television, and for ten years designed *The Ed Sullivan Show.* Recent television designs include *America's Funniest Home*

Videos, Everyday for Joan Lunden, award shows including the *1989 Emmy Awards, The Country Music Association Awards, Grammy Awards,* specials, and sitcoms. He also designs children's shows, including the series *Mathnet* for Children's Television Workshop, *The Electric Company,* and *Kids Are People Too,* telethons, game shows, live casino shows in Las Vegas, and many, many more.

Scenic Designs:
1984: *Doug Henning and His World of Magic*

Frank J. Boros

Frank J. Boros was born in Bridgeport, Connecticut on March 4, 1943. He attended the University of Connecticut and began designing there, starting with costumes for *Don Giovanni.* He received an M.F.A. at Yale in 1969 where he studied with Frank Poole Bevan. In 1975 he made his debut on Broadway with the openings of two plays at the same time. Besides designing costumes and scenery for the theatre, Mr. Boros is an art director in the film business.

Scenic Designs:
1975: *Lieutenant, The* **1981:** *Shakespeare's Cabaret*

Costume Designs:
1975: *Lieutenant, The*; *P.S. Your Cat Is Dead*
1981: *Shakespeare's Cabaret*

Charles E. Boss

Charles E. Boss died at age 65 on March 17, 1940 in Mount Vernon, New York. He was a scenic artist active in early films, including D.W. Griffith's *Way Down East.* His Broadway credits include the Act III set for *You Never Can Tell* in collaboration with H.A. Vincent. He also built displays for the New York World's Fair for General Motors Corporation, and designed and painted scenery for summer stock, municipal stock companies and theatre chains.

Scenic Designs:
1915: *Arms and the Man*; *You Never Can Tell*
1932: *Carrie Nation*

Michael P. Bottari

Michael P. Bottari is from Philadelphia where he was born October 14, 1948, the son of Guido and Malvina Bottari. He studied for two years at Temple University and two years at New York University School of the Arts. His career in the theatre has been influenced by high school drama coach Francis A. Perri, apprentice leader Jack Batman, art teacher Robert Rabinowitz and designer Robert Green. He generally designs in collaboration with Ronald Case and has created sets and/or costumes for numerous touring productions, off-Broadway shows, productions in regional theatres, television and industrial promotions. Together they have been nominated twice for the Carbonell Award in south Florida for designs at the Burt Reynolds Theatre. In addition to his theatrical design, Michael Bottari has created a line of soft sculptured replicas of famous dance shoes, such as the Ruby Slipper, Gwen Verdon's boot, a toe shoe and others.

Scenic Designs:
1989: *Prince of Central Park*

Costume Designs:
1989: *Prince of Central Park*

Mel Bourne

Mel Bourne was born on November 22, 1923 and was reared in Chicago. He studied electrical engineering at Purdue and subsequently at LeHigh University before turning his attention to design. He studied with Frank Bevan at the Yale School of Drama and worked as an assistant to Robert Edmond Jones for four years. He made his New York debut with the Theatre Guild's production of *Seagulls over Sorento.* Mr. Bourne currently spends most of his time designing films, including art direction of *Rude Awakening, Manahttan, Annie Hall, Still of the Night, Fatal Attraction* and *Reversal of Fortune,* among many others. His designs have been regularly honored with Academy Award nominations for Art Direction. He also designs commercials and television productions.

Scenic Designs:
1952: *Male Animal, The*; *Seagulls Over Sorrento* **1953:** *End As a Man*

Lighting Designs:
1952: *Seagulls Over Sorrento*

Costume Designs:
1953: *End As a Man*

John Boyt

John Boyt has designed sets, costumes and/or lights for numerous productions in New York since 1946. Besides his designs for the theatre, he has created costumes and scenery for ballets, operas, and television. He designed the world premier of Aaron Copeland's *The Tender Land* and many other productions at the New York City Center. John Boyt was born in Newark, New Jersey on April 19, 1921 and was graduated from the University of Iowa in 1942. He also attended Northwestern University and studied at the Mohawk Drama Festival in Schenectady, New York.

Scenic Designs:
1946: *Playboy of the Western World, The* 1956: *Debut*

Lighting Designs:
1956: *Debut*

Costume Designs:
1946: *Flag Is Born, A*; *Playboy of the Western World, The*; *Years Ago* 1947: *Anthony and Cleopatra* 1955: *Wooden Dish, The* 1956: *Debut*; *Lovers, The*

John Braden

John Braden was born on January 20, 1935 in Frederick, Colorado and attended the California College of Arts and Crafts, Chicago Art Institute, Goodman Theatre School and and the Art Students League. He first worked in New York as a paint boy at the Metropolitan Opera. He subsequently assisted a stellar list of designers: Eldon Elder, Robert Randolph, William and Jean Eckart, Miles White, and Karinska, to name only a few. His New York debut was *Single Man at a Party* which opened in 1959 off-Broadway. In 1964 he designed *Shadow Ground* for the New York City Ballet, after which he ran the New York City Ballet shop for several years, also working on three worlds fair pavilions. He joined ABC-TV in 1970 where he remains as staff designer. He received an Emmy Award for an ABC network news special. John Braden has a twin brother, Herb, who designs for television and movies in California.

Scenic Designs:
1970: *Candida*

Lillian Bradley

Mrs. Lillian Trimble Bradley was a playwright and director. She wrote some of her plays in collaboration with her husband, George H. Broadhurst, including *The Red Falcon* in 1923 and *Izzy*, first produced in 1924. Born in Milton, Kentucky in 1875, she was educated in Kentucky and France. The playbill for *Keep it to Yourself* in 1918 recorded her contribution to the play as: "Scenery designed and color schemes selected by Mrs. Lillian Trimble Bradley, decorations and furnishings selected by Mrs. Lillian Trimble Bradley." She both directed and designed scenery for *The Wonderful Thing*. She also produced plays, including those written by herself, her husband and others in New York and London. Mrs. Bradley died in May 1961.

Scenic Designs:
1918: *Keep It to Yourself* 1919: *Crimson Alibi, The* 1920: *Wonderful Thing, The*

Scott Bradley

Scott Bradley was born on September 5, 1961 in St. Louis, Missouri into a family of commercial artists. He received a B.A. in stage design at the University of Illinois in 1983, studying Kabuki design and painting with Shozo Sato and an M.F.A. at Yale in 1986. He has studied with and been influenced by Ming Cho Lee, Jane Greenwood, Michael Yeargan and Dunya Ramicova. Related training includes a 1978 painting internship in St. Louis and a 1979 internship at the International Arts Conference in Lucerne, Switzerland. His first design was *The Birthday Party* in 1977. Recent designs include *Late Night with David Letterman*, *The Lost Boys* and *Road to Nirvana* for the American Repertory Theatre and *The Hostage* for Portland Stage. Honors include a Drama Desk Nomination for *Joe Turner's Come and Gone* and numerous American Watercolor Society purchase prizes.

Scenic Designs:
1988: *Joe Turner's Come and Gone*

William Bradley Studio

William Bradley began his career in theatre as a singer and dancer, appearing in 1885 in *The Little Tycoon* at the Old Standard Theatre. He left New York City to work in Ohio theatres but soon returned to New York in 1908 to work for Henry B. Harris. While supplying properties for productions he decided to open his own studio. William Bradley Studios specialized in properties and was located at 318 West 43rd Street, New York City. Through this business he supplied props for numerous productions of George C. Tyler and others. He served on the staff of the Hudson Theatre as Master of Properties in 1924. He was also author of *The American Stage of Today* (1910) which contained photographs of leading performers of the day.

Scenic Designs:
1929: *Guinea Pig, The*

Claude Bragdon

Claude Bragdon was a practicing architect for most of his life, specializing in railroad stations. He was born in Oberlin, Ohio on August 1, 1866 and received his education at the University of Michigan. He first designed buildings in Rochester, New York, and later in New York City. A prolific author and translator, Mr. Bragdon wrote twenty books on architecture and related topics. He served as art director for Walter Hampden's productions during the 1920s and 1930s, designing scenery and costumes for some of the shows. Mr. Bragdon died on September 17, 1946.

Scenic Designs:
1918: *Hamlet* **1923:** *Cyrano De Bergerac* **1925:** *Merchant of Venice, The*; *Othello* **1926:** *Caponsacchi*; *Cyrano De Bergerac*; *Immortal Thief, The*; *Servant in the House, The* **1927:** *Enemy of the People, An* **1928:** *Caponsacchi*; *Cyrano De Bergerac*; *Enemy of the People, An*; *King Henry V*; *Light of Asia, The* **1929:** *Bond of Interest*; *Caponsacchi*; *Richelieu* **1932:** *Cyrano De Bergerac* **1934:** *Hamlet* **1935:** *Achilles had a Heel* **1936:** *Cyrano De Bergerac* **1937:** *Enemy of the People, An*

Costume Designs:
1923: *Cyrano De Bergerac* **1925:** *Merchant of Venice, The*; *Othello* **1926:** *Caponsacchi* **1927:** *Enemy of the People, An* **1928:** *Caponsacchi*; *Cyrano De Bergerac*; *Enemy of the People, An*; *King Henry V*; *Light of Asia, The* **1929:** *Caponsacchi*; *Richelieu* **1935:** *Achilles had a Heel* **1936:** *Cyrano De Bergerac* **1937:** *Enemy of the People, An*

Charles Brandon

After graduating from the University of Iowa, Charles Brandon was staff designer for the Cleveland Playhouse for the 1957-58 season, and later resident designer for the Falmouth Playhouse. He designed productions in New York at the Cherry Lane Theatre, Actor's Playhouse, and Equity Library Theatre and also designed *The Smokeweaver's Daughter* in 1959.

Scenic Designs:
1957: *Simply Heavenly* **1963:** *Heroine, The*

H. George Brandt

H. George Brandt designed four productions on Broadway in the early 1920s. On one occasion he designed both sets and costumes for the production. He was born in Brooklyn, New York on October 1, 1916 and died in New York on November 12, 1963 at age 47. After leaving school he worked as an office boy on Wall Street before moving to Hollywood to write and produce films. Upon returning to New York he became involved in the movement to take Broadway hits on the road to smaller theatres. His Subway Circuit was very successful and large numbers of people gained access to the theatre though his efforts. He also produced shows on Broadway.

Scenic Designs:
1920: *Ladies Night* **1921:** *Demi-Virgin, The*; *Getting Gertie's Garter*

Costume Designs:
1921: *Demi-Virgin, The*

Ruth Brenner

Ruth Brenner contributed designs to two shows on Broadway in the 1920s.

Scenic Designs:
1925: *Starlight*

Costume Designs:
1925: *Starlight* **1929:** *Little Show, The*

Maurice Brianchon

Maurice Brianchon, a painter, designed scenery and/or costumes for two shows on Broadway in the early 1950s. He was born in 1899 at Fresnay-sur-Sarthe, France and studied at the Academy of Decorative Art. In 1937 he joined the faculty at the National Academy of Fine Arts in Paris continuing in that position until 1949. His paintings are mainly landscapes and portraits. As a young man in France he designed sets and costumes for plays and operas before turning his complete attention to painting and teaching.

Scenic Designs:
1952: *Les Fausses Confidences*; *Les Fourberies De Scapin*

Costume Designs:
1952: *Les Fausses Confidences*

Kenneth Bridgeman

Kenneth Bridgeman designed scenery and costumes for a 1963 Broadway production. He studied at the West of England College of Art and first worked professionally in advertising. Mr. Bridgeman has served as resident designer for the Belgrade Theatre and as a freelance designer for many repertory theatres in England. He has also worked as set decorator for several feature films and was art director for the 1985 film *Ordeal by Innocence*.

Scenic Designs:
1963: *Semi-Detached*

Costume Designs:
1963: *Semi-Detached*

Herbert Brodkin

Herbert Brodkin, who died at age 77 on October 31, 1990, received an M.F.A. from Yale University in 1940. He was born on November 9, 1921 in New York City and studied at the University of Michigan, receiving a B.A. in 1934. He designed sets for theatre and Hollywood studios prior to beginning in television, initially as a set designer but primarily as a producer in a career lasting some forty years. He was responsible for *The Defenders*, as well as shows for *Playhouse '90*, *The Elgin Hour*, and *Studio One*. With Robert Berger he formed Titus Productions in the 1960s and continued producing provocative productions including *Skokie*, *Mandela*, *Sakarov* and *Pueblo* until dissolving the company in 1989. A retrospective show in 1985 at the Museum of Broadcasting featured productions of his television career.

Scenic Designs:
1947: *Caribbean Carnival*; *This Time Tomorrow* **1948:** *Silver Whistle, The*

Lighting Designs:
1947: *Volpone* **1948:** *Silver Whistle, The*

Louis Bromberg

Louis Bromberg designed sets on Broadway between 1925 and 1940. An artist, his studio was located at 220 West 14th Street in New York City in the mid-1920s. In addition, he illustrated *The Outline of Man's Knowledge* by Clement Wood in 1925.

Scenic Designs:
1925: *Flesh* **1927:** *Field God, The* **1929:** *Broken Chair, The*; *Cortez* **1930:** *Noble Experiment, The* **1932:** *Blue Monday*; *Intimate Relations* **1934:** *Hipper's Holiday* **1936:** *Truly Valiant* **1937:** *Thirsty Soil* **1940:** *Russian Bank*

Lou Bromley

Lou Bromley was the son of Walter Lewis Bromley, a painter who exhibited in London between 1866 and 1892 at the Suffolk State Gallery. He worked with the Federal Theatre Project in one of twenty-two marionette units. His production, a variety show based on *Don Quixote*, toured Los Angeles parks in a puppet van.

Scenic Designs:
1936: *Don't Look Now*

Bernard Brooks

Bernard Brooks designed three sets for Broadway productions in the early 1930s.

Scenic Designs:
1932: *Moral Fabric* **1933:** *Fantasia/ A Temporary Husband/ Crescendo*; *One Wife Or Another*

Georgianna Brown

Georgianna S. Brown was active on Broadway in the 1920s. In private life she was Mrs. Charles H. Brown. In 1932 she resided at 4428 Carpenter Avenue in New York City.

Scenic Designs:
1922: *Greenwich Village Follies*

Costume Designs:
1922: *Greenwich Village Follies*

Jack Brown

Jack Brown is a lighting and scenic designer who has designed for the Opera Society of Washington and Boston Arts. Off-Broadway credits include: *Stephen D, Dylan* and *Slow Dance on the Killing Ground.* After graduating from Carnegie Tech with a major in acting, he operated the White Barn Theatre near Pittsburgh in 1963. For the Broadway production of *Invitation to a March* he served as assistant to William Pitkin.

Scenic Designs:
1972: *Heathen!*

Lighting Designs:
1963: *Natural Affection* **1964:** *Beeckman Place; Ben Franklin in Paris; Dylan; Slow Dance on the Killing Ground*

Ralph Brown

Ralph Brown designed scenery on Broadway in 1946.

Scenic Designs:
1946: *Song of Bernadette*

Zack Brown

Zack Brown, a designer of sets and costumes, was born on July 10, 1949 in Honolulu. He received a B.F.A. from Notre Dame in 1968 (where he began designing) and an M.F.A. from Yale. His New York debut came in 1977 with the opening of *Tartuffe* at Circle in the Square, for which he received a Drama Desk nomination for Best Costumes. With his Broadway debut, *The Importance of Being Earnest* (also in 1977), he received a Tony nomination for the setting. His designs for the settings and costumes for *La Gioconda* earned him two Emmys when the opera, performed by the San Francisco Opera, was broadcast. Among the regional theatres for which he has designed are the Williamstown Theatre Festival, The Guthrie Theatre, Arena Stage and the Yale Repertory Theatre.

Scenic Designs:
1977: *Importance of Being Earnest, The; Tartuffe* **1978:** *13 Rue De l'Amour; Man and Superman* **1979:** *Loose Ends* **1980:** *Major Barbara; Man Who Came to Dinner, The; Past Tense* **1983:** *On Your Toes* **1988:** *Devil's Disciple, The; Night of the Iguana, The*

Costume Designs:
1977: *Saint Joan; Tartuffe* **1978:** *13 Rue De l'Amour; Man and Superman* **1980:** *Major Barbara; Man Who Came to Dinner, The* **1983:** *On Your Toes* **1988:** *Devil's Disciple, The*

Catherine Browne

Catherine Browne designed sets, lights and costumes for a show which originated in London's West End and subsequently moved to Broadway.

Scenic Designs:
1966: *Killing of Sister George, The*

Lighting Designs:
1966: *Killing of Sister George, The*

Costume Designs:
1966: *Killing of Sister George, The*

Andrew and Margaret Brownfoot

Andrew and Margaret Brownfoot collaborated on the settings and costumes for a Broadway show in 1970. They were married after meeting as students at the Central School of Arts and Crafts. After completing school Andrew became the resident designer for the Puppet Theatre on BBC Television. The Brownfoots have designed numerous plays at Stratford East's Stage 60 Company where they have worked as resident designers. Designs include *Widower's Houses, Saint's Day* and *Little Winter Love.* Their designs have also been seen at the Palace Theatre in Watford and include a production of *As Dorothy Parker Once Said.*

Scenic Designs:
1970: *Boy Friend, The*

Costume Designs:
1970: *Boy Friend, The*

John Brunton

John Brunton, who died on February 15, 1951 in Yonkers, New York was a set designer and builder of sets and properties. He designed plays under his own name and through John Brunton Studios, which he operated in Atlantic City and at 226 West 41st Street in New York City. Floats and parade decorations were also created in his studios. He came to the United States from London as a youth and progressed from prop builder to scene designer. Undoubtedly he designed more productions than those for which he received credit, as he was on the staffs of Klaw & Erlanger and Florenz Ziegfeld. At the time of his death he was working for NBC-TV.

Scenic Designs:
1922: *Montmartre*; *Night Call, The*

John Brunton Studios

John Brunton Studios was located in Atlantic City and at 226 West 41st Street in New York City. John Brunton designed productions under his own name and through his studios where he also created floats and parade decorations. For additional information and credits, see "John Brunton".

Scenic Designs:
1919: *Burgomaster of Belgium, A* 1920: *Her Family Tree*

Robert Brunton

Robert Brunton operated a scenic studio and received credit for a production on Broadway in the mid 1930s. He operated a theatrical supply business on West 49th Street in the 1930s and resided in Long Island City, Queens. Also employed as a theatrical manager, his portrait appeared in the December 4, 1919 issue of *Dramatic Mirror*.

Scenic Designs:
1934: *Another Love*

Mabel A. Buell

Mabel A. Buell designed sets on Broadway between 1917 and 1939 and through her studio. For additional information, see "Mabel A. Buell Scenic Studio".

Scenic Designs:
1917: *Good Morning, Rosamond* 1919: *Love Laughs* 1921: *Triumph of X, The* 1922: *Bronx Express, The* 1924: *Plain Jane* 1926: *Judge's Husband, The* 1932: *Cradle Snatchers* 1933: *Blackbirds of 1933* 1937: *Sea Legs* 1939: *Lew Leslies' Blackbirds of 1939*

Mabel A. Buell Scenic Studio

The Mabel A. Buell Scenic Studio was located at 1402 Broadway in 1919 and was active between 1921 and 1937. The studio was operated by Mabel A. and Nina Buell.

Scenic Designs:
1921: *Squaw Man, The* 1928: *Straight Through the Door* 1932: *Blackberries of 1932* 1936: *Summer Wives* 1937: *Straw Hat*

Edward Burbridge

Edward Burbridge has designed many off-Broadway productions, operas, ballets, national tours, television and regional theatre productions. He was born in New Orleans on May 23, 1933 and studied at Pratt Institute and the Lester Polakov Studio and Forum of Stage Design. The recipient of the John Hay Whitney Fellowship to study European theatres, his career has been influenced by Boris Aronson. Among his many productions for The Negro Ensemble Company are *Summer of the Seventeenth Doll*, *Daddy Goddess* and *The First Breeze of Summer*. In addition, he was art director for the television series *Kojak*.

Scenic Designs:
1967: *Marat/Sade* 1968: *Jimmy Shine*; *Mike Downstairs*; *Summer of the 17th Doll* 1969: *Buck White*; *Does a Tiger Wear a Necktie?*; *Our Town* 1973: *Chemin De Fer*; *Holiday*; *Status Quo Vadis*; *Visit, The* 1974: *Absurd Person Singular* 1975: *First Breeze of Summer, The* 1980: *Reggae* 1988: *Checkmates*

Everett Burgess

Everett Burgess designed one set in 1940 on Broadway.

Scenic Designs:
1940: *Quiet Please*

Lloyd Burlingame

Lloyd Burlingame has been production designer for plays both on and off Broadway since he debuted in New York City with the opening of *Leave it to Jane*. Born in Washington, D.C. on December 31, 1934, the son of Harry and

Estelle Burlingame, he had an early introduction to the arts by his uncle, Lloyd Embry, a portrait painter. After study at Carnegie-Mellon he spent a year at La Scala in Milan on a Fulbright Scholarship, beginning the study of opera, which has remained of particular interest. Mr. Burlingame prefers to have responsibility for all of the design elements for a production, after the example set by Robert Edmond Jones, and has had that responsibility with all of his Broadway credits. Mr. Burlingame, in addition to actively designing, is a Master Teacher of Design and Chair, Department of Design at New York University. In 1985 a retrospective show of his scenic designs and touchable art was held in New York City, and a one-man show of recent work, "Once More with Feeling," was held at the Wadsworth Atheneum in Hartford, Connecticut in 1988.

Scenic Designs:

1964: *Alfie* **1966:** *First One Asleep, Whistle*; *Loves of Cass Mc Guire, The*; *Philadelphia, Here I Come* **1967:** *Astrakhan Coat, The*; *Keep It in the Family* **1968:** *Woman Is My Idea* **1969:** *Love Is a Time of Day* **1970:** *Not Now, Darling*

Lighting Designs:

1963: *Lady of the Camellias, The* **1965:** *Boeing-Boeing*; *Inadmissable Evidence*; *Right Honorable Gentleman, The* **1966:** *First One Asleep, Whistle*; *Help Stamp Out Marriage*; *Loves of Cass Mc Guire, The*; *Philadelphia, Here I Come* **1967:** *Brief Lives*; *There's a Girl in My Soup* **1968:** *Day in the Death of Joe Egg, A*; *Flip Side, The*; *Rockefeller and the Red Indians*; *Woman Is My Idea* **1969:** *Hadrian VII*; *Love Is a Time of Day* **1970:** *Not Now, Darling* **1971:** *Midsummer Night's Dream, A*; *Philanthropist, The* **1972:** *Vivat! Vivat Regina!*

Costume Designs:

1964: *Alfie* **1966:** *Philadelphia, Here I Come* **1967:** *Astrakhan Coat, The* **1968:** *Woman Is My Idea* **1969:** *Love Is a Time of Day* **1970:** *Not Now, Darling*

John Bury

John Bury was born in Aberystwyth, Wales on January 27, 1925. Originally an actor, he progressed to design work through various technical positions. His career began in 1946 at Joan Littlewood's Theatre Workshop with designs for many productions between 1954 and 1964. His first designs for the Royal Shakespeare Company in Stratford-upon-Avon were sets and costumes for *Julius Caesar* in 1963, and from 1964 until 1968 he was head of design for the RSC. Mr. Bury was appointed Head of Design at the National Theatre of Great Britain in 1973. Mr. Bury's work was first seen in New York City in 1974 when he designed the sets and lights for *Oh, What a Lovely War*. Mr. Bury has also designed for films and opera, and consulted on the design of theatres. In 1975 he received a Gold Medal for design in Prague which was followed by a Golden Troika in Prague in 1979. He was elected a fellow of the Royal Society of the Arts in England in 1968 and also has been honored with an O.B.E. *Amadeus* brought Mr. Bury a Tony nomination for outstanding costume design, and a Tony award for the set in 1981.

Scenic Designs:

1964: *Oh What a Lovely War*; *Physicists, The* **1967:** *Homecoming, The* **1970:** *Rothschilds, The* **1971:** *Old Times* **1972:** *Via Galactica* **1976:** *No Man's Land* **1980:** *Amadeus*; *Betrayal* **1986:** *Petition, The*

Lighting Designs:

1964: *Oh What a Lovely War*; *Physicists, The* **1967:** *Homecoming, The* **1971:** *Old Times* **1976:** *No Man's Land* **1980:** *Betrayal* **1986:** *Petition, The*

Costume Designs:

1964: *Physicists, The* **1967:** *Homecoming, The* **1970:** *Rothschilds, The* **1972:** *Via Galactica* **1976:** *No Man's Land* **1980:** *Amadeus*; *Betrayal* **1986:** *Petition, The*

Clara Butler

Clara Butler, known in private life as Mrs. Frank I. Frayne, was at one time the champion lady rifle shot of the world. Her husband was Frank Ives Frayne (1836-1891), an actor and champion short-range rifle shot of the world. They toured with Otis Skinner and performed an act in which Mr. Frayne shot an apple off Clara Butler's head. She was also a sculptor, and exhibited at the Royal Academy in London in 1881 and 1883. Born Miss Clehorow Caroline Butler, she resided at 224 Brooklyn Avenue in Valley Stream, Long Island in 1932.

Scenic Designs:

1925: *Handy Man, The*

Alexandra Byrne

Alexandra Byrne designed scenery and costumes for a play on Broadway in 1990. A British designer, she is active in regional theatres throughout the United Kingdom and as a costume designer and art director for British television. She has designed *Hamlet* and *Temptation* for the Royal Shakespeare Company. Productions in London also include *Life of Napoleon* and numerous productions at the Soho Poly Theatre.

Scenic Designs:
1990: *Some Americans Abroad*

Costume Designs:
1990: *Some Americans Abroad*

Gladys E. Calthrop

Gladys E. Calthrop (a.k.a. G. E. Calthrop) was born in Ashton, Devonshire, England in 1900, the daughter of Frederick and Mabel Treeby. After receiving her education in England, she married Major Everard Calthrop and spent her professional career designing sets and costumes both in England and the United States. She designed sets and costumes for the initial productions of nearly all of Noel Coward's plays. Gladys Calthrop began her career as a painter and has numerous credits for scenery, beginning with *Vortex* in London in 1925. She retired from designing in the late 1940s to pursue her interest in decorating, only to return to the theatre in the late 1950s to design a production of *The Edwardians* in London, set in a period which she had always found compelling. Gladys Calthrop, who died in 1980, also wrote fiction.

Scenic Designs:
1925: *Beware of Widows*; *Hay Fever*; *Master Builder*; *Vortex, The*; *Young Woodley* 1926: *John Gabriel Borkman*; *Master Builder, The*; *Red Blinds*; *This Was a Man*; *Three Sisters, The*; *Twelfth Night* 1927: *Cradle Song, The* 1928: *This Year of Grace* 1929: *Bitter Sweet* 1930: *Cradle Song, The* 1931: *Private Lives* 1933: *Design for Living* 1934: *Conversation Piece* 1935: *Point Valaine* 1936: *Tonight At 8:30* 1937: *Excursion* 1939: *Dear Octopus*; *Set to Music*

Costume Designs:
1925: *Hay Fever*; *Master Builder*; *Vortex, The*; *Young Woodley* 1926: *John Gabriel Borkman*;

Master Builder, The; *Saturday Night*; *Three Sisters, The* 1927: *Cradle Song, The*; *Inheritors* 1928: *This Year of Grace* 1929: *Bitter Sweet* 1930: *Cradle Song, The* 1934: *Conversation Piece* 1939: *Set to Music*

John P. Campbell

John P. Campbell was the son of Bartley Campbell, a playwright. He worked with producers, including Henry Miller and Oliver Morosco before joining a stock brokerage firm in New York as a secretary. He designed both sets and costumes for a production in 1919. Mr. Campbell died at the age of 67 on October 15, 1938.

Scenic Designs:
1919: *Dark Rosaleen*

Costume Designs:
1919: *Dark Rosaleen*

Patton Campbell

Born in Omaha, Nebraska on September 10, 1926, Patton Campbell received both a B.A. and an M.F.A. at Yale. His career has been principally as a costume designer, but he began as a scenic and costume designer in various summer stock theatres and as an assistant to Rouben Ter-Arutunian. He has designed for many companies, including the New York City Opera, the Santa Fe Opera and the Opera Company of Boston as well as national tours and productions at the New York City Center. His list of extensive costume and scenery credits includes many operas, both world premieres and works from the standard repertory. His designs for opera have also been broadcast on television, principally by WNET. Mr. Campbell was nominated for a Tony Award in 1977 for *Man of La Mancha*, which he designed with Howard Bay. In addition to his design activity Mr. Campbell is an educator, having taught at Barnard College, Juilliard, Columbia University, and the State University of New York at Purchase.

Scenic Designs:
1955: *Grand Prize, The*

Lighting Designs:
1955: *Grand Prize, The*

Costume Designs:
1955: *All in One, Trouble in Tahiti*; *Twenty Seven Wagons Full of Cotton* 1956: *Fallen Angels* 1957: *Hole in the Head, A*; *Makropoulos*

Secret, The **1958:** *Howie* **1960:** *There Was a Little Girl* **1961:** *All American; Conquering Hero, The* **1965:** *Glass Menagerie, The* **1966:** *Agatha Sue, I Love You* **1967:** *Come Live with Me; Natural Look, The* **1968:** *Loot* **1977:** *Man of La Mancha*

Emilio Carcano

Emilio Carcano began his career as an assistant to Renzo Mongiardino and Franco Zeffirelli for both films and theatres in his native Italy. He designed sets for Bertucelli's film *Paulina 1800.* His first production in Paris for "group TSE", who produced *Heartaches of a Pussycat* on Broadway, was *24 Heures.* He has also designed Herb Gardner's *La Fraîcher de l'Aube* and *L'Etoile du Nord* in Paris.

Scenic Designs:
1980: *Heartaches of a Pussycat*

Charles Carmello, Jr.

Charles Carmello, Jr. has designed scenery in summer stock and regional theatres. He is also the author of the play *Saints Alive* which was performed in New York in 1979.

Scenic Designs:
1976: *Wheelbarrow Closers*

Michael Carr

Michael Carr, born Michael Cohen on March 17, 1900 in Leeds, Yorkshire, England, appeared in the 1937 film *Let's Make a Night of It.* He also designed sets on Broadway, but should not be confused with the American actor of the same name who performed on Broadway. In 1922 he was associated with Blanding Sloan and Peter Larsen in an artists' studio called "Wits & Fingers Studio" at 17 East 14th Street in New York City. He died on September 16, 1968.

Scenic Designs:
1923: *Uptown West*

Edward Carrick

Edward Carrick (a.k.a.   Edward Anthony Craig), son of Gordon Craig and grandson of Ellen Terry, worked in New York City in the 1930s as a painter, producer and decorator. He was born in London on January 3, 1904 and studied painting in Italy from 1917 to 1926. His first exhibition in London was in 1928 where he signed his works "Edward Carrick". Undoubtedly influenced by his father's design activity, he was art director for Associated Radio Productions in 1932 and art director for Associated Talking Pictures in London from 1931 to 1935. He later worked with other film companies such as Ealing Films, and as an independent producer and stage director. In 1938 he founded the first school specializing in film studies in England. He also wrote widely on the subject of film design, including "Moving Picture Sets, A Medium for the Architect" in *Architectural Record* and "Designing for the Motion Pictures" in *Design* in 1950. In 1948 he designed *Macbeth* at Stratford-upon-Avon, a production which later toured the United States.

Scenic Designs:
1936: *Night Must Fall*

Earl Carroll

Earl Carroll is perhaps best remembered as a creator of musicals and revues, including several editions of *Earl Carroll Vanities* from 1923 to 1936 for which he was the major writer and composer. Many of his productions were performed in the Broadway theatre named for him, the Earl Carroll Theatre, located at 755 Seventh Avenue. He was born on September 16, 1893 in Pittsburgh and began his career in theatre selling programs. He moved to New York in 1912, after traveling in the Far East and serving as a pilot in the Army Air Service in World War I, to become a songwriter for a music publisher. After an appearance in vaudeville in 1917 he worked steadily in New York until 1938, when he moved to Hollywood to become an associate producer for 20th Century Fox Film Corporation. He contributed set designs to two plays, including *The Lady of the Lamp* in 1920, the first production which he managed. Mr. Carroll died in a plane crash on June 17, 1948 near Mt. Carmel, Pennsylvania at age 56.

Scenic Designs:
1916: *Lady's Name, A* **1920:** *Lady of the Lamp, The*

Lincoln J. Carter

Lincoln J. Carter was a playwright who supplied designs for the setting of a Broadway show in the teens. He was 61 years old when he died on July 13, 1926.

Scenic Designs:
1918: *American Ace, An*

Ronald Case

Ronald Case was born in Los Angeles on July 30, 1950, the son of Almon and Lois Case. He studied for two years at Rio Hondo Junior College in California and for two years at New York University's Tisch School of the Arts. Influences on his career include an acting teacher in high school, Squire Freidel, and designers Eoin Sprott and Robin Wagner. He assisted properties designer Eoin Sprott for several Broadway shows, including *Pippin, The Wise Child, Jesus Christ Superstar, Sgt. Pepper's on the Road* and *Antony and Cleopatra.* With Michael Bottari, a frequent collaborator, he designs sets and/or costumes for a variety of productions: tours, such as *Ballroom, The King and I, Showboat,* and *The Pirates of Penzance*; off-Broadway plays including *The Man who Shot Lincoln* and *Buddies*; and for regional theatres and industrial promotions.

Scenic Designs:
1989: *Prince of Central Park*

Costume Designs:
1989: *Prince of Central Park*

Julio Castellanos

The painter Julio Castellanos designed sets for a Broadway play in the 1930s.

Scenic Designs:
1938: *Mexicana*

William E. Castle

William E. Castle designed sets for several productions in the 1920s. He began his career as a paint boy for Gates and Morange in their scenic studio. The scenic design studio Dodge & Castle was formed by D. Frank Dodge and William E. Castle and operated at 241 West 62nd Street in New York City in the 1920s. They collaborated on several productions between 1914 and 1934 and painted the scenery for many additional productions. For additional credits, see the entry "Dodge & Castle."

Scenic Designs:
1922: *Clinging Vine, The* 1923: *Battling Buckler; Love Scandal, A; Magic Ring, The* 1924: *Lollipops; Magnolia Lady, The; Man in Evening Clothes, The; Merry Wives of Gotham* 1926: *Captive, The; Honest Liars; Square, The* 1927: *Celebrity; Interference; Love Is Like That; Pickwick; That French Lady* 1928: *Our Betters; Paris*

Cary Chalmers

Cary Chalmers first designed on Broadway in 1981.

Scenic Designs:
1981: *Marlowe*

Miss Ida Hoyt Chamberlain

Miss Ida Hoyt Chamberlain, the sister of Neville Chamberlain, contributed sets to a 1923 production on Broadway. She died in her home in Odiham, Hampshire, England in 1943 at age 72. Her musical comedy *Enchanted Isle* was performed at the Lyric Theatre in New York in 1927, starring Greek Evans and Madeline Grey. Miss Chamberlain also performed recitals of her compositions at the Hotel Biltmore. In 1932 she resided at 103 East 75th Street in New York City.

Scenic Designs:
1927: *Enchanted Isle*

Stewart Chaney

Stewart Chaney designed sets, sometimes costumes, and occasionally lights on Broadway. He was born in Kansas City, Missouri, and studied at Yale with George Pierce Baker and also in Paris with André L'Hote. He began his career as a scene designer in summer stock and made his Broadway debut with the opening of *The Old Maid* in 1935. For the following thirty years his designs for scenery, costumes and lights were seen regularly in plays, operas and ballets. During the 1940s Mr. Chaney designed two films, *Up in Arms* and *The Kid From Brooklyn.* He also worked in television during its early years. Mr. Chaney died on November 9, 1969 at the age of 59. His designs are included in the collections of the Smithsonian Institution in Washington, D.C.

Scenic Designs:

1934: *Bride of Torozko, The; Dream Child; Kill That Story* **1935:** *Ghosts; Old Maid, The; On to Fortune; Parnell; Times Have Changed* **1936:** *Aged 26; Hamlet; Hedda Gabler; New Faces of 1936; O Evening Star; Parnell; Spring Dance* **1937:** *But for the Grace of God; Having Wonderful Time* **1938:** *Wuthering Heights* **1939:** *Life with Father* **1940:** *International Incident, An; Suzanna and the Elders; Twelfth Night* **1941:** *Blithe Spirit; More the Merrier, The; Sunny River* **1942:** *Lady Comes Across, The; Morning Star* **1943:** *Blythe Spirit; Dark Eyes; Innocent Voyage, The; Three's a Family; Voice of the Turtle, The; World's Full of Girls, The* **1944:** *Down to Miami; Dream with Music; Duke in Darkness, The; Embezzled Heaven; House in Paris, The; Jacobowsky and the Colonel; Laffing Room Only; Late George Apley, The; Pretty Little Parlor; Public Relations; Trio* **1945:** *Dunnigan's Daughter; Many Happy Returns; Mr. Strauss Goes to Boston; One Man Show; Signature* **1946:** *Joy Forever, A; Obsession; Winter's Tale, The* **1947:** *Bathsheba; Craig's Wife; Druid Circle, The; Inspector Calls, An; Laura* **1948:** *Doctor Social; Life with Mother; Red Gloves; You Never Can Tell* **1949:** *I Know My Love; Ivy Green, The; My Name Is Aquilon* **1950:** *Design for a Stained Glass Window; Great to Be Alive* **1951:** *King of Friday's Men, The; Lo and Behold!; Moon Is Blue, The; Seventeen* **1952:** *Much Ado About Nothing* **1953:** *Girl Can Tell, A; Late Love; Sherlock Holmes* **1957:** *Hidden River, The* **1960:** *Forty-ninth Cousin, The* **1964:** *Severed Head, A*

Lighting Designs:

1944: *Down to Miami* **1946:** *Obsession* **1947:** *Bathsheba; Druid Circle, The; Inspector Calls, An* **1948:** *Doctor Social* **1949:** *I Know My Love* **1950:** *Design for a Stained Glass Window* **1951:** *King of Friday's Men, The; Lo and Behold!; Moon Is Blue, The* **1953:** *Late Love; Sherlock Holmes* **1957:** *Hidden River, The* **1960:** *Forty-ninth Cousin, The*

Costume Designs:

1935: *Ghosts; Old Maid, The; Parnell* **1936:** *Aged 26; Hamlet; Hedda Gabler; New Faces of 1936; Parnell* **1938:** *Wuthering Heights* **1939:** *Life with Father* **1940:** *Twelfth Night* **1942:** *Lady Comes Across, The* **1944:** *Duke in Darkness, The; Embezzled Heaven; Jackpot; Late George Apley, The* **1945:** *Dunnigan's Daughter, A; Winter's Tale, The* **1947:** *Bathsheba; Inspector Calls, An* **1948:** *Doctor Social; You Never Can Tell* **1949:** *I Know My Love; Ivy Green, The* **1950:** *Design for a Stained Glass Window; Great to Be Alive* **1951:** *King of Friday's Men, The; Lo and Behold!* **1952:** *Much Ado About Nothing* **1953:** *Sherlock Holmes* **1964:** *Severed Head, A*

David Chapman

David Chapman majored in architecture at the Georgia Institute of Technology. He was born in Atlanta, Georgia on November 11, 1938 and is principally known as a scenic designer, though he occasionally creates both sets and costumes for a production. Mr. Chapman, who received the Maharam Award for his set design for *The First*, includes designers Boris Aronson and Robin Wagner and the sculptor Steffan Thomas as major influences on his career. His film work includes art direction for *The Cotton Club, Legal Eagles* (New York locale) and production design for *Dirty Dancing* and *Mystic Pizza*. He is married to costume designer Carol Oditz.

Scenic Designs:

1969: *Red White and Maddox* **1972:** *Promenade, All!* **1973:** *Nash At Nine* **1974:** *Magic Show, The* **1981:** *First, The* **1982:** *Othello* **1983:** *Zorba* **1987:** *Cabaret*

Costume Designs:

1969: *Red White and Maddox*

Michael Chekhov

Michael Alexandrovich Chekhov began his career in the theatre in Russia, where he was a founding member of the Studio One Group at the Moscow Art Theatre and later its director. A nephew of the playwright Anton Chekhov, he was born in St. Petersburg, Russia in 1891. He left Russia in 1927, travelling throughout Europe and acting with various companies including Max Reinhardt's. He settled in England for a short time, beginning a school for training actors. He moved to the United States in 1927 and taught acting in his own studio, continuing to act and direct and also occasionally design. Michael Chekhov spent the last fifteen years of his life in California, appearing in numerous films and coaching actors. He died September 30, 1955.

Scenic Designs:
1941: *Twelfth Night*

Costume Designs:
1941: *Twelfth Night*

Alexander Chertov

Alexander Chertov was born in Minsk, Russia and as a youth emigrated to the United States. He began his career as a scenic artist in movies and worked in film studios in both Ft. Lee, New Jersey and Hollywood. He designed settings in New York mainly for Jewish plays and for the Yiddish Art Theatre. He died in Hollywood, California at age 79 on October 22, 1961.

Scenic Designs:
1933: *Yoshe Kalb* 1935: *Waiting for Lefty*

Alison Chitty

Alison Chitty, a British designer of sets and costumes, was born in 1948. From 1971 until 1974 she was assistant designer at Victoria Theatre, Stoke-on-Trent, serving as head of design from 1974 until 1977. She has designed for theatres throughout the United Kingdom, including productions for the Riverside Studios, the Royal Shakespeare Company, the Crucible Theatre in Sheffield, Theatre Royal and Stratford East. As resident designer at the National Theatre she has designed *A Month in the Country*, *Don Juan*, *Danton's Death*, *Tales from Hollywood* and many others, as well as *Orpheus Descending* for Peter Hall in 1988.

Scenic Designs:
1989: *Orpheus Descending*

Costume Designs:
1989: *Orpheus Descending*

André Chotin

André-Marcel Chotin was born in Paris on April 24, 1888 and died in Boulogne-Billancourt, France on December 20, 1969. He was a painter of still lifes and maritime scenes who exhibited regularly at the Salon des Indepéndants, the Salon d'Automne and Galeries Zak in Paris. He was also a pantomimist and dancer and in the early 1920s appeared in and contributed scenic designs to a Broadway production.

Scenic Designs:
1922: *Fantastic Fricassee, A*

Roy Christopher

As a prolific set designer for television for more than twenty years, Roy Christopher has been nominated for several Emmy Awards and received five, for the *Academy Awards Show* in 1981, 1984, 1986 and 1990 and *The Richard Pryor Show*. He currently is the production designer of the television series *Murphy Brown* and has designed others series such as *My Sister Sam*, *Chico and the Man*, *Valerie*, *Wings*, *Welcome Back Kotter* and *Growing Pains*. He received an M.A. at California State University at Fresno, where he subsequently taught. He was also artistic director at Cahuenga Playhouse in Los Angeles and worked as a scene painter for NBC-TV. His theatre designs, mainly on the West Coast, include *Peculiar Pastimes*, *The Boys from Syracuse*, *Jane Heights* and the West Coast revival of *Come Back Little Sheba*.

Scenic Designs:
1984: *Woman of Independent Means, A*

Cirker and Robbins

The partnership between Mitchell Cirker and Robert Nelson Robbins produced designs for numerous Broadway shows between 1919 and 1944 under the name of Cirker and Robbins Scenic Studios. As with most scenic studios of the era, the designs credited to Cirker and Robbins Scenic Studio were often for contemporary plays which required a simple single set. Within the firm, Mitchell Cirker was the business manager and Robert Robbins the creative and technical partner. Mitchell Cirker was born in New York City and studied painting at the National Academy of Design. He worked as a stage hand, electrician, and scene painter before joining R.N. Robbins. Throughout his life he continued to exhibit landscapes and seascapes but never received individual credit for the scenic design of a Broadway show. He died at age 70 on February 4, 1953. Robert Robbins also designed sets using his own name and additional information is available under his entry in this book.

Scenic Designs:
1919: *Penny Wise* **1920:** *Innocent Idea, An* **1926:** *Jay Walker, The; Little Spitfire, The* **1927:** *Four Walls; Gossipy Sex, The; Out of the Night* **1928:** *Eva the Fifth; Skull, The* **1929:** *All the King's Men; Borrowed Love; Diana; Family Affairs; How's Your Health; Let Us Be Gay; Mendel, Inc; Nice Women; Seven; Subway Express; Zeppelin* **1930:** *Ada Beats the Drum; Ballyhoo; Blue Ghost, The; London Calling; Luana; Many a Slip; Oh, Promise Me; Once in a Lifetime; Penal Law 2010; Pressing Business; Ritzy; This Man's Town; Who Cares?* **1931:** *As Husbands Go; Caught Wet; Fast and Furious; Great Barrington, The; Miss Gulliver's Travels; She Lived Next to the Firehouse; Society Girl; Woman Denied, A* **1932:** *20th Century; Black Tower; On the Make; Passionate Pilgrim, The; Take My Tip; That's Gratitude* **1933:** *Drums Begin, The; Four O'Clock; Ghost Writer; Heat Lightening; Party's Over, The* **1934:** *John Brown* **1935:** *Loose Moments; Play, Genius, Play; Squaring the Circle; Strip Girl* **1936:** *All Editions; Brother Rat; Lend Me Your Ears; Mimie Scheller; Pre-Honeymoon* **1937:** *Abie's Irish Rose; Blow Ye Winds; Brown Sugar; Penny Wise; Room Service* **1938:** *Lightnin'; What a Life* **1939:** *Farm of Three Echoes; Once Upon a Time; Primrose Path, The; See My Lawyer* **1940:** *Goodbye in the Night; Scene of the Crime* **1941:** *Out of the Frying Pan* **1942:** *Sweet Charity* **1943:** *Army Play By Play, The; Boy Meets Girl; Milky Way, The* **1944:** *Mrs. Kimball Presents*

Howard Claney

Howard Claney designed the set for a Broadway production in 1925. An actor, he appeared in many plays between 1921 and 1929, such as *Don Juan, Voltaire* and *The Little Poor Man*. In 1932 he was associated with the National Broadcasting Company. He returned to the New York stage in 1959 in *An Evening with George Bernard Shaw*, and appeared in both *Romeo and Juliet* and *Figuro in the Night* in 1962.

Scenic Designs:
1925: *Little Poor Man, The*

Jane Clark

Jane Clark has served as assistant art director for many commericals, as an illustrator of magazines, books and newspapers, and as a scenic designer in regional theatres, on, off- and off-off-Broadway. She graduated from the Yale School of Drama.

Scenic Designs:
1982: *Master Harold...and the Boys*

Peggy Clark

As with many designers, Peggy Clark's initial exposure to the theatre was as a performer. She gave up acting, however, and became a major force in the establishment of theatrical lighting design as an independent profession. Born in Baltimore, she graduated from Smith College and in 1938 received an M.F.A. at Yale University, where she was introduced to all areas of design. Only three months after graduation, Peggy Clark made her debut on Broadway, designing the costumes for *The Girl From Wyoming*. Although she continued to design costumes for a time she also served in various technical positions and designed scenery, while developing an expertise in stage lighting. During her career she has lit over one hundred productions on Broadway. Teaching has also been part of her life: at her alma mater, Smith College; at Yale; and at Lester Polakov's Studio and Forum of Stage Design. Peggy Clark was the first woman elected President of United Scenic Artists Local 829, in 1968. She was named a fellow of the United States Institute for Theatre Technology in 1978. Married to Lloyd R. Kelley from 1960 until his death in 1972, she is also known as Peggy Clark Kelley.

Scenic Designs:
1941: *Gabrielle* **1951:** *High Ground, The*

Lighting Designs:
1926: *Gentlemen Prefer Blondes* **1946:** *Beggar's Holliday* **1947:** *Brigadoon; High Button Shoes; Medea; Topaz* **1948:** *Love Life; Rape of Lucretia, The* **1949:** *Along Fifth Avenue; Gentlemen Prefer Blondes; Touch and Go* **1950:** *All You Need Is One Good Break; Bless You All* **1951:** *High Ground, The* **1952:** *Of Thee I Sing; Pal Joey* **1953:** *In the Summer House; Kismet; Maggie; Trip to Bountiful, The; Wonderful Town* **1954:** *On Your Toes; Peter Pan*

1955: *No Time for Sergeants; Plain and Fancy; Righteous Are Bold, The; Will Success Spoil Rock Hunter?* **1956:** *Auntie Mame; Bells Are Ringing; Mr. Wonderful; New Faces of '56* **1957:** *Eugenia; Nude with Violin; Potting Shed, The* **1958:** *Flower Drum Song; Present Laughter; Say, Darling* **1959:** *Billy Barnes Revue; Cheri; Goodbye Charlie; Juno* **1960:** *Bye, Bye, Birdie; Distant Bell, A; Under the Yum-Yum Tree; Unsinkable Molly Brown, The* **1961:** *Mary, Mary; Sail Away; Show Girl* **1962:** *Romulus* **1963:** *Girl Who Came to Supper, The* **1964:** *Bajour; Poor Richard* **1966:** *Best Laid Plans, The* **1968:** *Darling of the Day* **1969:** *Jimmy; Last of the Red Hot Lovers* **1971:** *How the Other Half Loves* **1980:** *Musical Chairs*

Costume Designs:
1942: *Great Big Doorstop, The; Uncle Harry* **1944:** *Ramshackle Inn* **1945:** *Dark of the Moon; Devil's Galore* **1951:** *High Ground, The*

Bill Clarke

Bill Clarke was born on October 9, 1950 in Landstuhl, Germany and was raised in Raleigh, North Carolina. He attended the University of Virginia, where he received a B.A. in 1980, and the Yale School of Drama where he received an M.F.A. in 1987. Related training includes courses at the Art Students League and the School of Visual Arts. The design for *A Walk in the Woods*, which premiered at the La Jolla Playhouse, was honored with a Drama Logue Award and the San Diego Theatre Critics Circle Award. Bill Clarke designs sets and occasionally costumes in New York and regional theatres including the Indiana Repertory Theatre and PlayMakers Repertory Company.

Scenic Designs:
1988: *Walk in the Woods, A*

T.M. Cleland

T.M. Cleland, who created sets and costumes for a production in the early 1920s was born Thomas Maitland Cleland in Brooklyn and studied at the Artist-Artisan Institute in New York City. A painter and illustrator, he spent most of his life working as a graphic artist designing books, brochures, and magazines. He worked as art editor for *Fortune* and *McClures*.

Mr. Cleland, who received a gold medal from the American Institute of Graphic Arts in 1940, died at age 84 on November 9, 1964.

Scenic Designs:
1923: *Scaramouche*

Costume Designs:
1923: *Scaramouche*

George Clisbee

George Clisbee was born in Chicago and studied in Paris at Julien's Studio. During World War I he served with the French ambulance service and the United States Army. From 1919 to 1926 he worked as art editor for *The Cleveland Daily News*. A prolific writer of short stories, mainly about cats, he was also a magazine illustrator. Mr. Clisbee died at age 41 on December 5, 1936.

Scenic Designs:
1923: *Salome*

Costume Designs:
1923: *Salome*

C. Clonis

Cleovulos Clonis was born in Greece in 1907. He studied at the University of Athens and has designed scenery not only in Greece but throughout Europe, including London and Frankfurt. Between 1932 and 1945 he designed numerous settings for the National Theatre in Greece, including *Agamemnon*, *Hamlet* and *Oedipus Rex*.

Scenic Designs:
1952: *Electra; Oedipus Tyrannus*

Warren Clymer

Warren Clymer first became involved with stage design as an undergraduate at the University of Iowa where he earned a B.A. He also attended Indiana University where he received an M.A. He was born on December 29, 1922 in Davenport, Iowa. In the early 1950s he worked for three years with Jo Mielziner and Howard Bay. Since then he has spent very little time working on stage productions, devoting his talents instead to design for television and feature films. His television designs have been honored with two Emmy Awards for Art Direction/Set Design.

Scenic Designs:
1961: *Write Me a Murder*

Norman Coates

The British designer Norman Coates–not to be confused with the American lighting designer of the same name– has been associated with Inter-Action and The Almost Free Theatre in England for the past several years. He has designed sets and costumes for the world premieres of many plays by Edward Bond, Robert Patrick, Heathcote Williams and James Saunders.

Scenic Designs:

1979: *Dogg's Hamlet, Cahoot's Macbeth*

Costume Designs:

1979: *Dogg's Hamlet, Cahoot's Macbeth*

Henry Ives Cobb, Jr.

Henry Ives Cobb, Jr., the eldest son of the distinguished American architect, designed settings for a Broadway play in 1917.

Scenic Designs:

1917: *Have a Heart*

Felix E. Cochren

Felix E. Cochren has designed not only settings but also costumes on Broadway. He studied art and theatre at Carnegie Mellon University and spent five years as resident costume designer and graphic artist at Brooklyn's Billie Holiday Theatre. His many sets for the Negro Ensemble Company include *A Soldier's Play*. In 1979 Mr. Cochren received the Audelco Award for sets and costumes, one of the five Audelco Awards for stage designs he has won during his career.

Scenic Designs:

1980: *Home* **1981:** *Inacent Black*

Costume Designs:

1983: *Amen Corner*

Franco Colavecchia

Franco Colavecchia is from Cham County, Durham, England where he was born in 1937. He was educated at London University and received specialized training in painting at the Lincoln School of the Arts and St. Martin's School in London. He studied set design at the Wimbledon Theatre School and at the Slade School. His professional debut occurred in two locations at the same time, with the opening of *The Homecoming* at the Oxford Playhouse and of *Cellini* at the Edinburgh Festival. Mr. Colavecchia designs both sets and costumes and has received awards in England and the United States, including a shared Emmy for the Set Design for "Pavarotti in Philadelphia: *La Boehme*," broadcast by PBS. Honors in England include an award by the British Arts Council and the Royal Society Award for Art and Industry.

Scenic Designs:

1974: *Treemonisha*

Costume Designs:

1974: *Treemonisha*

Paul Colin

Paul Colin, who died in Noigent-sur-Marne at age 92 on June 18, 1985, was a famous French posterist and theatrical designer. He designed over twelve thousand posters during his career, beginning in the early 1920s with commissions from the Theatre des Champs-Elysées, where he later designed scenery. Among the seven hundred settings he designed were those for the films *Lilliom* directed by Fritz Lang and *Carnet de Bal* directed by Julien Duvivier. He painted the setting for *La Revue Nègre* in 1925 which introduced Josephine Baker to Paris. His designs have been exhibited often, most recently in a retrospective at the Sorbonne in 1982.

Scenic Designs:

1929: *Wake Up and Dream*

Costume Designs:

1929: *Wake Up and Dream*

John Collette

John Collette was well known on the West Coast as a scenic artist associated with Oliver Morosco. He died in the great influenza epidemic of 1918, on November 19, 1918 in Los Angeles.

Scenic Designs:

1917: *Lombardi, Ltd.*

Harry Collins

Harry Collins designed costumes for numerous productions on Broadway between 1916 and

1921. In addition he also designed scenery for one production.

Scenic Designs:

1919: *First is Last*

Costume Designs:

1916: *Co-Respondent, The* **1917:** *De Luxe Annie; Furs and Frills; Going Up; Hitchy Koo; On with the Dance; Over the 'Phone; Tailor-Made Man, A* **1918:** *Oh, Lady! Lady!; Oh, My Dear* **1919:** *Adam and Eva; Exchange of Wives, An; First is Last; Little Whopper, The; Too Many Husbands* **1920:** *Anna Ascends; Innocent Idea, An* **1921:** *Dear Me; Wait Till We're Married*

Vincent Collins

In 1919 Vincent Collins designed sets for a show on Broadway. In 1920 he was President of Vincent Collins, Inc., Decorators, 749 Fifth Avenue, New York City.

Scenic Designs:

1919: *Nothing But Love*

Alvin Colt

Alvin Colt has been designing costumes steadily for the theatre and ballet since 1940. His costume designs have been seen on Broadway since *On the Town* opened at the Adelphi Theatre in 1944. Occasionally he has also contributed set designs to the productions he has costumed. Born in Louisville, Kentucky on July 15, 1915, he attended Yale, studying with Donald Oenslager, Frank Bevan and Pavel Tchlitchev. Two of the films he has designed, *Top Banana* and *Li'l Abner* were shows he had originally designed on Broadway. He has designed for television, most notably *The Adams Chronicles* series for WNET in 1976. Mr. Colt received the Tony Award for his costume designs in 1957 for *Pipe Dream* and has been nominated five other times.

Scenic Designs:

1947: *Music in My Heart*

Costume Designs:

1944: *On the Town* **1946:** *Around the World in Eighty Days* **1947:** *Barefoot Boy with Cheek; Music in My Heart* **1949:** *Clutterbuck* **1950:** *Guys and Dolls* **1951:** *Top Banana* **1953:** *Frogs of Spring, The* **1954:** *Fanny; Golden Apple, The* **1955:** *Lark, The; Phoenix '55; Pipe*

Dream **1956:** *Li'l Abner; Sleeping Prince, The* **1957:** *Copper and Brass; Rumple* **1958:** *Blue Denim; Say, Darling* **1959:** *Destry Rides Again; First Impressions* **1960:** *Christine; Greenwillow; Wildcat* **1961:** *Aspern Papers, The; Thirteen Daughters* **1962:** *Beauty Part, The* **1963:** *Here's Love* **1964:** *Crucible, The; Seagull, The; Something More!* **1967:** *Henry, Sweet Henry; Imaginary Invalid, The; Paisley Convertible, The; Tonight At 8:30; Touch of the Poet, A* **1968:** *Golden Rainbow; Goodbye People, The* **1972:** *Sugar* **1974:** *Lorelei or Gentlemen Still Prefer Blondes* **1980:** *Roast, The* **1981:** *Broadway Follies* **1990:** *Accomplice*

Giulio Coltellacci

Born in Rome on April 12, 1916, Giulio Coltellacci is one of that city's foremost men of the theatre. His stage designs have won many Passerelle d' Argento Awards in Rome. He originally studied sculpture and design before enrolling at the Academia de Belle Arti to study stage and costume design with V. Grassi. After serving as an assistant to the Italian designer Aldo Calvo in the early 1940s, he made his debut in 1945 with the set and costume design for *Rebecca*. Living alternately in Paris and Rome, he has designed numerous operas and plays in each city, in addition to designs in London and New York. As a painter and illustrator he has been a regular contributor to the Paris edition of *Vogue*, and *Rivista Teatro*, Rome. In 1958 his paintings were exhibited in a New York gallery.

Scenic Designs:

1964: *Rugantino*

Costume Designs:

1964: *Rugantino*

Homer B. Conant

For most of his years in the theatre Homer B. Conant worked for the Shubert Organization. He was born in Nebraska in 1887 and died in New York in 1927. Mr. Conant primarily painted stage scenery but was also a mural designer and painter. Between 1916 and 1920 he contributed costume designs to fifteen productions and settings to four productions on Broadway, generally in collaboration with other designers employed by the Shubert Organization.

Scenic Designs:

1916: *Girl from Brazil, The* **1917:** *May-time* **1920:** *Century Revue, The*; *Cinderella on Broadway*

Costume Designs:

1916: *Follow Me*; *Girl from Brazil, The*; *Passing Show of 1916, The* **1917:** *Barbara*; *Doing Our Bit*; *Maytime*; *Over the Top* **1918:** *Sinbad*; *Somebody's Sweetheart* **1919:** *Nothing But Love*; *Passing Show of 1919, The* **1920:** *As You Were*; *Century Revue, The*; *Cinderella on Broadway*; *Tick-Tack-Toe*

H.A. Condell

Born in Berlin, Germany in 1905, H.A. Condell studied there with Ernest Stern. Between 1925 and 1930 he designed for various theatres in Berlin and for films, before accepting a position as the chief stage and costume designer at the Mellini Theatre Hannover, and subsequently at the Civic Opera in Berlin. In 1933 he helped found the Culture Group Opera and Playhouse in Berlin, travelling when possible to the United States to design for the American League for Opera in New York. In 1940 Mr. Condell relocated to New York where he primarily designed operas and taught scene design at both the Dramatic Workshop and the New School for Social Research. A prolific designer, he created sets and occasionally costumes for many American opera companies, and designed regularly in New York City at City Opera and City Center. Mr. Condell died on November 6, 1951.

Scenic Designs:

1942: *Winter Soldiers* **1946:** *Yours Is My Heart* **1950:** *Barrier, The* **1951:** *Springtime for Henry*

Costume Designs:

1946: *Yours Is My Heart*

John Conklin

John Conklin was born on June 22, 1937 in Hartford, Connecticut, the son of William Palmer Conklin and Anne Marshall Conklin. He received both a B.A. and an M.F.A. at Yale University where he studied with and was influenced by Donald Oenslager. As an undergraduate at Yale he began to design with a production of *Tom Jones* and made his Broadway debut in

1963. Mr. Conklin prefers to design both sets and costumes for productions, and works regularly for the major opera companies and regional theatres throughout the United States. His designs have been seen at the Guthrie Theatre, the Santa Fe Opera, Pennsylvania Ballet, Seattle Repertory Theatre, San Diego Shakespeare Theatre, Willimastown Theatre, Houston Grand Opera, New York City Opera, the Opera Company of St. Louis and regularly at Hartford Stage, where he often collaborates with Mark Lamos and lighting designer Pat Collins. Mr. Conklin has also directed operas.

Scenic Designs:

1963: *Tambourines to Glory* **1971:** *Scratch* **1973:** *Au Pair Man, The* **1974:** *Cat on a Hot Tin Roof*; *Leaf People*; *Lorelei or Gentlemen Still Prefer Blondes* **1976:** *Rex* **1977:** *Bully* **1980:** *Bacchae, The*; *Philadelphia Story, The* **1984:** *Awake and Sing* **1988:** *Streetcar Named Desire, A*

Costume Designs:

1963: *Tambourines to Glory* **1976:** *Rex* **1977:** *Bully*; *Romeo and Juliet* **1980:** *Bacchae, The*

Connors and Bennett

Connors and Bennett received credit for a single Broadway production in 1926. James Connors resided at 133 West 67th Street in 1922. Bennett is perhaps H. Gordon Bennett.

Scenic Designs:

1926: *Half-Caste, The*

Continer and Golding

The team of Continer and Golding collaborated on the designs for a Broadway show in 1932. Both Anthony Continer and Stephen Golding designed productions individually. Anthony Continer (a.k.a. Antonio Contineri) designed sets for four productions on Broadway between 1929 and 1934 and was associated at one time with scene designer Homer F. Emens. Stephen Golding was president of Golding Scenic Studios in 1919.

Scenic Designs:

1932: *'Ol Man Satan*

Anthony Continer

Anthony Continer designed sets for four productions on Broadway between 1929 and 1934. In addition, he collaborated with Stephen Golding on a set design. Antonio Contineri was associated with the scenic design firm Homer F. Emens, Artists at 533 West 43rd Street in 1915 and resided in Union Hill, New Jersey.

Scenic Designs:
1929: *Decision; Great Scott; Uncle Vanya*
1934: *Africana*

John Marshall Coombs

John Marshall Coombs designed the sets and lights for a production on Broadway in 1930.

Scenic Designs:
1931: *No More Frontier*

Lighting Designs:
1931: *No More Frontier*

Theodore Cooper

Theodore Cooper has created sets and lights for two productions on Broadway.

Scenic Designs:
1949: *Texas, Li'l Darlin'* 1950: *Story for Sunday Evening, A*

Lighting Designs:
1949: *Texas, Li'l Darlin'* 1950: *Story for Sunday Evening, A*

Edward B. Corey

Edward B. Corey designed sets on Broadway in 1921. In 1925 Edward B. Corey was president of William A. Taylor, Inc., security brokers and insurance at 205 Columbus Avenue in New York.

Scenic Designs:
1921: *Only 38*

E. David Cosier, Jr.

E. David Cosier, Jr. was born in San Francisco on June 23, 1958. He received a B.A. in theatre from Santa Clara University and an M.F.A. from the Yale University School of Drama in 1988. Working primarily as a scenic designer, he has designed off-Broadway at the American

Jewish Theatre and the Theatre for the New City, among others. Regional theatre credits include *Social Security* for the Indiana Repertory Theatre, *Billy Bishop Goes to War* for the Missouri Repertory Theatre and *A Christmas Carol* and *As You Like It* for the Arts District Theatre of the Dallas Theatre Center. Television designs include *Saturday Night Live* for NBC-TV and *House Party*. He acknowledges both Eugene Lee and Ming Cho Lee as mentors. E. David Cosier is married to scenic designer Deb Booth.

Scenic Designs:
1990: *Piano Lesson, The*

Peter Cotes

Peter Cotes, an actor, director and occasional designer of sets and lights, was born Sydney Boulting in Maidenhead, England on March 12, 1912. He appeared on stage for the first time when he was four years old, as a page in *Henry V*. His credits as a director of plays in England are lengthy, and also include *A Pin to See the Peepshow* and *Hidden Stranger* in New York. Television and films have also been within his domain and he has adapted many of the works he has directed.

Scenic Designs:
1963: *Hidden Stranger*

Lighting Designs:
1963: *Hidden Stranger*

Robert Cothran

Robert M. Cothran was born in Detroit on May 9, 1930 and designed his first sets for *Antigone* at the Vanderbilt University Theatre in Nashville, Tennessee in 1949. He studied at Vanderbilt, the University of Tennessee and at Yale University with Donald Oenslager. He designs principally in regional theatres and serves as resident designer for the Clarence Brown Company at the University of Tennessee. Robert Cothran is also a graphic artist and spent ten years as owner and major designer of an industrial exhibit company.

Scenic Designs:
1986: *Honky Tonk Nights*

Derek Cousins

A freelance graphic designer in England, Derek Cousins works mainly in television and film. He studied at the Royal College of Art where he illustrated an edition of *Canterbury Tales*. He subsequently made his debut as a stage designer with a production of the play, *Canterbury Tales*. In 1951 his business, D. Cousins, Costumiers, was located at 172 Railway Approach in London.

Scenic Designs:
1969: *Canterbury Tales*

Miguel Covarrubias

Miguel Covarrubias, a painter, illustrator and caricaturist was born in Mexico City in 1902 and died there in 1957. He came to New York in 1923 and with the support of the Mexican Government quickly established himself as an enterprising and creative force. Within a short time of his arrival he published books of caricatures, contributed regularly to *Vanity Fair* and *The New Yorker*, and designed ballets and one play on Broadway. During his lifetime he also wrote and illustrated ethnological studies.

Scenic Designs:
1925: *Androcles and the Lion*; *Garrick Gaieties*; *Man of Destiny* 1926: *Garrick Gaieties*

Costume Designs:
1925: *Androcles and the Lion* 1926: *Garrick Gaieties*

Eugene Cox

Eugene Cox designed settings for a Broadway play in 1924. An artist, he lived in New York City in the early 1920s, but resided in London at 36 Great James Street by 1925.

Scenic Designs:
1924: *Easy Street*

Tom Adrian Cracraft

A set designer, Tom Adrain Cracraft (a.k.a. Cracraft) designed scenery for numerous plays on Broadway and contributed costumes to one. He spent the last ten years of his life in Hollywood designing for film and television studios and the Hilton Hotel chain. Mr. Cracraft died on Oct. 8, 1963 at the age of 58.

Scenic Designs:
1932: *Goodbye Again* 1933: *Hilda Cassidy*; *Kultur*; *Love and Babies*; *Shady Lady*; *They All Come to Moscow* 1934: *All Rights Reserved*; *Broomsticks, Amen!*; *I, Myself*; *Roll Sweet Chariot*; *Wednesday's Child* 1935: *Black Pit*; *Symphony* 1936: *American Holiday*; *Class of '29*; *Help Yourself*; *It Can't Happen Here*; *Murder in the Cathedral* 1937: *Hero Is Born, A* 1938: *Hill Between, The*; *Window Shopping* 1941: *Popsy* 1943: *Goodbye Again*; *Petrified Forest, The*

Costume Designs:
1936: *Murder in the Cathedral*

Gordon Craig

Although his name does not appear often in playbills documenting credits of designers and directors on the Broadway stage, Edward Henry Gordon Craig's influence and presence was felt nonetheless. He was born in 1872 in Stevenage, Hertfordshire, England, the son of Edward William Godwin and the actress Ellen Terry. He trained as an actor and joined Henry Irving's company in 1889, gaining experience with that company and with his mother's productions in all aspects of the theatre as he began formulating theories about production. His first scenic designs, *For Sword or Song*, were for Fred Terry and for his mother's production of *Much Ado About Nothing* in 1903, after which he moved to the continent, wrote, founded a theatre journal, ran a school of acting and contributed designs to productions for several years. His final designs were for *Macbeth* in New York in 1928. The author of many books on various aspects of the theatre, including acting, directing, and design, he was regarded by many as a twentieth century theatre prophet. His papers and library were obtained by the Rondel Collection in Paris shortly before his death on July 29, 1966 in Vence, France.

Scenic Designs:
1928: *Macbeth*

Costume Designs:
1928: *Macbeth*

Ned Crane

In 1932 Ned Crane designed the settings for a

Broadway play. As an actor, he appeared in the 1958 production *The Confederacy*.

Scenic Designs:
1932: *Triplets*

Crayon

Hermann Křehan's (a.k.a. Crayon-Křehan) debut in New York was as scenic and costume designer for *Manon Lescaut* in 1949, the first new production at the Metropolitan Opera of *Manon* in twenty years. He trained as an architect in Zurich, graduating from the Darmstadt School and designed his first settings for Max Reinhardt in Berlin in the late teens, later designing for the Theater an der Wien in Vienna. He came to the United States initially to design *l'Bohème* and *Old Maid and the Thief* for television. He also designed *Wieder Metropol* in 1926, and *At Heidelberg* in 1932.

Scenic Designs:
1948: *Morey Amsterdam's Hilarities*

Frederick Crooke

Born in Guilford, Surrey, England on October 27, 1908, Frederick Crooke is a painter and scene designer. He studied at the Heatherley School of Art in London and began designing for the theatre in the 1930s, starting with sets and costumes for *Primrose Time* at the Royal Theatre in Brighton. Additional designs appeared at Sadler's Wells, the Old Vic, Stratford-on-Avon, and the Svenska Theatre in Finland. The production he designed on Broadway in 1956 originated at the Old Vic in London.

Scenic Designs:
1956: *Troilus and Cressida*

Costume Designs:
1956: *Troilus and Cressida*

Bob Crowley

A British designer of sets and costumes, Bob Crowley has designed for the Bristol Old Vic, the Welsh National Opera, the Royal Shakespeare Company, and for the Royal Opera House at Covent Garden.

Scenic Designs:
1987: *Les Liaisons Dangereuses*

Costume Designs:
1987: *Les Liaisons Dangereuses*

Audrey Cruddas

Audrey Cruddas designed sets and costumes on Broadway for several plays by Shakespeare in the mid-1950s. She was born in Johannesburg, South Africa on Nov. 16, 1914 and studied at the St. John's Wood School of Art. Her first professional designs were the sets for *The White Devil* in 1948. Shortly after the opening of that production she was invited to design *King John* for the Royal Shakespeare Festival in Stratford-upon-Avon, which led in turn to numerous additional credits. Audrey Cruddas usually designs both sets and costumes for productions, which has been the case with each show she has designed on Broadway. Her designs for the opera, ballet and theatre have been seen around the world. She received the Donaldson Award for *Caesar and Cleopatra* in the 1951-52 season.

Scenic Designs:
1956: *Macbeth* **1958:** *Hamlet*; *Henry V*

Lighting Designs:
1958: *Hamlet*; *Henry V*

Costume Designs:
1951: *Antony and Cleopatra*; *Caesar and Cleopatra* **1956:** *Macbeth* **1958:** *Hamlet*; *Henry V*

Keith Cuerden

Keith Cuerden has designed sets and costumes for many plays at the Circle in the Square, including *Plays for Bleeker Street* and *The Grass Harp*.

Scenic Designs:
1954: *Girl on the Via Flamina, The*

Costume Designs:
1954: *Girl on the Via Flamina, The*

Brian Currah

Brian Mason Currah is from Plymouth, Devonshire, England where he was born on August 19, 1929. He is both a stage designer and teacher of design. His debut in theatre was in 1951 at the Hippodrome in Stockton, England and since then his sets have been seen throughout the British Isles, in Canada and the United States. He has taught at the Croydon College of Art, Worthing College of Art, Theatre Clwd and the University of Alberta.

Scenic Designs:
1964: *Caretaker, The* **1967:** *After the Rain*

Liz da Costa

Liz da Costa, a British designer of sets and costumes, became designer for the Royal Exchange Theatre in Manchester after studying at the Central School of Art and Design. Her first London production was *The Changeling* at Riverside Studios. She met choreographer Micha Bergere at Riverside Studios, which led to collaborations including *Solo Ride* at Contemporary Dance and additional productions. She has taught theatre design at Hounslow Borough College.

Scenic Designs:
1987: *Breaking The Code*

Costume Designs:
1987: *Breaking The Code*

Daffi

In 1970 Daffi created sets for a play on Broadway.

Scenic Designs:
1970: *Gloria and Esperanza*

Asadata Dafora

Asadata Dafora wrote, choreographed, provided the music, and designed the costumes for a play in the mid-1930s. She moved to New York in 1929 from Sierra Leone, and was the first African choreographer to present African dances on the American stage. Between 1930 and her death in New York in 1965 she created and staged works based on African traditions. In 1979 the Charles Moore Dancers and Drums of Africa honored her memory with a program of dances at the Marymount Manhattan Theatre.

Scenic Designs:
1934: *Kyundor*

Costume Designs:
1934: *Kyundor*

Warren Dahler

Warren Dahler, a painter and designer who was born in New York City on October 12, 1897, attended the University of Chicago and studied with George Grey Barnard. He designed murals, including one for the Missouri State Capitol, and many sets for Broadway plays from his studio at 611 West 127th Street in New York

City. He also participated in exhibits at the National Academy of Design and occasionally also designed costumes. Mr. Dahler died in 1961.

Scenic Designs:
1915: *Glittering Gate, The; Tethered Sheep*
1916: *Great Katherine; Inca of Perusalem, The; Queen's Enemies, The* **1922:** *Czarina, The*

Costume Designs:
1916: *Great Katherine*

Marjorie Dalmain

Marjorie Dalmain created sets for two plays on Broadway in 1922.

Scenic Designs:
1922: *Manhattan; Up the Ladder*

Daphne Dare

Daphne Dare, who was named Head of Design at the Stratford (Ontario) Festival in 1975, has designed costumes for dozens of shows there and in her native England. She was born in Yeovil, Somerset, England and attended the Bath Academy of Art and London University. Her first position in the theatre was as a scene painter at the Birmingham Repertory Theatre. She first designed costumes and sets in 1958 for *Amphitryon 38* at the Bristol Old Vic, and since that time while continuing to design settings has concentrated on costumes. She has also designed costumes for television, notably *Dr. Who* and *Fall of Eagles*, and for motion pictures.

Scenic Designs:
1988: *Macbeth*

Costume Designs:
1971: *Abelard and Heloise*

Jean Dary

Jean Dary designed one play on Broadway in 1926.

Scenic Designs:
1926: *Play's the Thing, The*

Leon Davey

Leon G. Davey was born in London on August 6, 1904 and designed sets on Broadway in the 1940s. His career began in the early 1920s with productions at the Glasgow Royal Theatre, the Lyceum Theatre in Edinburgh and for the Oxford Players. His production credits in London are extensive and include *The Man of Yesterday*, *The Two Mrs. Carrolls*, *A Woman Passed By*, *Sitting Pretty*, *The School for Spinsters*, *The Kid from Stratford*, *Miss Mabel*, *Two Dozen Roses*, *Top Secret*, and *The Green Bay Tree*. He also designed for the Hampstead Everyman Theatre, the Kingsway Theatre, Blackpool's Grand Theatre, and Brighton's Theatre Royal. During World War II he was active with the Entertainment National Service Association.

Scenic Designs:
1948: *Don't Listen Ladies*

Michael Davidson

Throughout the 1960s Michael C. Davidson was an active lighting designer. In addition to designing a production on Broadway in 1969, he lit off-Broadway productions such as *Adaptation-Next*, *Get Thee to Canterbury* and *3 from Column A*. He designed lights for the Berkshire Theatre Festival in 1967 and 1968. As a technical and lighting consultant, he also lit displays, industrial promotions, residences, building interiors, and sculpture .

Scenic Designs:
1969: *No Place to Be Somebody*

Lighting Designs:
1969: *No Place to Be Somebody*

Spencer Davies

Spencer Davies designed numerous productions for the Goodman Theatre in Chicago in the 1940s, including *Family Portrait* and *The Merry Wives of Windsor*.

Scenic Designs:
1961: *Billy Barnes People, The*

Richard Davis

Richard Davis designed sets in 1970 for one production on Broadway.

Scenic Designs:
1970: *Cherry Orchard, The*

Robert Peter Davis

In 1923 Robert Peter Davis was designer of the settings for a play on Broadway. He was president of the Brotherhood of Painters, Decorators & Paper Hangers of America in 1915, and resided at 216 East 59th Street, New York City.

Scenic Designs:
1923: *Roseanne*

Robert Davison

Robert Davison, scenic and costume designer, was born in Long Beach, California on July 17, 1922. After study at Los Angeles City College he moved to New York where he was influenced by the Russian Constructivists and the pre-World War I New Romantics. Although he made his debut on Broadway as a costume designer in 1944, Mr. Davison did not design his first set on Broadway until 1945. Notable designs include sets and costumes for *Galileo* for Brecht in Los Angeles in 1947, and *La Barca di Venezia per Padova* in Spoleto, Italy in 1963. He also exhibited three duco paintings at the E.B. Dunkel Scenic Studio along with designs and paintings by his colleagues.

Scenic Designs:
1945: *Day Before Spring, The* **1946:** *Around the World in Eighty Days*; *Flag Is Born, A*; *O Mistress Mine* **1947:** *Galileo*; *Miracle in the Mountains*

Costume Designs:
1944: *Hand in Glove*; *Song of Norway* **1947:** *Miracle in the Mountains*

Mercedes de Acosta

Mercedes de Acosta was a playwright and well-known screen writer in the 1920s and 30s. She was born in Paris, raised in New York and educated at several schools in Europe. Eva Le Gallienne starred in two of her plays which were produced in New York, *Sandro Borrecelli* and *Jeanne d'Arc*. She also wrote books of poetry. Mercedes de Acosta died in New York at age 75 on May 9, 1968.

Scenic Designs:
1924: *Assumption of Hannele, The*

Costume Designs:
1924: *Assumption of Hannele, The*

Jean Fournier de Belleval

Jean Fournier de Belleval designed sets and costumes for a play in 1951 on Broadway.

Scenic Designs:
1951: *Ti-Coq*

Costume Designs:
1951: *Ti-Coq*

Joan and David deBethel

Joan and David deBethel collaborated on the designs for a Broadway production in 1955.

Scenic Designs:
1955: *Joyce Grenfell Requests the Pleasure*

John Decker

John Decker was a successful caricaturist of New York and Hollywood personalities and had a brief career as an actor. Born in San Francisco, he died June 8, 1947 at age 52 in Hollywood. He worked for the newspaper *The Evening World* in New York City, but after it closed in 1928 moved to California where he was employed as a stand-in for actors playing artists. He painted and drew but found his greatest popular success transposing famous faces onto copies of famous paintings, such as Greta Garbo masquerading as Mona Lisa and W.C. Fields as Victoria Regina. His serious paintings were also successful and widely exhibited, bringing him honors including the John Barton Payne Medal for American painting.

Scenic Designs:
1929: *Top O' the Hill*

William DeForest

William DeForest was responsible for the design of the sets, lights and costumes for a play in 1948, and sets for an additional production in 1949.

Scenic Designs:
1948: *Rats of Norway, The* **1949:** *Diamond Lil*

Lighting Designs:
1948: *Rats of Norway, The*

Costume Designs:
1948: *Rats of Norway, The*

Edward DeForrest

Edward DeForrest designed costumes for one play and costumes for another in the 1940s.

Scenic Designs:
1943: *Victory Belles*

Costume Designs:
1946: *Apple of His Eye*

Laurie Dennett

Laurie Dennett, a British designer of sets, studied at the Wimbledon School of Art and has designed many West End productions. In 1964 she was awarded the Royal Society of Arts Bursary for theatrical design.

Scenic Designs:
1981: *Dresser, The*

Paul de Pass

Born in New York City on May 22, 1950, Paul de Pass began designing at age sixteen. He studied at the High School of Music and Art, Cooper Union, and Sarah Lawrence College and received a B.F.A. at Carnegie Mellon University in 1972. In 1973 he formed a co-design partnership, Associated Theatrical Designers, Ltd., with Michael J. Hotopp. Credits include over one hundred national television commercials and numerous industrial shows for major companies. In 1981 he received a Clio for the IBM commercial "Partners". As a graphic designer he created the show poster for *The 1940's Radio Hour.*

Scenic Designs:
1979: *Oklahoma!* **1980:** *Brigadoon* **1981:** *Oh, Brother* **1983:** *Tapdance Kid, The*

Lighting Designs:
1982: *Cleavage*

Jack Derrenberger

Jack Derrenberger designed sets for one show in 1954.

Scenic Designs:
1954: *Hayride*

Raymond Deshays

Raymond Deshays was responsible for one set design on Broadway in 1939. In collaboration with Marc Henri, Laverdet, Jean Gabriel Domergue and Arnaud he also created scenery for a revue on the London stage in 1921, *Fun of the Fayre*. His credits in France begin in 1910 with a production of *Faust* at the Odéon and continued with many productions for Opéra Comique through the 1920s, 1930s, 1940s and 1950s, including *Le Jongleur de Notre Dame*, *Gargantua*, *George Dandin* and *Pelléas et Mélisande*. He also designed for le Chatelet and the Folies Bergère.

Scenic Designs:
1939: *Folies Bergère*

Lowell Detweiler

Lowell Detweiler was born on June 29, 1947 in Bucks County, Pennsylvania. He received an M.F.A. from New York University in 1973 and spent a season at the Guthrie Theatre as Resident Assistant, working with Desmond Heeley, John Jensen, Hal George and Carl Toms. In addition he assisted John Conkin for two years. His professional design debut occurred during the first season of Syracuse Stage with a production of *An Enemy of the People*. Mr. Detweiler, who designs sets in addition to costumes, is also a painter. He received a Daytime Emmy Award for his costume designs for *Square One TV* for the Children's Television Workshop in 1988, and has designed for the Houston Opera, Goodspeed Opera, American Stage Festival, the Criterion Theatre, Alabama Shakespeare Festival, Minneapolis Children's Theatre and the Moscow Central Theatre, among others.

Scenic Designs:
1989: *Starmites*

Costume Designs:
1978: *Tribute* **1986:** *Corpse!*

Michael Devine

Michael Devine, a scenic designer for film, theater, and television works principally on the West Coast. He has designed sets and lights for plays on the West Coast and at Cafe La Mama and New Theatre For Now in New York City.

He attended the School of Theatre at San Francisco State College where he majored in scene design. His father was the playwright Jerry Devine. Michael Devine was art director for the 1989 film, *Criminal Law*.

Scenic Designs:
1970: *Paul Sills' Story Theatre*

Sophia Harris Devine

See Motley

Ernest De Weerth

Ernest De Weerth began his career in the theatre as an assistant stage manager at the Neighborhood Playhouse, and within six months was designing sets and costumes for the theatre. He was born in Paris on August 21, 1894 to an American mother, Helene Baltzell, and a German father, Ernest De Weerth, Sr. He studied at Eton and Oxford. During the rehearsals for *The Miracle* he was personal assistant to Max Reinhardt and continued to work with Reinhardt following that opening. Mr. De Weerth designed costumes for theatre and film and wrote many articles on stage design. He died in Rome on March 29, 1967.

Scenic Designs:
1921: *Great Way, The*; *Trial of Joan of Arc, The* **1923:** *Sandro Botticelli* **1926:** *Kwan Yin* **1928:** *'T Is to Blame for Everything*

Costume Designs:
1921: *Great Way, The* **1923:** *Sandro Botticelli* **1926:** *Kwan Yin* **1927:** *Grand Street Follies*; *Midsummer Night's Dream, A* **1928:** *'T Is to Blame for Everything*; *Peripherie* **1931:** *Thais*

Elsie de Wolfe

Born Ella Anderson de Wolfe in New York on December 20, 1865, Miss Elsie de Wolfe was an actress, author, and interior decorator. As Lady Mendl (after marriage to Sir Charles Mendl in 1926) she was also a society leader. She was educated in Scotland after which she returned to the United States where she participated in amateur theatricals. Her professional debut was in 1891 with an appearance in Sardou's play *Thermidor*. Believing herself to be a mediocre performer, she left the stage in 1905 to become

America's first female decorator and led a rebellion against drabness. In 1906 she established her reputation when she decorated the Colony Club, the first social club for women in New York City. She moved to France at the outbreak of World War I and served at the Ambrine Mission caring for gas burn victims. When the war ended, she settled in Versailles. After the outbreak of World War II she moved to California, returning to Versailles after the war where she lived until her death on July 12, 1950 at the age of 84.

Scenic Designs:
1915: *Common Clay; Nobody Home; Very Good, Eddie* **1917:** *Polly with a Past* **1918:** *Daddies*

Eileen Diss

Eileen Diss is a British designer of theater, film and television. She was born on May 13, 1931 and studied at the Central School of Art and Design. She designed for the British Broadcasting Corporation from 1952 to 1959 including series, operas adapted for television, and films. She recently designed the five-part series, *Jeeves and Wooster* for Masterpiece Theatre. At the National Theater in London her credits begin with the 1976 production of *Blithe Spirit* and include most of Harold Pinter's plays, beginning with *Exiles* in 1969 in the West End. Feature films include *Secret Places* in 1983 and Harold Pinter's *Betrayal* in 1982. She has been honored with awards for television design.

Scenic Designs:
1972: *Butley* **1977:** *Otherwise Engaged*

Mstislav Dobuzhinsky

Mstislav Valerianovich Dobuzhinsky (Dobujinsky) was born in St. Petersburg in 1875 and studied at the Imperial Russian Academy of Fine Arts before beginning his career as a designer of sets and costumes with Meyerhold in 1907. He designed ballets produced by Diaghilev, including *The Fairy Doll* for Anna Pavlova. With the onset of the Russian Revolution he left Russia for Lithuania and began working for theatres in Dresden, Prague, Brussels, and London. In 1939 he joined Michael Chekhov's Theatre in New York. He also designed sets and costumes for other companies

in the United States and Canada, and for the Metropolitan Opera Company in the 1940s and 1950s, including *Boris Gudonov* and *Un Ballo in Maschera*, and productions for the New York City Opera, such as *The Love for Three Oranges*. Mr. Dobuzhinsky died on November 21, 1957 at age 82 in New York City.

Scenic Designs:
1927: *Chauve Souris* **1930:** *Month in the Country, A* **1939:** *Possessed, The* **1941:** *Anne of England*

Costume Designs:
1930: *Month in the Country, A* **1941:** *Anne of England*

Peter Docherty

Peter Docherty, a British designer of sets and costumes, was born on June 21, 1944 in Blackpool, England. He trained at the Central School of Art and Design after which he specialized in dance (especially ballet), collaborating regularly with the choreographers Peter Darrell and Eric Hynd. He has also designed operas and concert shows.

Scenic Designs:
1977: *Side By Side By Sondheim*

Dodge and Castle

The scenic design studio Dodge and Castle was formed by D. Frank Dodge and William E. Castle and operated at 241 West 62nd Street in New York City. They collaborated on several productions between 1914 and 1934 and painted the scenery for many additional productions. D. Frank Dodge, who lived in Mt. Vernon, New York in 1916, was also associated with the P. Dodd Ackerman Scenic Studio at one time. William E. Castle also designed scenery under his own name.

Scenic Designs:
1914: *Mix-Up, A* **1915:** *90 in the Shade; Full House, A* **1916:** *Co-Respondent, The; Fast and Grow Fat; Getting Married* **1917:** *Broken Threads; Friend Martha; His Little Widows; Lodger, The; Over the 'Phone; When Johnny Comes Marching Home* **1918:** *Another Man's Shoes; Daddy Long Legs; Ladies First* **1919:** *Exchange of Wives, An; Good Morning, Judge; She's a Good Fellow* **1920:** *French Leave;*

Frivolities of 1920; Kissing Time; Night Boat, The; Oh, Henry; Tip Top **1921:** *Transplanting Jean* **1934:** *Only Girl, The*

D. Frank Dodge

D. Frank Dodge was partner with William E. Castle in the scenic studio Dodge and Castle, which was active between 1914 and 1934. For credits and additional information see "Dodge and Castle".

R. Paul Dodge

R. Paul Dodge designed scenery for a production on Broadway in 1927. An artist, he resided at 2441 Seventh Avenue, New York City in 1917.

Scenic Designs:
1927: *Comic, The*

Peter Dohanos

S. Peter Dohanos was a scenic designer for television, film and theater and a watercolor painter. He was born in Cleveland, Ohio, son of the artist Steve Dohanos. He grew up in Westport, Connecticut and graduated from Dartmouth. He designed many films including *Diary of a Mad Housewife*, and was active in television, notably as art director for *The Kraft Television Theatre* and as production designer for the *Bell Telephone Hour*. He died on December 27, 1988.

Scenic Designs:
1959: *Kataki* **1980:** *Tricks of the Trade*

Lighting Designs:
1980: *Tricks of the Trade*

Stephen Doncaster

Stephen Doncaster, a British designer who trained at the Old Vic School, has worked for many theatres including the Royal Shakespeare Company, the Royal Court and the English Stage Company. He has designed sets and supervised costumes for commercial television in England for series such as *The Avengers, Private Eye* and *Redcap*. Additional designs by Mr. Doncaster have been seen at the Nottingham Players, Glasgow Citizen's Theatre, the Actor's

Company, the Royal Exchange Theatre, and in London's West End.

Scenic Designs:
1958: *Epitaph for George Dillon*

Costume Designs:
1981: *Dresser, The*

Cushing Donnell

Captain Cushing Donnell wrote a play which was produced on Broadway in 1929. He also designed the sets and costumes for the show. Captain Donnell was said to be the first American to discharge a firearm in the First World War. He also wrote *Shadows of the Cross* which was produced in Dublin.

Scenic Designs:
1929: *Chinese O'Neill*

Costume Designs:
1929: *Chinese O'Neill*

John Dos Passos

The novelist John Dos Passos also wrote and designed plays. He was born on January 14, 1896 in Chicago and died on September 28, 1970. He received a Bachelor of Arts degree from Harvard in 1916. In the 1920s he was very active, travelling, painting with watercolors, writing plays, novels, poetry, and pamphlets and even designing scenery. Most of his talents, however, were devoted to writing, producing thirty books including *District of Columbia* and the acclaimed trilogy *U.S.A.* Interestingly his scenic designs were not limited to his own plays, although he did design scenery for all of his own plays.

Scenic Designs:
1926: *Moon Is a Gong, The* **1927:** *Belt, The; Centuries* **1928:** *International, The* **1929:** *Airways, Inc.*

Jay Doten

Jay Doten was the playwright and scene designer for a play produced at the Provincetown Playhouse in 1934.

Scenic Designs:
1934: *Green Stick*

Wade Douglas

Wade Douglas was a scenic designer in the teens and twenties. He was associated with the Joseph Physioc Studios.

Scenic Designs:
1919: *Thunder* **1921:** *Thank You; Wheel, The*

Hans Dreier

Hans Dreier was a prolific art director for motion pictures. He won three Academy Awards, in 1950 for *Sunset Boulevard* in the black and white category and for *Samson and Delilah* in the color category, and in 1945 for *Frenchman's Creek* among many nominations. At Paramount Studios he was supervising art director from 1927 to 1950, working often with Rouben Mamoulian and Cecil B. DeMille. A native of Germany, he was born on August 21, 1885 in Bremen and studied architecture and engineering at Munich University. He served in the German Army during World War I, beginning his film career in Berlin prior to coming to the United States in 1921. He died on October 24, 1966 in Bernardsville, New Jersey at the age of 71.

Scenic Designs:
1929: *Marriage Bed, The*

Henry Dreyfuss

Henry Dreyfuss was a set designer who also designed theatre interiors. Born in New York City in 1904 he designed numerous sets for plays on Broadway, occasionally also designing the costumes and lights as well as the interiors of theatres. He also worked as art director for companies which presented films. An industrial designer, he formed Henry Dreyfuss and Associates to manufacture and merchandise products. He died a suicide with his wife, Mrs. Doris Marks Dreyfuss, on October 5, 1972. He was 68.

Scenic Designs:
1924: *Two Strangers from Nowhere* **1926:** *Beau Gallant; Beau-Strings* **1927:** *Manhatters, The* **1928:** *Hold Everything* **1929:** *Remote Control* **1930:** *Affair of State, An; Blind Mice; Boundary Line, The; Fine and Dandy; Kiss of Importance, A; Last Mile, The; Pagan Lady; Sweet Stranger; This Is New York* **1931:** *Cat and the Fiddle, The; Gang's All Here, The; Man on Stilts, The; Philip Goes Forth; Shoot the Works* **1933:** *Strike Me Pink* **1934:** *Continental Varieties* **1935:** *Continental Varieties; Paths of Glory*

Lighting Designs:
1931: *Shoot the Works*

Costume Designs:
1927: *Manhatters, The* **1928:** *Merry Wives of Windsor, The* **1930:** *Affair of State, An*

Raoul Pène Du Bois

Raoul Pène Du Bois launched his career on Broadway in 1930 with the contribution of one costume to the *Garrick Gaities*. This design was the beginning of 50 years creating creative and colorful costumes and imaginative sets. He trained briefly at the Grand Central Art School, but coming from a family rich in artistic heritage his natural talents found ready employment in theatre and films. His grandfather, Henri Pène Du Bois, was an art and music critic; his uncle, Guy Pène Du Bois, a painter; and cousin, William Pène Du Bois, a book illustrator. He received a Tony Award for the costumes for *No, No, Nanette* in 1973 with three additional nominations, and a Tony Award for set design in 1953 for *Wonderful Town*. In addition to his Broadway credits he designed in London and Paris. Raoul Pène Du Bois' costumes and scenery graced films, ice shows, ballets, night clubs, aquacades, the Rockettes, and commercial illustrations. He was born on Staten Island and died in New York on January 1, 1985 at age 72.

Scenic Designs:
1934: *Thumbs Up* **1939:** *Du Barry Was a Lady; One for the Money* **1940:** *Hold Onto Your Hats; Panama Hattie; Two for the Show* **1941:** *Liberty Jones; Sons O'Fun* **1948:** *Heaven on Earth; Lend An Ear* **1950:** *Alive and Kicking; Call Me Madam* **1951:** *Make a Wish* **1952:** *In Any Language; New Faces of 1952* **1953:** *John Murray Anderson's Almanac; Maggie; Wonderful Town* **1954:** *Mrs. Patterson* **1955:** *Plain and Fancy; Vamp, The* **1956:** *Bells Are Ringing* **1957:** *Ziegfeld Follies* **1963:** *Student Gypsy, or The Prince of Liederkrantz* **1964:** *P.S. I Love You* **1971:** *No, No, Nanette* **1973:** *Irene* **1975:** *Doctor Jazz* **1979:** *Sugar Babies*

Lighting Designs:
1948: *Lend An Ear*

Costume Designs:

1930: *Garrick Gaieties* **1934:** *Keep Moving*; *Life Begins At 8:40*; *Ziegfeld Follies: 1934* **1935:** *Jumbo* **1936:** *Ziegfeld Follies: 1936* **1937:** *Hooray for What!* **1938:** *Leave It to Me!* **1939:** *Du Barry Was a Lady*; *Leave It to Me!*; *One for the Money*; *Too Many Girls* **1940:** *Hold Onto Your Hats*; *Panama Hattie*; *Two for the Show* **1941:** *Liberty Jones*; *Sons O'Fun* **1943:** *Carmen Jones* **1945:** *Are You with It?*; *Firebrand of Florence,the* **1948:** *Heaven on Earth*; *Lend An Ear* **1950:** *Alive and Kicking*; *Call Me Madam* **1951:** *Make a Wish* **1952:** *In Any Language* **1953:** *Maggie*; *Wonderful Town* **1954:** *Mrs. Patterson* **1955:** *Plain and Fancy*; *Vamp, The* **1956:** *Bells Are Ringing* **1957:** *Music Man, The*; *Ziegfeld Follies* **1959:** *Gypsy* **1963:** *Student Gypsy, or The Prince of Liederkrantz* **1964:** *P.S. I Love You* **1968:** *Darling of the Day* **1971:** *No, No, Nanette* **1973:** *Irene* **1974:** *Gypsy* **1975:** *Doctor Jazz* **1979:** *Sugar Babies* **1980:** *Reggae*

Caroline Dudley

Caroline Louise Carter Dudley was born in Lexington, Kentucky on June 10, 1862 and reared in Ohio. After nine years of marriage and the birth of one son she divorced Leslie Carter, became an actress and retained his name for stage use, appearing as Mrs. Leslie Carter. David Belasco created *The Heart of Maryland* and other plays for her which proved to be great successes. After losing Belasco's support she moved to England for a time, returning occasionally to the New York stage. Her career never regained the level of success achieved under Belasco and they remained unreconciled. She died in Santa Monica, California on November 13, 1937.

Scenic Designs:

1915: *Earth, The* **1917:** *Peter Ibbetson*

Costume Designs:

1917: *Claim, The*; *Hamilton*; *Peter Ibbetson*

John H.M. Dudley

Retired army officer Colonel John H.M. Dudley died at the age of 77 on August 25, 1954 in Elizabeth, New Jersey. He was born Henry Carter in Bristol, England, the son of two musicians. He came to Boston in 1895, becoming a citizen in 1901. Beginning in theatre as an actor, he established a business in Elizabeth, New Jersey for architecture, theatrical scene painting and clay modeling in 1902, one of many varied activities in his life. From 1932 to 1954, he served as director of the Board of Freeholders of Union County, New Jersey.

Scenic Designs:

1919: *Nothing But Love* **1922:** *Monster, The*

William Dudley

William Dudley, a British painter and designer of sets and costumes, has credits for a wide range of theatre and opera pieces, beginning with *Hamlet* for the Nottingham Playhouse in 1970 and including five years in residence with the Royal Court Theatre in London. He was born on March 4, 1947 in London and studied marine painting at St. Martin's School of Art, the Slade School of Art and with Nicholas Georgiadis. He first worked in amateur theatre as a scene painter and actor. He gradually began designing and working with professional theatres in the West End, for the National Theatre and the Royal Shakespeare Company. He designed a new production of *Der Ring der Nibelungen*, directed by Peter Hall in 1984 at Bayreuth and the setting for *Billy Budd* at the Metropolitan Opera. In addition to a production on Broadway in 1990, recent credits in the United States include sets and costumes for *Lucia Di Lammermoor* at the Lyric Opera of Chicago.

Scenic Designs:

1990: *Cat on a Hot Tin Roof*

Lady Duff Gordon

See Lucile

C.B. DuMoulin

C.B. DuMoulin designed sets for a Broadway play in the mid-1920s. An electrician named Eugene DuMoulin resided at 522 East 156th Street, New York City in 1925.

Scenic Designs:

1925: *Fall of Eve, The*

Boyd Dumrose

Boyd Dumrose is the set designer of the soap opera *Loving*, which features eighty-five working sets. He received a design award in 1984 from the Broadcast Designers Association for the television movie which launched *Loving*. He received a degree in Theater Arts from the University of California, Los Angeles and began in the theatre as an actor. He moved to New York City in 1957 and has designed often in summer stock and off-Broadway. He has served as a design assistant to George Jenkins and Robert Randolph.

Scenic Designs:
1969: *Three Men on a Horse*

Clarke Dunham

Clarke Dunham is a prolific designer of both sets and lighting, with more than three hundred productions to his credit. He received a Maharam Award for *The Me Nobody Knows*, Tony nominations for the settings for *End of the World* and *Grind* and has worked often in collaboration with Harold Prince. He designs in regional theatres such as the Goodman and received a Jefferson Award for *Twentieth Century*. Additional credits include numerous operas, such as the New York City Opera production of *Candide*, *Madame Butterfly* at the Lyric Opera of Chicago and design and direction of *Das Liebesverbot* at the 1983 Waterloo Festival. Raised on Philadelphia's Main Line, he is married to the poet, playwright, and lyricist Barbara Tumarkin Dunham.

Scenic Designs:
1970: *Me Nobody Knows, The*; *Place for Polly, A* **1973:** *Iceman Cometh, The*; *Waltz of the Toreadors, The* **1976:** *Bubbling Brown Sugar* **1984:** *End of the World*; *Play Memory* **1985:** *Grind* **1987:** *Late Nite Comic*

Lighting Designs:
1967: *Girl in the Freudian Slip, The*; *Ninety-day Mistress, The* **1970:** *Me Nobody Knows, The*; *Place for Polly, A* **1977:** *Something Old, Something New*

E.B. Dunkel Studios

Eugene B. Dunkel operated his studio in New York City to produce his own designs and those of other designers. For additional information, see "Eugene B. Dunkel".

Scenic Designs:
1942: *Chocolate Soldier, The*

Eugene B. Dunkel

Eugene B. Dunkel (a.k.a. E. B. Dunkel) was a set designer and mural painter born on April 30, 1890 in Verny (Alma-Ata), Russian Turkestan. He studied painting in Moscow, St. Petersburg and Vilna and also worked in the theatre there. After leaving Russia he came to the United States where he designed sets and built and painted the scenery for the Ballet Russe de Monte Carlo from 1930 to 1940. He had his own studio, E.B. Dunkel Studios, where he executed his own work and that of other designers. He designed and executed sets for many designers and companies, including the American Ballet and the Ballet Moderne and also for television and opera. He died in Pelham, New York at age 81 in April 1972.

Scenic Designs:
1933: *One Sunday Afternoon*; *Scorpion, The* **1934:** *Fools Rush in* **1937:** *Fireman's Flame, The*; *Naughty Naught '00* **1938:** *Bridal Crown*; *Girl from Wyoming, The* **1940:** *Man Who Killed Lincoln, The*

Thomas F. Dunn

Thomas F. Dunn designed sets in 1920 for a production on Broadway. In 1924 he designed *Bunty Pulls the Strings* with Sydney Cook in London. An architect, he had studios in New York City in 1922.

Scenic Designs:
1920: *Don't Tell*

Jacques Du Pont

Jacques Du Pont designed sets and costumes for ballets, operas and plays in the United States, France and England. He was born in Charou, France on January 16, 1909 and died in Paris on April 21, 1978. His debut in Paris was scenery for *La Sonate des Spectres* in 1934 at the Rideau de Paris where he subsequently designed many additional productions. He also designed for the Opéra Comique, Théâtre de la

Reine (Versailles), Festival d'Aix-en-Provence, Théâtre Hérbertot and the Festival de Bordeaux. Additional New York productions include *Faust* and *Carmen*, directed by Jean-Louis Barraultat at the Metropolitan Opera.

Scenic Designs:
1963: *Phaedre* 1965: *La Grasse Valise*

Costume Designs:
1963: *Phaedre* 1965: *La Grasse Valise*

Paul du Pont

Paul du Pont was born in Bradford, Pennsylvania, the son of an opera singer and a chemist. Originally trained to be a singer, he changed to painting and then to ballet. A serious fall through an open trap door while on tour with a ballet troupe cut short his dancing career. His first costume designs were for ballet, after which he designed for the Group Theatre and the Theatre Guild. In addition to his designs of scenery, costumes and lighting for the theatre, he designed extensively for television, including the Sid Caesar–Imogene Coca Variety series. Mr. du Pont died at age 51 on April 20, 1957.

Scenic Designs:
1951: *Diamond Lil*

Lighting Designs:
1951: *Diamond Lil*

Costume Designs:
1936: *Johnny Johnson* 1939: *Time of Your Life, The* 1940: *Another Sun; Fifth Column, The; Retreat to Pleasure; Time of Your Life, The* 1942: *All Comforts of Home; Chocolate Soldier, The; Kiss for Cinderella, A; Let Freedom Sing; Porgy and Bess; Strings, My Lord, Are False, The; Time, the Place, and the Girl, The* 1943: *First Million, The; One Touch of Venus; Porgy and Bess* 1944: *Anna Lucasta; Porgy and Bess; Pretty Little Parlor* 1949: *Diamond Lil* 1950: *All You Need Is One Good Break* 1951: *Diamond Lil* 1953: *Oh, Men! Oh, Women!*

Duke Durfee

Duke Durfee was born on September 9, 1952 in Wheaton, Illinois and received a B.A. degree from Mankato State College, as well as an M.F.A. from Pennsylvania State University where he studied with Anne A. Gibson. After

completing college he held an his internship at The Guthrie Theatre. His first design was *The Tempest* at Mankato State. He moved to New York in 1981 to assist Karl Eigsti and Lawrence Miller and has worked on Broadway and in regional theaters. He designs videos, industrial promotions, commercials and films such as *The Flamingo Kid* for which he was art director.

Scenic Designs:
1989: *Metamorphosis*

Harry Dworkin

Harry Dworkin designed sets in 1944 for a single production on Broadway.

Scenic Designs:
1944: *Slightly Scandalous*

John T. Dwyer

John T. Dwyer was an actor who occasionally also contributed set designs while appearing in roles in the 1920s. Off-Broadway stage appearances included roles in *Over the Hill to the Poor House* in 1920 and *Jack O'Hearts* and *The Man In The Shadow* in 1926. John T. Dwyer was born in 1877 and died on December 7, 1936.

Scenic Designs:
1922: *Billeted* 1926: *Nic Nax of 1926*

Chris Dyer

Chris Dyer is a British designer of scenery and costumes. After attending art school in Bromley he was a scene painter at the Bristol Old Vic from 1971 to 1973, and subsequently worked at Stratford-upon Avon with Hayden Griffin, Abd'el Farrah and John Napier. Since 1975, as Associate Designer for the Royal Shakespeare Company, he has designed over thirty productions including new plays such as *The Bundle* and classic works such as *The Roaring Girl* and *Macbeth*. Designs for opera include productions at La Scala, the Scottish Opera, and the Royal Opera House. He has also designed at the Stratford (Ontario) Festival and for the English Shakespeare Festival.

Scenic Designs:
1989: *Merchant of Venice, The*

Costume Designs:
1989: *Merchant of Venice, The*

Michael Eagan

Michael Eagan is a set designer who works primarily in Canada. He designed the 1978 summer season for Theatre Plus in Ontario.

Scenic Designs:
1980: *Happy New Year*

Holmes Easley

Holmes Easley is a set designer with credits at the Roundabout, the GEVA Theatre, the Asolo Theatre and many other off-Broadway and regional theatres. He was born September 24, 1934, in San Saba, Texas, and studied with Freda Powell at Sul Ross College in Texas and with Donald Oenslager at the Yale Drama School. His initial professional design was the set for *Anastasia* at the Alley Theatre in Houston in 1957. He taught stage design for three years at Stanford University and at Colgate University after completing his own degree at Yale. For the past twenty years he has been set decorator for *The Guiding Light* and *As the World Turns* as well as for many other productions at CBS-TV.

Scenic Designs:
1973: *Play's the Thing, The*

Arthur Ebbetts

Arthur Ebbetts designed lighting on Broadway between 1917 and 1918 and sets on Broadway in 1924. He worked as a stage director in the late teens and in the early 1930s worked as a stage manager, residing at 4611 Spuyten, Duyvil Parkway in New York City.

Scenic Designs:
1924: *Main Line, The*

Lighting Designs:
1917: *Why Marry?* **1918:** *Why Marry?*

Marsha L. Eck

Marsha L. Eck works as a set designer for opera, often in collaboration with Tito Capobianco. Their joint work includes *Manor* and *Lucia di Lammermoor* at the New York City Opera and *Falstaff* at the Chilean National Opera. Her designs have been seen at Circle in the Square, at the New York Shakespeare Festival for *The Corner* and *The Children* and at the Juilliard School of Music and Drama Theatre. She is married to costume designer Joseph G. Aulisi.

Scenic Designs:
1969: *Trumpets of the Lord* **1972:** *Mourning Becomes Electra* **1973:** *Molly*

William and Jean Eckart

Since 1951 William and Jean Eckart have provided designs for some of Broadway's most popular shows. That year they designed sets and lights for *Glad Tidings* and *To Dorothy a Son*. William Eckart was born in 1920 in New Iberia, Louisiana and received a B.S. in architecture from Tulane University in 1942 and an M.F.A. in stage design at Yale in 1949. He married Jean Levy in 1943 and they have two children. She was born in Chicago on August 18, 1921 and received a B.F.A. at Newcomb College and an M.F.A. at Yale. The majority of their design work has been done in collaboration and includes theatre, film, television and industrial productions. Their design credits are generally for scenery and lighting, but occasionally they also contribute costumes to a production. In 1954 they received the Donaldson Award for *The Golden Apple* for their scenery. In 1976 Jean Eckart returned to school, receiving a M.S.W.S. from the University of Texas at Arlington, and from 1978 to 1986 worked in the mental health field at the Community Psychotherapy Center in Dallas and in private practice. She also continues to lecture on theatrical design, teaching recently on costume design. William continues to design, including a production in summer 1990 for the Colorado Shakespeare Festival.

Scenic Designs:
1951: *Glad Tidings; To Dorothy, a Son* **1952:** *Gertie* **1953:** *Dead Pigeon; Oh, Men! Oh, Women!* **1954:** *Golden Apple, The; Portrait of a Lady; Wedding Breakfast* **1955:** *Damn Yankees* **1956:** *Li'l Abner; Mister Johnson* **1957:** *Copper and Brass* **1958:** *Body Beautiful, The* **1959:** *Fiorello* **1960:** *Viva Madison Avenue* **1961:** *Happiest Girl in the World, The; Let It Ride!; Take Her, She's Mine* **1962:** *Never Too Late* **1963:** *Here's Love; Oh Dad, Poor Dad, Mamma's Hung You...; She Loves Me* **1964:** *Anyone Can Whistle; Fade Out-Fade In* **1965:**

Fade Out-Fade In; Flora, the Red Menace; Zulu and the Zayda, The 1966: *Agatha Sue, I Love You; Mame* 1967: *Hallelujah, Baby!* **1968:** *Education of H.Y.M.A.N. K.A.P.L.A.N., The; Maggie Flynn* 1969: *Fig Leaves Are Falling, The* 1970: *Norman, Is That You?* 1974: *Of Mice and Men*

Lighting Designs:

1954: *Portrait of a Lady; Wedding Breakfast* 1956: *Li'l Abner* 1957: *Copper and Brass* 1958: *Body Beautiful, The* 1959: *Fiorello* 1960: *Viva Madison Avenue* 1961: *Happiest Girl in the World, The; Let It Ride!; Take Her, She's Mine* 1962: *Never Too Late* 1963: *She Loves Me* 1964: *Fade Out-Fade In* 1965: *Fade Out-Fade In; Zulu and the Zayda, The* 1966: *Agatha Sue, I Love You* 1974: *Of Mice and Men*

Costume Designs:

1955: *Damn Yankees* 1956: *Mister Johnson* 1959: *Fiorello* 1974: *Of Mice and Men*

Eddie Eddy

Edward J. Eddy was a set designer on Broadway in the 1920s and 1930s. He worked as a laborer in the teens and resided at 1267 Park Avenue in 1915.

Scenic Designs:

1927: *Love in the Tropics* 1928: *Potiphar's Wife* 1929: *Broken Dishes; Come-On Man, The; Comedy of Women, A; Indiscretion; Patriarch, The; Town's Woman, The* 1930: *Nancy's Private Affair; Room 349; Room of Dreams; Troyka* 1931: *Privilege Car* 1932: *Singapore* 1933: *Late One Evening* 1934: *First Legion, The* 1935: *This Our House*

Serge Edgerly

Serge Edgerly designed one set on Broadway in 1932.

Scenic Designs:

1932: *Tree, The*

Kate Edmunds

Kate Edmunds was born in Detroit, Michigan on March 20, 1952. She received a B.F.A. from Wayne State University where she studied drawing, painting and printmaking, and received an M.F.A. from the Yale School of Drama. An admirer of the work of Boris Aronson, she continued her study of design through an apprenticeship with Tony Straiges. The last fifteen years have been spent primarily on the regional theater circuit, with additional credits off and off-Broadway. Her designs have been honored with Drama Logues on the West Coast.

Scenic Designs:

1980: *Charlie and Algernon*

Ben Edwards

Ben Edwards, born George Benjamin Edwards in Union Springs, Alabama on July 5, 1916, studied in New York City at the Feagin School of Dramatic Arts, the Kane School of Art, and through association with Gordon Craig, Robert Edmond Jones and Jo Mielziner. He first designed sets and lights at the Barter Theater in Abingdon, Virginia and first designed on Broadway in 1938. His credits for settings and lighting design are extensive both in the theatre and for television. Mr. Edwards also produces plays. He is married to costume designer Jane Greenwood.

Scenic Designs:

1938: *Cap't Jinks of the Horse Marines; Coriolanus; Diff'rent; No More Peace; Pygmalion* 1940: *Another Sun* 1947: *Medea* 1948: *Sundown Beach* 1949: *Diamond Lil* 1950: *Captain Brassbound's Conversion* 1952: *Sunday Breakfast; Time of the Cuckoo, The* 1953: *Remarkable Mr. Pennypacker, the* 1954: *Anastasia; Lullaby; Travelling Lady, The* 1955: *Honeys, The; Tonight on Samarkind* 1956: *Ponder Heart, The; Someone Waiting* 1957: *Dark At the Top of the Stairs, The; Waltz of the Toreadors, The* 1958: *Disenchanted, The; Jane Eyre; Touch of the Poet, A; Waltz of the Toreadors, The* 1959: *God and Kate Murphy; Heartbreak House* 1960: *Face of a Hero; Second String, A* 1961: *Aspern Papers, The; Big Fish, Little Fish; Midgie Purvis; Purlie Victorious; Shot in the Dark, A* 1962: *Harold* 1963: *Ballad of the Sad Cafe, The* 1964: *Hamlet* 1965: *Family Way, The; Race of Hairy Men, A* 1966: *How's the World Treating You?; Nathan Weinstein, Mystic, Connecticut; Where's Daddy* 1967: *More Stately Mansions* 1969: *Mother Lover, The* 1970: *Hay Fever; Purlie* 1972: *Purlie* 1973: *Finishing Touches; Moon for the*

Misbegotten, A **1976:** *Matter of Gravity, A*; *Texas Trilogy, A* **1977:** *Almost Perfect Person, An*; *Anna Christie*; *Touch of the Poet, A* **1981:** *To Grandmother's House We Go*; *West Side Waltz, The* **1982:** *Medea* **1984:** *Death of a Salesman* **1985:** *Iceman Cometh, The* **1988:** *Long Day's Journey Into Night* **1989:** *Few Good Men, A*

Lighting Designs:

1950: *Captain Brassbound's Conversion* **1952:** *Time of the Cuckoo, The* **1954:** *Anastasia*; *Lullaby*; *Travelling Lady, The* **1955:** *Tonight on Samarkind* **1956:** *Ponder Heart, The*; *Someone Waiting* **1957:** *Waltz of the Toreadors, The* **1958:** *Ages of Man*; *Touch of the Poet, A*; *Waltz of the Toreadors, The* **1959:** *God and Kate Murphy*; *Heartbreak House* **1960:** *Face of a Hero*; *Second String, A* **1961:** *Aspern Papers, The*; *Big Fish, Little Fish*; *Midgie Purvis*; *Purlie Victorious*; *Shot in the Dark, A* **1962:** *Harold* **1965:** *Family Way, The*; *Race of Hairy Men, A* **1966:** *How's the World Treating You?*; *Nathan Weinstein, Mystic, Connecticut*; *Where's Daddy* **1969:** *Mother Lover, The* **1970:** *Hay Fever* **1973:** *Finishing Touches*; *Moon for the Misbegotten, A* **1976:** *Texas Trilogy, A* **1977:** *Almost Perfect Person, An*; *Anna Christie*; *Touch of the Poet, A*

Costume Designs:

1938: *Cap't Jinks of the Horse Marines*; *Coriolanus*; *Diff'rent*; *No More Peace*; *Pygmalion* **1950:** *Bird Cage, The*; *Legend of Sarah* **1952:** *Desire Under the Elms*; *Sunday Breakfast* **1953:** *Emperor's Clothes, The*; *Remarkable Mr. Pennypacker, the* **1954:** *Anastasia*; *Travelling Lady, The* **1957:** *Waltz of the Toreadors, The* **1958:** *Touch of the Poet, A*; *Waltz of the Toreadors, The*

Larry Eggleton

William Lawrence Eggleton was born in 1920 and became a member of United Scenic Artists in 1949. He died on September 16, 1990. While he sometimes designed for theatre, he devoted his talents to commercials and television, working at one time for the Columbia Broadcasting System.

Scenic Designs:

1950: *Black Chiffon*

Stephen Ehlers

Stephen Ehlers designed his first Broadway production in 1989.

Scenic Designs:

1989: *Wizard of Oz*

Karl Eigsti

Karl Eigsti has designed sets and costumes on Broadway since 1977. He is principally a set designer who has on occasion also designed costumes and lights. Mr. Eigsti was born on September 19, 1938 in Goshen, Indiana and studied at Indiana and American Universities and at the School of Visual Arts in New York City. In 1964 he received an M.A. from Bristol University in England while on a Fulbright Award. He first designed sets professionally for *Billy Budd* at Arena Stage in 1964. He first designed costumes professionally at The Guthrie Theatre in 1968 for *Sgt. Musgrave's Dance*. Since 1969, he has designed sets for over two hundred productions on and off-Broadway and in regional theatres, worked as an art director for television productions, and taught design at New York University. Awards include the Maharam Award and a Tony nomination for *Knockout* in 1979, a Los Angeles Drama Critics Award in 1986 for *Tartuffe*, and a Helen Hayes in 1988 for *Les Blancs*.

Scenic Designs:

1970: *Henry V*; *Inquest*; *Othello* **1974:** *Yentl* **1975:** *Sweet Bird of Youth* **1977:** *Cold Storage* **1978:** *Eubie*; *Once in a Lifetime* **1979:** *Knockout*; *Murder At the Howard Johnson's* **1980:** *American Clock, The* **1982:** *Almost An Eagle*; *Joseph and the Amazing Technicolor Dreamcoat*; *World of Shalom Aleichem, The* **1983:** *Amen Corner* **1984:** *Accidental Death of An Anarchist*; *Alone Together*

Costume Designs:

1977: *Cold Storage* **1982:** *Almost An Eagle*

Eldon Elder

Eldon Elder is a setting and lighting designer who occasionally contributes costumes to plays and operas. He was born March 17, 1921 in Atchison, Kansas. He studied at Kansas State Teachers College (now Emporia State College) with Professor R. Russell Porter and at the University of Denver. He received an M.F.A. from Yale in 1950, studying with Donald Oenslager and subsequently assisting him for one year. His first professional designs were for the Provincetown Playhouse in 1949 and he first designed on Broadway in 1951 for *The Long Days* (sets and lights.) He designed sets, costumes and lights for many of the New York Shakespeare Festival's productions in the Belvedere Lake Theatre in the late 1950s and early 1960s. A teacher of design and an author, Mr. Elder also consults on the design of theatres. At the invitation of the Chinese Stage Decoration Institute he toured China and lectured while on a Guggenheim Foundation grant. Mr. Elder is the author of *Will It Make a Theatre?* and *Eldon Elder: Designs for the Theatre.*

Scenic Designs:

1951: *Legend of Lovers; Long Days, The* **1952:** *Grey Eyed People, The; Hook 'n Ladder; Time Out for Ginger* **1953:** *Take a Giant Step* **1954:** *Girl in Pink Tights, The; One Eye Closed* **1955:** *All in One, Trouble in Tahiti; Heavenly Twins, The; Phoenix '55; Twenty Seven Wagons Full of Cotton; Young and Beautiful, The* **1956:** *Fallen Angels* **1957:** *Shinbone Alley* **1962:** *Affair, The; Fun Couple, The* **1965:** *Mating Dance* **1967:** *Of Love Remembered* **1974:** *James Whitmore in Will Rogers' U.S.A.* **1976:** *Music Is* **1989:** *Hizzoner*

Lighting Designs:

1951: *Long Days, The* **1952:** *Grey Eyed People, The; Time Out for Ginger* **1953:** *Take a Giant Step* **1954:** *Girl in Pink Tights, The; One Eye Closed* **1955:** *All in One, Trouble in Tahiti; Heavenly Twins, The; Twenty Seven Wagons Full of Cotton* **1956:** *Fallen Angels* **1962:** *Affair, The; Fun Couple, The* **1967:** *Of Love Remembered* **1974:** *James Whitmore in Will Rogers' U.S.A.*

Costume Designs:

1974: *James Whitmore in Will Rogers' U.S.A.*

Charles Elson

Charles Elson was born September 5, 1909 in Chicago and received degrees at the Universities of Illinois, Chicago, and Yale. He designed numerous settings, also insisting on control over the lighting for those same productions. As producer-designer for a production he

would contribute costumes as well. He worked regularly as an assistant to Donald Oenslager. An author and committed educator, Mr. Elson taught at Hunter College of the City University of New York from 1948 to 1974, when he became Professor Emeritus. While on the Hunter College faculty he designed forty-eight productions for their theatre. He also served on the design faculties of the University of Iowa, Yale, and the University of Oklahoma.

Scenic Designs:

1946: *Hidden Horizon* **1947:** *Duet for Two Hands; First Mrs. Fraser, The* **1948:** *Cup of Trembling; Kathleen; Power Without Glory; Private Lives* **1950:** *Enemy of the People, An* **1951:** *Borscht Capades; Nina* **1952:** *Collector's Item; Deep Blue Sea, The* **1954:** *His and Hers* **1955:** *Champagne Complex* **1956:** *Lovers, The*

Lighting Designs:

1945: *Pygmalion* **1946:** *Born Yesterday; Hidden Horizon; Land's End; Loco; Present Laughter; Three to Make Ready; Years Ago* **1947:** *As You Like It; Duet for Two Hands; First Mrs. Fraser, The; Message for Margaret* **1948:** *Cup of Trembling; Kathleen; Power Without Glory; Private Lives* **1949:** *Regina* **1950:** *Enemy of the People, An; Lady's Not for Burning, The; Out of This World* **1951:** *Borscht Capades; Nina; Rose Tattoo, The* **1952:** *Collector's Item; Deep Blue Sea, The* **1953:** *Little Hut, The* **1954:** *His and Hers* **1955:** *Champagne Complex* **1956:** *Lovers, The* **1957:** *Compulsion* **1958:** *Blue Denim; Maria Golovin* **1959:** *First Impressions* **1960:** *Wildcat* **1962:** *Perfect Setup, The* **1963:** *Photo Finish* **1967:** *Mother Courage*

Costume Designs:

1951: *Nina* **1955:** *Champagne Complex*

Homer Emens

Homer Farnham Emens was born on May 9, 1862 in Volney, New York and died on September 15, 1930. He was known as a scene painter and watercolorist and often designed one or two sets within multi-set plays, specializing in outdoor scenes. He started as an apprentice to Philip Goatcher at Madison Square Garden and worked for the American Opera Company. In 1893 he opened his own paint studio at 533 West 43rd Street, while continuing to design, notably the Metropolitan Opera's production of *Parsifal*, the first performance of the opera in the

United States. Many of the productions Homer Emens designed were produced before 1915 and included *Blue Jeans* in 1890, *Mavourneen* and *Alabama* in 1891, *Babes in Toyland* in 1903, *Twelfth Night* in 1904, *Mlle. Modiste* in 1905, *Red Mill* in 1906, and *Kismet* in 1911.

Scenic Designs:

1915: *Celebrated Case, A; Chief, The; Cock O' the Walk; Duke of Killicrankie, The; Natural Law, The; Our Mrs. McChesney* **1916:** *Betty; Margaret Schiller; Sybil* **1917:** *Belinda/New Word, The/Old Friends/Old Lady; Case of Lady Camber, The; Jack O'Lantern; Lady of the Camellias, The; Rambler Rose; Seremonda; Three Bears, The* **1918:** *Belinda; Dear Brutus; Humpty Dumpty; Off Chance, The; Saving Grace, The* **1919:** *Come Along; Declassee; Mis' Nelly of N'Orleans* **1920:** *Mary Rose; Pietro; Sacred and Profane Love*

Entwisle

"Entwisle" designed lights for one production in 1924 on Broadway. Robert C. Entwistle, an electrician, was associated with Charles Schmitz and the Rialto Stage Lighting Company, located in 1925 at 304 West 52nd Street in New York City. He resided at 1425 Amsterdam Avenue. He also designed scenery and lights for productions in collaboration with Louis Kennel between 1919 and 1931. For additional credits see the entry "Kennel and Entwisle".

Scenic Designs:

1924: *Leah Kleschna*

Erté

Erté (born Romain de Tirtoff) had a long, varied career designing costumes and fashions under the name derived from the French pronunciation of his initials. He was born in St. Petersburg, Russia on November 10, 1892 and after studying painting in Russia went to Paris. He worked originally for an undistinquished fashion designer, Caroline, but quickly joined Paul Poiret as a sketch artist. His first designs for the theatre were produced in 1914, although he worked primarily as a fashion designer prior to World War I. In the early 1920s he came to the United States to design for Florenz Ziegfield and other producers, finding success as a stage designer throughout the 1920s and 1930s. In 1967

many of his drawings, paintings, sculptures, decorative arts, and designs were exhibited in New York and later purchased by the Metropolitan Museum of Art. His creative works are widely collected in museums and books, such as *Erté at Ninety-Five*, published in 1987. He died in Paris at age 97 on April 21, 1990.

Scenic Designs:

1922: *Greenwich Village Follies*

Costume Designs:

1922: *George White's Scandals* **1923:** *George White's Scandals; Topics of 1923* **1924:** *George White's Scandals* **1925:** *Artists and Models; George White's Scandals* **1926:** *George White's Scandals; Night in Paris, A* **1927:** *Manhattan Mary* **1928:** *George White's Scandals* **1929:** *George White's Scandals*

Diane Esmond

Diane Esmond contributed sets and costumes to a Broadway play in 1963.

Scenic Designs:

1963: *Berenice*

Costume Designs:

1963: *Berenice*

Manuel Essman

Manuel Essman (a.k.a. Easman, Essmann) died in April 1967 at age 68. He worked on Broadway, at the Federal Theatre, the Provincetown Playhouse, and for the New Playwrights Theatre. He studied at the Carnegie Institute of Technology and designed the film *Rhapsody in Steel* for the Ford Motor Company. He was a set designer for the Columbia Broadcasting System with numerous television designs to his credit including *The Ed Sullivan Show*. During World War II he was a photographer and writer for *Stars and Stripes*. At the time of his death he was devoting his energies to sculpture.

Scenic Designs:

1928: *Singing Jailbirds* **1936:** *Conjur Man Dies, The; Walk Together Chillun* **1937:** *Processional* **1938:** *Androcles and the Lion* **1939:** *Coggerers, The/Mr. Banks of Birmin/The Red Velvet Coat*

Eleanor Eustis

Eleanor Eustis designed one set in 1929 on Broadway.

Scenic Designs:
1929: *Paolo and Francesca*

Charles Evans

Charles Evans began professional life as an artist but changed to scene design, beginning with productions at the Playhouse in the Park in Philadelphia. Mr. Evans also has his own company, Design Associates, in Lambertville, New Jersey which builds sets for shows. He has served as designer and artistic director at the Vancouver Playhouse Theatre Company in British Columbia. During his career he has occasionally provided costume designs to productions for which he has also designed scenery.

Scenic Designs:
1965: *Me and Thee*

Costume Designs:
1965: *Me and Thee*

James B. Fagan

James Bernard Fagan made his first stage appearance in 1895 as an actor in Sir Frank R. Benson's Company, and while he continued to act off and on throughout his life, he is remembered principally as a producer and playwright. He was born in Belfast, Ireland on May 18, 1873 and attended Clongowes Wood College and Trinity College, where he considered a career in law. J. B. Fagan acquired the Big Game Museum in Oxford and converted it into the Oxford Playhouse, giving John Gielgud, Tyrone Guthrie, Raymond Massey and other young actors their start and developing a reputation as a Shakespearean director. *And So to Bed* and *The Improper Duchess* are among the plays he wrote. He died on February 17, 1933 in Hollywood, California at age 59 shortly after adapting *Smilin' Through* for Norma Shearer.

Scenic Designs:
1927: *And So to Bed* 1928: *Cherry Orchard, The*

Sven Fahlstelt

Sven Fahlstelt designed a production on Broadway in 1962.

Scenic Designs:
1962: *Father, The*

John Falabella

John Falabella was born in New York City on Oct. 9, 1952. At the age of ten he began designing fashions, and received his formal training at New York University, earning a B.F.A. in 1974. He worked as an assistant to Oliver Smith for four years and made his Broadway debut as a set designer in 1976 for *Kings* and as a costume designer in 1980 for *The Lady from Dubuque*. Recent costume designs include for *Rhymes with Evil* for the American Stage Festival in New Hampshire, *Beetle Bailey - The Musical* for Candlewood Playhouse, and *All's Well That End's Well* for the Huntington Theatre Company. He has also designed settings for *The Chalk Garden* for the Berkshire Theatre Festival, *Candide* for the Repertory Theatre of St. Louis, and was production designer for *TAD* for Great Performances/Dance in America and art director for *Happy New Year USA* on PBS. Mr. Falabella teaches scene design at Boston University.

Scenic Designs:
1976: *Kings* 1980: *Perfectly Frank* 1982: *Blues in the Night* 1983: *Caine Mutiny Court-martial, The*; *Guys in the Truck, The* 1987: *Barbara Cook: A Concert for the Theatre*; *Safe Sex*

Costume Designs:
1980: *Lady from Dubuque, The*; *Perfectly Frank* 1983: *Guys in the Truck, The*; *Man Who Had Three Arms, The* 1985: *Home Front*

Gabriella Falk

In addition to designing scenery and costume for the theatre, Gabriella Falk is an active film designer with credits including *In Search of Gregory* and *The Adding Machine*. From 1971 to 1973 she was a design consultant for Inter-Action Productions in London's West End. She has also designed in regional theatres throughout the United Kingdom.

Scenic Designs:
1977: *Dirty Linen/ New Found Land*

Costume Designs:
1977: *Dirty Linen/ New Found Land*

Charles B. Falls

Charles B. Falls (C.B. Falls), a graphic artist, designed sets and costumes on Broadway between 1919 and 1935. He designed posters for "Victory" book campaigns in World War I and World War II. He was born in Ft. Wayne, Indiana in 1874 and died on April 15, 1960 at age 85. At age twenty-one he moved to Chicago and worked for an architect before joining the art staff at the *Chicago Tribune.* Mr. Falls specialized in illustrations, posters (including show posters) and large-scale murals. A writer and book illustrator, he also designed fabrics and furniture. In 1922 he served as president of the Guild of Free Lance Artists in New York City. During the last years of his life he worked to develop art talent in disabled veterans.

Scenic Designs:
1919: *Greenwich Village Follies* **1926:** *Henry IV, Part I*

Costume Designs:
1926: *Henry IV, Part I* **1935:** *Macbeth; Othello*

Abd'el Farrah

Abd'el Elkader Farrah was born in Boghari, Algeria on March 28, 1926 and designed his first production in 1953 in Amsterdam. A designer of both sets and costumes, he has had a long association with the Royal Shakespeare Company in London and at Stratford-upon-Avon. A prolific designer with over three hundred productions to his credit, he has taught design in France and Canada.

Scenic Designs:
1973: *Emperor Henry IV*

Costume Designs:
1973: *Emperor Henry IV*

Thomas Farrar

Thomas Prince Farrar was born in New Orleans. He studied architecture at Tulane University and in Europe prior to becoming a set designer on Broadway. He was art director for Ringling Brothers & Barnum and Bailey Circus, where he was associated with costume designer Miles White. Also an industrial designer, he was a member of the firm Van Doren, Nowland and Schladermundt. Thomas Farrar died at age 50 on June 11, 1951.

Scenic Designs:
1928: *Perfect Alibi, The* **1929:** *Michael and Mary* **1930:** *Mrs. Moonlight* **1931:** *Give Me Yesterday; Roof, The* **1934:** *Mahogony Hall*

Eleanor Farrington

Eleanor Farrington, primarily known as a set designer, created sets, costumes and lights for a Broadway show in 1945, a remarkable accomplishment for a woman at that time.

Scenic Designs:
1938: *Michael Drops In* **1945:** *Deep Mrs. Sykes, The*

Lighting Designs:
1945: *Deep Mrs. Sykes, The*

Costume Designs:
1945: *Deep Mrs. Sykes, The*

A. H. Feder

A. H. (Abe) Feder has been well known as a lighting and scenery designer throughout a career which began in 1932 with the lighting design for *Trick or Trick.* He was born in Milwaukee, Wisconsin on June 27, 1909 and studied at Carnegie Institute of Technology with Woodman Thompson and Alexander Wykcoff. Mr. Feder has designed the lighting for plays, ballets and operas throughout the United States and lectures extensively. He has been consultant for the lighting of interiors of theatres, museums, galleries, and buildings, including the Kennedy Center in Washington, D.C., the Israel National Museum in Jerusalem and Rockefeller Plaza in New York City. He was instrumental in the development of the profession of lighting design, as it progressed from relying on electricians for the presence of light on stage to relying on designers for the quality of light on stage.

Scenic Designs:
1950: *Gioconda Smile, The* **1963:** *Once for the Asking* **1964:** *Blues for Mr. Charley*

Lighting Designs:
1934: *Calling All Stars; Four Saints in Three Acts* **1935:** *Ghosts; Hook-Up, The* **1936:** *Conjur Man Dies, The; Hedda Gabler; Macbeth;*

New Faces of 1936 **1937:** *Native Ground; Without Warning* **1938:** *Androcles and the Lion; Big Blow, The; Cap't Jinks of the Horse Marines; Coriolanus; Cradle Will Rock, The; Diff'rent; Here Come the Clowns; No More Peace; Prologue to Glory; Pygmalion; Sing for Your Supper* **1940:** *Hold Onto Your Hats; Johnny Belinda; Passenger to Bali, A* **1941:** *Angel Street* **1942:** *Autumn Hill; Magic/ Hello, Out There; Walking Gentleman* **1943:** *Winged Victory* **1950:** *Gioconda Smile, The* **1951:** *Sleep of Prisoners, A* **1952:** *Three Wishes for Jamie* **1953:** *Pin to See the Peepshow, A* **1954:** *Boyfriend, The; Flowering Peach, The; Immoralist, The* **1955:** *Inherit the Wind; Seventh Heaven; Skin of Our Teeth, The; Young and Beautiful, The* **1956:** *My Fair Lady* **1957:** *Clearing in the Woods, A; Orpheus Descending; Time Remembered; Visit to a Small Planet, A* **1958:** *Cold Wind and the Warm, The; Goldilocks* **1959:** *Loss of Roses, A* **1960:** *Camelot; Greenwillow* **1962:** *Tiger Tiger Burning Bright* **1963:** *Once for the Asking* **1964:** *Blues for Mr. Charley; Three Sisters, The* **1965:** *On a Clear Day You Can See Forever* **1971:** *Scratch* **1975:** *Doctor Jazz; Goodtime Charley* **1979:** *Carmelina*

Costume Designs:
1964: *Blues for Mr. Charley*

Richard Ferrer

Richard Ferrer designed sets for a Broadway play in 1974. A native of Louisiana, he studied at Tulane University and received a B.A. in architecture from the University of Southwestern Louisiana. He began his professional career as an architect for the Vieux Carre Commission of the City of New Orleans, renovating and restoring historic structures in the French Quarter. He has designed scenery for theatre, television and the ballet in New Orleans, and for the American Theatre in Washington, D.C. in addition to other locations.

Scenic Designs:
1974: *Rainbow Jones*

David Ffolkes

David Ffolkes was born October 12, 1912 in Hagley, Worchestershire, England. He began to study architecture in Birmingham but left to

pursue a career in theatre. His first designs were for the Cambridge Arts Theatre. He spent a year in residence at the Old Vic where he met and often designed for Maurice Evans. In 1936 Mr. Ffolkes came to New York with the Evans Company and stayed in the United States to design sets and costumes for additional productions. He has extensive design credits in both the U.S. and England. In addition to plays, David Ffolkes has designed ballets and films including *Journey to the Center of the Earth* and *Alexander The Great*. His designs for *Henry VIII* were honored with a Tony Award for outstanding costume design.

Scenic Designs:
1937: *King Richard II; Young Mr. Disraeli* **1938:** *Hamlet* **1939:** *Hamlet; Henry IV, Part I* **1940:** *King Richard II* **1946:** *Henry VIII* **1948:** *Where's Charley* **1951:** *Where's Charley* **1953:** *Men of Distinction*

Costume Designs:
1937: *King Richard II; Young Mr. Disraeli* **1938:** *Hamlet* **1939:** *Hamlet; Henry IV, Part I* **1940:** *King Richard II* **1943:** *Richard III* **1946:** *Henry VIII; What Every Woman Knows* **1947:** *Brigadoon; Man and Superman* **1948:** *Sleepy Hollow; Where's Charley* **1949:** *Along Fifth Avenue; Browning Version, The and A Harlequinade* **1951:** *Flahooey; Seventeen; Springtime for Henry; Where's Charley* **1953:** *Men of Distinction*

Tazeena Firth

Tazeena Firth is a British designer of both sets and costumes who works primarily in Europe. From 1954 to 1957 she designed for the Theatre Royal, Windsor, England before working for other theatres including the Royal Shakespeare Company and the English Stage Company. Since 1961 she has designed in partnership with Timothy O'Brien, although she occasionally designs independently. Together they have designed numerous plays and operas. She was born in Southampton, England on November 1, 1935 and educated at St. Mary's, Wantage and the Chatelard School. Honors include the Gold Medal for set design at the 1975 Prague Quadriennale, shared with Timothy O'Brien, Ralph Koltai and John Bury. Timothy O'Brien and Tazeena Firth received Tony Award nominations for both scenery and costumes for *Evita*.

Scenic Designs:
1979: *Bedroom Farce*; *Evita* **1982:** *Doll's Life, A*

Costume Designs:
1979: *Evita*

Eugene C. Fitsch

Eugene Camille Fitsch (a.k.a. Eugene C. Fritsch) was born December 11, 1892 in Alsace, France and studied at the Albright Art School and with Mahonri Young, Frank V. DuMond and Joseph Pennell. He was on the faculty of the Art Students League of New York, teaching graphic arts. He was a painter, graphic artist and set designer who occasionally also designed costumes. In 1932 he maintained a studio at 5 East 14th Street in New York City.

Scenic Designs:
1928: *Him* **1929:** *Winter Bound* **1931:** *Ladies of Creation* **1932:** *When Ladies Meet* **1934:** *Whatever Possessed Her*

Costume Designs:
1928: *Him*

Edward Fitzgerald

Edward Fitzgerald was born in Dublin, Ireland in 1876 and spent his career in the theatre as an actor and business manager. He was educated at Uppingham School and Dublin University. As an actor, he appeared in New York with the Richard Mansfield Company from 1902 to 1905. He went back to England in 1905 but quickly returned to New York, staying until called to military service for World War I.

Scenic Designs:
1937: *Wall Street Scene*

Robert Fletcher

Robert Fletcher was born Robert Fletcher Wyckoff on August 23, 1922 in Cedar Rapids, Iowa and studied at Harvard and the University of Iowa. He entered the theatre as a director and designer for the Council Bluffs (Iowa) Little Theatre. After service in World War II he appeared on Broadway as an actor before concentrating his talents on designing sets and costumes. His credits are extensive and varied.

He has designed for the Stratford (Ontario) Festival, the Brattle Theatre in Cambridge, Massachusetts (which he helped found), the Spoleto Festival, San Francisco Ballet, Boston Opera, and many others. Robert Fletcher has designer regularly for television since the late 1950s when he was a staff designer for NBC-TV.

Scenic Designs:
1960: *Farewell, Farewell, Eugene* **1964:** *High Spirits* **1969:** *Hadrian VII* **1980:** *Life, A* **1985:** *Doubles*

Costume Designs:
1958: *Firstborn, The* **1960:** *Farewell, Farewell, Eugene* **1961:** *Happiest Girl in the World, The*; *How to Succeed in Business Without Really Trying* **1962:** *Family Affair, A*; *Little Me*; *Moon Beseiged, The*; *Nowhere To Go But Up* **1964:** *Foxy*; *High Spirits* **1966:** *Walking Happy* **1969:** *Hadrian VII* **1970:** *Cry for Us All* **1980:** *Life, A* **1982:** *Othello*; *Seven Brides for Seven Brothers* **1985:** *Doubles*

Frank Hallinan Flood

Frank Hallinan Flood graduated from the National College of Art and Design in 1978 and held the Robert Smithson Memorial Scholarship at the Brooklyn Museum of Art from 1978 to 1979. He worked as a design assistant at the Abbey Theatre in Dublin, Ireland for a year and as assistant to Hayden Griffen at Covent Garden. He was designer at the National Opera in the 1980-81 season but currently concentrates on designing for theatre and film. He was art director for the film *Da*.

Scenic Designs:
1988: *Juno And The Paycock*

Chris Flower

Chris Flower designed the settings for a show on Broadway in 1980.

Scenic Designs:
1980: *Quick Change*

Frederick Foord

See Frederick Ford

Frederick Ford

In the early 1920s Frederick Leslie Ford was the scenic designer for a show produced on Broadway, although the playbill spelled his surname incorrectly. He was born in New Bedford, Massachusetts in 1894 and received as B.S. in architecture from the Massachusetts Institute of Technology in 1924. He began professional life as a draftsman for other architects, but ultimately established his own firm. A specialist in residences and public and commercial buildings, he designed many churches (principally in Massachusetts) including the Weymouth Universalist Church, the Auburndale Congregational Church and the Wollaston Methodist Church.

Scenic Designs:
1923: *Time*

R. Forester

R. Forester created sets for a show on Broadway in the mid-1920s. He appeared in *The Whirl of the World* at the London Paladium in 1925.

Scenic Designs:
1925: *Chivalry*

Stanley Fort

In 1933 Stanley Fort designed sets on Broadway for one production. In 1925 he worked as a plasterer from his residence at 2658 Eighth Avenue in New York City.

Scenic Designs:
1933: *Mountain, The*

Thomas Fowler

Thomas Fowler received credit as the scenic designer for a Broadway show in 1934. He was proprietor of Fowler's Scenic Studios, located at 261 West 54th Street in New York City in 1932, a supplier of "theatrical supplies and equipment".

Scenic Designs:
1934: *Legal Murder*

Frederick Fox

Frederick Fox is a scenic and lighting designer who occasionally contributes costume designs to a production as well. Born in 1910 in New York

City, he studied at Yale and worked initially as an architect. Before his New York debut, *Farewell Summer* in 1937, he designed many summer stock productions. A prolific designer of plays and operas, Mr. Fox now concentrates on creating designs for television. He designed numerous films between 1936 and 1961, as a scenic designer and lighting director, and received additional credits as a producer and costume designer. The setting for *Darkness At Noon* won him a Donaldson Award in 1951.

Scenic Designs:
1937: *Bat, The; Farewell Summer; Orchids Preferred* **1938:** *Man from Cairo, The; There's Always a Breeze* **1940:** *Blind Alley; Johnny Belinda; Strangler Fig, The* **1941:** *All Men Are True; Brooklyn Biarritz; Good Neighbor; Junior Miss; Snookie* **1942:** *Doughgirls, The; Johnny on a Spot; Magic/ Hello, Out There; Wine, Women and Song; Yankee Point* **1943:** *Lady, Behave; Land of Fame; Men in Shadow; Naked Genius, The; Snark Was a Boojum, The; Those Endearing Young Charms; Two Mrs. Carrolls, The* **1944:** *Anna Lucasta; Day Will Come, The; Dear Ruth; Decision; Hickory Stick; Man Who Had All the Luck, The; Odds on Mrs. Oakley, The; Only the Heart; Ramshackle Inn* **1945:** *Alice in Arms; Calico Wedding; Good Night Ladies; Goose for the Gander, A; Kiss Them for Me; Marriage is for Single People; Wind is Ninety, The* **1946:** *Little Brown Jug; Mr. Peebles and Mr. Hooker* **1947:** *John Loves Mary* **1948:** *Light Up the Sky; Make Mine Manhattan* **1949:** *They Knew What They Wanted* **1950:** *Southern Exposure* **1951:** *Angels Kiss Me; Darkness At Noon; Never Say Never* **1952:** *Climate of Eden, The; Seven Year Itch, The* **1953:** *Room Service* **1954:** *Anniversary Waltz; King of Hearts; Lunatics and Lovers; Reclining Figure* **1955:** *Wayward Saint, The* **1956:** *Speaking of Murder* **1957:** *Fair Game; Greatest Man Alive, The* **1958:** *Howie* **1959:** *Golden Fleecing; Warm Peninsula, The* **1960:** *Hostage, The; Mighty Man Is He, A; Send Me No Flowers* **1961:** *From the Second City; Mandingo*

Lighting Designs:
1943: *Men in Shadow* **1944:** *Career Angel* **1945:** *Alice in Arms; Good Night Ladies; Secret Room, The* **1946:** *Little Brown Jug* **1947:** *John Loves Mary* **1950:** *Southern Exposure* **1951:** *Angels Kiss Me; Darkness At Noon* **1952:** *Seven Year Itch, The* **1953:** *Room Service* **1954:** *An-*

niversary Waltz; *King of Hearts*; *Lunatics and Lovers*; *Reclining Figure* **1955**: *Wayward Saint, The* **1956**: *Speaking of Murder* **1957**: *Greatest Man Alive, The* **1958**: *Howie* **1959**: *Golden Fleecing*; *Warm Peninsula, The* **1960**: *Hostage, The*; *Mighty Man Is He, A*; *Send Me No Flowers* **1961**: *From the Second City*; *Mandingo*

Costume Designs:

1942: *Johnny on a Spot* **1944**: *Only the Heart* **1945**: *Alice in Arms* **1949**: *They Knew What They Wanted* **1952**: *Seven Year Itch, The* **1954**: *King of Hearts*; *Lunatics and Lovers*; *Reclining Figure* **1957**: *Greatest Man Alive, The* **1959**: *Golden Fleecing* **1960**: *Send Me No Flowers* **1961**: *Mandingo* **1965**: *La Grasse Valise*

Miss Mary Fox

Miss Mary Fox designed the settings for a single Broadway show in 1925. She appeared in two movies in the 1920s, *Don't Bother Mother* and *Gambling*.

Scenic Designs:

1925: *Don't Bother Mother*

Kenneth Foy

Kenneth Foy was born on July 22, 1950 in New York City and received a B.F.A. at Cooper Union. He first became involved with theatre while attending summer camp, where he created sets for *The Mikado*. He has served as resident designer for the Kenyon (Ohio) Festival and the Berkshire Theatre Festival. He also designed for the Manhattan Theatre Club, Juilliard, Studio Arena Theatre, Long Wharf Theatre and the Lyric Opera of Chicago among others, and designed the world premiere of Thomas Passatiere's opera *The Three Sisters*. Since the late 1980s he has been a member of the staff at the Metropolitan Opera. Recent designs include the October 1990 revival of *Oh! Kay*.

Scenic Designs:

1981: *Candida* **1982**: *Macbeth* **1989**: *Gypsy*

Millard France

Millard H. France designed sets for two shows in the mid-1920s. He was also the proprietor of Millard H. France Company, a scenic studio through which he probably designed additional productions. He operated a scenic studio with his son, Chester A. France, which initially provided storage for stage settings, but subsequently became a scene painting studio and ultimately a scenic construction business. In 1931 the company became known as Millard H. France Sons, Inc., and was operated at the same location by Chester, Edward and Raymond France and continued to provide theatrical scenery. In 1925 Millard France resided at 461 Fort Washington Avenue in New York City.

Scenic Designs:

1918: *Awakening, The* **1924**: *Fatal Wedding, The* **1927**: *One for All*

Earl Payne Franke

Earl Payne Franke (a.k.a. Erle Franke) designed sets and costumes for one show in 1922 and costumes for an additional production in 1924. In 1925 Erle Studios, Inc., a firm of decorators, was located at 161 East 60th Street in New Work City, with Erle Franke as President.

Scenic Designs:

1922: *Greenwich Village Follies*

Costume Designs:

1922: *Greenwich Village Follies* **1924**: *No Other Girl*

P.T. Frankl

Paul T. Frankl, a native of Vienna emigrated to the United States in 1914 after study at the University of Vienna, the University of Munich and art schools in Paris and Munich. In addition to working as an interior decorator he created modern settings for plays and designed modern furniture for the Johnson Company of Grand Rapids, Michigan. He was president of a Madison Avenue art gallery and interior design studio (the Frankl Galleries), lectured at the Metropolitan Museum, New York University, and the University of Southern California, and wrote books on contemporary design. Prior to World War I, he was important in the modern art movement. He died on March 21, 1958, at age 71 in Palos Verdes Estates, California.

Scenic Designs:

1921: *Sonya*

C. Lovat Fraser

C. Lovat Fraser was a British graphic artist and theatrical designer. He was born Lovat Claud Fraser on May 15, 1890 and died suddenly in 1921 at thirty-one years of age. A talent for drawing and a fondness for bright colors made him an influential designer early in this century. He designed for the Lyric Theatre, Hammersmith where he collaborated with actor-manager Nigel Playfair. He carried his pencils along while serving in World War I and recorded battle scenes at Ypres, France. Both an illustrator and an artist, Mr. Fraser, who loved the eighteenth century, was a book illustrator and wrote poetry under the pen name "Honeywood." A book chronicling his life and art, *The Book of Lovat* by Haldane MacFall, was published in 1923.

Scenic Designs:
1920: *Beggar's Opera, The* **1928:** *Beggar's Opera, The*

Costume Designs:
1920: *Beggar's Opera, The* **1928:** *Beggar's Opera, The*

Charles Friedman

Born in Russia on September 20, 1902, Charles Friedman was raised on the Lower East Side of New York City where he died on July 18, 1984. He directed plays wherever he found the opportunity, in settlement houses and small theatres. Representative productions include *Pins and Needles, Carmen Jones, Street Scene* and the Federal Theatre production of *Sing for Your Supper* in 1939. We wrote the script and lyrics for *My Darlin' Aida*. Charles Friedman was also a director, producer and writer for television.

Scenic Designs:
1927: *Rutherford and Son* **1928:** *Waltz of the Dogs* **1929:** *Silver Tassie, The*

Lighting Designs:
1935: *Mother*

Ralph Funicello

Ralph Funicello, while originally from New York, works extensively on the West Coast. He studied at Boston University and graduated from New York University in 1970, studying with Ming Cho Lee and Wolfgang Roth. He

designed the first two productions at the Denver Theatre Center in 1980 and received the Los Angeles Drama Critics Circle Award for the set design for *Misalliance* at South Coast Repertory in 1988. His designs for sets have also appeared on the stages of the American Conservatory Theatre and the Pacific Conservatory of the Performing Arts (where he has been resident designer), the Mark Taper Forum, The Guthrie Theatre, California Actors' Theatre, the New York Shakespeare Festival and the McCarter Theatre. He also designed the American premiere of Jean Anouilh's play *Dear Antoine* at the Loeb Drama Center in Boston.

Scenic Designs:
1980: *Division Street*

Roger Furse

Roger Kemble Furse, a British designer and painter was born September 11, 1903 in Ightham, Kent, England. He has extensive credits for scenery and costumes in England for plays at the Old Vic and in London's West End. He began professional life as a portraitist in Paris and in New York. In 1931 he became associated with Laurence Olivier and thereafter devoted his talents to theatrical design. He designed several films, including *Ivanhoe, The Road to Hong Kong* and *The Prince and The Show Girl*, winning an Oscar for the design of Laurence Olivier's *Hamlet* in 1948. In 1951 his business, W.J. Furse and Company, Limited, supplied "Cinema and Theatre Lighting" from its location at 7 Carteret Street, Westminster, England. Roger Furse died in August 1972 on the island of Corfu, Greece.

Scenic Designs:
1938: *Spring Meeting* **1950:** *Daphne Laureola* **1951:** *Antony and Cleopatra; Caesar and Cleopatra* **1952:** *Venus Observed* **1960:** *Duel of Angels; Tumbler, The*

Costume Designs:
1946: *Henry IV, Part II; Henry IV, Part I* **1965:** *Pickwick*

Lillian Gaertner

Lillian Gaertner designed scenery and costumes for many operas and plays in addition to her work as an illustrator and painter. Her designs for *Egyptian Helen* by Richard Strauss were seen at the Metropolitan Opera House in 1928. The settings for that production were designed by Joseph Urban, with whom she often worked. She also designed murals, including those decorating the lobby of the New Ziegfeld Theater at its opening in 1928. Born in New York City on July 5, 1906, she studied painting with Joseph Hoffman and Ferdinand Schmutzer. She was married to Harold Palmedo on January 19, 1930.

Scenic Designs:
1926: *Straw Hat, The*

Costume Designs:
1926: *Straw Hat, The*

Raimonda Gaetani

Raimonda Gaetani first designed scenery and costumes on Broadway in 1974. An Italian theatrical designer, she was born in Naples, Italy in 1942 and studied at the Architecture University there, where she became interested in the theatre. Her film designs include Federico Fellini's *Casanova* (with fellow Italian designer Danilo Donati) and G. Ferrara's *Un Coeur Simple*. She has additional credits for productions at the Teatro Alla Scala in Milan and the Quirius Theatre in Rome. She often designs sets and costumes for theatre and television plays written by Eduardo de Filippo, author of *Filumena*.

Scenic Designs:
1980: *Filumena*

Costume Designs:
1974: *Saturday Sunday Monday* **1980:** *Filumena*

David S. Gaither

David S. Gaither was principally a set designer who also created lights and costumes on Broadway between 1924 and 1933. He served as President of United Scenic Artists in the late 1930s. He was also a painter and in 1932 resided at 29 Perry Street in New York City.

Scenic Designs:
1923: *Rivals, The* **1924:** *Wonderful Visit, The* **1925:** *Episode; Nocturne* **1926:** *Ghosts; Old Bill, M.P.* **1927:** *Ghosts* **1929:** *Queen Bee* **1930:** *Gold Braid* **1932:** *Riddle Me This* **1933:** *Foolscap; Riddle Me This; Two Strange Women*

Lighting Designs:
1927: *Ghosts*

Costume Designs:
1927: *Ghosts* **1930:** *Gold Braid*

J.F. Gallagher

J.F. Gallagher designed one set in 1928 on Broadway. In 1925 he resided at 50 Union Avenue in New York City.

Scenic Designs:
1928: *Age of Innocence, The*

Leo Gambacorta

Leo Gambacorta was scenic, costume and lighting designer for one show on Broadway in 1980.

Scenic Designs:
1980: *Black Broadway*

Lighting Designs:
1980: *Black Broadway*

Costume Designs:
1980: *Black Broadway*

Frank Garrison

Frank Garrison designed sets on Broadway between 1924 and 1927. He was a primarily a producer who worked with Al G. Fields, John W. Vogel, and others on various minstrel shows. He died on April 11, 1933 in Columbus, Ohio at age 50.

Scenic Designs:
1924: *Blind Alleys* **1927:** *Banshee, The*

William George Gaskin

William George Gaskin designed sets and costumes on Broadway in 1930. He was also a much exhibited watercolorist and oil painter in the late 1920s. He was born in San Francisco in 1892. His painting, "San Francisco Scene," is in the collection of the San Francisco Art Commission.

Scenic Designs:
1928: *Hoboken Blues* **1930:** *General John Regan; Playboy of the Western World, The*

Costume Designs:
1930: *Playboy of the Western World, The*

Mordecai Gassner

Mordecai (Mordi) Gassner contributed the designs for sets and costumes for a play in 1948. He was principally a scenic designer, beginning his career at the Westchester Playhouse in Mt. Kisco, New York. He was also art director for films produced by Douglas Fairbanks, Sr. Mr. Gassner received two Guggenheim Fellowships to study painting in Europe, and often had his own paintings exhibited.

Scenic Designs:
1948: *Gone Tomorrow/Home Life of a Buffalo/Hope is the Thing*; *Minnie and Mr. Williams*

Costume Designs:
1948: *Minnie and Mr. Williams*

Gates and Morange

Gates and Morange were active on Broadway for four decades. In 1894 Frank E. Gates, a native of Chicago, and Edward A. Morange from Cold Springs, New York painted a curtain, "Leaving for the Masked Ball" at the Court Square Theatre in Springfield, Massachusetts, which led to their partnership. Their first stage set was *Off the Earth* in 1894 for the American Travesty Company. Frank Gates' brother Richard later joined the firm. Scenic artists (and scenic designers) Alexander Grinager, Arne Lundborg, William E. Castle, Orestes Raineiri, and Thomas Benrimo were employed at Gates and Morange, among others. Both Frank Gates and Edward Morange studied at the School of Fine Arts at Washington University in St. Louis, Missouri. In 1919 Gates and Morange was located at 155 West 29th Street. By 1931 it had relocated to 220 West 42nd Street, and later operated at 530 W. 47th. This active studio supplied the designs for settings for numerous productions and painted additional productions, such as *The Garden of Allah, Citizen Pierre, The Daughter of Hearn*, and *Joseph and His Brother*. Edward A. Morange also designed settings under his own name. Additional information may be found under this entry.

Scenic Designs:
1915: *Treasure Island* 1916: *13th Chair, The*; *Rio Grande*; *See America First*; *Turn to the Right* 1917: *Colonel Newcome*; *Disraeli*; *Gay Lord Quex, The*; *Our Betters* 1918: *April*; *Garden of Allah, The*; *Head Over Heels*; *Her Country*; *Service*; *Success* 1919: *Come Along*; *Forbidden* 1920: *Bat, The*; *Daddy Dumplins*; *First Year, The*; *Genius and the Crowd*; *Three Showers* 1921: *Alias Jimmy Valentine*; *Bill of Divorcement, A*; *Good Morning, Dearie*; *Straw, The*; *Wake Up, Jonathan* 1922: *Bunch and Judy, The*; *Pinch Hitter, A*; *To the Ladies* 1923: *Cymbeline*; *Dice of the Gods, The*; *Exile, The*; *Mad Honeymoon, The*; *Mary Jane McKane*; *Wildflower* 1924: *New Brooms*; *Paradise Alley*; *Rose-Marie* 1927: *Behold This Dreamer*; *Jimmie's Women*; *Money from Home*; *Much Ado About Nothing* 1928: *Diplomacy*; *Merry Wives of Windsor, The*; *Rainbow*; *Sherlock Holmes* 1929: *Among the Married*; *Great Day*; *Houseparty*; *Ladies of the Jury*; *Mrs. Bumpstead-Leigh*; *Sherlock Holmes*; *Sweet Adeline*; *Your Uncle Dudley* 1930: *Mr. Samuel*; *Rivals, The*; *Well of Romance, The* 1931: *Admirable Crichton, The*; *Colonel Satan*

Philip Gelb

Philip Gelb, a producer, set designer and artist, produced plays on Broadway such as *A-Hunting We Will Go* in 1940, and *Honky Tonk - L'Historie de la Burlesque* in 1941. He also produced *Swing Chamber Music* at the Hotel Times Square Grill and *Who Do* at the 1939 World's Fair. In 1932 his studio was located at 48 West 48th Street.

Scenic Designs:
1930: *Life Is Like That* 1932: *Anybody's Game*; *Jamboree* 1933: *Come Easy* 1934: *Geraniums in My Window*; *Halfway to Hell*; *Wind and the Rain, The* 1935: *Triumph*

Peter Gennaro

Peter Gennaro is well known as a dancer and choreographer. He was born in 1924 in Metairie, Louisiana. After studying dance with Katherine Dunham and José Limon, he joined the ballet company of the San Carlo Opera. He danced on Broadway in musicals including *Make Mine Manhattan* and *Kiss Me, Kate*, and choreographed *Fiorello!*, *Irene* (for which he received a Tony nomination for choreography) and *The Unsinkable Molly Brown*. In 1948 he married

Jean Kinsella, a former ballet dancer. His credits as a dancer and choreographer also extend to films and television. He not only choreographed *Mr. President* in 1962, but also designed the scenery and lighting. In 1964 Peter Gennaro received an award from *Dance Magazine.*

Scenic Designs:

1962: *Mr. President*

Lighting Designs:

1962: *Mr. President*

Rolf Gérard

Rolf Gérard, a set designer who also designs costumes, was born in Berlin on August 9, 1909. His mother was the famous Italian soprano, Mafalder Salvatini, and his father, Dr. Walter Gérard, a German scientist of French descent. He attended school in Germany and studied medicine in Heidelberg and Paris, receiving his M.D. in Switzerland in 1937. He practiced medicine in England where he moved in 1936. His London debut was in 1944 for *Awake and Sing*, soon after designing *Romeo and Juliet* at Stratford-upon-Avon directed by Peter Brook. He has since designed extensively for theater, ballet and opera in Europe and the United States, including twenty productions for the Metropolitan Opera. An officer of the French Legion of Honor and a British subject, Mr. Gérard currently resides in Switzerland where he continues to paint.

Scenic Designs:

1949: *Caesar and Cleopatra; That Lady* 1952: *Evening with Beatrice Lillie, An* 1953: *Love of Four Colonels, The; Strong Are Lonely, The* 1959: *Fighting Cock, The* 1960: *Irma La Douce* 1963: *Tovarich*

Costume Designs:

1949: *Caesar and Cleopatra; That Lady* 1953: *Love of Four Colonels, The; Strong Are Lonely, The* 1959: *Fighting Cock, The* 1960: *Irma La Douce*

Zvi Geyra

Zvi Geyra was born in Jerusalem and studied art at Bezalel in Israel . He moved to New York City in 1950 to study design at the Dramatic Workshop. He left New York to serve in the Israeli Army and design in Tel Aviv, but later returned to the Dramatic Workshop to teach. Off-Broadway credits include *Uncle Vanya* and plays at Equity Library Theatre. He has also designed for television, and in the late 1950s was in residence at La Jolla Playhouse for a summer season.

Scenic Designs:

1958: *Edwin Booth* 1960: *Long Dream, The*

Lighting Designs:

1958: *Edwin Booth*

Edward Gilbert

Edward Gilbert is a native of New York City who studied at the Parsons School and the Art Students League. His first professional designs were costumes for his sister, the actress Ruth Gilbert in the original production of *The Iceman Cometh.*

Scenic Designs:

1939: *Straw Hat Revue* 1940: *All in Fun* 1942: *New Faces of 1943* 1944: *No Way Out; While the Sun Shines* 1945: *Next Half Hour, The; Overtons, The; Star Spangled Family* 1946: *Icetime; If the Shoe Fits; Toplitzky of Notre Dame* 1947: *Icetime of 1948* 1948: *Hold It* 1949: *All for Love; Metropole; Yes, My Lord* 1950: *Day After Tomorrow, The* 1953: *Solid Gold Cadillac, The*

Costume Designs:

1942: *New Faces of 1943* 1949: *Yes, My Lord*

Enid Gilbert

Enid Gilbert designed scenery, costumes and lights for plays on Broadway in the mid 1940s.

Scenic Designs:

1946: *Bees and the Flowers, The*

Lighting Designs:

1946: *Bees and the Flowers, The*

Costume Designs:

1945: *Assassin, The* 1946: *Bees and the Flowers, The*

Ernest Glover

Ernest Glover designed settings for five productions on Broadway in the early 1940s.

Scenic Designs:

1940: *Every Man for Himself; Suspect* 1942: *Sun Field, The; Vickie* 1944: *School for Brides*

Peter Goffin

Peter Goffin, a British stage designer and director, began professional life as an interior decorator and mural painter. He was born February 28, 1906 in Plymouth, Devonshire, England.
Employment in various theaters, including the
Barn Theatre, Chesham Bois, England in the
1935-36 season, led him to design for the D'Oyly
Carte Opera Company in 1949. He remained as
resident designer until being appointed Artistic
Director in 1961. An author and educator, Mr.
Goffin lectured widely on theater design and theater education before his death in 1974.

Scenic Designs:
1948: *Yeomen of the Guard* **1955:** *Mikado,
The*; *Ruddigore*; *Yeomen of the Guard*

Costume Designs:
1948: *Yeomen of the Guard* **1955:** *Ruddigore*;
Yeomen of the Guard

Stephen Golding

Stephen Golding designed one set in 1935 on
Broadway. In 1919 he was president of Golding Scenic Studios, Inc., 1493 Broadway in New
York City with William Golding, Vice President
and Bert LaMont, Secretary.

Scenic Designs:
1935: *Mulatto*

Lawrence L. Goldwasser

As a partner in Televideo Productions in New
York City, Lawrence L. Goldwasser designed, directed and produced hundreds of television commercials. He was born on August 4, 1916 in
Yonkers, New York, the son of Ida L. and Ben
Goldwasser, and studied at Yale University with
Donald Oenslager. While at Yale he was the
official designer for the WPA in Connecticut.
His credits also include interiors, summer stock,
and productions for the 1939 World's Fair. His
career as a scenic designer was just beginning
when interrupted by World War II. After the
war he became involved in television and gradually began directing. He designed and directed
live television at ABC-TV and directed live and
filmed productions for the J. Walter Thompson
Agency. He also taught design at Marymount
College, Tarrytown, New York. Now retired,

Mr. Goldwasser resides in Chapel Hill, North
Carolina.

Scenic Designs:
1938: *Devil Takes a Bride, The*; *Ringside
Seat*; *Washington Jitters* **1939:** *Streets of Paris*
1940: *At the Stroke of Eight*; *Passenger to Bali,
A* **1946:** *Made in Heaven*

Costume Designs:
1946: *Made in Heaven*

Natalia Gontcharova

Natalia Gontcharova, a Russian/French artist,
was born in Ladyzhino, Tonla, Russia on June
4, 1881. She studied at the School of Painting,
Sculpture and Architecture in Moscow. Early
in her career she met the painter Mikhail Larinov. They later married and together led the
Primitive Movement in Moscow. Her first stage
designs were produced in Moscow in 1909. She
designed for Diaghilev and the Russian Ballet
and also produced marionettes. Her productions of *Le Coq d'Or* (1914), *Les Noces d'Aurore*
(1922) and *Nuit sur le Mond Chauve* (1923) for
the Ballets Russes were widely admired. She
spent much of her life in Paris where she moved
with Larinov in 1917, becoming a French citizen
in 1938. A much honored painter and stage designer, her creative works, paintings, sculptures
and designs are widely exhibited and collected.
She died in Paris on October 17, 1962.

Scenic Designs:
1931: *New Chauve-Souris*

Costume Designs:
1931: *New Chauve-Souris*

Ruby Goodnow

Ruby Ross Goodnow designed a set on Broadway in 1922. In the mid-1920s she resided at
160 East 38th Street, New York City.

Scenic Designs:
1922: *Plot Thickens, The*

Steven Gordon Scenic Studio

Steven Gordon was a set designer active in 1932.

Scenic Designs:
1932: *New York to Cherbourg*

Mordecai Gorelik

Mordecai (Max) Gorelik, a scenic designer, director, author and educator, also occasionally designed costumes during his long, distinguished career. He attended the Pratt Institute and studied with Norman Bel Geddes, Robert Edmond Jones and Serge Soudeikine. He was born on August 25, 1899 in Shchedrin, Russia. His family emigrated to New York in 1905 and Max worked in his father's newsstand. His first professional production was *King Hunger* at the Hedgerow Theatre in Moylan, Pennsylvania in 1924. He made his Broadway debut with scenic designs for *Processional* in 1925, after working at the Neighborhood Playhouse as a scene painter and technician and at the Provincetown Playhouse. He served as principal designer for The Group Theatre from 1937 to 1940. The author of over one hundred articles and the books *New Theaters for Old* and *Toward a Larger Theatre*, he taught design and lectured widely. From 1960 to 1972 he was on the faculty of Southern Illinois University, which awarded him an honorary degree in 1988. Mordecai Gorelik died on March 23, 1990 at age 90.

Scenic Designs:
1925: *Processional* 1926: *Moon Is a Gong, The* 1927: *Loud Speaker* 1928: *Final Balance, The* 1931: *1931*- 1932: *Success Story* 1933: *All Good Americans*; *Big Night*; *Little Ol' Boy*; *Men in White* 1934: *Gentlewoman*; *Sailors of Cattaro* 1935: *Let Freedom Ring*; *Mother*; *Young Go First, The* 1938: *Casey Jones*; *Rocket to the Moon*; *Tortilla Flat* 1939: *Thunder Rock* 1940: *Night Music* 1947: *All My Sons* 1952: *Desire Under the Elms* 1954: *Flowering Peach, The* 1955: *Hatful of Rain, A* 1957: *Sin of Pat Muldoon, The* 1960: *Distant Bell, A*

Lighting Designs:
1947: *All My Sons* 1955: *Hatful of Rain, A*

Costume Designs:
1925: *Processional* 1929: *Fiesta* 1955: *Hatful of Rain, A*

Edward Gorey

Edward Gorey is an author and artist. He applied his considerable talents to designing sets and costumes for a Broadway show in 1977, and won a Tony Award for the costumes. A native of Chicago, he was born there on February 22,

1925, studied at the Art Institute of Chicago and graduated from Harvard with a degree in French. His many books have attracted a loyal and devoted following, due mainly to his unique view of the world. He has designed for Les Ballets Trocadero de Monte Carlo and created the opening segment for the *Mystery* series on PBS.

Scenic Designs:
1977: *Dracula* 1978: *Gorey Stories*

Costume Designs:
1977: *Dracula*

Maria Gortinskaya

Maria Gortinskaya designed costumes and scenery for a Broadway show in the mid-1920s.

Scenic Designs:
1925: *Daughter of Madame Angot, The*

Costume Designs:
1925: *Daughter of Madame Angot, The*

Jane Graham

Jane Graham was the scenic designer for a 1963 Broadway production.

Scenic Designs:
1963: *Rehearsal, The*

Victor Graziano

Victor Graziano designed one set in 1934 on Broadway. He was also a scenic artist and in 1915 worked as a shoemaker on St. Nicholas Avenue in New York City.

Scenic Designs:
1934: *Errant Lady*

Andrew Greenhut

Andrew Greenhut was born on June 15, 1935 in Philadelphia. He received both Bachelor of Arts and Master of Arts degrees at the University of Miami, where he began designing. He has taught at the University of Miami, Southwest Missouri State University and the University of Delaware. He won a Clio Award for the design of a television commercial for the Minnesota Mining and Manufacturing Company (3M).

Scenic Designs:
1976: *Best Friends*

Howard Greenley

Howard Greenley designed galleries, residences and hotels during his career as an architect. He was born in Ithaca, New York on May 14, 1874 and died in Middlebury, Vermont on November 24, 1963. After studying at Trinity College in Hartford, Connecticut, he attended the Ecole des Beaux Arts in Paris and the American School of Fine Arts in Fontainebleu, France. Before entering private practice, he worked as a draftsman, and designed scenery.

Scenic Designs:
1917: *Lord and Lady Algy*

Howard Greer

Howard Greer was born in Nebraska in 1886 and died in Los Angeles in 1964. He started his career working for the haute couture designer Lucile, but after service in World War I worked as an assistant to Paul Poiret and Molyneux in Paris. It was during this time in Europe that he began designing theatrical costumes in addition to fashion. When he returned to the United States he contributed costume and occasionally scenic designs to Broadway shows and also worked again for Lucile for a time. His designs for the *Greenwich Village Follies* led to a position as Chief Designer at the West Coast Studios of Famous Players-Lasky (later Paramount Pictures Corporation). His film credits are extensive between the years 1923 and 1953. He also had his own couture house, Greer, Inc. which catered to movie stars and private customers. Mr. Greer retired in 1962. His autobiography, *Designing Male* chronicles his career.

Scenic Designs:
1922: *Greenwich Village Follies*

Costume Designs:
1921: *Ziegfeld Midnight Follies* 1922: *Greenwich Village Follies* 1923: *Jack and Jill* 1933: *Lake, The* 1936: *Reflected Glory* 1940: *Quiet Please*

Ivan Gremislavsky

Ivan Iakovlevich Gremislavsky was born in 1886 in Moscow. His parents were Iakov Ivanovich and Maria Alekseevna Gremislavski, make-up artists for the Moscow Little Theatre and later for the Moscow Art Theatre. He studied at the Artists-Industrial School, the School of Painting, Scupture and Architecture, and with Konstantin A. Korovin. He was influenced by his family and Alexander N. Benois, although Stanislavski was his great mentor. His first designs were for *World Holiday* and *Burial of Hope* at the Moscow Art Theatre in 1913. From 1922 to 1924 he toured Europe and America with the Moscow Art Theatre, and between 1926 and 1930 designed sets and cosutmes for two major works in conjunction with A. Golovin, *Marriage of Figaro* and *Othello*. He also worked for many years in the technical departments of the Moscow Art Theatre Musical Studio. In 1967 a collection of articles, illustrations, essays and additional materials about Ivan Gremislavsky was published in Moscow.

Scenic Designs:
1925: *Love and Death/ Aleko/ Fountain of Bakkchi Sarai/ etc.*

Costume Designs:
1925: *Love and Death/ Aleko/ Fountain of Bakkchi Sarai/ etc.*

Hayden Griffin

Hayden Griffin designed sets for two shows on Broadway, one in 1968 and another in 1978. He has designed professionally since 1967 after taking a design course at Sadler's Wells. His credits range throughout the United States, in Europe and his native England from the Royal Court, the Metropolitan Opera, the National Theatre, Chichester, the Aarhus Theatre in Denmark, York, Stratford-upon-Avon and Edinburgh to the West End and Vienna. In addition to earning extensive credits designing operas, plays and ballets, he teaches design. The students who take his courses and his design assistants often credit him as a mentor.

Scenic Designs:
1968: *Rockefeller and the Red Indians* 1978: *Players*

Costume Designs:
1968: *Rockefeller and the Red Indians* 1978: *Players*

Grinager and Beardsley

Grinager and Beardsley, a scenery studio owned by Alexander Grinager and Rudolph Beardsley, was active on Broadway in 1914 and 1915.

For additional information see the entries under their respective names.

Scenic Designs:
1914: *Silent Voice, The* **1915:** *Just Outside the Door*

Alexander Grinager

Alexander Grinager studied painting in Denmark, France, Norway, Italy and Sicily. He was born in Albert Lea, Minnesota on January 26, 1865. He studied at the Royal Academy in Copenhagen, Denmark for four years and in Paris at the Julien Academy. A member of the Allied Artists of America, Artists League of Minneapolis and the American Federation of the Arts, his murals adorned many buildings, including the United States Department of Commerce, the New York Central Rail Road and Grand Central Palace. He designed and painted many productions during his long association with David Belasco, including *Ben-Hur* and *Chanticleer* starring Maude Adams. He worked as a scene painter for Gates and Morange, Ernest Albert, and Castle & Harvey and also worked in collaboration with Rudolph Beardlsey in 1914 and 1915. He died March 8, 1949 at age 84. For additional information see the entries "Beardsley" and "Grinager and Beardsley".

Scenic Designs:
1920: *Call the Doctor; One*

David Gropman

David Gropman has designed sets on Broadway and in Europe for the theatre, major motion pictures, and dance. He was born on June 16, 1952 in Los Angeles to Helen and Paul Gropman. His father works in advertising and public relations. He attended San Francisco State University where he studied with Eric Sinkonnen and received a B.A. He studied with Ming Cho Lee at the Yale School of Drama, which he attended as a recipient of the Donald Oenslager Scholarship, and earned an M.F.A. He began designing in the second grade with *The Nutcracker*, and his most recent credit is James Ivory's *Mr. and Mrs. Bridge* starring Paul Newman and Joanne Woodward. The setting for *Mr. and Mrs. Bridge* was designed by his wife, scenic designer Karen Schultz. Other films include *Slaves*

of New York, Key Exchange, Sweet Lorraine and *Come Back to the Five and Dime, Jimmy Dean, Jimmy Dean.* He has also designed sets for ...*Byzantium, Snow White* and *Danbury Mix* for the Paul Taylor Dance Company.

Scenic Designs:
1979: *1940s Radio Hour, The* **1980:** *Passione* **1981:** *Mass Appeal* **1982:** *Come Back to the 5 & Dime, Jimmy Dean, Jimmy Dean; Little Family Business, A* **1984:** *Open Admissions* **1987:** *Death and the King's Horseman*

Ernest M. Gros

Ernest M. Gros designed settings for numerous productions for David Belasco, who admired his realistic painting style. Many of the productions he designed were produced prior to 1915 and included *El Capitan* (1896), *Sherlock Holmes* and *Ben Hur* (1899), *Under Two Flags* (1901), *The Darling of the Gods* (1902), *The Music Master* (1904), *Adrea, Peter Pan* and *The Girl of the Golden West* (1905), *Salvation Nell* (1908), *The Easiest Way* (1909), and *The Bird of Paradise* (1912). Ernest Gros was born in Paris and painted murals of panoramic views, a popular art form in the 1880s and 1890s.

Scenic Designs:
1915: *Boomerang, The; Marie Odile; Peter Pan* **1916:** *Heart of Wetona, The; Little Lady in Blue; Music Master, The; Seven Chances* **1917:** *Polly with a Past; Tiger Rose; Very Minute, The* **1918:** *Auctioneer, The; Remnant* **1919:** *Gold Diggers, The; Son-Daughter, The* **1920:** *Deburau; One* **1921:** *Easiest Way, The; Grand Duke, The; Return of Peter Grimm, The* **1922:** *Merchant of Venice, The; Shore Leave; Spite Corner* **1923:** *Comedian, The; Mary, Mary, Quite Contrary; Nifties of 1923; One Kiss* **1925:** *Grand Duchess, The/ The Waiter*

Grosvois and Lambert

In 1939 Grosvois and Lambert collaborated on scenic designs for a Broadway play.

Scenic Designs:
1939: *Folies Bergère*

Anton Grot

Anton Grot, an art director for films, created the first practical stairway used in motion pictures. His prolific movie career began in 1913 with *The Mouse and the Lion*, included *Mildred Pierce* and *The Private Lives of Elizabeth and Essex* in 1939, and culminated in 1950 with *Backfire*. He retired in 1947, ending a career in which he designed over one hundred films, most of them for Warner Brothers and many of them directed by Cecil B. DeMille. Born Antocz Franciszek Grosvewski on January 18, 1884 in Kelbasin, Poland he came to the United States in 1909 at the age of 25. He studied at the Cracow Academy of Arts and at the Technical College in Koenigsberg, Germany. He was hired in 1913 by Sigmund Lubin to design sets for the Lubin Company in Philadelphia, which led to assignments for additional movies and to Hollywood in 1922, where he designed Douglas Fairbanks' and Mary Pickford's films. Unlike many of the scenic designers and art directors of his era, he was trained as an artist and did not have a background in construction. Instead of just building a set, he created designs, rendering them in charcoal and pen and ink before construction. He received a special Academy Award for a "ripple machine" in 1940. Anton Grot died in 1974 at age 90.

Scenic Designs:
1920: *Hole in the Wall, A*

Jules Guerin

Jules Guerin, an artist, was born in St. Louis in 1896. The winner of many prizes and awards, he specialized in decoration for buildings, banks, opera houses, state capitol buildings and theatres, including the Lincoln Memorial in Washington, D.C. and the Pennsylvania Railroad Station in New York City. His paintings received the Silver Medal at the 1904 St. Louis Exhibition and the Gold Medal at the 1915 Panama Exposition. In 1928 he contributed designs to a play on Broadway and in 1931 was elected to the National Academy of Design. Jules Guerin died in Neptune, New Jersey on June 13, 1946.

Scenic Designs:
1928: *Beaux Stratagem, The*

Costume Designs:
1928: *Beaux Stratagem, The*

Robert Guerra

Robert Guerra was art director for the 1989 films *Family Business* and *See You in the Morning*. He also served as art director for *Annie*

and *Heaven Help Us*. His designs for settings on Broadway were first seen in 1973, followed by additional productions in the 1980s.

Scenic Designs:
1973: *Warp* 1980: *Manhattan Showboat* 1981: *America*

Art Guild

Art Guild (sic) designed a set on Broadway in 1954.

Scenic Designs:
1954: *Hayride*

Robert Gundlach

Robert Gundlach graduated from the Art School of The Cooper Union in 1937. Except for a brief stint as a commercial artist and service in World War II, he has been working as a designer ever since. His work in theatre, television and film is extensive, although he has only a single Broadway credit. Early in his career he was scenic designer and technician for the Chekhov Theatre Studio. In the late 1940s he designed the stage and auditorium to convert an old theatre on Bleeker Street from motion picture usage to legitimate stage productions for NEW STAGES, INC. For ANTA Experimental Theatre at NEW STAGES, he designed *The Four Horsemen of the Apocalypse*. He served as staff designer for NBC-TV in the late 1940s and early 1950s and for CBS-TV from 1954 to 1958. The majority of his career has been as an art director and production designer, principally for feature films and made-for-television movies. Productions include: *Rachel, Rachel; Bang the Drum Slowly; Oliver's Story; Eyes of Laura Mars; See No Evil, Hear No Evil; Fighting Back; I, The Jury; Hero at Large; Firepower* and *Married to It*. He has also designed countless commercials.

Scenic Designs:
1948: *Happy Journey, The/ Respectful Prostitute, The*

John Gunter

John Gunter is a British designer of sets and costumes with extensive credits for the Royal Shakespeare Company, the Royal Court Theatre, in London's West End and other theatres in England and on the continent. Born in England in 1938, he spent three years as resident designer for the Schauspiel Haus, Zurich and has designed plays and operas in Berlin, Vienna and Hamburg. Mr. Gunter has also served as the Head of the Theatre Design Department at the Central School of Art and Design in London from 1974 to 1982, where he studied. Recent productions in London include *The Rivals* and *The Government Inspector*. For the Royal Shakespeare Company he has designed *Julius Caesar, Juno and the Paycock* and *Jingo* among others. His opera credits include *Peter Grimes* in Buenos Aires, *Andrea Chenier* for the Welsh National Opera, *The Turn of the Screw* for the Munich State Opera and *Die Meistersinger* in Cologne.

Scenic Designs:
1971: *Philanthropist, The* **1981:** *Rose* **1983:** *All's Well That Ends Well*; *Plenty* **1986:** *Wild Honey*

Costume Designs:
1976: *Comedians*

David Guthrie

David Guthrie, who specializes in ballet design, was born in Glasgow, Scotland on May 18, 1922. Between 1958 and 1976 he worked primarily as Oliver Smith's assistant. He has also worked for and trained under William and Jean Eckart, Boris Aronson and Jo Mielziner. His first professional costume designs were for the American Ballet Theatre. David Guthrie also has over one hundred commercials and industrial shows to his credit, including the design for the theatre for the Du Pont Pavillion at the 1965 New York World's Fair. He designs sets and costumes regularly for the Cleveland Ballet Company.

Scenic Designs:
1972: *Different Times* **1973:** *Pajama Game, The*

Costume Designs:
1972: *Different Times* **1973:** *Pajama Game, The*

Michel Gyarmathy

Michel Gyarmathy was born in Hungary and went to Paris as a young artist to study and paint. He designed for the Folies Bergère in Paris from the mid-1930s to the mid-1960s. He was awarded the Prix de Rome for design and decor. In 1964 he not only designed settings and costumes for the *Folies Bergère* on Broadway, but also produced and directed the production. He has been associated with the *Folies Bergère* since the late 1930s and in the mid-1970s was appointed Artistic Director, while continuing his duties as designer.

Scenic Designs:
1964: *Folies Bergère*

Costume Designs:
1964: *Folies Bergère*

George Haddon

George Haddon (Hadden) was active on Broadway between 1923 and 1930 as a setting and costume designer. He appeared in the 1920 film *Beyond the Horizon* and in 1933 was dialogue director for *Cavalcade*.

Scenic Designs:
1923: *Other Rose, The*

Costume Designs:
1923: *Laugh, Clown, Laugh* **1926:** *Lulu Belle* **1928:** *Minna* **1930:** *Tonight Or Never*

James Hamilton

James Hamilton designed lighting and settings for a Broadway show in 1969, and designed a set for an additional production in 1979.

Scenic Designs:
1969: *New Music Hall of Israel, The* **1979:** *Got Tu Go Disco*

Lighting Designs:
1969: *New Music Hall of Israel, The*

Aubrey Hammond

Aubrey Hammond designed sets for two productions on Broadway in 1934. He was born in Folkestone, England on September 18, 1893, studied at Bradfield College and also studied art in Paris and London. His first design in 1913 led to numerous productions in London, plays and operas in New York, and films. After service in World War I, where he assisted in developing camouflage and illustrated military publications, he resumed his design career. He also created theatrical posters. He was scenic supervisor for the opening of the Shakespeare Memorial Theatre in Stratford-upon-Avon. In 1936 he became an art director for films and joined the faculty of the Westminister School of Art. He died on March 19, 1940 at age 46.

Scenic Designs:
1934: *Shining Hour, The*; *Successful Calamity, A*

Natalie Hays Hammond

Natalie Hays Hammond, a painter and museum director studied with Sergi Soudeikine. Born in Lakewood, New Jersey on January 6, 1905, she designed sets and costumes in the mid 1930s for theatrical productions. She has had numerous one-woman shows and is founder and director of the Hammond Museum in North Salem, N.Y. An author and illustrator, she wrote *Elizabeth of England, Anthology of Pattern* and *New Adventure in Needlepoint Design.*

Scenic Designs:
1931: *Social Register, The*

Costume Designs:
1933: *La Nativite*

Carolyn Hancock

Carolyn Hancock, a designer of scenery and costumes, started her career as technical director for the Theatre Guild in its early days. She did the settings for numerous Broadway plays, including *Windows* and *An American Tragedy.* She not only designed the sets and costumes for the Garrick Gaieties in 1925 but also appeared in the show. She was active in developing the Costume Institute at the Metropolitan Museum of Art. Carolyn Hancock, who died on April 19, 1951, was married to scene designer Lee Simonson.

Scenic Designs:
1923: *Devil's Disciple, The*; *Race with the Shadow, The*; *Windows* **1924:** *Locked Door, The*; *They Knew What They Wanted* **1925:** *Ariadne*; *Garrick Gaieties*; *Man of Destiny* **1926:** *American Tragedy, An*; *At Mrs. Beam's*; *Garrick Gaieties* **1935:** *Taming of the Shrew, The* **1940:** *Taming of the Shrew, The* **1945:** *Secret Room, The*

Costume Designs:
1923: *Devil's Disciple, The*; *Race with the Shadow, The* **1924:** *They Knew What They Wanted* **1925:** *Ariadne*; *Garrick Gaieties*; *Man of Destiny* **1926:** *At Mrs. Beam's*; *Garrick Gaieties* **1943:** *Family, The*

William Hanna

William Hanna was responsible for one set design in 1916 on Broadway.

Scenic Designs:
1916: *Turn to the Right*

Mrs. Ingeborg Hansell

Mrs. Ingeborg Hansell designed sets and costumes on Broadway in the 1920s. For the 1922 and 1924 versions of *Greenwich Village Follies* Mrs. Ingeborg Hansell designed both sets and costumes. Her husband Nils Hansell was a civil engineer and they resided at 5012 Waldo Avenue with their son, Nils, Jr. in 1932.

Scenic Designs:
1922: *Greenwich Village Follies* **1924:** *Greenwich Village Follies*

Costume Designs:
1922: *Greenwich Village Follies* **1924:** *Greenwich Village Follies*

Joseph Hansen

Joseph Hansen was set designer for one production in 1933 on Broadway. In 1930 he was associated with Ernot Blitzen in Hansen & Blitzen, purveyors of theatrical goods. The business continued in 1932 from his residence at 423 West 43rd Street in New York City where he lived with his wife, Mercy Hansen.

Scenic Designs:
1933: *Fly By Night*

Emilie Hapgood

Emilie B. Hapgood and her husband, Emory Hutchins Hapgood, were active members of the Greenwich Village arts community. Emilie Hapgood was president of the New York Stage Society in 1914 when she invited Harley Granville-Barker to direct a play in New York. He chose *Androcles and the Lion* with sets and costumes by his English designer, Norman Wilkinson. Soon after arriving in New York, Granville-Barker met Robert Edmond Jones at an exhibition of theatrical designs sponsored by the New York Stage Society, where his scenic designs for *The Man Who Married A Dumb Wife* were on display. The play was added as a curtain raiser to the production of *Androcles and the Lion* and the two plays opened on January 27, 1915. The production of *The Man Who Married a Dumb Wife* is generally regarded as the beginning of the modern Broadway era, and the designs by Robert Edmond Jones the introduction of the New American Stagecraft.

Scenic Designs:
1917: *Magic, The*

Gerry Hariton

Gerry Hariton was born August 1, 1951 in New York City, the son of Lucie and Harry Hariton. He attended Brandeis University and received a Bachelor of Arts degree summa cum laude in 1973. He subsequently received an M.F.A. from Brandeis University under Howard Bay. Based in Los Angeles, he has worked almost exclusively with Vicki Baral since 1978. Together they have received five Los Angeles Drama Critics Circle Awards, including one for *Mail*, which later played on Broadway.

Scenic Designs:
1986: *Raggedy Ann* 1988: *Mail*

Joseph C. Harker

Joseph C. Harker was born in Manchester, England on October 17, 1855. His first production was *Hamlet* with the Theatre Royal, Glasgow in 1881. In 1888 he designed and painted *Macbeth* for Henry Irving in London followed by several more productions for Irving at the Lyceum Theatre. He also worked for Herbert Beerbohm-Tree as a designer and scenic painter. Joseph C. Harker helped established his family as the stars of the English school of scenic artists. Author of *Studio and Stage*, he had four sons, Joseph, Roland, Colin and Phil who joined him as scene painters. Joseph C. Harker died at age 71 on April 15, 1927, but his descendants continues the family association with scenery.

Scenic Designs:
1917: *Colonel Newcome*

Joseph and Phil Harker

Joseph C. Harker and son Phil Harker worked together as scene painters and designers in London. Between 1919 and 1922 three productions designed and painted by Joseph C. and Phil Harker were transferred from London to New York. Phil Harker travelled with the set, and because he was responsible for the necessary alterations to the scenery received co-design credit with his father. After the death of Joseph C. Harker in 1927, Phil Harker and his brothers Joseph, Colin and Roland continued the family business. After Phil died in 1933, Joseph became head of the company. In 1951 Harker Brothers, Scenic Artists still operated in London from a shop on Horsely Street, almost seventy-five years after the family entered the theatre business. With descendants of Joseph and Phil Harker, scenic designer David Homan formed Harker, Homan and Bravery Limited in 1953. Both Joseph C. and Phil Harker designed independently as well as in collaboration in England. Their designs, particularly for the D'Oyly Carte Opera, continued in use after their deaths, which accounts for the posthumous credits listed below.

Scenic Designs:
1915: *Quinneys* 1919: *Aphrodite* 1920: *Mecca* 1922: *Voice from the Minaret, The* 1938: *Flashing Stream, The* 1948: *H.M.S. Pinafore* 1951: *Trial By Jury/ H.M.S. Pinafore* 1955: *H.M.S. Pinafore; Trial By Jury*

Donald Harris

Donald Harris designed settings on Broadway in the mid 1970s. He has designed in regional theatres including the Mark Taper Forum, Ahmanson Theatre, Westwood Playhouse, StageWest, and The Company Theatre. He received the Los Angeles Drama Critics Circle Award for *Cyrano de Bergerac*. In 1974 he was resident lighting designer for the Old Globe Shakespeare Festival and was art director for the televison show *On The Rocks*. He served as art director for the 1979 film *Swap Meet*.

Scenic Designs:
1974: *Me and Bessie* 1976: *I Have a Dream*

George W. Harris

George W. Harris was a painter, etcher and

scenic designer who developed new techniques for scenic painting. He was born in 1876 and died on February 14, 1929. He was credited with scenic design, costume design, properties, and/or scene painting for more than fifty plays in London in the 1920s, many for Basil Dean. The production he designed on Broadway, *Hassan*, originated in London and was featured in the 1990 exhibit "Theatre on Paper" at The Drawing Center in New York City.

Scenic Designs:
1924: *Hassan*; *Peter Pan* 1925: *Easy Virtue*
1926: *Constant Nymph, The*; *This Was a Man*

Costume Designs:
1924: *Hassan*; *Peter Pan*

Margaret Harris

See Motley

Mrs. Sidney Harris

Mrs. Sidney Harris, (a.k.a. Miriam Cole Harris) died in 1925 in Pau, France at age 92. She was born on the Island of Dosoris near Hen Cove, New York, and was a direct descendant of early American settlers. She was a prolific writer whose work included the books *The Sutherlands* and *Rutledge*.

Scenic Designs:
1919: *Toby's Bow*; *Up from Nowhere*

Llewellyn Harrison

Llewellyn Harrison, a set designer, has worked off-Broadway, for the Negro Ensemble Company, and for the New Federal Theatre among others in New York City. He has also designed in London for the American Arts Festival, in Washington, D.C. for Ford's Theatre, and in Rome for Teatro Umberto. He owns and operates Techprops, a theatrical properties business.

Scenic Designs:
1987: *Don't Get God Started*

Hartmann & Fantana

Louis Hartmann collaborated with Fantana on a production in 1926 for the Broadway stage. Hartmann was known primarily as a lighting designer although he also designed sets. He became David Belasco's chief electrician in 1901 and worked with him until Belasco's death in 1931. He developed many techniques including the first incandescent spotlights, indirect overhead lighting, and silvered reflectors. At the time of his death at age 64 on February 9, 1941, Hartmann was on the sound staff at Radio City Music Hall. He was the author of *Theatre Lighting: A Manual of the Stage Switchboard*, a book which documented some of the developments he pioneered.

Scenic Designs:
1926: *Not Herbert*

Peter Hartwell

Peter Hartwell has designed for the Royal Court Theatre, the National Theatre, and in the West End in London. Off-Broadway his credits include *Aunt Dan and Lemon*. He was born in Canada and has designed productions at the New York Shakespeare Festival as part of an exchange with the Royal Court Theatre. He worked with Hayden Griffen as an assistant and then co-designer and has designed scenery and costumes for Caryl Churchill plays in London including *Top Girls*, *Serious Money* and the original production of *Cloud 9*.

Scenic Designs:
1988: *Serious Money*

Costume Designs:
1988: *Serious Money*

Peter Harvey

Peter Harvey was born January 2, 1933 in Quiriqua, Guatemala, a descendant of British colonials. He studied in Central America, North America and Europe and moved permanently to the United States in 1958. A set and costume designer, he has designed numerous ballets for companies including the New York City Ballet, the Washington National Ballet and the Metropolitan Opera Ballet. Influenced by the work of Léon Bakst, Christian Bérard, Oliver Messel and Cecil Beaton, his mentor is Rouben Ter-Arutunian. His first production was *Pantomime for Lovers* for the Miami Ballet in 1954, and he has also designed summer stock for companies in Maine, Rhode Island, Connecticut and

Florida. In 1969 he received the Drama Critics Award in Los Angeles for *Boys in the Band*. He taught set design, costume design, scene painting and costume history at Pratt Institute in Brooklyn from 1970 to 1987. While he has credits in various milieu, his most important work has been for the New York City Ballet and off-Broadway.

Scenic Designs:
1964: *Baby Wants a Kiss* 1970: *Park; Water Color/ Criss Crossing* 1975: *Letter for Queen Victoria, A* 1978: *Effect of Gamma Rays on Man-in-the-Moon Marigolds, The*

Costume Designs:
1964: *Baby Wants a Kiss* 1965: *All in Good Time* 1970: *Gloria and Esperanza; Park; Water Color/ Criss Crossing* 1975: *Letter for Queen Victoria, A* 1978: *Effect of Gamma Rays on Man-in-the-Moon Marigolds, The*

Walter M. Harvey

Walter M. Harvey attended the Cincinnati Art School in his hometown of Cincinnati, Ohio. He was principally a scene painter and was a partner in Wood & Harvey Studios, 502 West 38th Street, New York, New York where he painted *Irene, Tobbaco Road,* and *Earl Carroll's Vanities* among other productions. Examples of his work as a mural painter adorn the walls of the Polyclinic Hospital in New York City. Walter M. Harvey died on October 27, 1945 in Englewood, New Jersey.

Scenic Designs:
1930: *First Night* 1931: *Papavert; Unexpected Husband* 1932: *Through the Years; Trick for Trick* 1933: *It Happened Tomorrow* 1934: *Ship Comes In, A*

John F. Hawkins

John F. Hawkins designed sets and costumes on Broadway in the late 1920s. An artist, Mr. Hawkins paintings were exhibited posthumously at the Argent Galleries in New York in 1940. At the time of his death on May 22, 1939 in Santa Monica, California, he worked in the drafting department of Metro Studios.

Scenic Designs:
1927: *Connecticut Yankee, A* 1928: *Chee-Chee*

Costume Designs:
1927: *Connecticut Yankee, A*

William Hawley

William Hawley was the set designer in 1930 for a Broadway play. Principally a set designer, he also painted scenery, including *The Victoria Cross* in 1894.

Scenic Designs:
1930: *Jonica*

Richard L. Hay

Richard L. Hay has been principal scenic and theatre designer at the Oregon Shakespeare Festival since 1969. He is also Associate Artistic Director for Design for the Denver Center Theatre Company. He was born May 28, 1929, in Wichita, Kansas, and has a B.A. in architecture and an M.A. in theatre arts from Stanford University. During the past twenty-five years he has designed over one hundred seventy productions at the Oregon Shakespeare Festival since his association began in 1950, including the entire Shakespeare canon. He also has designed over seventy-five other productions in many regional theaters around the United States. In addition to his stage designs he has designed three theatres for the Ashland Festival, two theatres for the Old Globe and two theatre spaces for the Denver Center Theater. He has received five Hollywood Drama Logue Critics Awards and in 1989 the Oregon Governor's Award for the Arts.

Scenic Designs:
1968: *Resistible Rise of Arturo Ui, The*

Costume Designs:
1968: *Resistible Rise of Arturo Ui, The*

David Hayes

David Hayes was managing director in 1973 of *Showboat*, a floating children's theatre and learning center at the Eugene O'Neill Theatre Center. He made his Broadway debut as a scenic designer in 1981.

Scenic Designs:
1981: *Kingdoms*

Dermot Hayes

Dermot Hayes designed one set in 1981. He is a British set designer.

Scenic Designs:
1981: *Life and Adventures of Nicholas Nickleby, The*

Edward Haynes

Edward Haynes, a native of Burleson, Texas attended the University of Texas where he received both bachelor and master's degrees in fine arts. He also studied at Yale University and at Lester Polakov's Studio and Forum of Stage Design. He has assisted on Broadway shows, including *Anya*, *The Royal Hunt of the Sun*, and *Fiddler on the Roof*. He is, in addition, a draftsman at Feller Scenery Studios.

Scenic Designs:
1976: *Going Up*

David Hays

David Arthur Hays, a scenic and lighting designer and producer, was born on June 2, 1930 in New York City. He has worked during his career with many great designers, actors and directors, including Roger Furse, Leslie Hurry, Oliver Gielgud and Peter Brook. He attended Harvard, receiving a B.A. in 1952 and held a Fulbright to the Old Vic in 1952. He attended the Yale University School of Drama from 1953 to 1954 and then Boston University, where he earned an M.F.A. in 1955 under Raymond Sovey and Horace Armistead. He was an apprentice at the Brattle Theatre in Cambridge, Massachusetts from 1949 to 1952 where he worked with Robert O'Hearn. His first design, *Hay Fever* in 1951, was at the Brattle Theatre. His inspiration has come from Jo Mielziner, George Balanchine and Tyrone Guthrie. With fifty Broadway plays and thirty ballets for George Balanchine to his credit, it is little wonder he has received two Obie Awards, (for *The Quare Fellow* and *The Balcony*), several Tony nominations, two honorary doctorates, and the New York Drama Critics Award for *No Strings*. His book *Light on the Subject* was published by Limelight Editions in 1990.

Scenic Designs:
1956: *Innkeeper, The*; *Long Day's Journey Into Night* 1958: *Night Circus, The* 1959: *Rivalry, The*; *Tenth Man, The*; *Triple Play* 1960: *All the Way Home*; *Love and Libel*; *Roman Candle* 1961: *Gideon*; *Look: We've Come Through*; *No Strings*; *Sunday in New York* 1962: *Family Affair, A*; *In the Counting House* 1963: *Lorenzo*; *Strange Interlude* 1964: *Hughie*; *Last Analysis, The*; *Marco Millions*; *Murderer Among Us, A*

1965: *Diamond Orchid*; *Drat! the Cat!*; *Mrs. Dally*; *Peterpat* 1966: *Dinner At Eight*; *We Have Always Lived in the Castle* 1967: *Dr. Cook's Garden* 1968: *Cry of Players, A*; *Goodbye People, The* 1969: *National Theatre of the Deaf, The* 1970: *Gingerbread Lady, The*; *Songs from Milkwood*; *Two By Two* 1978: *Platinum*

Lighting Designs:
1956: *Innkeeper, The* 1959: *Tenth Man, The*; *Triple Play* 1960: *All the Way Home*; *Love and Libel*; *Roman Candle* 1961: *Gideon*; *Look: We've Come Through*; *No Strings*; *Sunday in New York* 1962: *Family Affair, A*; *In the Counting House* 1963: *Lorenzo*; *Strange Interlude* 1964: *Baby Wants a Kiss*; *Hughie*; *Last Analysis, The*; *Marco Millions*; *Murderer Among Us, A* 1965: *Diamond Orchid*; *Drat! the Cat!*; *Mrs. Dally*; *Peterpat* 1966: *Dinner At Eight*; *We Have Always Lived in the Castle* 1967: *Dr. Cook's Garden* 1968: *Goodbye People, The* 1981: *Bring Back Birdie*

Douglas Heap

Douglas Heap was appointed head of design at the Royal Academy of Dramatic Art in 1969. He was born in London on August 7, 1934, the son of Clifford Vernon Heap, who entertained with miniature theatres. He studied at the Byam Shaw School of Drawing and Painting and initially designed professionally for *Bid Time Return* in 1958. Beginning with *Boesman and Lena* in 1971 he has designed all of Athol Fugard's plays in London. He has numerous additional credits in London and throughout the United Kingdom. Recent opera designs include productions in Wexford, for the Kent Opera, and at the Coliseum. He also designed *Run For Your Wife* and *Pygmalion* for the Theatre of Comedy.

Scenic Designs:
1987: *Pygmalion*

H. Heckroth

Hein Heckroth was a German painter and stage and film designer born in Giessen, Germany on April 14, 1901. After meeting with success in Germany in the early 1930s as a scenic designer, he travelled throughout the world concentrating on designing film settings. He won two Oscars for sets: for *The Red Shoes* in 1943 and *Tales of*

Hoffman in 1951. His paintings and designs have been widely exhibited and collected and have been the subject of numerous books and articles. He was director of settings for the Frankfurt City Stage for the thirteen years prior to his death on July 6, 1970.

Scenic Designs:

1942: *Big City, The*; *Green Table, The*

Costume Designs:

1942: *Big City, The*; *Green Table, The*

Desmond Heeley

A noted designer, Desmond Heeley's designs for both sets and costumes have been widely seen in his native England, in Canada, and in the United States. He was born in West Bromwich, Staffordshire, England, on June 1, 1931 and trained at the Ryland School of Art, drawn to the theatre in part because of his admiration for the work of Oliver Messell. His first professional designs were for the Birmingham Repertory Theatre. He then proceeded to design for all the major theatre companies in England, beginning with the Royal Shakespeare Company in 1948. He has had a long association with the director Michael Langham, and has designed numerous productions both for Mr. Langham and others in Stratford, Ontario and at The Guthrie Theatre in Minneapolis. He has designed for the American Ballet Theatre, the Australian Ballet, the Houston Ballet, the London Festival Ballet, the National Ballet of Canada, Sadler's Wells Royal Ballet and the Stuttgart Ballet Companies among others. His opera credits in England and in the United States include the much praised production of *Brigadoon* at the New York City Opera in 1985 and *Manon Lescaut, Don Pasquale, Pelleas and Melisande* and *Norma* for the Metropolitan Opera, as well as productions at Covent Garden, the Vienna State Opera and the English National Opera. Mr. Heeley won two Tony awards in 1967, one for the costumes and another for the scenery of *Rosencrantz and Guildenstern are Dead.*

Scenic Designs:

1958: *Twelfth Night* 1967: *Rosencrantz and Guildenstern Are Dead* 1979: *Teibele and Her Demon* 1980: *Camelot* 1981: *Camelot* 1987: *South Pacific* 1989: *Circle, The*

Costume Designs:

1958: *Twelfth Night* 1967: *Rosencrantz and Guildenstern Are Dead* 1973: *Cyrano* 1979: *Teibele and Her Demon* 1980: *Camelot* 1981: *Camelot* 1987: *South Pacific*

W. Emerton Heitland

Wilmont Emerton Heitland designed costumes for a play on Broadway in 1916 and scenery for a play in 1944. A painter and illustrator, he was born in Superior, Wisconsin on July 5, 1893. For most of his career he worked as an illustrator of magazines, including *Delineator* and *Harper's Bazaar*. He also taught at the Art Students League. Mr. Heitland was widely exhibited and the winner of many awards for his paintings and illustrations. He died in 1969.

Scenic Designs:

1944: *Earth Journey* 1916: *Six Who Passed While the Lentils Boiled*

Costume Designs:

1916: *Six Who Passed While the Lentils Boiled*

John Held, Jr.

John Held, Jr., an author and illustrator, used his considerable talents to record the Jazz Age. His woodcuts and cartoons published in *The New Yorker, Life*, and *College Humor* captured the spirit of the age. Author of short stories and novels as well as a comic strip, he was born in Salt Lake City, Utah, on January 10, 1889, and died in Belmar, New Jersey on March 2, 1958. In the early 1940s he was artist in residence at two major universities in the United States.

Scenic Designs:

1926: *American*

Costume Designs:

1926: *American* 1928: *Americana*

Robert P. Heller

Robert P. Heller designed one set on Broadway in 1930. During the 1940s he was director of radio programming for CBS. He assisted Frank Capra during World War II with *Why We Fight*, an army orientation film. After the war he returned to CBS and from 1946 to 1948 was head of the documentary unit. In 1954 he moved to

Great Britain and began working in television. At his death at age 60 in London in 1975 he was head of documentary and factual programming for the Associated Television Corporation of Britain.

Scenic Designs:
1930: *Petticoat Influence*

William Penhallow Henderson

William Penhallow Henderson, an architect and painter, was born in Medford, Massachusetts in 1877 and studied at the Massachusetts Normal Art School and at the Boston Museum of Fine Arts. He painted portraits, landscapes, and murals. His exhibitions included one in the Museum of Navajo Ceremonial Art in Santa Fe, New Mexico. In 1915 he designed scenery and costumes for a play on Broadway. Mr. Henderson died on October 15, 1943.

Scenic Designs:
1915: *Alice in Wonderland*

Costume Designs:
1915: *Alice in Wonderland*

Stephen Hendrickson

Stephen Hendrickson is a set designer who is also on the faculty at New York University. He trained as a theatre designer but works mainly in television and film. He has been art director for films including *The Boys From Brazil, Live and Let Die* and *Fletch Lives*, and production designer for *Arthur* and the third "Muppet" movie.

Scenic Designs:
1972: *Wild and Wonderful*

Marc Henri

Marc Henri, a prolific British designer, was active on Broadway in the 1920s. He has extensive credits on the London stage for scene design between 1915 and 1919, including *Samples!* (1915), *Look Who's Here!, The Best of Luck* (1916), *Suzette, Cheep, Bubbly* (1917), *Flora, The Beauty Spot, The Officer's Mess* (1918), *The Very Idea, Kissing Time, Cinderella, The Kiss Call* and *Baby Bunding* (1919) among many

others. His name also appeared in playbills for over seventy productions in London in the 1920s, with credits such as scenic painter, scenic designer, scene builder and costume designer.

Scenic Designs:
1924: *Andre Charlot's Revue of 1924* 1925: *Charlot Revue* 1928: *This Year of Grace* 1929: *Wake Up and Dream'*

Costume Designs:
1929: *Wake Up and Dream*

Henry Herbert

Henry Herbert, an actor from England, was known for portrayals of roles in Shakespearean plays. He first appeared with the Ben Greet Company and subsequently appeared with F.R. Benson's Company in England. He also managed Benson's companies. He first appeared in New York City in 1912 in *The 'Mind-the-Paint' Girl* after which he remained in the United States appearing in additional plays and occasionally designing. One of the original members of The Elizabethean Stage Society, he was Associate Director of Stratford-on-Avon for a time. He died on February 20, 1947.

Scenic Designs:
1922: *Bavu*

Jocelyn Herbert

Jocelyn Herbert, a British designer of sets and costumes, was born on February 22, 1917. She studied in England and France with George Devine and Michel St. Denis, who have been influential during her career. She did not begin to design until the age of 40, with *The Chairs* for the English Stage Company at the Royal Court Theatre. Since that time she has designed countless productions, working extensively in theatre and opera. Companies for which she has designed include the National Theatre, Royal Shakespeare Company, Metropolitan Opera, Paris Opera, and Sadler's Wells in addition to productions in London's West End and on Broadway. While Jocelyn Herbert's film designs have been few they have been notable, including *Tom Jones, Hamlet, If...* and *The Hotel New Hampshire*.

Scenic Designs:
1963: *Chips with Everything; Luther* 1965: *Inadmissable Evidence* 1969: *Hamlet Starring*

Nichol Williamson **1970:** *Home* **1977:** *Merchant, The* **1989:** *3Penny Opera*

Lighting Designs:

1963: *Chips with Everything; Luther*

Costume Designs:

1963: *Chips with Everything; Luther* **1965:** *Inadmissable Evidence* **1969:** *Hamlet Starring Nichol Williamson* **1970:** *Home* **1977:** *Merchant, The* **1989:** *3Penny Opera*

Hjalmar Hermanson

Hjalmar Hermanson is known principally as a designer for NBC-TV where he designed sets for news anchors. He was born in Finland on January 20, 1907, and as a youth washed paint brushes for a scenic artist. He studied at the National Academy of Design, the Grand Central Art School and Columbia University. He had hoped to be a commercial artist, but a broken right index finger limited his ability to do fine work. He turned to scene painting for theatrical productions and gradually began to design. As designer for the Works Progress Administration's Federal Theatre Unit, he designed *The Living Newspaper, Triple A Plowed Under* and *Injunction Granted*. After service as an anti-aircraft sergeant during World War II he returned to CBS-TV, where his designs have included the sets for the second Nixon-Kennedy debate.

Scenic Designs:

1936: *Living Newspaper, The*

B. Russell Herts

Benjamin Russell Herts lived from May 27, 1908 until November 3, 1954. He created set designs for three shows in 1915 and was scenic and costume designer for an additional show in 1916. He spent his life mainly as an interior decorator and was president of Herts Brothers Co., Inc., Interior Decorators at 37 West 57th Street in New York City in 1919, moving in 1931 to 20 West 57th Street. He also wrote books including *A Female of the Species, The Son of Man* and *Grand Slam*. In addition he edited the magazine *Moods* from 1908 to 1909 and *Forum* from 1909 to 1910.

Scenic Designs:

1915: *Husband and Wife; Liars, The; New York Idea, The* **1916:** *Merry Christmas, Daddy*

Costume Designs:

1916: *Merry Christmas, Daddy*

Hewlett & Basing

Brothers Arthur T. and J. Monroe Hewlett and associate Charles Basing formed the scenic studio Hewlett & Basing. Between 1919 and 1920 they collaborated on the designs for three productions on Broadway. Charles Basing was a mural painter who also designed plays under his own name. Arthur T. Hewlett, a mural painter, worked with his brother J. Monroe Hewlett, an architect, on the scenery for many productions by Maude Adams. Both of the Hewletts were born in the family home on Long Island and attended Columbia College. For additional credits and information, see the entries "Charles Basing," "A.T Hewlett" and "J. Monroe Hewlett."

Scenic Designs:

1919: *For the Defense* **1920:** *Beyond the Horizon; Letter of the Law, The*

Arthur T. Hewlett

Arthur Thomas Hewlett died at age 81 on November 11, 1951. He was principally a mural painter who created murals at the Eastman School of Music in Rochester, New York, in the main office of the Bank of New York, and on the ceiling of the Grand Central Station, featuring signs of the Zodiac. He collaborated with his brother J. Monroe Hewlett on the scenery for many productions by Maude Adams. A 1892 graduate of Columbia College, he was a descendant of the family for whom the village of Hewlett on Long Island was named. His family imported tea and sugar, and Arthur Hewlett was involved with their business, Hewlett & Co., 79 Wall Street throughout his life.

Scenic Designs:

1920: *All Soul's Eve*

J. Monroe Hewlett

J. Monroe Hewlett was born in the family home at Lawrence, Long Island on August 1, 1868. He graduated from Columbia University in 1890 and joined the architectural firm of McKim, Mead and White. After further study in Paris he founded Lord & Hewlett, Architects at 2 West

45th Street in New York City. From 1932 to 1935 he was resident director of the American Academy in Rome. He designed hospitals in Brooklyn, New York and Danbury, Connecticut as well as libraries, churches, houses and country estates. As a member of the committee for the Beaux Arts Ball in New York he designed settings for their events, and with brother A.T. Hewlett designed for Maude Adams. With Bassett Jones, who supervised lights for Maude Adams, he developed a technique to create depth by using light zones between gauze drops and a black velvet backdrop. This technique was first used in *Chanticleer*, designed by John W. Alexander. J. M. Hewlett died in 1941.

Scenic Designs:
1918: *Freedom* **1920:** *All Soul's Eve*

Douglas Higgins

Douglas Higgins, a native of Canada, attended the University of British Columbia and Yale University. He has designed off-Broadway at the American Place Theatre and the Chelsea Theatre among others, and in regional theatres as well as for films and commercials. He was art director for the 1984 film *Runaway*.

Scenic Designs:
1974: *Love for Love*; *Rules of the Game, The*
1975: *Member of the Wedding, The*

Girvan Higginson

Girvan Higginson was a lighting designer, scenic designer and director who was active on Broadway in the 1940s. He graduated from Yale where he specialized in stage lighting. His father was the architect Augustus Higginson, who worked in Chicago and Santa Barbara, California. He was the nephew of John Higginson, founder of the Boston Symphony. Girvan Higginson also directed *Speak of the Devil* and produced *Eye on the Sparrow* and *The Nightingale* in New York City and appeared in *1776* and *Gentlemen, the Queen* in the mid-1920s.

Scenic Designs:
1942: *Willow and I, The*

Lighting Designs:
1942: *Willow and I, The* **1947:** *Story of Mary Surratt, The*

Charles E. Hoefler

Charles E. Hoefler, who has designed sets on and off-Broadway and for stock companies, makes his living designing industrial promotions. He was born on May 25, 1930 in Detroit and attended the University of Michigan, where he received a B.A. in 1952 and an M.F.A. in 1953. He served an apprenticeship with Tobins Lake Studios, South Lyon, Michigan when it was a design and construction shop. His first Broadway experience was with projections for the Oliver Smith design for *Jimmy* in 1970. His designs have been honored with the Drama Critics Award and Bronze, Silver and Gold Awards at the New York International Film and Television Festival.

Scenic Designs:
1980: *It's So Nice to Be Civilized*

Lighting Designs:
1980: *It's So Nice to Be Civilized*

Emil Holak

Before coming to the United States, Emil Holak designed with Ernst Stern and Oscar Strnad for Max Reinhardt in Berlin. Along with George H. Holak he was proprietor of Holak Studios, Theatrical Supplies at 451 First Avenue in New York.

Scenic Designs:
1942: *I Killed the Count*

Klaus Holm

Klaus Holm is a scenic and lighting designer, although the majority of his Broadway credits are for lighting. He was born Klaus Kuntze in Dresden, Germany on June 27, 1920, the son of sculptor and painter Martin Kuntze and dancer and choreographer Hanya Holm. He attended New York University, receiving a B.S. in 1948, and earned an M.F.A. at Yale in 1951. He designed as well as acted in college and stock productions. He has designed scenery for many productions off-Broadway at the Phoenix Theatre and Circle in the Square, New York City Center, Goodspeed Opera House, and New York City Opera among others. Between 1961 and 1962 he was lighting design consultant at the New York State Theatre and Lincoln Philharmonic Hall at Lincoln Center. His designs for television include the set for *The Kate Smith Show* in

1951 for NBC. He shared the 1956 Obie Award for design and lighting with Alvin Colt.

Scenic Designs:

1962: *Moby Dick*; *Private Ear, The/ The Public Eye*

Lighting Designs:

1954: *Girl on the Via Flamina, The*; *Golden Apple, The* **1955:** *Phoenix '55* **1960:** *Advise and Consent*; *Semi-Detached* **1961:** *Donnybrook!*; *Once There Was a Russian* **1962:** *Private Ear, The/ The Public Eye*; *Something About a Soldier* **1963:** *Heroine, The*

Glen Holse

Glen Holse was born in Beresford, South Dakota and graduated from Washington University in St. Louis, Missouri. His early designs were for a wallpaper firm and as a network television staff designer creating sets for shows featuring Eddie Fisher and Steve Allen. He designed in Las Vegas as art director for revues at the Tropicana, the Thunderbird Hotel, Aladdin Hotel and for Liberace. International credits include sets in Korea, Puerto Rico and Rio de Janeiro. He also designed settings for wax museums in Buena Park, California, Tokyo and Osaka, Japan. Glen Holse died on February 14, 1983 in Bakersfield, California at the age of 52.

Scenic Designs:

1959: *Billy Barnes Revue*

David Homan

David Homan was born in Christiana, Norway on September 10, 1907 and studied at the Glasgow Art School, in Cornwall and in Rome. He first worked as a scene painter in the early 1930s and subsequently as set designer for many productions before service in World War II. In the late 1940s he became managing director of Ambassador's Scenic Studios, a company which supplied sets for productions throughout the United Kingdom. With descendants of Joseph and Phil Harker he formed Harker, Homan and Bravery Limited in 1953, serving as the firm's director and secretary.

Scenic Designs:

1934: *And Be My Love*

Hiram Hoover

Hiram Hoover designed one set in 1932 for the Broadway stage.

Scenic Designs:

1932: *Devil's Little Game, The*

Harry Horner

Before devoting his talents to the theatre Harry Horner, was an architect. Known primarily as a scenic designer and director, he was born on July 24, 1912 in Holic, Czechoslovakia and studied acting and directing with Max Reinhardt. In the early 1930s he acted, directed and occasionally designed settings, lighting and costumes. After coming to the United States in 1935 he assisted Max Reinhardt and Norman Bel Geddes in New York. His credits for set design in theatre and opera are numerous and he has also continued to direct for theatre and television. His film designs have garnered him Academy Awards for the art direction of *The Hustler*, *The Heiress* and *They Shoot Horses, Don't They?*

Scenic Designs:

1938: *All the Living*; *Escape This Night* **1939:** *Family Portrait*; *Jeremiah*; *World We Make, The* **1940:** *Burning Deck, The*; *Reunion in New York*; *Weak Link, The* **1941:** *Banjo Eyes*; *Five Alarm Waltz*; *In Time to Come*; *Lady in the Dark*; *Let's Face It* **1942:** *Kiss for Cinderella, A*; *Let's Face It*; *Lily of the Valley*; *Star and Garter*; *Under This Roof*; *Walking Gentleman* **1943:** *Lady in the Dark*; *Winged Victory* **1946:** *Christopher Blake* **1948:** *Joy to the World*; *Me and Molly* **1953:** *Hazel Flagg* **1961:** *How to Make a Man*

Lighting Designs:

1942: *Lily of the Valley* **1946:** *Christopher Blake* **1953:** *Hazel Flagg* **1961:** *How to Make a Man*

Costume Designs:

1939: *Family Portrait*; *Jeremiah*

Michael J. Hotopp

Michael J. Hotopp works primarily in association with fellow designer Paul de Pass. They have extensive credits for productions on and off-Broadway, fashion shows, industrial promotions and television commercials as "Associated

Theatrical Designs, Limited". Michael Hotopp studied at Carnegie Mellon and New York Universities. The national tours of *Evita* and *Annie* are also among their credits as well as designs in regional theatres such as the Goodspeed Opera House, the Baltimore Opera, and Pittsburgh Playhouse. Michael Hotopp created the environment for *CBS This Morning* and has designed music videos. Awards include a Clio for an IBM commercial. For additional information see "Paul de Pass"

Scenic Designs:
1979: *Oklahoma!* **1980:** *Brigadoon* **1981:** *Oh, Brother* **1983:** *Tapdance Kid, The*

Lighting Designs:
1982: *Cleavage*

Norris Houghton

Norris Houghton was born Charles Norris Houghton on December 26, 1909 in Indianapolis, Indiana. He attended Princeton University where he received a Bachelor of Arts degree, Phi Beta Kappa in 1931. He was assistant to Robert Edmond Jones at Radio City Music Hall in 1932. After serving in the United States Naval Reserve from 1942 to 1945 he turned his talents to directing. In September 1953 he founded the Phoenix Theatre with T. Edward Hambleton and became co-managing director. The first production at the Phoenix was *Madame, Will You Walk* which opened December 1, 1953. In 1963 he resigned as managing director but remained on the Board of Directors and as Vice-President of the Phoenix Corporation. In 1967 he was appointed professor and Dean, Division of Theatre Arts, State University of New York at Purchase, where he remained until his retirement. Lee Simonson was his mentor and he acknowledges Gordon Craig and Robert Edmond Jones as major influences. His memoirs, *Entrances and Exits*, are scheduled to be published by New York Limelight Editions in 1991.

Scenic Designs:
1937: *In Clover* **1938:** *Dame Nature; Good Hunting; How to Get Tough About It; Stop-Over, Waltz in Goose Steps; White Oaks* **1956:** *Sleeping Prince, The* **1957:** *Makropoulos Secret, The*

Pamela Howard

Pamela Howard, a British designer, was born in Birmingham, England on January 5, 1939 and

studied at the Slade School of Fine Art and University College, London. She began designing in 1959 and has designed for many theatres in the United Kingdom, including the Royal Shakespeare Company, the Old Vic, the National Theatre, Theatre Clwyd, and Lyric Hammersmith. With Peter Gill she helped to create the Riverside Studios where she designed *The Cherry Orchard* and *Tree Tops*. At London's Central School of Art and Design she holds the position of lecturer in theatre design.

Scenic Designs:
1984: *Kipling*

Costume Designs:
1984: *Kipling*

George W. Howe

George Howe was born George Hauthalen in Salzburg, Austria in 1896 and ran away to America when he was fourteen. He was known primarily as an illustrator for *Collier's, American, Good Housekeeping, Women's Home Companion* and other magazines. He studied art in Paris and worked in various positions before devoting himself to serial illustrations. He also designed and painted scenery for motion picture studios. Just before his death in 1941 he executed a series of paintings which were subsequently used as posters for the Barnum and Bailey Circus.

Scenic Designs:
1923: *White Cargo* **1924:** *Garden of Weeds* **1926:** *White Cargo*

Wilson Hungate

Wilson Hungate designed one set on Broadway in 1924. He resided at 325 East 57th Street in Manhattan. A member of the Lotus Club, he died in April 1943 in New York City.

Scenic Designs:
1924: *Fake, The*

Leslie Hurry

Leslie Hurry, one of Britain's foremost designers, was born in London on February 10, 1909, and went to school at St. John's Wood Art School. He designed the ballet *Hamlet* in 1942, the first of numerous plays, ballets and operas for the major companies of Great Britain. He went to Canada to design sets and costumes in 1955 for the Stratford (Ontario) Festival and returned many times to design additional productions. His designs were well known for their lyrical quality of line and color. His theatrical designs and costumes have been exhibited often, most recently at the Royal Festival Hall in London. His final realized design was *Caesar and Cleopatra* at the Shaw Festival, Niagra-on-the-Lake, Ontario in 1975. At the time of his death on November 20, 1978, he was working on designs for *Mazeppa* for the Boston Opera, which were never produced.

Scenic Designs:
1956: *Richard III; Tamburlaine the Great*

Costume Designs:
1956: *Richard III; Tamburlaine the Great*

Wiard Boppo Ihnen

Wiard "Bill" Boppo Ihnen, a film art director, was born in Jersey City, New Jersey and joined the East Coast art department of Famous Players-Lasky in 1919. He soon moved to California and his first movie *Idols of Clay* was produced in 1920. It was followed by many others, notably *Becky Sharp* in 1935 which he designed with Robert Edmond Jones, *Stagecoach* in 1939, and his final movie *The Gallant Hours* in 1960. He won Academy Awards for Art Direction for *Wilson* and *Blood on the Sun* while working for Twentieth Century Fox. During World War I and World War II he served in the army as a camouflage expert. He was also a painter and an authority on early California architecture, and served a term as president of the Art Directors Guild. He met costume designer Edith Head while working on *Cradle Song* in 1933 and they were married in 1940, although she retained the name of her first husband for professional use. Bill Ihnen died in June 1979 at age 91.

Scenic Designs:
1925: *Hell's Bells* **1928:** *Bottled*

Josef Ijaky

Josef Ijaky designed one set on Broadway in 1970.

Scenic Designs:
1970: *Light, Lively, and Yiddish*

George Illian

George Illian, an artist and illustrator, designed the setting and collaborated on the costume design for a Broadway play in 1926. He was born in Milwaukee in 1894 and studied at the Art Institute of Chicago and the Royal Academy in Munich. One of the organizers of the Artist's Guild, he taught art to disabled veterans after World War I. He spent most of his life in New York City and Mt. Vernon, New York, where he lived with his wife Margaret. George Illian died in 1932.

Scenic Designs:
1926: *Henry IV, Part I*

Costume Designs:
1926: *Henry IV, Part I*

Ilmar and Tames

Ilmar and Samuel Tames together designed the setting and costumes for a single Broadway production in 1935. Samuel Tames was a painter who resided at 241 Madison Avenue in New York City in 1932.

Scenic Designs:
1935: *Bertha, The Sewing Machine Girl*

Costume Designs:
1935: *Bertha, The Sewing Machine Girl*

Christopher Ironside

Christopher Ironside, a British artist and designer, was born on July 11, 1913 and trained at London's Central School of Arts and Crafts. He has designed many medals, coins, reverses and coats-of-arms. His paintings are in public and private collections and he has exhibited in one-man shows. In collaboration with his brother, Robin C. Ironside, he also designed for the theatre.

Scenic Designs:
1954: *Midsummer Night's Dream, A*

Costume Designs:
1954: *Midsummer Night's Dream, A*

Robin C. Ironside

Robin C. Ironside was born on July 10, 1912 and studied at the Courtauld Institute and on the continent. He spent the majority of his professional career working at the Tate Gallery and writing. In addition, he was active with the Contemporary Art Society. He published several books in the 1940s, including *British Painting Since 1939* and *The Pre-Raphaelites*. In collaboration, brothers Christopher and Robin Ironside designed sets and costumes for many productions, beginning with *Der Rosenkavalier* at Covent Garden in 1948. Robin Ironside died on November 2, 1965.

Scenic Designs:
1954: *Midsummer Night's Dream, A*

Costume Designs:
1954: *Midsummer Night's Dream, A*

Lawrence Irving

Laurence Henry Foster Irving, painter, illustrator, and designer of scenery and costumes for the theatre and films, was born on April 11, 1897 in London. He studied at the Byam Shaw School and began designing with the sets and costumes for *Vaudeville Vanities* in London in 1926. He was in the service in World War I and World War II. He was art director in Hollywood for Douglas Fairbanks' films *The Man in the Iron Mask* (1928) and *The Taming of the Shrew* (1929) as well as other films. A governor of Stratford Memorial Theatre, Stratford-upon-Avon and the Royal Academy of Dramatic Art, he was awarded an Order of the British Empire in 1944. He was the biographer of his grandfather, Sir Henry Irving and helped inspire the formation of the Theatre Museum in London. Laurence Irving died in 1988.

Scenic Designs:
1932: *There's Always Juliet* **1933:** *Evensong* **1938:** *I Have Been Here Before*

Eiko Ishioka

Eiko Ishioka is a graphic designer from Japan. She initially studied industrial design at Tokyo National University of Fine Arts and Music and then changed to graphic and commercial design. She has designed a number of projects including the Parco Japanese shipping complexes. Her first film was *Mishima*, an American film directed by Francis Ford Coppola, which won a special jury prize for artistic achievement at the Cannes Film Festival in 1985. In 1986 she was production designer for the Faerie Tale Theatre's *Rip Van Winkle*. A book about her designs, *Eiko by Eiko* was published in 1982. Eiko Ishioka received nominations for Tony Awards for both the sets and costumes for *M. Butterfly* in 1988.

Scenic Designs:
1988: *M. Butterfly*

Costume Designs:
1988: *M. Butterfly*

Nikolai Iznar

Nikolai Iznar designed scenery and costumes on Broadway in 1925 in collaboration with another designer.

Scenic Designs:
1925: *Love and Death/ Aleko/ Fountain of Bakkchi Sarai/ etc.*

Costume Designs:
1925: *Love and Death/ Aleko/ Fountain of Bakkchi Sarai/ etc.*

Andrew Jackness

Andrew Jackness received an M.F.A. from the Yale University School of Drama in 1979 after studying with Ming Cho Lee. He has also studied at the Pratt Institute and Lester Polakov's Studio and Forum of Stage Design. He is the recipient of the Obie and Carbonell Awards and has in addition been nominated for Drama Desk and Maharam Awards. Andrew Jackness was born in New York City on September 27, 1952, the son of Jack and Meredith Jackness. His designs have been seen on and off-Broadway, at the Schiller Theatre in Berlin, the National Theatre in London, in major regional theatres in the United States, and during summers at the Williamstown Theatre Festival. As a production designer he has worked on the feature film *Longtime Companion*, *Blue Window* for American Playhouse and *Grownups* for Great Performances. His credits also include television commercials and videos for the MTV network.

Scenic Designs:
1979: *Wings* **1980:** *John Gabriel Borkman* **1981:** *Grown-ups; Little Foxes, The* **1982:** *Beyond Therapy; Whodunnit* **1986:** *Precious Sons* **1988:** *Michael Feinstein in Concert; Spoils of War*

Sally Jacobs

Sally Rich Jacobs, a British designer of sets and costumes, works frequently in the United States and the United Kingdom. She was born in London on November 5, 1932 and studied at Saint Martin's School of Art and the Central School of Arts and Crafts. She began her career working in the film industry, specializing in continuity. Her first professional design was *Five Plus One* at the Edinburgh Festival in 1961. Additional credits include designs for the Royal Shakespeare Company in London and Stratford-upon-Avon, in London's West End, and at the Mark Taper Forum. Films include *Nothing But the Best, Marat/Sade* and *Catch Us If You Can*. In 1970 she lectured on theatre design at the California Institute of the Arts in Los Angeles.

Scenic Designs:
1965: *Marat/Sade* **1971:** *Midsummer Night's Dream, A*

Costume Designs:
1971: *Midsummer Night's Dream, A*

John Jacobsen

John W. Jacobsen was born in Bronxville, New York on October 8, 1945 to Eric and Mary Jacobsen. He received a B.A. in art history at Yale University in 1967 and two years later an M.F.A. in stage design after study with Donald Oenslager. His first designs were for *Breaking Point* at Yale, where he also won an award for best undergraduate scenic design for *Dr. Faustus*. He has over sixty productions to his credit in regional and New York theatres, and extensive credits in Boston for companies including the Charles Playhouse, Goldovsky Opera, Opera Company of Boston and Boston Ballet. Since the mid-1970s his career has been committed to other forms of theatre, producing shows using advanced media technologies such as lasers and IMAX/OMNIMAX film, primarily for museums. Through his company White Oak Associates and as Associate Director of the Boston Museum of Sciences from 1985 to 1988, he has produced "New England Time Capsule" for the Boston Museum of Science Omni theatre, "Images: The New Astronomy" for the Charles Hayden Planetarium, DECWORLD '90 and many others. "Science Crossroads," produced for the Carnegie Science Center in Pittsburgh, is scheduled to open in 1991.

Scenic Designs:
1974: *Mourning Pictures*

Walter Jagemann

Walter Jagemann designed three sets in the late 1930s on Broadway. He generally worked in collaboration with designers Russell Patterson and Herbert Andrews.

Scenic Designs:
1935: *George White's Scandals* **1939:** *Swingin' the Dream; Yokel Boy*

Finlay James

Finlay James gave up a career in law to design for the theatre. He was born in Angus, Scotland and received a Diploma of Art in Dundee, Scotland. He has designed sets and costumes in Glasgow, Rome, Amsterdam, London (including the Old Vic and in the West End), and in Edinburgh among many other locations. His first designs on Broadway were seen in 1971. A teacher as well as a designer, he spent fourteen years as head of the School of Design in the College of Art and Design in Birmingham, England and has also been head of design at the City of Birmingham Polytechnic. In 1974 his costume designs for *Crown Matrimonial* were nominated for a Tony Award.

Scenic Designs:
1970: *Conduct Unbecoming* **1973:** *Crown Matrimonial* **1985:** *Aren't We All?* **1987:** *Blithe Spirit*

Lighting Designs:
1970: *Conduct Unbecoming*

Costume Designs:
1970: *Conduct Unbecoming* **1973:** *Crown Matrimonial*

Neil Peter Jampolis

Neil Peter Jampolis has numerous credits for designing lighting and sets on Broadway and for opera companies in the United States. He was born in Brooklyn on March 14, 1943 and received a B.F.A. from the Art Institute of Chicago in 1971. He occasionally also designs costumes for plays and operas. Mr. Jampolis received a Tony award for the lighting design for *Sherlock Holmes* in 1975. Recent designs include sets and lights for *Jackie Mason*, which opened in October 1990.

Scenic Designs:

1970: *Borstal Boy* 1971: *Earl of Ruston*; *To Live Another Summer* 1985: *Search for Signs/Intellegent Life...* 1986: *World According to Me, The* 1988: *World According to Me, The* 1989: *Sid Caesar and Company*

Lighting Designs:

1970: *Borstal Boy*, *Les Blancs* 1971: *Earl of Ruston*; *To Live Another Summer* 1972: *Butley*; *Wild and Wonderful*; *Wise Child* 1973: *Crown Matrimonial*; *Emperor Henry IV*; *Let Me Hear You Smile* 1974: *Sherlock Holmes* 1976: *Innocents, The* 1977: *Otherwise Engaged* 1979: *Knockout*; *Night and Day* 1980: *American Clock, The*; *Harold and Maude* 1984: *Kipling* 1985: *Search for Signs/Intellegent Life...* 1986: *Into The Light*; *World According to Me, The* 1988: *World According to Me, The* 1989: *Black and Blue*; *Merchant of Venice, The*; *Orpheus Descending*; *Sid Caesar and Company*

Costume Designs:

1971: *Earl of Ruston* 1972: *Butley* 1986: *Into The Light*

David Jenkins

David Jenkins has designed settings for major regional theatres and worked as an art director for the television productions *American Playhouse* and *Theatre in America*. Educated at Earlham College, Indiana University and the Yale School of Drama, he is married to stage designer, Leigh Rand, who often works as his assistant. David Jenkins was born on July 30, 1937 in Hampton, Virginia. He works principally as an art director for television commercials, and is currently associated with Wieden & Kennedy, where he has designed spots including the Bo Jackson and Spike Lee campaigns for Nike.

Scenic Designs:

1973: *Changing Room, The* 1974: *Freedom of the City, The* 1975: *Rogers and Hart* 1976: *Checking Out* 1977: *Saint Joan* 1979: *Elephant Man, The*; *Strangers* 1980: *I Ought to Be in Pictures* 1981: *Piaf* 1982: *Queen and*

the *Rebels, The*; *Special Occasions* 1983: *Total Abandon* 1987: *Sherlock's Last Case*; *Stardust*; *Stepping Out* 1989: *Welcome To The Club* 1990: *Accomplice*

George Clarke Jenkins

George Clarke Jenkins is a well-known scenery and lighting designer and art director for films. Occasionally during his career he has also contributed costume designs to a production. He was born in Baltimore on November 19, 1911 and studied architecture at the University of Pennsylvania. He worked as an architect and interior designer before assisting Jo Mielziner from 1937 to 1941. His first Broadway show was *Early to Bed* in 1943, for which he designed the sets and lights. This production was followed by many others in New York City and throughout the country, including designs for the San Francisco Opera Association. He is also an art director for films known for his detail and realistic sets, as evidenced in movies such as *All the President's Men* (Academy Award), *The Miracle Worker*, *The China Syndrome*, *The Subject Was Roses*, *Presumed Innocent*, *The Dollmaker* and *Sophie's Choice*. He received the Donaldson Award for his settings for *I Remember Mama* in 1945. From 1985 to 1988 he was Professor of Motion Picture Design at UCLA.

Scenic Designs:

1943: *Early to Bed* 1944: *Allah Be Praised*; *I Remember Mama*; *Mexican Hayride* 1945: *Are You with It?*; *Common Ground*; *Dark of the Moon*; *French Touch, The*; *Memphis Bound*; *Strange Fruit* 1948: *Time for Elizabeth*; *Tonight At 8:30* 1949: *Lost in the Stars* 1950: *Bell, Book and Candle*; *Curious Savage, The* 1952: *Three Wishes for Jamie* 1953: *Gently Does It*; *Touchstone* 1954: *Bad Seed, The*; *Immoralist, The* 1955: *Ankles Aweigh*; *Desk Set, The* 1956: *Happiest Millionaire, The*; *Too Late the Phalarope* 1957: *Rumple* 1958: *Cue for Passion*; *Once More, with Feeling*; *Two for the Seesaw* 1959: *Jolly's Progress*; *Miracle Worker, The*; *Tall Story* 1960: *Critics Choice*; *One More River* 1961: *Thirteen Daughters* 1962: *Step on a Crack*; *Thousand Clowns, A* 1963: *Jennie* 1965: *Catch Me If You Can*; *Generation* 1966: *Wait Until Dark* 1968: *Only Game in Town, The* 1972: *Night Watch* 1976: *Sly Fox*

Lighting Designs:
1943: *Early to Bed* **1944:** *Allah Be Praised;*
I Remember Mama **1945:** *Are You with It?;*
Common Ground; Dark of the Moon; French
Touch, The; Memphis Bound; Strange Fruit
1950: *Bell, Book and Candle; Curious Savage,*
The **1953:** *Gently Does It; Touchstone* **1954:**
Bad Seed, The **1955:** *Ankles Aweigh; Desk Set,*
The **1956:** *Happiest Millionaire, The; Too Late*
the Phalarope **1957:** *Rumple* **1958:** *Cue for*
Passion; Once More, with Feeling; Two for the
Seesaw **1959:** *Miracle Worker, The; Tall Story*
1960: *Critics Choice; One More River* **1961:**
Thirteen Daughters **1962:** *Step on a Crack;*
Thousand Clowns, A **1965:** *Catch Me If You*
Can; Generation **1966:** *Wait Until Dark* **1976:**
Sly Fox

Costume Designs:
1930: *So Was Napoleon* **1934:** *Anything Goes*
1945: *Common Ground; French Touch, The*
1950: *Curious Savage, The; Curious Savage,*
The **1955:** *Desk Set, The*

Donald Jensen

Donald F. Jensen, the son of Ernest and Margaret O'Conner Jensen, was born in Emporia, Kansas on October 2, 1931. He received a B.F.A. in the School of Drawing and Painting at the University of Kansas in 1953, and studied scenic design with Milton Smith at Columbia University and with Lester Polakov. Principally a costume designer, his first costume designs were for the opera *Gallantry* at Columbia and in 1957 he designed *Winkelburg* at the Renata Theatre in New York. He has assisted both Desmond Heeley and Theoni Aldredge in addition to his own designing. Other costume designs include the New York premiere of *Cock-a-Doodle Dandy* by Lucile Lortel. He was art director for the 1989 films *Dad* and *In Country*.

Scenic Designs:
1964: *Sunday Man, The*

Lighting Designs:
1964: *Sunday Man, The*

Costume Designs:
1964: *Sunday Man, The*

John Jensen

John Jensen is a set designer active in regional and repertory theatres who also serves as head of the design/tech program at Rutgers University. He was born on December 20, 1933 in Weiser, Idaho. After graduating from Hillsboro High School in Oregon he attended the University of Oregon where he received a B.S. degree in 1953. Over the years he has also taken courses at the Pratt Institute, Lester Polakov's Studio and Forum of Stage Design, the Art Students League and the School of Visual Arts. He spent two years as an assistant to Jo Mielziner and several years as an associate of Sir Tyrone Guthrie, Tanya Moiseiwitsch and Desmond Heeley, designing for The Guthrie Theatre and the American Conservatory Theatre. His first professional design was *Ardele* at the Guthrie Theatre in 1969.

Scenic Designs:
1973: *Cyrano* **1980:** *Watch on the Rhine* **1983:**
Man Who Had Three Arms, The

Jimnolds

Jimnolds (sic) designed one set on Broadway in 1923.

Scenic Designs:
1923: *Helen of Troy, New York*

Joel

Joel was responsible for the interiors of a 1936 Broadway production in collaboration with Lucile who designed the exterior settings.

Scenic Designs:
1936: *Life and Loves of Dorian Gray, The*

Tom John

Tom H. John is an art director for television and a scenic designer for theatre and dance. He has won five Emmy Awards, including one each for *My Name is Barbra* in 1965, *Much Ado About Nothing* in 1973 and *Beacon Hill* in 1976. He is the only art director to receive television's Peabody Award For Special Achievement, awarded in 1966 for art direction of *Death of a Salesman, Color Me Barbra* and *The Strollin' Twenties*. Recent television shows he has designed include *Tattinger's* and *Kate and Allie*. He has also designed for Radio City Music Hall, Alvin Ailey, Dance Theatre of Harlem and the San Francisco Ballet among other companies.

His film work includes art direction for *Zoot Suit* and *Thank God it's Friday.*

Scenic Designs:

1968: *George M!* **1971:** *Frank Merriwell (or Honor Changed)* **1972:** *Selling of the President, The* **1975:** *Wiz, The* **1976:** *Guys and Dolls* **1983:** *Five-Six-Seven-Eight...Dance!*; *Marilyn*; *Peg*

Martin Johns

Martin Johns, a British designer, is head of design at the Leicester Haymarket Theatre. He has also been head of design at theatres in Newcastle and York. Production credits in London's West End include *Rolls Hyphen Royce* and *Let the Good Times Roll.* In addition, he designed *Romans in Britain* at the National Theatre. *Me and My Girl* started at the Leicester Haymarket, moved to the West End and later opened in New York City.

Scenic Designs:

1986: *Me and My Girl*

Albert R. Johnson

Albert Richard Johnson was primarily a set designer who also occasionally designed lights. He began designing in 1929 and his final production opened in in October 1967, just prior to his death on December 21, 1967. He was born in La Crosse, Wisconsin on February 1, 1910 and first worked in theatre at the age of fifteen as a scene painter for the Farmington, Long Island Opera House. His first New York design was *The Criminal Code* in 1929 at the age of nineteen, after which he studied with Norman Bel Geddes. During his busy career he was a consultant on productions and designs for the New York World's Fair, Radio City Music Hall, Ringling Brothers & Barnum and Bailey Circus, and Jones Beach. He also directed and designed lights for industrial promotions.

Scenic Designs:

1929: *Criminal Code, The*; *Half Gods* **1930:** *Three's a Crowd* **1931:** *Band Wagon, The* **1932:** *Americana*; *Face the Music*; *Foreign Affairs*; *Mad Hopes, The* **1933:** *As Thousands Cheer*; *Face the Music*; *Let 'em Eat Cake* **1934:** *Great Waltz, The*; *Life Begins At 8:40*; *Revenge with Music*; *Union Pacific*; *Ziegfeld Follies: 1934* **1935:** *Great Waltz, The*; *Jumbo*

1937: *Betweeen the Devil* **1938:** *Great Lady*; *Leave It to Me!*; *You Never Know* **1939:** *George White's Scandals*; *Leave It to Me!* **1940:** *John Henry* **1941:** *Crazy with the Heat* **1942:** *Proof Through the Night*; *Skin of Our Teeth, The* **1943:** *My Dear Public* **1944:** *Sing Out, Sweet Land* **1945:** *Girl from Nantucket, The*; *Live Life Again* **1947:** *Dear Judas* **1949:** *Two Blind Mice* **1950:** *Pardon Our French* **1952:** *Chase, The*; *Fancy Meeting You Again*; *Of Thee I Sing*; *Shuffle Along* **1958:** *Cloud 7* **1962:** *Night Life* **1967:** *What Did We Do Wrong?*

Lighting Designs:

1932: *Americana* **1941:** *Crazy with the Heat* **1945:** *Girl from Nantucket, The*; *Live Life Again* **1947:** *Dear Judas* **1958:** *Cloud 7* **1962:** *Night Life*

Doug Johnson

Doug Johnson, a painter, illustrator and theatrical designer, was born in Toronto, Canada in 1940 and studied painting in Europe after attending the Ontario College of Art. He moved to New York City in 1968 to work with advertising agencies and for magazines including *Sports Illustrated, Look* and *Playboy.* His advertising consulting firm, Performing Dogs, has worked on several Broadway shows. As Creative Director of the Chelsea Theatre Center he has won several awards. Doug Johnson has exhibited widely in both group and individual shows and has taught at the School of Visual Arts. He was art director for the 1979 film *Take Down.*

Scenic Designs:

1982: *Pump Boys and Dinettes*

Virginia Johnston

Virginia Johnston supervised the set design for a 1960 Broadway production.

Scenic Designs:

1960: *World of Carl Sandburg, The*

Edovard Jonas

Edovard Jonas designed the set in 1926 for a Broadway show. He was the curator and wrote the catalogue copy for a 1930 exhibition at the Museum Cognacq-Jay in Paris. In 1932 he was President, Secretary and Treasurer of "Edovard

Jonas of Paris, Inc.," a business devoted to pictures and engraving, located at 9 East 56th Street in New York City.

Scenic Designs:
1926: *Mozart*

Jones and Erwin

Jones and Erwin collaborated on the set design for a Broadway play in 1928. Frederick W. Jones III and Hobart S. Erwin were partners in Jones & Erwin, interior decorators located at 729 Madison Avenue in 1927. In 1931 the directors of the company (which had moved to 15 East 57th Street) were Hobart S. Erwin, William J. Muldowney and Adolph M. Dick. As was common in the era, interior decorators supplied settings for contemporary production and received credit in the playbill. Frederick W. Jones III also designed productions under his own name and additional information is available under his entry in this book.

Scenic Designs:
1928: *Phantom Lover, The*

Bassett Jones

Bassett Jones was born in New Brighton, Staten Island on February 6, 1877 and died at the age of 82 on January 25, 1960. He studied engineering at the Stevens Institute of Technology and the Massachusetts Institute of Technology and spent his life principally designing elevators and architectural lighting systems. He designed lights for the New York World's Fair, the Empire State Building, the Chrysler Building, and the Irving Trust Company. Bassett Jones also made several contributions to stage lighting, creating the first floodlight units and also devising other special equipment. He supervised stage lighting for Maude Adams' plays and was consultant for *Peter Pan* in 1912.

Scenic Designs:
1925: *Cain*

Lighting Designs:
1925: *Cain*

Costume Designs:
1925: *Cain*

Frederick W. Jones III

Frederick W. Jones III was active as a setting and occasional costume designer on Broadway throughout the 1920s. His sets were featured in the September 1923 issue of *Theater Magazine.* He was, in addition, an interior decorator, associated with National Interior Decorators located at 2575 Broadway in New York City in 1922, and an actor. In 1927 he was associated with Jones & Erwin, interior decorators at 729 Madison Avenue. Jones occasionally designed in collaboration with Hobart S. Erwin.

Scenic Designs:
1923: *Dagmar; Jack and Jill* **1924:** *Man Who Ate the Popomack, The; Paolo and Francesca* **1925:** *Caesar and Cleopatra; Captain Jinks; Hamlet; Starlight* **1926:** *Shanghai* **1928:** *Shanghai Gesture; Unknown Warrior, The*

Costume Designs:
1923: *Jack and Jill*

Robert Edmond Jones

Robert Edmond Jones, designer and producer, was born in Milton, New Hampshire on December 12, 1887 and began designing for the theatre in 1911. He studied at Harvard and brought great originality of design and color to the theatre, perhaps influenced by his admiration of Max Reinhardt. While working on a pageant in Madison Square Garden he became acquainted with one of Reinhardt's artists, who invited him to Germany to see the producer's methods. The outbreak of war forced his return to America in 1915. Jones' designs for *The Man Who Married A Dumb Wife,* included at the last moment as a curtain raiser for *Androcles and the Lion,* are generally regarded as marking the beginning of the "New American Stagecraft." He was associated with Kenneth MacGowan and Eugene O'Neill in the production of many plays at the Greenwich Village Playhouse, and directed and designed many of O'Neill's plays. A prolific designer, he had many productions to his credit, well beyond the list included here. He was art director for the opening production at Radio City Music Hall. His book, *The Dramatic Imagination,* is a classic. Robert Edmond Jones died on November 26, 1954.

Scenic Designs:
1915: *Devil's Garden, The; Man Who Married a Dumb Wife, The; Trilby* **1916:** *Caliban*

By the Yellow Sands; Good Gracious, Annabelle; Happy Ending, The 1917: Deluge, The; Rescuing Angel, The; Rider of Dreams, The/ Granny Maumee/ Simon; Successful Calamity, A 1918: Be Calm, Camilla; Gentile Wife, The; Hedda Gabler; Redemption; Wild Duck, The 1919: Jest, The 1920: George Washington; Samson and Delilah; Tragedy of Richard III, The 1921: Anna Christie; Claw, The; Daddy's Gone A-Hunting; Idle Inn, The; Macbeth; Mountain Man, The; Swords 1922: Deluge, The; Hairy Ape, The; Hamlet; Romeo and Juliet; Rose Bernd; S.S. Tenacity, The; Voltaire 1923: Hamlet; Laughing Lady, The; Launzi; Royal Fandango, A 1924: Desire Under the Elms; Fashion; George Dandin, Or the Husband Confounded; Living Mask, The; Saint, The; Spook Sonata, The; Welded 1925: Beyond; Buccaneer, The; Fountain, The; In a Garden; Love for Love; Michel Auclair; Trelawney of the Wells 1926: Great God Brown, The; Jest, The; Love 'em and Leave 'em 1927: Claw, The; House of Women, The; Paris Bound; Trelawney of the Wells 1928: Holiday; Machinal; Martine; Money Lender, The; Mr. Moneypenny; Salvation; These Days 1929: Becky Sharpe; Channel Road, The; Commodore Marries, The; Cross Roads; Ladies Leave; See Naples and Die; Serena Blandish; Week-End 1930: Children of Darkness; Green Pastures, The; Rebound; Roadside 1931: Camille; Lady with a Lamp, The; Mourning Becomes Electra; Passing Present, The 1932: Camille; Lucrece; Mourning Becomes Electra; Night Over Taos 1933: Ah, Wilderness; Green Bay Tree, The; Mary of Scotland; Nine Pine Street 1934: Dark Victory; Joyous Season 1935: Green Pastures 1937: Othello 1938: Devil and Daniel Webster, The; Everywhere I Roam; Seagull, The; Susanna, Don't You Cry 1939: Kindred; Philadelphia Story, The; Summer Night 1940: Juno and the Paycock; Love for Love 1942: Without Love 1943: Othello 1944: Helen Goes to Troy; Jackpot 1946: Iceman Cometh, The; Lute Song 1950: Enchanted, The 1951: Green Pastures

Lighting Designs:

1933: Mary of Scotland 1938: Devil and Daniel Webster, The; Susanna, Don't You Cry 1939: Summer Night 1940: Romeo and Juliet 1942: Without Love 1943: Othello 1944: Helen Goes to Troy 1946: Iceman Cometh, The; Lute Song

Costume Designs:

1915: Devil's Garden, The; Man Who Married a Dumb Wife, The 1916: Caliban By the Yellow Sands 1917: Rider of Dreams, The/ Granny Maumee/ Simon 1920: George Washington; Tragedy of Richard III, The 1921: Macbeth; Swords 1922: Hamlet; Romeo and Juliet; Voltaire 1923: Hamlet; Launzi 1924: Fashion; George Dandin, Or the Husband Confounded; Living Mask, The; Spook Sonata, The; Welded 1925: Beyond; Buccaneer, The; Fountain, The; Love for Love; Trelawney of the Wells 1926: Great God Brown, The; Jest, The; Little Eyolf 1927: House of Women, The 1928: Martine; Mr. Moneypenny 1929: Becky Sharpe; Channel Road, The; See Naples and Die 1930: Children of Darkness 1931: Camille; Mourning Becomes Electra; Passing Present, The 1932: Lucrece; Mourning Becomes Electra; Night Over Taos 1933: Mary of Scotland; Nine Pine Street 1935: Green Pastures 1937: Othello 1938: Devil and Daniel Webster, The; Everywhere I Roam; Seagull, The; Susanna, Don't You Cry 1939: Summer Night 1942: Without Love 1943: Othello 1946: Iceman Cometh, The; Lute Song 1950: Enchanted, The 1951: Green Pastures

Gerald Jongerius

Gerald Jongerius designed one set in 1982 on Broadway.

Scenic Designs:
1982: Herman Van Veen: All of Him

Jonel Jorgulesco

Jonel Jorgulesco designed costumes and sets on Broadway in 1932. He was born in Berlin on August 18, 1904 and studied stage design in Berlin and Frankfurt. During the 1920s he was resident designer for the Boston Repertory Theatre, and in the 1930s he designed for the Broadway stage, creating many settings for the Metropolitan Opera including Don Pasquale, Die Walküre, La Traviata and La Nozze di Figaro. A contributor to several books about scenic design, Mr. Jorgulesco served as art director and design consultant for various companies. In 1960 he moved to St. Thomas, Virgin Islands to pursue a career in architectural design. He died in St. Thomas on November 7, 1966.

Scenic Designs:
1932: *Child of Manhattan; Too True to Be Good*

Costume Designs:
1932: *Too True to Be Good*

James Leonard Joy

James Leonard Joy designed sets on the Broadway stage beginning in 1981. He was born in Detroit, Michigan in 1949 and received a B.A. in theatre from the University of Michigan. Instead of attending law school, he received an M.F.A. at Carnegie-Mellon in theatrical design. He spent three years as an assistant to Ben Edwards and three years as an assistant to José Varona. He has extensive regional theatre experience, including productions during lengthy associations with the Goodspeed Opera, Huntington Theatre, Missouri Repertory Theatre, Kansas City Lyric Opera, and Alliance Theatre. His professional career began at the Chautauqua Opera. Recent productions include *Travesties* at the Huntington and productions at Cinncinati Playhouse and Arena Stage. He designed the "fantasy" scenes in the 1990/91 Broadway production of *Peter Pan* starring Cathy Rigby.

Scenic Designs:
1981: *Ned and Jack* **1985:** *Take Me Along*

Philipp Jung

Philipp Jung was born on June 10, 1949 in Cleveland, Ohio and studied at Ohio University, the Yale School of Drama and in the English National Opera Design Program. His designs have been honored with the English Arts Council Design Bursary. His design work has been influenced by the creativity of Boris Aronson.

Scenic Designs:
1979: *Madwoman of Central Park West, The* **1989:** *Eastern Standard; Mastergate*

Theodore Kahn

Theodore Kahn was a set designer who received credit for five plays between 1928 and 1934 on the Broadway stage. The Theodore Kahn Scenic Studio was located at 155 West 29th Street, New York City in 1927.

Scenic Designs:
1928: *K Guy, The* **1930:** *Brown Buddies* **1931:** *Sugar Hill* **1932:** *Barrister, The* **1934:** *Good-Bye Please*

Myer Kanin Scenic Studios

Myer Kanin Scenic Studios received credit for a scenic design on Broadway in 1932. Myer Kanin was an artist with a studio located at 1236 Boynton Avenue in New York in the early 1930s. His play, *The Willoughbys*, written in collaboration with Harry Ingram, was published in 1938.

Scenic Designs:
1932: *Blackberries of 1932*

Nat Karson

Nat Karson, a scenic designer and television producer, was Art Director at Radio City Music Hall from 1936 to 1943. He was born in Zurich, Switzerland, the son of an architect who was a refugee from Russia. At a young age he moved with his family to Chicago where he won an art prize in high school and a scholarship to the Art Institute of Chicago. His debut in the theatre as a designer occurred with *Hamlet* as conceived by John Houseman and Orson Welles. In addition he designed the so-called "voodoo" *Macbeth* for Houseman and Welles for the Federal Theatre Project. He considered his design for the *Hamlet* produced in Elsinore, Denmark in 1949 a great personal success. His credits as a set designer were numerous and he occasionally contributed costumes and lighting as well. Mr. Karson also spent several years designing in London. He died at age 46 on September 29, 1954.

Scenic Designs:
1934: *Calling All Stars* **1935:** *Hook-Up, The* **1936:** *Macbeth; White Man* **1937:** *Arms for Venus* **1938:** *Journeyman; Right This Way; Roosty* **1939:** *Hot Mikado, The* **1940:** *Keep Off the Grass; Liliom* **1941:** *High Kickers* **1943:** *Connecticut Yankee, A* **1946:** *Front Page, The; Nellie Bly* **1948:** *Ballet Ballads*

Lighting Designs:
1943: *Connecticut Yankee, A* **1946:** *Nellie Bly* **1948:** *Ballet Ballads*

Costume Designs:
1936: *Macbeth; White Man* **1939:** *Hot Mikado, The* **1940:** *Keep Off the Grass; Liliom* **1946:** *Nellie Bly* **1948:** *Ballet Ballads*

John Kasarda

John Kasarda has numerous credits as a scenic designer in regional theatres such as The Philadelphia Drama Guild, where he has been resident designer; the American Stage Festival in New Hampshire; the Goodman Theatre, and Center Stage. Off-Broadway credits include productions at The Public Theatre and Manhattan Theatre Club. He has designed for opera, television, and the 1984 Louisiana World Exposition in New Orleans. His most extensive credits, however, are as an assistant designer. He has worked on Broadway shows including *Chicago*, *Mack & Mabel*, *The Good Doctor*, *The Mooney Shapiro Songbook*, *Good* and *Seesaw*. He was art director for the 1982 film *The Verdict*.

Scenic Designs:

1983: *All's Well That Ends Well* **1984:** *Cyrano De Bergerac; Much Ado About Nothing*

Frances Keating

Frances Keating, an interior decorator, designed one set in 1929 on Broadway. She resided at 215 West 51st Street in 1924 and at 150 East 54th Street in 1932.

Scenic Designs:

1929: *Dragon, The*

John William Keck

World Wide Christmas was John William Keck's debut as Art Director at Radio City Music Hall in 1973. He has designed numerous productions at Radio City including rock concerts for major acts. His first position after joining United Scenic Artists in 1954 was as a scenic artist at Radio City Music Hall. He was born in New York City on December 4, 1929 and studied at the High School of Music and Art and the Pratt Institute. He began his career in the theatre as a scenic artist for McDonald-Stevens and Nolan Scenery Studios.

Scenic Designs:

1979: *Snow White and the Seven Dwarfs* **1980:** *It's Spring; Rockette Spectacular with Ginger Rogers, A*

William Kellam

William Kellam began working at age fourteen building stage scenery for the company his father founded in 1890, the William Kellam Company. He left the business only once (for service in World War I) and took over the company in 1934 when his father retired. The William Kellam Company built sets for Group Theatre productions, *Life With Father*, and many productions designed by Howard Bay. When he died at age 48 on April 22, 1944, several of the productions running on Broadway had been constructed by his scenic studio: *Twentieth Century, Subway Express, Room Service*, and *Earl Carroll's Vanities*

Scenic Designs:

1943: *Patriots, The*

Marjorie Bradley Kellogg

Marjorie Bradley Kellogg is a creative, prolific designer of sets whose credits include major regional theatres, on and off-Broadway, films and television. She won the Los Angeles Drama Logue Award in 1988 for *Babbitt*, the Boston Theatre Critics Circle Best Design Award for the 1983-84 season, the American Council on the Arts Young Artists Award in 1983 and Drama Desk nominations for outstanding design in the 1982-83 and 1984-85 seasons. She was born in Cambridge, Massachusetts on August 30, 1946, the daughter of Mr. and Mrs. Jarvis Phillips Kellogg. After receiving a Bachelor of Arts degree at Vassar College in 1967 and after one year in graduate school, she left formal education behind to learn design by assisting Ming Cho Lee. She has designed many productions for Circle in the Square, for Hartford Stage and The Acting Company. In addition to designing she has written several science fiction novels, including *Lear's Daughters* and *A Rumor of Angels*.

Scenic Designs:

1974: *Where's Charley?* **1975:** *Death of a Salesman* **1976:** *Poison Tree, The* **1978:** *Best Little Whorehouse in Texas, The; Da* **1979:** *Spokesong* **1981:** *Father, The* **1982:** *Best Little Whorehouse in Texas, The; Present Laughter; Solomon's Child; Steaming* **1983:** *American Buffalo; Heartbreak House; Misanthrope, The; Moose Murders* **1985:** *Joe Egg; Requiem for a Heavyweight* **1986:** *Arsenic and Old Lace* **1987:** *Month of Sundays, A*

Robert Kelly

Robert Kelly was a lighting designer in 1962 on Broadway.

Scenic Designs:
1962: *Egg, The*

Lindsay Kemp

Lindsay Kemp studied art, mime, and ballet in London, and also studied mime with Marcel Marceau. He appeared with the Charles Weidman Dance Company and in 1964 formed the Dance Mime Company. A man of many talents, he has acted in and directed many productions in London and Edinburgh (among other locations) and also appeared in films. Mr. Kemp is, in addition, a choreographer, set designer and painter. *Flowers* – a play which he devised, directed and designed – was originally done at Edinburgh's Traverse Theatre, later moving to the Regent Theatre in London before arriving in New York City in 1974.

Scenic Designs:
1974: *Flowers*

Costume Designs:
1974: *Flowers*

Kennel and Entwistle

Louis Kennel and Robert C. Entwistle designed settings for productions on Broadway betwen 1919 and 1931. Robert Entwistle worked primarily as an electrician and Louis Kennel as a scenic designer and builder. For additional information and individual credits see the entries under their names.

Scenic Designs:
1919: *Phantom Legion, The* 1920: *Skin Game, The* 1922: *Nest, The; Swifty* 1927: *Lady Do* 1931: *Savage Rhythm*

Lighting Designs:
1920: *Skin Game, The* 1922: *Nest, The* 1927: *Lady Do*

Louis Kennel

Louis Kennel has Broadway credits as a costume and lighting designer, but his major activity in the theatre was as a scenic designer. He was born in North Bergen, New Jersey on

May 7, 1886 and studied painting with George Bridgman, Charles Graham, Ernest Gros, and William Lippincott. In 1940 he organized theatre technicians and director Royce Emerson into Louis Kennel, Inc. to produce and support play production by other producers. His primary business, however, was Louis Kennel Scenic Studios, 1427 44th Street in North Bergen, New Jersey, specializing in "Designing, Building and Painting for Theatre and T.V." His solo credits range from the twenties through the fifties. He also designed in collaboration with Robert C. Entwistle through "Kennel and Entwistle" from 1919 to 1931, and in collaboration with Rollo Peters through "Peters and Kennel" in 1918.

Scenic Designs:
1924: *Leah Kleschna* 1926: *Hangman's House; One Man's Woman* 1928: *Falstaff* 1930: *Apron Strings; Plutocrat, The; That's Gratitude; Those We Love* 1932: *Little Black Book, The* 1934: *Moor Born; Order Please; Re-Echo* 1935: *Moon Over Mulberry Street* 1936: *Black Widow; Halloween* 1937: *London Assurance* 1938: *Day in the Sun; Don't Throw Glass Houses* 1940: *Horse Fever* 1941: *Brother Cain; First Stop to Heaven* 1947: *Magic Touch, The* 1949: *Anybody Home; Twelfth Night* 1951: *Springtime Folly; Springtime for Henry* 1957: *Waiting for Godot*

Lighting Designs:
1949: *Anybody Home*

Costume Designs:
1934: *Re-Echo* 1949: *Anybody Home; Twelfth Night*

Sean Kenny

Sean Kenny was an Irish designer and architect. He was born in Portoe, Tipperary, Ireland on December 23, 1932 and studied architecture in Dublin and with Frank Lloyd Wright. He designed settings for the first time in Hammersmith, England but it was *The Hostage* in London which gave him his real entrance into the theatre--thanks to the offer of work from an old Irish friend, Brendan Behan. His credits for settings, and occasionally costumes, were extensive in England. He also designed for film, television and night clubs. He continued to practice as an architect when his schedule allowed, especially for new theatres and theatre renovations. Mr

Kenny, who received a Tony Award for the sets for *Oliver!* in 1963, died on June 11, 1973.

Scenic Designs:
1962: *Stop the World, I Want to Get Off* **1963:** *Oliver!* **1965:** *Oliver!*; *Pickwick*; *Roar of the Greasepaint – The Smell of the Crowd* **1973:** *Here Are Ladies* **1984:** *Oliver!*

Lighting Designs:
1962: *Stop the World, I Want to Get Off* **1965:** *Roar of the Greasepaint – The Smell of the Crowd* **1973:** *Here Are Ladies*

Costume Designs:
1963: *Oliver!* **1965:** *Oliver!* **1973:** *Here Are Ladies* **1984:** *Oliver!*

Carl Kent

Carl Kent, a set, lighting and costume designer and a native of New York City, was born on January 28, 1918. He studied at the Art Students League and the National Academy of Design. Also well known as a jazz pianist, he entered theatre as a technical supervisor and assistant to scenic designer Harry Horner. His credits for sets on Broadway were numerous and he occasionally designed costumes as well. Mr. Kent also designed sets for NBC-TV and CBS-TV. In addition to the theatre he designed for ballet, including *The New Yorker* for Ballet Russe in 1940. Mr. Kent died in New York City on December 13, 1959.

Scenic Designs:
1940: *'Tis of Thee* **1944:** *Career Angel* **1945:** *Concert Varieties* **1949:** *Leaf and Bough*

Lighting Designs:
1944: *Peepshow*

Costume Designs:
1945: *Concert Varieties*

Leo Kerz

Leo Kerz was a scenic, lighting, and costume designer, as well as a producer and director. He was born November 1, 1912 in Berlin, and studied there with Bertolt Brecht, Erwin Piscator and Laszlo Moholy-Nagy. His first settings were produced in Berlin in 1932, after which he designed throughout Europe and in South Africa. He came to the United States in 1942 and assisted Jo Mielziner, Watson Barratt and Stewart Chaney. He also designed sets for numerous operas, including *The Magic Flute* and *Parsifal* for the Metropolitan Opera, and the premieres of *The Moon* by Carl Orff and *The Tempest* by Frank Marin at New York City Opera in collaboration with Erich Leinsdorf. He also designed for films and television, including a stint as a CBS-TV staff designer between 1949 and 1954. Mr. Kerz, who lectured widely and wrote on trends in design, died on November 4, 1976 in New York City.

Scenic Designs:
1947: *Anthony and Cleopatra*; *Open House* **1948:** *Bravo*; *For Heaven's Sake, Mother* **1949:** *Biggest Thief in Town, The* **1950:** *Edwina Black* **1952:** *Sacred Flame, The*; *Whistler's Grandmother* **1954:** *Hit the Trail* **1959:** *Moonbirds* **1961:** *Rhinoceros* **1973:** *Children of the Wind*

Lighting Designs:
1944: *According to Law*; *Strange Play, A* **1946:** *Christopher Blake*; *Flamingo Road* **1947:** *Heads Or Tails*; *Little A*; *Lousianna Lady*; *Open House* **1948:** *For Heaven's Sake, Mother*; *Me and Molly* **1949:** *Biggest Thief in Town, The* **1950:** *Edwina Black* **1951:** *Ti-Coq* **1952:** *Sacred Flame, The*; *Whistler's Grandmother* **1954:** *Hit the Trail* **1959:** *Moonbirds* **1961:** *Rhinoceros* **1973:** *Children of the Wind*

Costume Designs:
1947: *Open House*

Philip Kessler

Philip Kessler designed sets and costumes for a Broadway play in 1947.

Scenic Designs:
1947: *Trial Honeymoon*

Costume Designs:
1947: *Trial Honeymoon*

Frederick J. Kiesler

Frederick John Kiesler lived from September 22, 1892 to December 27, 1965 and worked as an architect and scenic designer. He was born in Vienna and came to the United States in 1926. He was head of set design at the Juilliard School of Music from 1933 to 1957 and director of the Laboratory at the Columbia University School of Architecture. His first set was for *R.U.R.* in 1922 in Berlin. He received credit for numerous designs at Juilliard, exhibited architectual and theatrical designs, and influenced the emerging environmental theatre with plans and design for "Endless Theatre." He also designed the first projected scenery at the Metropolitan Opera, for *In the Pasha's Garden* in 1935. He was a member of United Scenic Artists from 1934 to 1965.

Scenic Designs:

1946: *No Exit*

Lighting Designs:

1946: *No Exit*

Alan Kimmel

A scene designer for stage and television, Alan Kimmel designed his first production in New York City the year before he received a B.F.A. in Scene Design from the Carnegie Institute of Technology in June 1959. His debut production, *Sweeney Todd* (the melodrama) in September 1958, opened the Sullivan Street Playhouse, shortly after the home of the *Fantastics*. From 1972 to 1982 he was staff designer for ABC-TV. In 1983 he won an Emmy Award for the set design of *The Morning Show* on ABC-TV. He received a grant from the state of New York to implement a practical internship program allowing senior design majors from the State University of New York at Fredonia to spend a resident semester in New York City. Alan Kimmel, who currently lectures at Fordham University on "Language and Knowing," was born on April 9, 1938 in Cedarhurst, New York. Recent theatre designs include *Carnal Knowledge* at the Kaufman Theatre.

Scenic Designs:

1971: *You're a Good Man, Charlie Brown*
1972: *Mother Earth*

Costume Designs:

1971: *You're a Good Man, Charlie Brown*

Alexander King, Jr.

Alexander King, Jr. designed interiors for a Broadway show in collaboration with Joseph Physioc. He was born Alexander Konig in Vienna on November 13, 1899 and came to the United States with his parents prior to World War I, becoming a citizen in 1920. He studied painting and began illustrating magazines

and books, including a special edition of Eugene O'Neill's plays. Between 1930 and 1955 he stopped painting, became an editor, was associated with *Americana, Stage, Life* and *Vanity Fair* and began writing. In 1959 he appeared on the Jack Parr television show and was a big success with his witty, irreverent commentary, which he used to a good effect on many subsequent television appearances until his death on November 17, 1965. Volumes in his memoirs include *Mine Enemy Grows Older, May this House Be Safe from Tigers* and *Rich Man, Poor Man,* and *Freud and Fruit.*

Scenic Designs:

1920: *Scrambled Wives*

Lawrence King

has designed sets and costumes on Broadway since 1975. A native of Wichita, Kansas, he received a B.A. at Wichita State University and his M.F.A at Yale. *The Rivals* for the Yale Rep was his first professional design assignment. He has designed many productions for regional theatres, off-Broadway theatres, and opera companies. Recent credits include *Hothouse* and *The Contractor* at the Chelsea Theatre Company. Mr. King often works in collaboration with designer Michael Yeargan and director Robert Drivas.

Scenic Designs:

1974: *My Sister, My Sister* **1975:** *Ritz, The*
1976: *Me Jack, You Jill* **1977:** *Night of the Tribades, The*; *Something Old, Something New*
1978: *Cheaters* **1981:** *It Had to Be You*

Costume Designs:

1975: *Ritz, The* **1976:** *Me Jack, You Jill* **1977:** *Something Old, Something New*

Sam Kirkpatrick

Sam Kirkpatrick was born on October 25, 1940 in County Fermanagh, Ireland. After completing his "A" level exams he studied at the Belfast College of Art for two years, and in 1962 received a diploma with distinction after three years of study at the Central School of Arts and Crafts. *Philoctetes* in 1964 at the National Theatre in London was his professional debut. His designs for costumes and scenery have been seen in Japan, Great Britain, Canada and throughout the United States. He has designed costumes for films including Orson Welles' *Chimes at Midnight*, and productions such as *Rip Van Winkle* and *The Dancing Princess* for Faerie Tale Theatre. The recipient of two Los Angeles Drama Logues for costume design, for *The Misanthrope* in 1982 and *Undiscovered Country* in 1985, he has designed sets and costumes for many productions at the Alabama Shakespeare Festival, The Old Globe, The Guthrie Theatre and the Stratford (Ontario) Festival.

Scenic Designs:
1985: *Wind in the Willows*

Harriet Klamroth

Harriet Klamroth designed one set in 1918 on Broadway. Her designs were included in an exhibit of American designers of the "New Stagecraft" at the Bourgeois Galleries in New York in 1919.

Scenic Designs:
1918: *Crops and Croppers* 1921: *Playboy of the Western World, The*

Alonzo Klaw

Alonzo Klaw, son of Marc Klaw of the producing firm Klaw & Erlanger, was himself a theatrical producer. He was born on April 15, 1885 in Louisville, Kentucky and studied at the New York School of Art and the Art Students League. He designed a single set on Broadway in 1924. He died on January 12, 1944 in Winter Park, Florida at age 58.

Scenic Designs:
1924: *Hell Bent*

William Kline

William Kline was the set designer for the Abbey Theatre Players performances in New York City in the late 1930s. An artist, he resided and had a studio at 244 West 14th Street, New York City in 1920.

Scenic Designs:
1927: *Good Hope, The* 1937: *Honor Bright*

Clayton Knight

Clayton Knight, an illustrator, contributed costume and scenic designs to a Broadway play in 1925. He illustrated several books on aviation and others based on his experiences as an American aviator in World War I. He also illustrated adventure books for boys. He died July 17, 1969 at age 78 in Danbury, Connecticut.

Scenic Designs:
1926: *Henry IV, Part I*

Costume Designs:
1926: *Henry IV, Part I*

H.P. Knight Scenic Studio

The H.P. Knight Scenic Studio received credit for scenic design of two Broadway plays in the teens.

Scenic Designs:
1915: *When the Young Vine Blooms* 1918: *Awakening, The*

Willis Knighton

Willis Knighton was active on Broadway between 1944 and 1949. He first worked in the theatre as a technical director. A teacher of design, Mr. Knighton was associated with the University of Utah and the Dramatic Workshop at the New School for Social Research. In the 1940s he also held the position of summer art director at the Chapel Theatre at Great Neck, Long Island. Knighton Studios was located at 157 Houndsditch, London, England in 1951.

Scenic Designs:
1944: *Meet a Body* 1945: *Brighten the Corner* 1946: *Song of Bernadette* 1949: *Gayden; Shop At Sly Corner, The*

Costume Designs:
1944: *Meet a Body* 1949: *Shop At Sly Corner, The*

John Koenig

John Koenig was born in Berlin in 1911 and brought to the United States as a toddler. He studied at the University of Pennsylvania, Grand Central School of the Arts and the Yale

Drama School. He designed sets and/or costumes for shows in New York, Pasadena, California and for Orson Welles' Mercury Theatre. As Private John Koenig he designed *This is the Army* for Irving Berlin. He served as designer at the Virginia Museum of Fine Arts between 1956 and his death on February 1, 1963.

Scenic Designs:

1937: *Many Mansions* **1938:** *Gloriana; Glorious Morning; Heartbreak House; Here Come the Clowns; Missouri Legend* **1940:** *Charley's Aunt* **1941:** *Little Dark Horse* **1942:** *This Is the Army*

Costume Designs:

1938: *Missouri Legend* **1940:** *Charley's Aunt; Pal Joey* **1941:** *In Time to Come; Pal Joey* **1942:** *This Is the Army*

Fred Kolo

Fred Kolo was born on September 27, 1942 in Columbus, Nebraska, the son of Fred T. and Helen Paulson Kolouch. He received a B.A. at Dartmouth College and attended the Yale University School of Drama, Lester Polakov's Studio and Forum of Stage Design and the Art Students League. He worked as an assistant at the Metropolitan Opera for Raoul Pène Du Bois and made his New York debut with Robert Sealy's *Meat and Potatoes* at Cafe La Mama. He has received two Joseph Jefferson Award nominations in Chicago for productions at the Academy Festival Theatre and three Carbonell Awards in Miami. A designer of scenery, costumes and lights for theatre, television, industrial promotions and film, he also directs, produces and writes. Fred Kolo is also known for his collaborations with Robert Wilson: *The Life and Times of Sigmund Freud* at the Brooklyn Academy of Music; *Deafman Glance* at the Brooklyn Academy of Music, the University of Iowa, the Nancy Festival, Holland Festival and in Paris; and scenery for *The Life and Times of Joseph Stalin* at the Brooklyn Academy of Music and the Teatro Municipal, São Paulo, Brazil.

Scenic Designs:

1990: *Truly Blessed*

Lighting Designs:

1990: *Truly Blessed*

Ralph Koltai

Ralph Koltai, a designer of Hungarian-German descent, was born in Berlin on July 31, 1924 and studied there and at London's Central School of Arts and Crafts, where he was head of theatre design from 1965 to 1973. His first design assignment was the opera *Angelique* in 1950 and since that time he has designed sets and costumes for nearly two hundred plays, operas and ballets around the world. An Associate of the Royal Shakespeare Company from 1963 to 1966 and since 1975, he has also designed for the National Theatre, Royal Opera House, and English National Opera. He directed and designed *The Flying Dutchman* in Hong Kong in 1987 and *Metropolis* in 1988. The recipient of numerous awards, he was co-winner of an Individual Gold Medal for Stage Design and co-winner of the Golden Troika National Award at the 1975 Prague Quadriennale, as well as recipient of the 1979 Designer of the Year Award from the Society of the West End Theatres for *Brand*.

Scenic Designs:

1968: *Soldiers* **1974:** *As You Like It* **1984:** *Cyrano De Bergerac; Much Ado About Nothing* **1985:** *Pack of Lies* **1988:** *Carrie*

Lighting Designs:

1968: *Soldiers*

Costume Designs:

1968: *Soldiers* **1974:** *As You Like It* **1985:** *Pack of Lies*

Theodore Komisarjevsky

Theodore Komisarjevsky, born Fyodor Fyodorovich Komissarzhevsky, began his theatre career in czarist Russia where his sister Vera was one of the great Russian actresses and his father a noted tenor. He was born in Venice on May 23, 1882 and began professional life as an architect, leaving his practice to manage his sister's theatre and gradually directing more and more plays. In 1918 he moved to England, became a British subject, and directed, designed, choreographed, and produced plays with great success at Stratford-upon-Avon and in London. The Theatre Guild initially brought him to New York to stage productions in 1922, and he subsequently returned to the United States to design plays including *Russian Bank* in 1940, *Crime and Punishment* in 1947 and *Love for Three Oranges* at the City Center, leaving when ill health forced his withdrawal. He was the second husband of British actress Peggy Ashcroft and exerted considerable influence on twentieth century theatre interpretations of classical repertory. He died on April 17, 1954.

Scenic Designs:
1922: *Tidings Brought to Mary, The* **1935:** *Escape Me Never*

Pierre Kontchalovsky

Pierre Kontchalovsky designed sets and costumes for a Broadway play in 1925. A major Russian Impressionist painter, he was born Pyotr Konchalovsky. His grandson, Andrei Kontchalovsky emigrated to the United States in 1980 and has directed the films *Duet for One, Runaway Train, Maria's Lovers* and *Shy People*.

Scenic Designs:
1925: *La Perichale*

Costume Designs:
1925: *La Perichale*

Jay Krause

Jay Krause designed sets, lights and costumes for a production on Broadway in 1955.

Scenic Designs:
1955: *Day By the Sea, A*

Lighting Designs:
1955: *Day By the Sea, A*

Costume Designs:
1955: *Day By the Sea, A*

Arnold Kraushaar

Arnold A. Kraushaar designed one set on Broadway in 1920. He operated an art gallery at 680 Fifth Avenue in New York City in 1922. In the mid-1920s he worked as an engineer and resided at 11 Vermilye Avenue in New York City.

Scenic Designs:
1920: *Lady Billy*

Hermann Křehan

See Crayon

Howard Kretz

Howard Kretz designed one set on Broadway in 1916 with Warren Dahler.

Scenic Designs:
1916: *Queen's Enemies, The*

Félix Labisse

Félix Louis Victor Léon Labisse was a painter and scenic designer who founded the Club du Cinema in Ostend, Belgium. He served as editor-in-chief for *Tribord* in Ostend from 1927 to 1931 after which he settled in Paris. Born in Marchiennes, France on March 9, 1905, he exhibited paintings widely in Europe, South America, the Far East and the United States. His works are in the permanent collections of New York City's Museum of Modern Art, Paris' Musée d'Art Moderne, and the Museé de Lille. In addition to scenic design on Broadway he has created theatrical settings for the Comédie Française, the Ballets de Monte-Carlo, and for theatre companies in Lyon, Geneva and Lausanne. He began designing in Paris in 1935 and designed numerous productions through the thirties, forties and fifties.

Scenic Designs:
1952: *Le Process*; *Occupe Toi d'Amelie*

Lighting Designs:
1952: *Le Process*

Paul Laighton

Paul Laighton was responsible for one scenic design in 1915 on Broadway. In 1918 he was the manager of the Bramhall Playhouse, 138 East 27th Street, New York City.

Scenic Designs:
1915: *Importance of Coming and Going, The*

Suzanne Lalique

Suzanne Lalique designed two shows on Broadway in 1955. A French designer, she was the daughter of the French glass artist. She made her debut in Paris with sets and costumes for the Comédie Française production of *Chacun Sa Vérité* in 1937, and designed many additional productions at the Comédie Française during the 1940s and 1950s. Her film work includes *Le*

Bourgeois Gentilhomme (1958) and *Le Marriage de Figaro* (1959) with the director Jean Meyer. Her exotic still-lifes were exhibited at Bergdorf Goodman in 1933.

Scenic Designs:
1955: *Le Bourgeois Gentilhomme*

Costume Designs:
1955: *Le Bourgeois Gentilhomme*; *Le Jeu De l'Amour et Du Hasard*

Sir Osbert Lancaster

Sir Osbert Lancaster became a cartoonist for the *Daily Express* in 1939. He was born in London on August 4, 1908, and after studying law and English literature attended the Slade School of Art. He also created illustrations for book jackets, large murals, and posters for the London Transport System. He was a member of the editorial board of the *Architectural Review* and also wrote on architecture. Beginning in the early 1950s Sir Osbert Lancaster designed sets and costumes for many companies including the Royal Ballet at Covent Garden, the Glyndebourne Opera, the D'Oyly Carte Opera, and for ballets such as *Pineapple Poll*, *Bonne Bouche*, *Coppélia* and *La Fille Mal Gardée*. Sir Osbert Lancaster, who was knighted in 1975, died in 1986.

Scenic Designs:
1957: *Hotel Paradiso*

Costume Designs:
1957: *Hotel Paradiso*

Jack Landau

Jack Landau, a director and producer, was born on January 5, 1925 in Braddock, Pennsylvania and studied in the United States and England, including a year at the Old Vic in London. During the 1940s and 1950s while designing sets, costumes, and occasionally lights for plays, he gradually began directing. In 1956 he joined the American Shakespeare Festival Theatre and Academy as associate director and directed numerous plays for the company. He has also designed, produced and directed for television. Mr. Landau died on March 16, 1967 in Boston at 42 years of age.

Scenic Designs:
1950: *Phoenix Too Frequent, A* 1951: *Buy Me Blue Ribbons* 1952: *Dear Barbarians*

Lighting Designs:
1944: *War President*

Costume Designs:
1950: *Phoenix Too Frequent, A* 1951: *Buy Me Blue Ribbons* 1952: *Dear Barbarians*

Heidi Landesman

Heidi Landesman was born on August 16, 1951 in San Francisco to Richard Prentice Ettinger and Barbara Lynn Ettinger. She received a B.F.A. at Occidental College in Los Angeles where her first design assignment was *King David*. Heidi Landesman designs both sets and costumes for plays when possible, but has additional credits for set design. Productions include *A Midsummer Nights' Dream* at the Delacorte Theatre, and *Painting Churches, American Passion* and many other productions off-Broadway and in regional theatres. She received an Obie for the sets for *Painting Churches* and Drama Desk, Maharam and Tony Awards for the sets for *Big River*. She is also a producer. Recent credits include scenery for the 1991 Broadway production of *The Secret Garden*, which she also co-produced with Richard Steiner, Elizabeth Williams, Frederic H. Mayerson and Dodger Productions.

Scenic Designs:
1983: *'Night Mother* 1985: *Big River*

Costume Designs:
1983: *'Night Mother*

Henry Landish

Henry Landish created one scenic design on Broadway in 1932.

Scenic Designs:
1932: *House of Doom, The*

Hugh Landwehr

Hugh Landwehr is a scenic designer who studied at Yale University, where he received a B.A. in 1972. For five years he was an assistant designer for the Hartford Stage Company. Although based in New York City, he designs extensively for Center Stage in Baltimore, an association which began with *The Runner Stumbles* in 1977. In 1982 he received a grant from the

National Endowment of the Arts to be artistic associate at Center Stage where he worked on over two dozen productions. He has designed many off-Broadway productions such as *Snow Orchid* at Circle Rep, *Lady House Blues, Chekov Sketchbook, Tazi Tales* at the Century Theatre and *Marion* at the Juilliard School. Regional theatre credits include productions at the Milwaukee Repertory Theatre, Alaska Rep, and the Santa Fe Festival.

Scenic Designs:

1983: *View from the Bridge, A* **1987:** *All My Sons*

Edgar Lansbury

Edgar George McIldowie Lansbury was born in London on January 12, 1930 and came to the United States in 1941, becoming a naturalized citizen in 1953. Known primarily as a film producer and art director, he began in theatre as an apprentice at the Windham (New Hampshire) Playhouse in 1947, where he returned to design in 1953-54. His New York debut was *The Wise have not Spoken* at the Cherry Lane Theatre in 1954. He served as art director for ABC-TV in 1955, and CBS-TV from 1955 to 1962, and in 1964 formed Edgar Lansbury Productions, a motion picture and theatre production company. He has subsequently produced many shows on Broadway, including *Gypsy* (1974), *American Buffalo* (1977), and *Broadway Follies* (1981). Films include *Godspell* (1973), *The Subject Was Roses* (1968), and *The Clairvoyant* (1982). *The Subject Was Roses*, which he produced, won a Tony Award as Best Play in 1963. His most recent production was *All The Queen's Men* at the Westport Country Playhouse in 1989.

Scenic Designs:

1964: *Subject Was Roses, The*

Roy LaPaugh

Roy LaPaugh designed one set on Broadway in 1933.

Scenic Designs:

1933: *Mountain, The*

Peter Larkin

Peter Larkin, a designer of sets, lights and sometimes costumes, was born in Boston on August 25, 1926. He studied at Yale University and with Oliver Larkin. His Broadway debut as a scenic designer was in 1952 but he made his New York debut a year earlier with *The Wild Duck* at City Center. He has been honored for outstanding set design with Tony Awards for *Teahouse of the August Moon* and *Ondine* in 1954 and *Inherit the Wind* and *No Time for Sergants* in 1956, as well as a Maharam Award for *Les Blancs* (1970). Additional credits include production design for the films *Tootsie, Compromising Positions* and *Three Men and a Baby*, and art direction for *Reuben, Reuben* among others.

Scenic Designs:

1952: *Dial M for Murder* **1953:** *Teahouse of the August Moon, The* **1954:** *Ondine; Peter Pan* **1955:** *Inherit the Wind; No Time for Sergeants* **1956:** *New Faces of '56; Protective Custody; Shangri-La* **1957:** *Compulsion; Good As Gold; Miss Isobel* **1958:** *Blue Denim; Goldilocks; Shadow of a Gunman, The* **1959:** *First Impressions; Only in America* **1960:** *Greenwillow; Wildcat* **1962:** *Giants, Sons of Giants; Nowhere To Go But Up* **1963:** *Marathon '33* **1964:** *Crucible, The; Seagull, The* **1966:** *Great Indoors, The; Hail Scrawdyke!* **1970:** *Les Blancs; Sheep of the Runway* **1971:** *Twigs* **1972:** *Wise Child* **1973:** *Let Me Hear You Smile* **1974:** *Thieves* **1977:** *Ladies At the Alamo* **1978:** *Dancin'* **1979:** *Break a Leg* **1981:** *Broadway Follies* **1983:** *Doonesbury* **1984:** *Rink, The* **1986:** *Big Deal*

Lighting Designs:

1952: *Dial M for Murder* **1953:** *Teahouse of the August Moon, The* **1955:** *Damn Yankees* **1956:** *Shangri-La*

Costume Designs:

1956: *Protective Custody*

Johannes Larsen

A scenic and lighting designer, Johannes Larsen designed one Broadway show in 1940. He designed the scenery for four additional shows between 1939 and 1942. He worked in the construction trade in the early 1930s and resided at 636 West 138th Street in New York City.

Scenic Designs:
1939: *Three Sisters, The* **1940:** *Boyd's Daughter; Return Engagement* **1942:** *First Crocus, The*

Lighting Designs:
1940: *Boyd's Daughter*

Yngve Larson

Yngve Larson designed one set in 1962 for a Broadway production.

Scenic Designs:
1962: *Miss Julie*

Lee Lash

Through the Lee Lash Studios, Lee and Samuel Lash designed theatrical productions and constructed those designed by others. The studio was located in Mt. Vernon, New York in the late twenties and at 1476 Broadway in 1931. Lee Lash was born in San Fransisco in 1864 and was active as a scenic artist in New York City at the turn of the century. He participated in a painting exhibition in 1893 in New York City.

Scenic Designs:
1934: *Tomorrow's Harvest*

Margaret Lathem

Margaret Lathem was active on Broadway as a scenic designer in the mid-1920s.

Scenic Designs:
1924: *Try It with Alice*

Alice Laughlin

Alice Denniston Laughlin designed one set in 1933 on Broadway. A painter, muralist, designer of stained glass and woodcuts, and an expert on medieval art, she was born on October 19, 1895 in New York City and died on July 30, 1952 in Pittsburgh, Pennsylvania. She studied with Vassily Shoukhoeff in Paris and at the New York Art Students League and participated in many exhibitions of stained glass and woodcuts.

Scenic Designs:
1933: *La Nativite*

Jules Laurentz

Jules Laurentz designed one set in 1936 on Broadway. His scenery construction business, J. Laurentz Studios, was active in New York before World War II.

Scenic Designs:
1936: *To My Husband*

Laverdet

Laverdet (a.k.a London Laverdet) was a French set designer who worked as a scenic artist and occasionally designed for the Comédie Française. He was active in New York between 1924 and 1929 creating sets and costumes. Laverdet also received credit for scenery and/or costumes for some thirty-six productions on the London stage during the 1920s, and designed scenery for *Mieux que Nue!* with Deshayes and Arnaud, Ronsin, Roger and Durand, and Canut at the Moulin Rouge Music-Hall in Paris in 1925.

Scenic Designs:
1924: *Andre Charlot's Revue of 1924* **1925:** *Charlot Revue* **1928:** *This Year of Grace* **1929:** *Wake Up and Dream*

Costume Designs:
1929: *Wake Up and Dream*

Lavignac & Pellegry

Lavignac & Pellegry collaborated on the design for a Broadway set in 1939. The production originated in France.

Scenic Designs:
1939: *Folies Bergère*

Roger LaVoie

Roger LaVoie designed scenery for the concert version of *Sally* performed on Broadway at the Academy Theatre. He was born on December 12, 1947 in Fitchburg, Massachusetts, the son of John J. LaVoie and Dorothy E. LeGére. He received a B.A. at Emerson College and an M.F.A. at the Yale University School of Drama. Roger LaVoie includes director Tom Haas and designer John Conklin as influential figures in his life and on his designs. His career began at Emerson College in 1967 with a production of *Peer Gynt*.

Scenic Designs:
1987: *Sally*

H. Robert Law

H. Robert Law designed scenery and also worked in collaboration with others, including P. Dodd Ackerman. For example, for *World of Pleasure* he designed Act I, Scenes 1, 3, 4 and Act II, Scene 2, with Ackerman doing Act I, Scene 2 and Act II, Scenes 1, 3, and 4. He designed many productions under his own name and also had an active studio where his own designs were produced as well as others. He also produced vaudeville productions and is credited with the scenery in collaboration with Marc Henri and Oliver Bernard, for the two-part revue *The Rainbow* in 1923 in London. H. Robert Law died on October 20, 1925 at age 49, although the studio bearing his name remained active on Broadway through 1931.

Scenic Designs:
1915: *Maid in America; Three of Hearts; Ware Case, The; White Feather, The; World of Pleasure, A* **1916:** *David Garrick; Fixing Sister; Man Who Came Back, The; Robinson Crusoe, Jr.* **1917:** *Out There; When Johnny Comes Marching Home* **1918:** *Her Country; Hitchy Koo 1918; Oh, Look!* **1919:** *At 9:45* **1921:** *Intimate Strangers, The* **1923:** *Sun Showers* **1924:** *Keep Kool*

H. Robert Law Studio

H. Robert Law began his Broadway career in 1915 and designed both under his own name and through a scenic studio. The H. Robert Law Studio was located at 502 West 138th Street in New York City and continued in operation until 1931.

Scenic Designs:
1915: *Mr. Myd's Mystery* **1916:** *His Majesty Bunker Bean; Master, The* **1917:** *Eileen* **1918:** *Listen Lester; Stitch in Time, A* **1919:** *Hitchy Koo 1919; Luck in Pawn; Velvet Lady, The* **1920:** *As You Were; Look Who's Here; Poldekin; Scandals of 1920* **1921:** *Dulcy; Golden Days; Peg O' My Heart; Two Little Girls* **1922:** *Endless Chain, The; French Doll, The; Just Because; Molly Darling; Our Nell; Persons Unknown; Queen O'Hearts* **1923:** *Runnin' Wild* **1924:** *Be Yourself; Dawn; I'll Say She Is; New Poor, The* **1925:** *Kosher Kitty Kelly; Tell Me More* **1931:** *Little Women*

Joseph Law

Joseph Law designed one set in 1922 on Broadway. A carpenter, he resided at 1018 Avenue A in New York City in 1916.

Scenic Designs:
1922: *Spice of 1922*

Les Lawrence

Les Lawrence, a sculptor and ceramist, was born Edwin Lawrence in Corpus Christi, Texas on December 17, 1940. He attended Southwestern State College in Weatherford, Oklahoma where he received a B.A. He also attended Arizona State University where he received an M.F.A. in ceramics in 1970 and served on the faculty as a guest artist. He has exhibited in numerous art shows and has received many prizes and awards.

Scenic Designs:
1972: *Jacques Brel Is Alive and Living in Paris*

Kate Drain Lawson

Kate Drain Lawson, a scenic designer, actress, theatre executive and costume designer, was born Kate Drain in Spokane, Washington on July 27, 1894. She attended art school in Paris and first appeared on stage as a dancer in Paris in 1921. She was married to playwright John Howard Lawson from 1918 to 1924. She began on Broadway as an assistant stage manager and during her career served in various capacities such as assistant to the designer, technical director, musical director and designer. During World War I she served with the Ambulance Americaine and in World War II served with the Red Cross in India. This multi-talented artist appeared in numerous films, designed for television and organized the costume department on the West Coast for NBC-TV, retiring in 1976. She died at age 83 on November 14, 1977.

Scenic Designs:
1926: *Chief Thing, The* **1927:** *Mr. Pim Passes By* **1930:** *Garrick Gaieties* **1934:** *Four Saints in Three Acts; Valley Forge* **1935:** *Eden End; Slight Case of Murder, A; To See Ourselves* **1936:** *Holmses of Baker Street, The; Love from a Stranger* **1937:** *Point of Honor, A*

Costume Designs:
1923: *Roger Bloomer* **1930:** *Garrick Gaieties* **1934:** *Four Saints in Three Acts* **1935:** *Slight*

Case of Murder, A; *Stick-in-the-Mud* **1937:**
Point of Honor, A **1938:** *Knights of Song* **1940:**
Meet the People

Mark Lawson

Mark Lawson was born in Stockholm, Sweden,
but came to Chicago with his parents when he
was six months old. He later lived in St. Paul
and Minneapolis, Minnesota where he learned
to paint scenery from Paul Clausen, at that
time the region's premier scenic artist. He subsequently worked at Boston's Stetson's Globe
Theatre before moving to New York City, where
he was active on Broadway as a set designer from
1919 to 1922. He joined the staff of the New
York Hippodrome when it opened and spent
fourteen years working there, initially with art
director Arthur Voeglin and later as head scenic
artist. He was also on the staff of the Ernest
Grau Studio and the Oden Waller Studio. Mark
Lawson died in New York City at age 62 in May
1928.

Scenic Designs:
1919: *Miss Millions* **1922:** *Better Times*

H.B. Layman

H. Bernard Layman was active on Broadway in
the mid-1920s. In 1921 he was manager of the
exposition department of John H. French Co.,
general building contractors, in New York City.

Scenic Designs:
1926: *Sure Fire*

Wilford Leach

Born Carson Wilford Leach on August 26, 1929
in Petersburg, Virginia, Wilford Leach was the
principal director of the New York Shakespeare
Festival from 1977 until his death on June 18,
1988 at age 59. He taught at Sarah Lawrence
College and was "artistic director" at La Mama
where he created many projects for Ellen Stewart, though always crediting her as artistic director. He attended the College of William and
Mary (A.B., 1949) and the University of Illinois
(M.A., 1954, Ph.D., 1957). A workshop production at the Public Theatre of *The Mandrake*
led to his initial New York Shakespeare Festival
in the Park productions, *All's Well That Ends*

Well and *The Taming of the Shrew.* In the fall of
1979 he gave up teaching and joined the Public
Theatre full-time. He received Tony Awards for
directing for *The Pirates of Penzance* and *The
Mystery of Edwin Drood.*

Scenic Designs:
1981: *Pirates of Penzance, The*

Jean-Guy Lecat

Jean-Guy Lecat has been technical director for
Peter Brook since 1976, in charge of adapting
the many different spaces where Brook's company has performed around the world. He entered theatre in 1967 as assistant set designer at
the Théâtre du Vieux Colombier and the Avin-
gon Festival. An experienced stage manager,
scenographer, lighting and scenic designer, he
has worked at La Mama and The Living Theatre
and designed productions for Jean-Louis Barrault, Jean-Pierre Vincent, Dario Fo, Jean Vilar
and others.

Scenic Designs:
1983: *La Tragedie De Carmen*

Eugene Lee

Eugene Lee has many recent design credits for
television including *Night Music, Kids in the
Hall,* and *House Party.* He is a proponent of real
items instead of façades and of environmental
settings which encompass not only the stage but
the entire theatre space, including the relationship between actor and audience. Eugene Lee
is well known as the designer of *Saturday Night
Live,* which he initially designed in collaboration
with his former wife, Franne Lee. He has been
principal designer at Trinity Square since 1968
and with David Rotundo is co-owner of Scenic
Services, a lighting and design company located
in Providence, Rhode Island. His first professional designs were *A Dream of Love* and *Belch*
at the Theatre of the Living Arts in Philadelphia
in 1966. Eugene and Franne Lee received the
"most promising designers" Drama Desk Award
in 1970-71 and each recieved a Tony, Marharam
and Drama Desk Award for *Candide.* Their
scenic design for *Sweeney Todd* also garnered a
Tony Award. Born on March 9, 1939, he studied at Carnegie-Mellon and Yale and has been
married to Brooke Lutz since 1981.

Scenic Designs:
1970: *Wilson in the Promise Land* 1972: *Dude*
1974: *Candide* 1975: *Skin of Our Teeth, The*
1977: *Some of My Best Friends* 1979: *Gilda
Radner Live from N.Y.*; *Sweeney Todd* 1981:
Merrily We Roll Along 1982: *Agnes of God*;
Hothouse, The

Lighting Designs:
1982: *Hothouse, The*

Franne Lee

Franne Lee has designed many productions both
on and off-Broadway, concentrating mainly on
costumes. She began her career with the Theatre of the Living Arts in Philadelphia, and since
then has designed throughout the United States
and in Europe for Peter Brook's International
Center for Theatre Research. Franne Lee has
received two Tony awards, for *Candide* in 1974
and for *Sweeney Todd* in 1979. Born Franne
Newman on December 30, 1941 in the Bronx
she received an M.F.A. from the University of
Wisconsin-Madison. She went to Madison in-
tending to study art, but while assisting an art
instructor paint a set, discovered the theatre.
Her first design was *Oh Dad, Poor Dad, Mama's
Hung You in the Closet and I'm Feeling So Bad*.
She has designed costumes for films, including
*One Trick Pony, Dead Ringer, The Local Stig-
matic* and *Baby, It's You*. Television credits include *The Scarlet Letter* on PBS and the first
five years of *Saturday Night Live* on NBC-TV,
designed in conjunction with her former husband, Eugene Lee.

Scenic Designs:
1972: *Dude*

Costume Designs:
1974: *Candide*; *Love for Love* 1975: *Skin of
Our Teeth, The* 1977: *Some of My Best Friends*
1979: *Gilda Radner Live from N.Y.*; *Sweeney
Todd* 1981: *Moony Shapiro Song Book, The*
1982: *Rock 'n Roll! The First 5,000 years*

Ming Cho Lee

Ming Cho Lee began designing in New York
City in 1958 with *The Infernal Machine* at the
Phoenix Theatre. He was born in Shanghai on
October 3, 1930 and received a B.A. at Occidental College. He attended the University of California at Los Angeles from 1953 to 1954. He
studied with Chinese watercolorist Kuo-Nyen
Chang and spent five years working as assistant
to Jo Mielziner. Ming Cho Lee's productions on
Broadway are barely representative of his design
work which has been seen for opera, dance and
theatre in major companies around the country.
His originality is remarkable and he has influenced countless students at New York University and at the Yale University School of Drama,
where he is now Co-Chair of Design. He likes to
work with students he has trained and regularly
hires them as assistants. His list of awards is
also long and includes a 1990 Distinguished Career Achievement Award from the National Endowment for the Arts, the Peter Zeisler Award
at Arena Stage in 1987, Maharam Awards for
Electra in 1965 and *Ergo* in 1968, a Tony Award
for *K-2*, a Guggenheim in 1988, and a Los Angeles Drama Critics and Hollywood Drama Logue
Critics Awards for *Traveller in the Dark* in 1985.
His wife, the former Betsy Rapport, works as his
assistant and they have three sons.

Scenic Designs:
1962: *Moon Beseiged, The* 1963: *Mother
Courage and Her Children* 1966: *Slapstick
Tragedy*; *Time for Singing, A* 1967: *Little
Murders* 1968: *Here's Where I Belong* 1969:
Billy; *La Strada* 1972: *Much Ado About Noth-
ing*; *Two Gentlemen of Verona* 1975: *All
God's Chillun Got Wings*; *Glass Menagerie, The*
1976: *For Colored Girls Who Have Considered
Suicide When the* 1977: *Caesar and Cleopa-
tra*; *Romeo and Juliet*; *Shadow Box, The* 1978:
Angel 1979: *Grand Tour, The* 1983: *Glass
Menagerie, The*; *K2* 1986: *Execution of Jus-
tice,*

Lighting Designs:
1962: *Moon Beseiged, The*

Thomas Bailey Lee

Thomas Bailey Lee, an interior and industrial
designer, was born in Costa Rica. He studied at the Traphagen School and the National
Academy. In the late 1930s he was display director at Bonwit Teller, and at the same time
a set and costume designer for the American
Ballet Company. After service in World War
II he formed his own firm and designed exhibitions for the Metropolitan Museum of Art, the
Smithsonian Museum and other museums, and

showrooms for fashion designers. This experience led to hotel design, beginning with Colonial Williamsburg's first motor lodge, and then for hotels all over the world. He completed the design for the interior of the Park-Lane Hotel in New York shortly before his death in July 1971.

Scenic Designs:

1940: *Lousiana Purchase*

Costume Designs:

1940: *Lousiana Purchase; Walk with Music*

Honor Leeming

Honor Leeming supervised the setting for a Broadway play in 1930. She resided at 123 West 57th Street in 1932.

Scenic Designs:

1930: *Out of a Blue Sky*

Charles LeMaire

Charles LeMaire, known primarily as a costume and fashion designer, was born in Chicago and entered the theatre as a vaudeville actor. He became interested in costume design through shopping for and painting fabrics. Known for the glitter and extravagance of his costumes, he first designed costumes in 1919 on Broadway. He made his Broadway debut as a scenic designer as "Sergeant Charles LeMaire" during World War I, but all subsequent scenic designs were in combination with costume designs. In addition to his Broadway credits he designed costumes for Brooks Costume Company and headed its costume department until 1929, when he organized his own firm. After service in World War II he settled in Hollywood and from 1943 to 1960 was Executive Director of Wardrobe at 20th Century Fox Studios. He won three Academy Awards for film designs. Mr. Le Maire died on June 8, 1985 in Palm Springs, California.

Scenic Designs:

1918: *Atta Boy* **1923:** *Hammerstein's Nine O'Clock Revue*

Costume Designs:

1919: *Elsie Janis and Her Gang* **1920:** *Broadway Brevities of 1920* **1922:** *Daffy Dill; Elsie Janis and Her Gang; Ziegfeld Follies: 1922* **1923:** *Hammerstein's Nine O'Clock Revue; Mary Jane McKane; Poppy; Wildflower* **1924:** *Artists and Models; Be Yourself; Betty Lee; Grab Bag, The; Hassard Short's Ritz Revue; Magnolia Lady, The; Rose-Marie; Sitting Pretty; Vogues of 1924* **1925:** *Cocoanuts, The; Earl Carroll's Vanities; Greenwich Village Follies; Merry, Merry; Tell Me More* **1926:** *Betsy; Earl Carroll's Vanities; Ramblers, The; Twinkle, Twinkle* **1927:** *Africana; Five O'Clock Girl; Love Call, The; My Princess; New Yorkers, The; Rufus LeMaire's Affairs; Take the Air* **1928:** *George White's Scandals; Get Me in the Movies; Hello, Daddy; Hello, Yourself; New Moon, The; Rain Or Shine; Rainbow; Three Cheers* **1929:** *Fioretta; George White's Scandals; Midnite Frolics; Murray Anderson's Almanac; Ned Wayburn's Gambols; Sons O' Guns; Sweet Adeline* **1930:** *Ballyhoo; Earl Carroll's Vanities; Fine and Dandy; Flying High; Luana; New Yorkers, The; Princess Charming; Ripples; Strike Up the Band* **1931:** *America's Sweetheart; Earl Carroll's Vanities; East Wind; George White's Scandals; Of Thee I Sing; Shoot the Works; Wonder Bar, The* **1932:** *Ballyhoo of 1932; George White's Music Hall Varieties; Hot-Cha!; Take a Chance* **1933:** *Blackbirds of 1933; Both Your Houses; Melody; Of Thee I Sing* **1934:** *Say When; Ziegfeld Follies: 1934* **1935:** *George White's Scandals* **1936:** *Mainly for Lovers*

Jacques Le Marquet

Jacques Le Marquet designed one setting on Broadway in 1958. He is also the author of *Jardins à la Française*, published in 1972 by Gallimard.

Scenic Designs:

1958: *Theatre National Populaire*

Gertrude Lennox

Actress Gertrude Best Lewin was known during her stage career as Gertrude Lennox. She received credit for a single scenic design on Broadway in 1923 and died on July 11, 1940.

Scenic Designs:

1923: *Meet the Wife*

Jean le Seyeux

Jean le Seyeux wrote musical revues and designed settings in Europe and the United States

United States for productions such as *Femmes en Folie* at the Folies Bergère in the 1935-36 season. Occasionally he designed costumes and scenery as well. Beginning in 1945 he wrote revues for the Casino de Paris in Monte Carlo, continuing there until his death in 1957. He spent the years during World War II in New York writing and designing.

Scenic Designs:
1940: *Earl Carroll's Vanities*

Costume Designs:
1940: *Earl Carroll's Vanities*

Lew Leslie

The producer Lew Leslie was born Lew Lessinsky and started in show business as a vaudeville performer. Beginning in 1928 he produced a series of successful revues on Broadway featuring black performers: *Blackbirds, Rhapsody in Black* and subsequent editions in following seasons. Lew Leslie introduced future stars Ethel Waters, Lena Horne, Bill Robinson, Aida Ward, Billie Cortez and others though these productions, beginning with the hit 1922 *Plantation Revue* starring Florence Mills, which he later produced in London. He died on March 11, 1963 at age 73.

Scenic Designs:
1922: *Plantation Revue*

Samuel Leve

Samuel Leve, a scenic designer who has also occasionally designed costumes and lighting, was born on December 7, 1910 near Pinsk, Russia. He came to the United States in 1920 and studied at Yale University and art schools in New York before beginning his career in theatre designing summer stock. He has designed sets for over one hundred productions on Broadway and at the Metropolitan Opera, the Mercury Theatre, and the Theatre Guild, among others. He has designed throughout the world as well, including productions in Rio de Janeiro, Canada, Israel, and London. He has also designed spectacles and two synagogues; lectured at Yale, New York University, and Florida State University, and written books, including *On Jewish Art.* Samuel Leve's many awards include the 1985 Goldie, named for Abraham Goldfadn, the father of Yiddish Theatre.

Scenic Designs:
1937: *The Miser/ The Great Cat/ Snickering Horses*; *Cherokee Night*; *Julius Caesar*; *Tobias and the Angel* 1938: *Big Blow, The*; *Shoemaker's Holiday, The* 1940: *Medicine Show* 1941: *Beautiful People, The*; *Distant City, The*; *Macbeth* 1942: *All in Favor*; *Beat the Band*; *Life of Reilly, The*; *Mr. Sycamore*; *They Should Have Stood in Bed* 1943: *Apology* 1944: *Dark Hammock*; *Hand in Glove*; *Last Stop*; *Sophie*; *Thank You, Svoboda*; *Wallflower* 1945: *It's a Gift*; *Oh, Brother*; *Round Trip*; *Sound of Hunting, A* 1946: *Family Affair, A* 1947: *Story of Mary Surratt, The* 1949: *Clutterbuck* 1950: *All You Need Is One Good Break* 1951: *Dinosaur Wharf*; *Lace on Her Petticoat* 1952: *Buttrio Square* 1953: *Fifth Season, The* 1955: *Hear! Hear!* 1956: *Double in Hearts*; *Goodbye Again* 1963: *Have I Got a Girl for You* 1964: *Cafe Crown* 1982: *Dybbuck, The*

Lighting Designs:
1937: *Julius Caesar* 1938: *Shoemaker's Holiday, The* 1940: *Medicine Show* 1943: *Apology* 1944: *Hand in Glove* 1948: *Madwoman of Chaillot* 1951: *Dinosaur Wharf* 1952: *Buttrio Square* 1963: *Have I Got a Girl for You*; *Cafe Crown* 1982: *Dybbuck, The*

Costume Designs:
1951: *Dinosaur Wharf*

Michael Levine

Michael Levine was born in Toronto, Canada in 1960 and studied at the Ontario College of Art and the Central School of Art and Design in London. He has designed numerous productions for the Glasgow Citizen's Theatre. Honors include a Dora Mavor Moore Award for the scenic design of *Springs Awakening* at Centerstage in Canada in 1986.

Scenic Designs:
1985: *Strange Interlude*

Pamela Lewis

Pamela Lewis designed one set on Broadway in 1964. She has also designed scenery for two touring productions in Capetown, South Africa: *The Birthday Party* and *Night of the Iguana.*

Scenic Designs:
1964: *Sponomo*

Walter Lewis

Walter Lewis designed scenery in 1927 on Broadway. He was a partner with James Van Sickler in Manhattan Scenic Studios, located at 260 West 10th Street, New York City in the early 1920s and at 28 West 63rd Street in the mid-1920s.

Scenic Designs:
1927: *Africana*

Alice and Irene Lewisohn

Sisters and collaborators Alice and Irene Lewisohn founded the Neighborhood Playhouse, where they directed, designed, adapted and performed numerous plays. Together they also nurtured the talents of countless other designers and performers. They not only designed but directed *Jephthah's Daughter* on Broadway in 1915. Irene, who was active in the Museum of Costume Art and served as its president, died on April 4, 1944. Alice, who married the artist (and occasional costume designer) Herbert E. Crowley, lived in Switzerland after the Neighborhood Playhouse closed. She published the chronicle *The Neighborhood Playhouse* in 1959 and died in Switzerland on January 6, 1972 at age 88.

Scenic Designs:
1915: *Jephthah's Daughter* 1916: *Thanksgiving*

Costume Designs:
1915: *Jephthah's Daughter* 1916: *Thanksgiving*

Hervig Libowitzky

Hervig Libowitzky, a scene designer and art director works primarily in Europe. He was born in Vienna and studied at the Vienna Academy of Fine Art. He has been art director for the films *The Prisoner of Zenda, The Girl From Petrovka, The Fifth Musketeer* and *Permission to Kill*.

Scenic Designs:
1986: *Into The Light*

Oscar Liebetrau

Oscar Liebetrau designed scenery for three plays in the 1920s. He was associated with Cleon Throckmorton, Inc., 102 West 3rd Street, New York City in the early 1930s.

Scenic Designs:
1923: *Sun-Up; Sylvia* 1928: *Sun-Up*

James Light

James "Jimmy" Light was born in Pittsburgh, Pennsylvania where his father, a British contractor, was constructing a building. Raised in England, he returned to the United States at age fourteen, later studying painting and architecture at the Carnegie Institute of Technology and Ohio State University. He moved to New York to attend Columbia University and shared a room over the Neighborhood Playhouse in Greenwich Village with designer Charles Ellis. A chance encounter with Eugene O'Neill at a public swimming pool led to continued interaction and to Light's involvement with the theatre, initially as an actor. In the early 1920s he began directing the plays of August Strindberg and O'Neill, including the first production of *S.S. Glencairn* and a controversial production of *All God's Chillun Got Wings* starring Paul Robeson. He was director of the Experimental Unit of the New York Federal Theatre Project and directed plays including *Chalk Dust*. He served as Dean of the Drama faculty at the New School for Social Research from 1939 to 1942 where he continued to direct. The founder of Reader's Theatre, Jimmy Light died on February 10, 1964 at the age of 69.

Scenic Designs:
1929: *Earth Between, The/ Before Breakfast*

Margaret Linley

Margaret Linley graduated from Smith College. She began her career as an actress at the Pasadena Playhouse and became a casting agent in California. She moved to New York to become casting director for the Theatre Guild, subsequently joined A.&.S Lyons Theatrical Agency and designed one set on Broadway in 1931. Margaret Linley Delima died at age 67 on May 27, 1969 in Altadena, California.

Scenic Designs:
1931: *Jack and the Beanstalk*

Charles Lisanby

Charles Lisanby has created lighting and scenic designs on Broadway since 1955. His television credits are extensive and include *The Garry Moore, Red Skelton,* and *Jack Benny* shows and more than one hundred specials. He has been nominated for nine Emmy Awards and won two, including one for *Baryshnikov on Broadway.* He has designed productions at Radio City Music Hall (including the 1984 *MTV Awards), Night of 100 Stars,* television commercials, and the *Folies Bergère* in Las Vegas. He also designed a Hilton Hotel in Australia.

Scenic Designs:
1957: *Hotel Paradiso* **1979:** *Magnificent Christmas Spectacular, The* **1980:** *Magnificent Christmas Spectacular, The* **1988:** *Christmas Spectacular*

Lighting Designs:
1955: *Little Glass Clock, The* **1956:** *Glass Clock, The*

John Robert Lloyd

John Robert Lloyd, a scenic and sometimes costume and lighting designer, began his career in the theatre as an actor performing in Italian productions. Born in St. Louis on August 4, 1920, he studied at the Art Students League, the Hadley Art School, Washington University and the University of Missouri. He assisted Robert Edmond Jones, Lemuel Ayers and Nat Karson and developed an early specialization in masks, make-up and sculptural stage elements. After working as a designer in summer stock he made his New York debut in 1948 off-Broadway with *The Duenna* at the Greenwich Mews Theatre. His Broadway debut was in 1949. Since that time he has designed numerous industrials, exhibits, films and television shows, both freelance and as staff designer for NBC-TV. John Robert Lloyd has served as production designer for the films *The Boys in the Band, The Owl and the Pussycat,* and *The Exorcist.*

Scenic Designs:
1949: *Touch and Go* **1951:** *Stalag 17* **1952:** *Bernadine* **1955:** *Almost Crazy* **1957:** *Holiday for Lovers; Monique* **1958:** *Drink to Me Only* **1960:** *Laughs and Other Events*

Lighting Designs:
1951: *Stalag 17* **1952:** *Bernadine* **1955:** *Almost Crazy* **1957:** *Holiday for Lovers* **1958:** *Drink to Me Only* **1960:** *Laughs and Other Events*

Costume Designs:
1949: *Mrs. Gibbon's Boys; Touch and Go* **1960:** *Laughs and Other Events*

Adrianne Lobel

Adrianne Lobel was educated at the Yale University School of Drama and has worked as a scenic artist at Chicago's Goodman Theatre and Lyric Opera. She has designed scenery for the American Repertory Theatre, the Juilliard School of Music, the La Jolla Playhouse, Arena Stage, Hartford Stage, the Manhattan Theatre Club, the American Place Theatre and many other off-Broadway and regional theatres. Her awards include the Joseph Jefferson Award for *Play Mas* at the Goodman Theatre. She has often collaborated with Peter Sellars and together they have done *The Government Inspector* at Yale; *The Mikado* for the Chicago Lyric Opera, and *The Visions of Simone Machard* at La Jolla. She has also worked with directors Andrei Serban, Lee Breuer, and Andrei Belgrader and with choreographer Mark Morris, most recently on a production of *The Nutcracker* in Brussels. In 1977 her book, *A Small Sheep in a Pear Tree,* was published by Harper and Row.

Scenic Designs:
1983: *My One and Only*

Robert E. Locher

Robert Evans Locher (a.k.a. Locker), architect and interior designer, was born on November 1, 1888 in Lancaster, Pennsylvania. He designed interiors of public buildings in New York City, Washington, D.C. and other cities, and was associate editor for *House and Garden* at one time. He also created illustrations for *Vogue* and *Vanity Fair,* designed book jackets, and produced industrial designs for Lunt Silversmiths, Sargent Hardware, and Imperial Paper & Color Corporation. He also designed costumes and scenery on Broadway during the 1920s. His work is in the collection of the Whitney Museum of American Art. Robert Locher died on June 18, 1956.

Scenic Designs:
1920: *Greenwich Village Follies* **1921:** *Greenwich Village Follies* **1923:** *Greenwich Village Follies*

Costume Designs:

1920: *What's in a Name* **1921:** *Greenwich Village Follies* **1923:** *Greenwich Village Follies; Jack and Jill* **1929:** *Murray Anderson's Almanac*

Bernard Lohmuller

Bernard Lohmuller designed a set on Broadway in 1927. He resided at 123 West 57th Street in the early 1930s.

Scenic Designs:

1927: *Allez-Oop*

Santo Loquasto

Santo Loquasto received a Liberal Arts degree at King's College and an M.F.A. from Yale. A designer of plays, ballets and operas, he designs both sets and costumes for many of his productions. A native of Wilkes-Barre, Pennsylvania, he was born July 26, 1944. He began designing professionally with *Cat on a Hot Tin Roof* at the Williamstown Theatre Festival in 1965 and designed in New York for the first time in 1970. He is a busy, prolific designer, well-known for the wide range of his talents and his designs for modern playwrights, including Sam Shepard, David Rabe and David Mamet, and modern choreographers such as Twyla Tharp. Often acknowledged as an influence on an emerging generation of designers, he credits Michael Annals and John Conklin as his own mentors. His work in film includes: production design for *Desperately Seeking Susan* and *Alice*; costumes for *Zelig* and *A Midsummer Night's Sex Comedy*; and art direction for *Crimes and Misdemeanors, New York Stories* and *She-Devil*. He is the recipient of numerous awards, including four Tonys (one for scenic design, three for costume design), a Maharam, Drama Desk, American Theatre Wing, Obie, and Outer Critics Circle Awards, and a British Academy Award for the production design of the film *Radio Days*. Recent credits include scenery and costumes for the 1991 Broadway production of Neil Simon's *Lost in Yonkers*.

Scenic Designs:

1972: *Miss Margarida's Way; Sticks and Bones; That Championship Season* **1975:** *Murder Among Friends; Kennedy's Children* **1976:** *Legend* **1977:** *American Buffalo; Cherry Orchard, The; Golda; Miss Margarida's Way*

1978: *King of Hearts; Mighty Gents, The* **1979:** *Bent; Goodbye People, The; Sarava* **1980:** *Suicide, The* **1981:** *Floating Light Bulb, The* **1982:** *Wake of Jamie Foster, The* **1985:** *Singin' in the Rain* **1987:** *Sweet Sue* **1989:** *Cafe Crown; Secret Rapture, The; Tenth Man, The*

Costume Designs:

1975: *Kennedy's Children* **1977:** *American Buffalo; Cherry Orchard, The; Golda; Miss Margarida's Way* **1979:** *Sarava* **1980:** *Suicide, The* **1981:** *Floating Light Bulb, The* **1989:** *Cafe Crown; Grand Hotel, The Musical; Miss Margarida's Way*

David L. Lovett

David L. Lovett designed scenery and costumes on Broadway for the first time in 1980. He has designed for many theatres in Canada, including the Citadel, Rice Theatre and Edmonton Opera. Recent designs include *Most Happy Fella, Komagata Maru Incident*, and *Bedroom Farce*. He also teaches in the Drama Department at the University of Alberta.

Scenic Designs:

1980: *Mister Lincoln*

Costume Designs:

1980: *Mister Lincoln*

Colin Low

Colin Low, a documentary director and animator, was born in 1926 in Cardston, Alberta, Canada. He studied at the Calgary School of Fine Arts and worked initially as a graphic artist for the National Film Board of Canada, gradually changing his focus to animation and directing. He has won numerous awards for his films which include *The Age of the Beaver, Days of Whiskey Gap* and *The Winds of Fogo*.

Scenic Designs:

1961: *Do You Know the Milky Way?*

Lucile

Lucile (a.k.a. Lady Duff Gordon) was born in London in 1862 as Lucy Kennedy and ran an influential fashion house in London, with branches in New York (opened in 1909) and Paris (opened in 1911). Married to Sir Cosmo Duff Gordon, she parlayed her fashion knowledge and insight into an even more successful business venture using her title, Lady Duff Gordon. This pioneering woman designer created gowns which were flamboyant, but were also softly colored and romantic. She often dressed dancers and actresses for Broadway productions, including Irene Castle, and worked regularly for Florenz Ziegfeld. She also designed scenery for a Broadway production in 1936. In 1932 she published her autobiography, *Discretions and Indiscretions*, but died in relative obscurity in 1936 in London.

Scenic Designs:
1936: *Life and Loves of Dorian Gray, The*

Costume Designs:
1915: *Great Lover, The; Ned Wayburn's Town Topics; Shadow, The* **1916:** *Bunny; Cohan Revue, The; Fear Market, The; His Bridal Night* **1917:** *Furs and Frills; Gipsy Trail, The; Her Husband's Wife; Lord and Lady Algy; Miss 1917; Why Marry* **1918:** *Ideal Husband, An; Riddle: Woman, The; Three Faces East; Why Marry?* **1919:** *Curiosity; First is Last; Lady in Red, The; Scandal* **1920:** *Broken Wing, The; Outrageous Mrs. Palmer, The; Sally* **1921:** *Circle, The; Nice People; White Peacock, The; Ziegfeld's 9 O'clock Frolic*

John Plummer Ludlum

John Plummer Ludlum designed one set in 1935 on Broadway.

Scenic Designs:
1935: *Provincetown Follies*

A.J. Lundborg

A.J. Lundborg (Arne Jansteen Lundborg) designed sets for eight Broadway productions between 1928 and 1938. He worked at one time for Gates and Morange, and maintained a studio for painting at 326 West 55st Street in 1932.

Scenic Designs:
1928: *Big Pond, The* **1929:** *Nut Farm, The* **1933:** *World Waits, The* **1934:** *False Dreams, Farewell; Page Miss Glory* **1935:** *Boy Meets Girl* **1936:** *Illustrator's Show, The* **1938:** *School Houses on the Lot*

Kert Lundell

Kert Lundell was born in Malmö, Sweden on June 17, 1936. Mr. Lundell, who studied at Yale, came to New York after study at the Goodman School of Drama. He is a scenic designer who occasionally also contributes costume and lighting designs to productions. His sets for theatre have been seen throughout the United States and in Europe. He served as consultant to the American Place Theatre in 1971 when its new space was built. He has also taught, designed films (including *They All Laughed* in 1981) and designed for television.

Scenic Designs:
1966: *Investigation, The; Under the Weather* **1968:** *Carry Me Back to Morningside Heights* **1971:** *Ain't Supposed to Die a Natural Death; Solitaire/ Double Solitaire* **1972:** *Don't Play Us Cheap; Lincoln Mask, The; Sunshine Boys, The* **1975:** *Hughey/ Duet; Night That Made America Famous, The* **1976:** *1600 Pennsylvania Avenue; Rockabye Hamlet* **1978:** *November People, The* **1982:** *Waltz of the Stork* **1989:** *Shenandoah*

Lighting Designs:
1968: *Carry Me Back to Morningside Heights*

Costume Designs:
1966: *Under the Weather* **1968:** *Carry Me Back to Morningside Heights*

Sir Edwin Lutyens

Sir Edwin Lutyens, a British architect, designed a set on Broadway in 1929. He is best known as the architect of the National Theatre in London, which he designed with Cecil Massey. He is also credited with scenic design for such London productions as *Quality Street* (1921) and *Berkeley Square* (1929). Known for his wide range of talents, he was born in London in March 1869, studied at the Royal College of Art and was influenced early in his career by landscape gardener Gertrude Jekyll. He died on January 1, 1944.

Scenic Designs:
1929: *Berkeley Square*

Tom Lynch

Thomas Michael Lynch was born in Asheville, North Carolina on February 19, 1953 and received B.A. and M.F.A. degrees at Yale University. Influenced by Ming Cho Lee and Robin Wagner, he has also studied painting and printmaking. Awards for his scenic designs include Joseph Jefferson Awards for *Pal Joey* (1988) and *The Time of Your Life* (1989), and a Tony nomination for *The Heidi Chronicles* (1989). His designs for *A Quiet Place*, which he created for the Vienna State Opera, were included in the 1987 Prague Quadrennial Scenography Exhibition. His designs for opera have also been seen in the United States and the Netherlands. He has designed the off-Broadway production and national tour of *Driving Miss Daisy*, the musical version of *Kiss of the Spiderwoman* directed by Hal Prince at the State University of New York at Purchase, and for the New York Shakespeare Festival.

Scenic Designs:
1980: *Tintypes* **1984:** *Design for Living* **1985:** *Arms and the Man* **1986:** *You Can Never Tell* **1989:** *Heidi Chronicles, The*

Molly MacEwan

Molly MacEwan designed sets for two Broadway plays in 1948.

Scenic Designs:
1948: *John Bull's Other Island; Where Stars Walk*

Ian Lloyd MacKenzie

In 1930 Ian Lloyd MacKenzie designed sets for a Broadway play. An actor, he returned to New York in 1940 to appear in *King Lear* and *Macbeth* and had also planned to make a film of *Richard III*.

Scenic Designs:
1930: *Marigold*

Woods Mackintosh

Woods Mackintosh has designed off-Broadway at the New York Shakespeare Festival, Proposition and The Hudson Guild. He has been art director for numerous films, including *Remo Williams: The Adventure Begins*, *Jaws 3-D*, *The World According to Garp* and *One Trick Pony*. Recent credits include *Struck Dumb* by

Jean-Claude van Itallie at the American Place Theatre.

Scenic Designs:
1978: *Runaways*

Elizabeth MacLeish

Elizabeth MacLeish designed one set in 1977 on Broadway.

Scenic Designs:
1977: *Ipi Tombi*

Jack Maclennan

Jack Maclennan designed sets and lights for one play in 1935. An electrician, he resided at 4523 Barnes Avenue in New York City with his wife Mary in 1932.

Scenic Designs:
1935: *Something More Important/The Old Woman/etc.*

Lighting Designs:
1935: *Something More Important/The Old Woman/etc.*

Michael MacLiammoir

Michael MacLiammoir (a.k.a. Micheál M'Liammóir), known primarily as an actor and director, was born on October 24, 1899 in County Cork, Ireland. He studied painting at the Slade Art School in London. He occasionally designed sets and costumes for plays in which he acted or directed. His credits at Dublin's Gate Theatre – which he founded with Hilton Edwards – were extensive. He performed onstage as a child in 1911 and on Broadway in 1948 when the Gate Theatre Company toured in a play he designed. He appeared often in London and Ireland in films and on television. An author of poems, plays and short stories, usually in Gaelic, he died on March 6, 1978 in Dublin.

Scenic Designs:
1948: *Old Lady Says "No", The*

Costume Designs:
1948: *Old Lady Says "No", The*

Georg Magnusson

Georg Magnusson designed sets for a production on Broadway in the early 1960s presented by the Royal Dramatic Theatre of Sweden.

Scenic Designs:
1962: *Long Day's Journey Into Night*

Bruno Maine

Bruno Jalmar Manninen was born in Finland and came to the United States at age thirteen, changing his name when he became a citizen in 1923. He apprenticed at a scenic studio and subsequently designed for John Murray Anderson. In 1933 he succeeded Vincent Minnelli as Art Director at Radio City Music Hall, where he remained for eighteen years. His Christmas and Easter Pageants were well known, as were the ice shows he designed for Sonja Henie and the inaugural balls he created for Dwight D. Eisenhower in 1953 and 1957. Bruno Maine died at age 65 on July 30, 1962.

Scenic Designs:
1942: *Stars on Ice* 1944: *Hats Off to Ice* 1947: *Icetime of 1948* 1948: *Howdy, Mr. Ice* 1949: *Howdy Mr. Ice of 1950*

Lighting Designs:
1951: *Bagels and Yox*

Alexander Maissel

Alexander Maissel has directed musicals including *Trial by Jury* and *Iolanthe* at the Cherry Lane Theatre. In the early 1960s he was musical director of *Pirates of Penzance* at the Light Opera of the Provincetown Playhouse, where he also directed *Ruddigore*. In the 1930s he was a partner with Aida Maissel and John F. Grahame in Theatre Art Productions, theatrical producers, located at 147 West 46th Street in New York City.

Scenic Designs:
1934: *Wrong Number*

Jean-Denis Malclès

Jean-Denis Malclès designed scenery and costumes on Broadway in the 1950s. Born in Paris on May 15, 1912, the son of a sculptor, he is a painter, lithographer and theatrical designer.

He studied with Louis Gognot and Rulhmann and has exhibited at Salon d'Automne and the Salon des Artistes Décorateurs. Honors include the Chevalier de la Légion d'Honneur. He has designed for many theatres, including the Opéra de Paris, Comédie Française, La Scala, Covent Garden, Le Théâtre de Jean Anouilh and Cie Renaud-Barrault.

Scenic Designs:
1952: *La Repetition Ou l'Amour Puni* 1957: *Romanoff and Juliet*

Costume Designs:
1952: *La Repetition Ou l'Amour Puni; Occupe Toi d'Amelie*

Vincent Mallory

Vincent Mallory designed sets on Broadway in the mid-1930s. He wrote *Sound in the Theatre* in collaboration with Harold Burris-Meyer and Lewis S. Goodfriend. Mallory died shortly after the first edition was published in 1959 by Theatre Arts Books.

Scenic Designs:
1934: *Green Stick*

Philip Maltese

Philip Maltese designed one set in 1932 on Broadway.

Scenic Designs:
1932: *Show-Off, The*

Lawrence Mansfield

Lawrence Mansfield designed one set in 1951 on Broadway.

Scenic Designs:
1951: *Springtime for Henry*

James Maronek

James Maronek is from Milwaukee, Wisconsin where he was born on December 4, 1931. He studied at the Layon School of Art in Milwaukee and earned an M.F.A. at the Art Institute of Chicago. He has received Chicago's Joseph Jefferson Award for Best Scenic Design for *Guys and Dolls* at the Goodman Theatre, and anoather Jefferson for Best Lighting Design for *Beckoning Fair One* at the Organic Theatre. He has also been active as a member and officer of United Scenic Artists.

Scenic Designs:

1982: *Do Black Patent Leather Shoes Really Reflect Up?*

Luis Marquez

Luis Marquez designed the scenery for one play on Broadway in 1942.

Scenic Designs:

1949: *Cabalagata (a.k.a. A Night in Spain)*

Reginald Marsh

Reginald Marsh, a painter of realistic scenes of New York life, was the son of artists. His paintings hang in the Metropolitan Museum of Modern Art and the Whitney Museum, among others. He was born in Paris on March 14, 1898 and moved with his family to Nutley, New Jersey when he was two. He graduated from Yale in 1920 and studied at the Art Students League. In the early 1920s he drew illustrations for magazines and "cartoonicle chronicles" of the vaudeville circuit. In the mid-twenties he began illustrating in *The New Yorker* and continued to contribute to the magazine throughout his life. He also designed sets while beginning to seriously paint and develop his artistic style. In addition to the scenery he designed in the mid-1920s on Broadway productions for movie houses and dance centers and the curtain for Otis Skinner's *Sancho Panza.*

Scenic Designs:

1922: *Greenwich Village Follies* **1924:** *Fashion*

Martin

Martin designed sets for one Broadway show in 1933.

Scenic Designs:

1933: *Tattle Tales*

Hugh Mason

Hugh Mason designed a set on Broadway in the mid-1930s. He resided with his wife Elizabeth at 3120 Bainbridge Avenue in New York City in 1932.

Scenic Designs:

1933: *Raw Meat*

Richard Mason

Richard G. Mason was born in New York City in 1929, the son of Dr. and Mrs. G. R. Mason. He received a B.A. from Swarthmore College in 1950 and an M.F.A. from the Yale University School of Drama. His teachers and mentors include Donald Oenslager, Frank Poole Bevan, H.A. Condell and Mordecai Gorelik, whom he also assisted. He designed costumes for *Uncle Vanya* at the Fourth Street Theatre in the mid-1950s, and scenery and costumes for several productions for the Columbia Players, Falmouth Playhouse, Allenberry Playhouse, Ivoryton and Tamiment. He also has taught and worked as an interior decorator.

Scenic Designs:

1973: *Bette Midler*

Michael Massee

Michael Massee first designed sets and costumes for a production on Broadway in 1988. In 1979 he designed the sets and costumes for *The End of All Things Natural,* one of many productions he has designed for opera, film, television and theatre. He was born on December 2, 1937 in Corvallis, Oregon, graduated from Portland State University and received an M.F.A. from the Mason Gross School of the Arts at Rutgers University. His career as a scenic desginer began in 1959 with *Man and Superman* at Portland State University. He is Head of the Design Program at Fordham University at Lincoln Center and is married to Carol Rosenfeld, an actress, teacher, and director.

Scenic Designs:

1988: *Paul Robeson*

Costume Designs:

1988: *Paul Robeson*

André Masson

André Masson, a French surrealist painter and stage designer, was born in Balagny, France on January 4, 1896. He made his professional debut with *Les Présages* for the Ballets de Monte Carlo in 1933 and has collaborated often with Jean Louis Barrault in France. His paintings have been widely exhibited in Europe and the United States. The themes of his paintings are echoed in books he has written, which include

Mythology of Nature, Mythology of Being and *Nocturnal Notebook.* In 1952 he provided designs for sets and costumes for a Broadway production.

Scenic Designs:
1952: *Hamlet*

Costume Designs:
1952: *Hamlet*

William Henry Matthews

William Henry Matthews designed costumes for numerous Broadway shows. His earliest credit was for *Ziegfeld Follies* in 1907. He was the son of a Presbyterian minister who was pastor at the Greenwich Church in New York City in the early years of this century. Mr. Matthews often worked in collaboration with Cora McGeachy, Gladys Monkhouse and Will R. Barnes. In 1923 he designed sets as well as costumes for a Broadway production.

Scenic Designs:
1923: *Deep Tangled Wildwood, The*

Costume Designs:
1915: *Arms and the Man*; *Hip-Hip-Hooray*; *Modern Eve, A* 1916: *Century Girl, The* 1917: *Eyes of Youth* 1918: *Everything*; *Kiss Burglar, The* 1919: *Young Man's Fancy, A* 1920: *Girl in the Spotlight, The*; *Lady of the Lamp, The*; *Respect for Riches* 1922: *Better Times*; *Frank Fay's Fables*; *Marjolaine* 1923: *Deep Tangled Wildwood, The* 1924: *Magnolia Lady, The*; *Merry Wives of Gotham* 1926: *Slaves All* 1928: *Earl Carroll's Vanities*; *Elmer Gantry* 1929: *Fioretta*; *Silver Swan, The* 1930: *King Lear* 1931: *Hamlet*; *Julius Caesar*; *Merchant of Venice, The*

Mayo

Paul Mayo, a British designer, was born in Bristol, England on December 13, 1918. His designs in London's West End include *The Cherry Orchard* and the *Silver Curlew*. In the late 1940s and throughout the 1950s he designed productions for the London Masque Theatre, Westminster Theatre and the New Theatre. He has also designed for television. His credits in Paris include *Orpheus* at the Ballets des Champs Élysées and *La Bonne Compagnie* and *L'Homme Qui a Perdu Son Ombre*, both at Mathurins.

Scenic Designs:
1952: *Baptiste*

Duane F. Mazey

Duane F. Mazey designed scenes and lighting for one play in 1976.

Scenic Designs:
1976: *Let My People Come*

Lighting Designs:
1976: *Let My People Come*

R. McCleery

Robert M. McCleery was a British designer who regularly created settings for the Theatre Royal, Drury Lane. He often worked in collaboration with other designers including Bruce Smith, Robert Caney, Harry Emden, and Harry Brooke among others. *Jack and the Beanstalk* (1899) and *Babes in the Wood* were among the pantomimes he designed. He was especially active in London during the 1920s. The production he designed in New York moved from the Theatre Royal, Drury Lane.

Scenic Designs:
1915: *Stolen Orders*

Charles McClennahan

Charles Henry McClennahan graduated in 1984 from Yale University where he was the recipient of the Donald Oenslager Scholarship. At Yale he also received a Graduate Commitment Award from the Afro-American Cultural Center for his contribution to the Center and the black community at Yale. He founded MINDTECK (Minority Designers and Technicians Network), a placement service for minorities in media and theatre. He has designed many productions in New York and the surrounding area for film, theatre and video. Recent credits include *A Tribute to Harry Chapin* at Carnegie Hall.

Scenic Designs:
1984: *Ma Rainey's Black Bottom*

Langdon McCormick

Playwright Langdon McCormick was born in Port Huron, Michigan and studied at Albion

College. An actor, he appeared with Otis Skinner in the late 1890s and in his own plays. He designed sets and lights for a 1919 Broadway production which he also wrote and in 1926 repeated the feat. His many plays included *How Hearts Are Broken, The Life of an Actress, Wanted by the Police* and *Toll Gate Inn.* Langdon McCormick died in June 1954.

Scenic Designs:
1919: *Storm, The*

Lighting Designs:
1919: *Storm, The* **1926:** *Ghost Train, The*

Jack McCullagh

Jack McCullagh designed sets for one Broadway show in 1962.

Scenic Designs:
1962: *Perfect Setup, The*

Paul McGuire

Paul McGuire designed costumes for a play in 1955 and scenery for a production in 1966. Known primarily as a set designer, he occasionally designs costumes for plays. He assisted Howard Bay, Motley, and Rolf Gerard at the Metropolitan Opera. He has many summer stock credits, including *Carousel* in 1965.

Scenic Designs:
1966: *Annie Get Your Gun*

Costume Designs:
1955: *Southwest Corner, The*

Reid McGuire

R. Reid McGuire was the scenic designer for a 1923 Broadway show.

Scenic Designs:
1923: *Sharlee; Vanities of 1923*

Robert T. McKee

Robert Tittle McKee was active on Broadway between 1917 and 1920. An architect, he resided at 42 East 78th Street in 1922 and at 225 East 79th Street in 1932.

Scenic Designs:
1917: *L'Elevation* **1918:** *Indestructible Wife, The* **1920:** *"Ruined" Lady, The*

Tom McPhillips

Tom McPhillips debuted as a scenic designer on Broadway in 1986. A British designer and art director, he studied at St. Martin's School in London. He began his theatre career working for the Young Vic and the National Opera and as a scenic artist. Since 1977 he has operated his own scenic studio. He is a prolific art director of commercials and music videos in England. He has designed sets for the concert tours of Ozzy Osbourne, Culture Club, Judas Priest, Luther Vandross, and Jennifer Holiday. He also designed *Sing, Mahalia, Sing.*

Scenic Designs:
1986: *Uptown...It's Hot*

Robert McQuinn

Robert McQuinn designed costumes and scenery on Broadway between 1915 and 1924. He was an artist and scenic designer who occasionally designed costumes as well. He also illustrated for magazines including *Vogue* and *Vanity Fair.* Robert McQuinn died on June 24, 1975 at the age of 92.

Scenic Designs:
1915: *Hip-Hip-Hooray; Stop! Look! Listen!* **1916:** *Big Show, The* **1917:** *Canary Cottage; Love O' Mike* **1918:** *Madonna of the Future*

Costume Designs:
1915: *Hip-Hip-Hooray; Stop! Look! Listen!* **1916:** *Betty; Big Show, The* **1917:** *Canary Cottage; Eyes of Youth* **1918:** *Everything* **1922:** *Better Times* **1923:** *Stepping Stones* **1924:** *Stepping Stones*

Kenneth Mellor

Kenneth Mellor was born in Yorkshire, England and trained as an architect. Productions of *'Tis Pity She's a Whore, The Wood Demon, Phantom of the Opera, You Never Can Tell, Country Life, Eastward Ho, Hobson's Choice* and *The Rules of the Game* are only a small portion of his recent activity in Great Britain. He has designed for the Actor's Company, the Lyric Hammersmith and in London's West End. Kenneth Mellor also designs industrial projects, including the lighting on the Thames Bridge.

Scenic Designs:
1984: *Beethoven's Tenth*

William Mensching

Three generations of men named William Mensching have been involved constructing (and occasionally designing) scenery for opera, theatre and television. William H. Mensching operated Mensching & Kilcoyne Studios with Joseph Kilcoyne, constructing opera scenery at 108 W. 15th Street in New York City. He was head carpenter for the original Shubert organization and for Billy Rose. For CBS-TV he worked with his son William G. Mensching, John De Verna and fifty-seven carpenters building scenery for approximately twenty-five shows a week for Jackie Gleason, Arthur Godfrey and Ed Sullivan, among others. William G. Mensching also worked as a carpenter for the Studio Alliance, for Feller Scenic Studios, Studio 3, and as production manager for Radio City from 1975 until his death on July 28, 1980. Apparently both William H. (who died in 1975) and William G. occasionally designed sets as "William Mensching," as well as through the William H. Mensching Studios during the early 1930s. The third generation, William M. Mensching, is president of Showtech, Incorporated, a theatrical construction shop in Norwalk, Connecticut which he operates with his brother Peter. They have built sets for *Starlight Express* and Universal Studio's film *The Hard Way* among many others as they carry on the family tradition, which actually began with a great-grandfather who hauled scenery for vaudeville by horse and buggy.

Scenic Designs:
1932: *Bidding High* 1934: *Good-Bye Please*

William H. Mensching Studios

William H. Mensching Studios received credit for scenery on Broadway in the mid-1930s. For additional information, see "William Mensching".

Scenic Designs:
1933: *Sellout, The* 1934: *Wife Insurance*

William Cameron Menzies

In 1928 William Cameron Menzies won the first Oscar for art direction in film for *The Dove*

and *The Tempest*. He spent most of his career as a film production designer, occasionally producing and directing. Born William Howe Cameron Menzies on July 29, 1896 in New Haven, Connecticut, he attended Yale University, the University of Edinburgh and the Art Students League and worked initially an as illustrator. He became Anton Grot's assistant at the Fort Lee, New Jersey Studios of Famous Players-Lasky and collaborated with Grot on his first movie, *The Naulahka*. He worked mostly as an independent art director during his long and prolific career, only occasionally hiring on with a major studio. William Cameron Menzies, who designed *Gone with the Wind* with Lyle Wheeler, was instrumental in developing the fields of art director and production designer for films and was widely regarded for his use of realism and carefully controlled details. He died on March 5, 1957 in Hollywood at the age of 60.

Scenic Designs:
1923: *Lullaby, The*

Costume Designs:
1923: *Lullaby, The*

Mercedes

Mercedes designed settings for two plays on Broadway in 1938 and 1941.

Scenic Designs:
1938: *Who's Who* 1941: *Tanyard Street*

Mary Merrill

Mary Merrill was born in Skowhegan, Maine on November 9, 1907. She started her career as a scenic designer and shifted to costumes. A graduate of Wheaton College, she studied at the Parsons School of Design and at Yale with Donald Oenslager and Frank Poole Bevan. After two years at Yale she succeeded Mr. Bevan as designer for the Hampton Players. She designed for Broadway, the Federal Theatre, and U.S.O. wartime shows overseas. She designed and taught costume design and history at the Provincetown Theatre in New York, and was a staff member of the Studio Theatre which Hallie Flanagan transferred to Vassar College for National Theatre productions. While at Vassar she designed the costumes for *One Third of a Nation*. Her film designs include *Patterns, The*

Bargain Stick and *Uncle Vanya*. In 1940 she left theatrical design for display design and was display manager at Bergdorf Goodman from 1942 to 1947. In 1950 she joined the CBS-TV costume department as designer for *You Are There, The Defenders, Man Against Crime* and hundreds of style shows. In 1970 she designed and mounted a huge exhibition of theatre costumes at the Museum of the City of New York.

Scenic Designs:
1933: *Double Door*

Costume Designs:
1933: *Double Door* **1934:** *Post Road; Wednesday's Child* **1935:** *Kind Lady* **1936:** *Double Dummy; Laughing Woman, The* **1937:** *Cherokee Night; Tobias and the Angel* **1938:** *Big Blow, The; Prologue to Glory; Sing for Your Supper*

Michael Merritt

Michael Merritt designed the films *House of Games* and *Things Change.* He received a B.A. degree in art history from the University of Chicago and has taught at Columbia College in Chicago. He has designed many sets for the Goodman Theatre and received several Joseph Jefferson Awards. At Lincoln Center he designed *Prairie du Chien* and *The Shawl.* Michael Merritt has also designed scenery for regional theatres including the Milwaukee Repertory Theatre, Woodstock Music Theatre Festival, Arizona Theatre Company and the North Light Repertory, among others.

Scenic Designs:
1984: *Glengarry Glen Ross*

Oliver Messel

Oliver Messel was born on January 13, 1904 in London and studied at the Slade School of Art. Well-known for his designs of sets and costumes for the British theatre, his first designs in London appeared in 1926. He first designed costumes and scenery in New York in 1928. He designed numerous plays in London's West End, and at the Old Vic, operas in Europe and for film. A designer of exquisite silhouette and detail, his designs for the stage were admired by his peers and by audiences. In 1955 he won a Tony Award for his set for *House of Flowers.*

Mr. Messel died on July 14, 1978. A biography by Charles Castle, *Oliver Messel,* was published by Thames and Hudson in 1987.

Scenic Designs:
1928: *This Year of Grace* **1929:** *Wake Up and Dream* **1936:** *Country Wife, The* **1948:** *Play's the Thing, The* **1950:** *Lady's Not for Burning, The* **1951:** *Romeo and Juliet* **1953:** *Little Hut, The* **1954:** *House of Flowers* **1955:** *Dark Is Light Enough, The* **1959:** *Rashomon* **1964:** *Traveller Without Luggage*

Costume Designs:
1928: *This Year of Grace* **1929:** *Wake Up and Dream* **1930:** *Symphony in Two Flats* **1936:** *Country Wife, The* **1950:** *Lady's Not for Burning, The* **1951:** *Romeo and Juliet* **1954:** *House of Flowers* **1959:** *Rashomon* **1964:** *Traveller Without Luggage* **1973:** *Gigi*

Leo B. Meyer

Leo B. Meyer has designed scenery and lights, taught design, painted scenery and produced plays during his thirty-five years in the theatre. He has worked throughout the United States and designed hundreds of plays. As president and owner/operator of Atlas Scenic Studios, Ltd. in Bridgeport, Connecticut he has supervised the construction of productions which have collectively won seven Tony Awards, five Pulitzer Prizes and one Emmy. He was born on July 10, 1934, was graduated in 1955 from Carnegie Mellon and also studied at the Pratt Institute. He was the son of a textile designer and began designing in 1953 at the White Barn Theatre with *The Moon is Blue.*

Scenic Designs:
1963: *Pajama Tops* **1967:** *Girl in the Freudian Slip, The; Minor Adjustment, A* **1972:** *All the Girls Come Out to Play*

Lighting Designs:
1963: *Pajama Tops* **1967:** *What Did We Do Wrong?* **1972:** *All the Girls Come Out to Play*

Gordon Micunis

Gordon Micunis was born in Lynn, Massachusetts on June 16, 1933. After receiving his B.A. at Tufts University he studied at Yale University with Donald Oenslager and Frank Poole Bevan, receiving an M.F.A. He has had a varied career creating contract and residential interior designs, historic renovations and rehabilitations, museum and exhibit installations, logotype and graphic designs, and theatrical and apparel designs. Gordon Micunis' first New York design was *Madame Butterfly* for New York City Opera in 1962, and he has since designed operas for many other companies throughout the United States. He has lectured on design at Barnard College, at the Fashion Institute of Technology, Lester Polakov's Studio and Forum of Stage Design and at C.W. Post College.

Scenic Designs:
1983: *Ritz, The*

Jo Mielziner

Jo Mielziner, known primarily as a scenic designer, created numerous costume and lighting designs as well, a common occurrence for designers of his generation. He was born on March 19, 1901 in Paris and attended art schools, including the Art Students League. His father, Leo Mielziner, was a portrait painter and his mother a journalist. He began his career in the theatre as an actor, stage manager and scene designer, first in stock and then for the Theatre Guild. His collaborations with Elia Kazan for plays by modern American playwrights are examples of his enormous influence on theatre and the quality of design. He received many awards including five Tonys for set design, Drama Desk awards, Critics Awards, Maharam Awards and Donaldson Awards, and a number of honorary degrees, all for his outstanding contributions to the theatre. Mr. Mielziner, who died on March 15, 1976, has also received posthumous credit for designs including the revival of *Slaughter on Tenth Avenue* at the New York City Ballet during the 1985-86 season.

Scenic Designs:
1924: *Guardsman, The; Nerves* 1925: *Caught; First Flight; Lucky Sam McCarver; Wild Duck, The* 1926: *Little Eyolf; Masque of Venice, The; Pygmalion; Seed of the Brute* 1927: *Doctor's Dilemna, The; Fallen Angels; Mariners; Marquise, The; Right You Are If You Think You Are; Saturday's Children; Second Man, The* 1928: *Cock Robin; Grey Fox, The; Jealous Moon, The; Lady Lies, The; Most Immoral Lady, A; Saturday's Children; Servant of Two*

Masters; Strange Interlude 1929: *Amorous Antic, The; First Mortgage; Jenny; Judas; Karl and Anna; Little Show, The; Meet the Prince; Skyrocket; Street Scene; Young Alexander* 1930: *Mr. Gilhooley; Second Little Show, The; Solid South; Sweet and Low; Uncle Vanya* 1931: *Anatol; Barretts of Wimpole Street, The; Brief Moment; House Beautiful, The; I Love An Actress; Of Thee I Sing; Third Little Show, The* 1932: *Biography; Bloodstream; Bridal Wise; Distant Drums; Gay Divorce; Hey, Nonny Nonny; Never No More* 1933: *Champagne Sec; Dark Tower, The; Divine Drudge, A; I Was Waiting for You; Lake, The; Of Thee I Sing* 1934: *Accent on Youth; Biography; By Your Leave; Dodsworth; Merrily We Roll Along; Pure in Heart, The; Romeo and Juliet; Spring Song; Yellow Jack* 1935: *Barretts of Wimpole Street, The; Deluxe; Flowers of the Forest; It's You I Want; Jubilee; Kind Lady; Panic; Pride and Prejudice; Romeo and Juliet; Winterset* 1936: *Co-Respondent Unknown; Daughters of Atreus; Ethan Frome; Hamlet; On Your Toes; Postman Always Rings Twice, The; Room in Red and White, A; Saint Joan; St. Helena; Wingless Victory, The; Women, The* 1937: *Barchester Towers; Father Malachy's Miracle; High Tor; Star Wagon, The; Susan and God; Too Many Heroes* 1938: *Boys from Syracuse, The; I Married An Angel; Knickerbocker Holiday; No Time for Comedy; On Borrowed Time; Save Me the Waltz; Sing Out the News; Yr. Obedient Husband* 1939: *Christmas Eve; Key Largo; Mornings At Seven; Mrs. O'Brien Entertains; Stars in Your Eyes; Too Many Girls* 1940: *Flight to the West; Higher and Higher; Journey to Jerusalem; Pal Joey; Two on An Island* 1941: *Best Foot Forward; Candle in the Wind; Cream in the Well; Land Is Bright, The; Mr. and Mrs. North; Pal Joey; Seventh Trumpet, The; Talley Method, The; Watch on the Rhine; Wookey, The* 1942: *By Jupiter; Solitaire* 1943: *Susan and God* 1945: *Barretts of Wimpole Street, The; Beggars Are Coming to Town; Carib Song; Carousel; Dream Girl; Firebrand of Florence,the; Foolish Notion; Glass Menagerie, The; Hollywood Pinafore; Rugged Path, The* 1946: *Annie Get Your Gun; Another Part of the Forest; Happy Birthday; Jeb* 1947: *Allegro; Barefoot Boy with Cheek; Chocolate Soldier, The; Command Decision; Finian's Rainbow; Street Scene; Streetcar Named Desire, A* 1948: *Anne of 1000*

Days; Mr. Roberts; Sleepy Hollow; Summer and Smoke; Summer and Smoke **1949:** *Death of a Salesman; South Pacific* **1950:** *Burning Bright; Dance Me a Song; Guys and Dolls; Innocents, The; Man from Mel Dinelli, The; Wisteria Trees, The* **1951:** *King and I, The; Point of No Return; Top Banana; Tree Grows in Brooklyn, A* **1952:** *Flight Into Egypt; Gambler, The; Wish You Were Here* **1953:** *Can-Can; Kind Sir; Me and Juliet; Picnic; Tea and Sympathy* **1954:** *All Summer Long; By the Beautiful Sea; Fanny* **1955:** *Cat on a Hot Tin Roof; Island of Goats; Lark, The; Pipe Dream; Silk Stockings* **1956:** *Happy Hunting; Middle of the Night; Most Happy Fella, The* **1957:** *Look Homeward, Angel; Miss Lonely Hearts; Square Root of Wonderful, The* **1958:** *Day the Money Stopped, The; Gazebo, The; Handful of Fire; Oh Captain!; Whoop-Up; World of Suzie Wong, The* **1959:** *Gang's All Here, The; Gypsy; Silent Night, Lonely Night; Sweet Bird of Youth* **1960:** *Best Man, The; Christine; Little Moon of Alban; Period of Adjustment; There Was a Little Girl* **1961:** *All American; Devil's Advocate, The; Everybody Loves Opal* **1963:** *Milk Train Doesn't Stop Here Anymore, The* **1964:** *Owl and the Pussycat, The* **1965:** *Playroom, The* **1966:** *Don't Drink the Water; My Sweet Charley* **1967:** *Daphne in Cottage D; Paisley Convertible, The; That Summer-That Fall* **1968:** *I Never Sang for My Father; Prime of Miss Jean Brodie, The; Seven Descents of Myrtle, The* **1969:** *1776* **1970:** *Child's Play; Georgy; Look to the Lilies* **1971:** *Father's Day* **1972:** *Children! Children!; Voices* **1973:** *Out Cry* **1974:** *In Praise of Love*

Lighting Designs:

1934: *Romeo and Juliet* **1935:** *Panic* **1937:** *Too Many Heroes* **1938:** *Boys from Syracuse, The* **1939:** *Too Many Girls* **1940:** *Journey to Jerusalem; Pal Joey; Two on An Island* **1941:** *Best Foot Forward; Candle in the Wind; Land Is Bright, The; Pal Joey; Seventh Trumpet, The* **1942:** *By Jupiter* **1945:** *Beggars Are Coming to Town; Carib Song; Dream Girl; Firebrand of Florence,the; Foolish Notion; Glass Menagerie, The; Hollywood Pinafore; Rugged Path, The* **1946:** *Annie Get Your Gun; Another Part of the Forest; Happy Birthday; Jeb* **1947:** *Allegro; Barefoot Boy with Cheek; Chocolate Soldier, The; Command Decision; Finian's Rainbow; Street Scene; Streetcar Named Desire, A* **1948:** *Anne of 1000 Days; Mr. Roberts; Sleepy Hol-*

low **1949:** *Death of a Salesman; South Pacific* **1950:** *Burning Bright; Guys and Dolls; Man from Mel Dinelli, The* **1951:** *King and I, The; Tree Grows in Brooklyn, A* **1952:** *Gambler, The; Wish You Were Here* **1953:** *Can-Can; Kind Sir; Me and Juliet; Picnic; Tea and Sympathy* **1954:** *All Summer Long; By the Beautiful Sea; Fanny* **1955:** *Cat on a Hot Tin Roof; Island of Goats; Lark, The; Pipe Dream; Silk Stockings* **1956:** *Happy Hunting; Middle of the Night; Most Happy Fella, The* **1957:** *Look Homeward, Angel; Miss Lonely Hearts; Square Root of Wonderful, The* **1958:** *Day the Money Stopped, The; Gazebo, The; Handful of Fire; Oh Captain!; Whoop-Up; World of Suzie Wong, The* **1959:** *Gang's All Here, The; Gypsy; Rashomon; Silent Night, Lonely Night; Sweet Bird of Youth* **1960:** *Best Man, The; Christine; Little Moon of Alban; Period of Adjustment; There Was a Little Girl* **1961:** *All American; Everybody Loves Opal* **1963:** *Milk Train Doesn't Stop Here Anymore, The* **1964:** *Owl and the Pussycat, The* **1965:** *Playroom, The* **1966:** *Don't Drink the Water; My Sweet Charley* **1967:** *Daphne in Cottage D; Paisley Convertible, The; That Summer-That Fall* **1968:** *I Never Sang for My Father; Prime of Miss Jean Brodie, The; Seven Descents of Myrtle, The* **1969:** *1776* **1970:** *Child's Play; Georgy; Look to the Lilies* **1971:** *Father's Day* **1972:** *Children! Children!; Voices* **1973:** *Out Cry* **1974:** *In Praise of Love*

Costume Designs:

1924: *Guardsman, The* **1925:** *Wild Duck, The* **1926:** *Little Eyolf; Pygmalion* **1927:** *Right You Are If You Think You Are* **1929:** *Karl and Anna* **1931:** *Admirable Crichton, The; Anatol; Barretts of Wimpole Street, The; Brief Moment; House Beautiful, The* **1932:** *Hey, Nonny Nonny* **1933:** *Divine Drudge, A* **1934:** *Romeo and Juliet* **1935:** *Barretts of Wimpole Street, The; Pride and Prejudice; Romeo and Juliet* **1936:** *Ethan Frome; Hamlet; Saint Joan; St. Helena; Wingless Victory, The* **1937:** *Barchester Towers; Father Malachy's Miracle; High Tor* **1938:** *Wild Duck, The; Yr. Obedient Husband* **1939:** *Christmas Eve; Mrs. O'Brien Entertains* **1945:** *Barretts of Wimpole Street, The; Dream Girl*

Lawrence Miller

Lawrence Miller's first New York design was for *Liza Minnelli in Concert* at Carnegie Hall in

1979. He made his New York debut shortly after serving three seasons as resident designer at the Repertory Theatre in Loretto Hilton Center in St. Louis. He was born on August 20, 1944 in Yonkers, New York, and received a B.F.A. at Carnegie Mellon University in graphic arts and a M.F.A. in theatre design in 1969, also at Carnegie Mellon. He assisted scenic designers Ming Cho Lee in 1975, Jo Mielziner in 1976 and Tony Walton from 1976 to 1977. He received a Tony nomination for the set for *Nine* and a Drama Logue Award for the 1985 production of *Teaneck Tanzi: The Venus Flytrap* in Los Angeles. He has designed off-Broadway productions including *Cloud Nine*, and films such as *Equus, Overboard, True Believer* and *The King of Comedy*. He has also designed ballets, operas, and MTV videos.

Scenic Designs:
1982: *Nine* 1983: *Teaneck Tanzi: The Venus Flytrap* 1985: *Loves of Anatol, The*

Costume Designs:
1983: *Teaneck Tanzi: The Venus Flytrap*

Michael Miller

Michael Miller was born on June 24, 1953 in Wellington, Kansas. He received a B.F.A. from Southern Oregon State College and an M.F.A. from the University of Washington. He was an intern and assistant designer at the American Conservatory Theatre in San Francisco and launched his design career with *Ghosts* at the Intiman Theatre in Seattle, Washington in 1977. Career influences have included John Jensen, Santo Loquasto, Spud Hopkins, William Forrester, Robert Dahlstrom and Margaret Booker. He has also designed in regional and off-Broadway theatres.

Scenic Designs:
1982: *Eminent Domain* 1986: *Boys in Autumn, The*

Robert Milton

Born Robert Milton Davidor in 1885 in Dinaburg, Russia, Robert Milton came to the United States as a child. He entered theatre as an actor with Richard Mansfield, moving on to assisting, stage management, and directing for Mansfield, Mrs. Fiske and William Harris. He directed

numerous plays and musicals in New York, beginning in 1911 with *The Return to Jerusalem* and including *Very Good, Eddie, Leave It to Jane, The Charm School, Bride of the Lamb* and *The Dark Angel*. He also designed settings for plays he directed using the acronym "R.M." In the late 1920s he began directing films, mainly for Paramount Studios, beginning with *The Dummy*. Mr. Milton died on January 13, 1956 at age 70.

Scenic Designs:
1918: *Oh, My Dear* 1920: *Unwritten Chapter, The*

Fania Mindell

Fania Mindell came to the United States from Russia around 1908 and ran a small shop off Washington Square in New York City, where she sold Russian objects and artifacts. When Robert Edmond Jones was designing the set for *Redemption* in 1918 he discovered the shop and its proprietor. He encouraged her interest in the theatre and asked Fania Mindell to assist him on the production - - she ultimately designed the costumes and assembled the required properties. This initial collaboration with Robert Edmond Jones led to other design assignments, mainly for costumes and occasionally also for sets.

Scenic Designs:
1919: *Night Lodging* 1922: *Candida*

Costume Designs:
1918: *Redemption* 1920: *Medea* 1925: *Morals*; *Rosmersholm* 1926: *Easter*; *Hedda Gabler*; *Sandalwood* 1927: *Brother's Karamazov, The*; *Mariners* 1928: *Grey Fox, The* 1929: *Bond of Interest* 1930: *Inspector General, The*; *Uncle Vanya* 1931: *House of Connelly, The*; *Wonder Boy*

Vincente Minnelli

Known primarily as a film director of musicals and large extravaganzas, Vincente (Vincent) Minnelli started his theatrical career as a designer. He began in the Midwest creating sets and costumes for the stage shows which accompanied films. In 1930 he relocated to New York City to design at the Paramount movie theatre. He made his Broadway debut as a costume designer for *Earl Carroll's Vanities* in 1931. Appointed art director at Radio City Music Hall for the 1933-34 season, he had responsibility for designing sets, costumes and lights for the weekly stage shows. Gradually he turned his talents to directing and creating revues. His last Broadway designs were costumes for *Very Warm for May* in 1939, which he also staged. After moving to Hollywood he directed many award-winning films and won an Oscar for the direction of *Gigi* in 1958. Vincent Minnelli was born in Chicago in 1910 and died July 25, 1986 at age 76.

Scenic Designs:

1931: *Earl Carroll's Vanities* **1932:** *Dubarry, The*; *Earl Carroll's Vanities* **1935:** *At Home Abroad* **1936:** *Show Is On, The*; *Ziegfeld Follies: 1936* **1937:** *Hooray for What!*; *Show Is On, The* **1939:** *Very Warm for May*

Costume Designs:

1930: *Earl Carroll's Vanities*; *Lew Leslie's Blackbirds* **1931:** *Earl Carroll's Vanities* **1932:** *Dubarry, The*; *Earl Carroll's Vanities* **1935:** *At Home Abroad* **1936:** *Show Is On, The*; *Ziegfeld Follies: 1936-1937* **1937:** *Show Is On, The*

David Mitchell

David Mitchell has won Tony Awards for the scene design of *Annie* and *Barnum* and received several Tony nominations since his Broadway debut in 1970. He was born on May 12, 1932 in Howesdale, Pennsylvania and studied at Pennsylvania State and Boston Universities. His initial design in New York was *Henry V* for the New York Shakespeare Festival in 1965. He has also designed costumes, notably for the Pennsylvania Ballet, and for *The Steadfast Tin Soldier* for the PBS series *Dance in America*. Films include *One Trick Pony*, *Rich Kids* and *My Dinner with Andre*. Among his other credits are operas, ballets, and plays. He has also received a Maharam Award for *Barnum* (1970), Drama Desk Award for *Short Eyes* (1974), and an Outer Critics Circle Award for *Annie* (1977). Recent credits include scenery for the 1991 Broadway production of *The Big Love*.

Scenic Designs:

1970: *Grin and Bare It!/ Postcards* **1971:** *How the Other Half Loves*; *Incomparable Max, The* **1976:** *Trelawney of the "Welles"* **1977:** *Annie*; *Gin Game, The*; *I Love My Wife* **1978:** *Working* **1979:** *I Remember Mama*; *Price, The* **1980:** *Barnum* **1981:** *Bring Back Birdie*; *Can-Can*; *Foxfire* **1983:** *Brighton Beach Memoirs*;

Dance a Little Closer; *La Cage Aux Folles*; *Private Lives* **1985:** *Biloxi Blues*; *Boys of Winter, The*; *Harrigan 'n Hart*; *Odd Couple, The* **1986:** *Broadway Bound* **1988:** *Legs Diamond* **1989:** *Tru*

Robert D. Mitchell

Robert D. Mitchell received a B.A. at Yale University in 1951 after study with Donald Oenslager. From 1963 to 1968 he assisted Jo Mielziner and from 1964 assisted Boris Aronson until Aronson's death. He was born in Rutherford, New Jersey on April 14, 1929 the son of Roger I. and Anna L. Mitchell. He was the first American designer invited by the Greek government to design for the National Theatre of Greece at Epidaurus, and later represented Greece at the Europalia Festival in Brussels and the 1984 Olympic Arts Festival in Los Angeles. He has designed theatre and ballet throughout the United States, Canada and Europe since his professional debut at the York Theatre in 1959 with the set design for *The Saintliness of Margery Kempe*.

Scenic Designs:

1968: *Sudden and Accidental Reeducation of Horse Johnson, The* **1973:** *Medea* **1977:** *Basic Training of Pavlo Hummel, The* **1979:** *Meeting in the Air, A* **1989:** *Chu Chem*

Mr. Mitchell

Mr. Roy Mitchell moved to New York in 1916 to study theatre and later taught folklore at New York University, where he was a member of the Dramatic Art faculty from 1930 until his death in 1944. He was born in St. Clair County, Michigan of Canadian parents in 1884 and studied at the University of Toronto. After working in amateur theatre and as a reporter, he began in 1908 to direct plays for the Arts and Letters Club in Toronto. He subsequently moved to New York and worked as a stage manager on Broadway and as technical director of the Greenwich Village Theatre. Mitchell then moved to Canada and worked in the Canadian film industry, becoming director of the Harthouse Theatre at the University of Toronto from 1919 until 1930. He designed sets for those productions that he also directed. Mr. Mitchell died on July 27, 1944 at age 60.

Scenic Designs:
1918: *Karen*; *Pan and the Young Shepherd*

J. Robin Modereger

J. Robin Modereger, a designer and painter from South Dakota, received an M.F.A. at the University of Utah. He was a design assistant to Jo Mielziner and has served as artistic director at the Candlewood Playhouse. In 1985 he taught at Long Island University. Additional credits in New York include *Winslow Boy*, *Thurber Carnival* and *Jacques Brel is Alive and Well and Living in Paris*.

Scenic Designs:
1980: *Of the Fields, Lately*

Tanya Moiseiwitsch

Tanya Moiseiwitsch, a British scenic designer, theatre designer and costume designer, was born in London on December 3, 1914. She attended the Central School of Arts and Crafts in London. Her first design assignment was *The Faithful* in London in 1934. A longtime colleague of Tyrone Guthrie, they often collaborated, notably to create the theatre for the Stratford (Ontario) Festival, The Guthrie Theatre and the Crucible Theatre in Sheffield, England. Known for her designs for opera and theatre in Europe and North America, she served as Principal Designer at The Guthrie Theatre from 1963 to 1969. Other companies for which she has worked include the Royal Shakespeare Company, the Old Vic, the Metropolitan Opera and the Abbey Theatre. Other designs include the 1984 film *King Lear* with Laurence Olivier. In 1975 her costume designs for *The Misanthrope* were nominated for a Tony Award. She was honored with a Commander of the British Empire in 1974 and a Distinguished Service Award from the United States Institute of Theatre Technology for fifty years of design in 1987.

Scenic Designs:
1946: *Critic, The*; *Uncle Vanya* 1955: *Matchmaker, The* 1968: *House of Atreus, The* 1975: *Misanthrope, The*

Lighting Designs:
1955: *Matchmaker, The* 1968: *House of Atreus, The*

Costume Designs:
1946: *Critic, The*; *Uncle Vanya* 1955: *Matchmaker, The* 1968: *House of Atreus, The* 1975: *Misanthrope, The*

William Molyneux

William Molyneux designed one set in 1954 on Broadway. In 1953 he designed scenery for the London premiere of Benjamin Britten's opera, *Billy Budd*. The production was broadcast by NBC-TV to open its fourth season of opera on television.

Scenic Designs:
1954: *Black-Eyed Susan*

E.H. Beresford Monck

See Chipmonck

Yves Montand

Yves Montand, a popular French actor and singer, was born Yves Livi on October 13, 1921 in Monsummano, Italy and educated in Marseilles. His first film appearance was in 1946 in *Les Portes de la nuit* and since then he has appeared in many French and American films, notably *On a Clear Day You Can See Forever*, *Is Paris Burning?*, and *Jean De Florette*. He was married to Simone Signoret from 1951 until her death in 1985. He contributed scene and lighting designs to a concert appearance he made on Broadway in 1961.

Scenic Designs:
1961: *An Evening with Yves Montand*

Lighting Designs:
1961: *An Evening with Yves Montand*

Elizabeth Montgomery

See Motley

Beni Montresor

Beni Montresor was born on March 31, 1926 near Verona, Italy and was reared in Venice. He studied at the Academy of Art in Venice. He designs extensively for opera companies around the world, specializing in opulence and fantasy and occasionally directs. He has also designed films, including the autobiographical *Pilgrimage* shown at the Cannes Film Festival in 1972. In 1962 he met Gian Carlo Menotti and subsequently designed Barber's *Vanessa*, his first opera, for the Spoleto Festival. His career was established with *Last Savage* by Menotti at the Metropolitan Opera in 1964 and was soon followed by numerous productions for the major opera companies around the world. His costume designs for *Marco Millions* were nominated for a Tony Award in 1964, as were his designs for *The Marriage of Figaro* in 1985.

Scenic Designs:
1965: *Do I Hear a Waltz?* 1985: *Marriage of Figaro, The* 1986: *Rags*

Lighting Designs:
1985: *Marriage of Figaro, The*

Costume Designs:
1964: *Marco Millions* 1965: *Do I Hear a Waltz?* 1985: *Marriage of Figaro, The*

Roger Mooney

Roger Mooney has designed many sets off-Broadway and in regional theatres. He designed the television version of *Look Back In Anger* and *The Killing of Sister George*, as well as productions at the Hudson Theatre Guild, PAF Playhouse and the Production Company. His scenic designs at the Roundabout Theatre include *The Master Builder*.

Scenic Designs:
1981: *Taste of Honey, A*

Herbert Moore

Herbert Moore designed scenery from 1919 to 1935 on Broadway. A painter, he was raised in Claymount, Delaware. *Links With Other Days*, a collection of pen drawings with some notes by Herbert Moore, was published in Melbourne, Australia in 1927 by C.S. Harvey and Company.

Scenic Designs:
1919: *Angel Face* 1929: *Wonderful Night, A* 1933: *Growing Pains* 1935: *Night of January 16*

John J. Moore

John Jay Moore received both a B.S. and an M.A. in drama from Syracuse University and

has designed scenery and lighting on Broadway since 1967. He assisted Jo Mielziner and Robert Randolph and was scenic consultant for Disneyland and Disney World. He has also been Professor of Theatre at Ramapo College in New Jersey. Film credits include art direction for *Black Rain, Just Tell Me What You Want* and *Sea of Love*.

Scenic Designs:
1972: *Don Juan* 1976: *Pal Joey*

Lighting Designs:
1967: *How to Be a Jewish Mother* 1969: *Teaspoon Every Four Hours, A*

Edward A. Morange

Edward A. Morange was born in Bronxville, New York. He attended the Chicago Art Institute, the Corcoran School of Fine Arts and the School of Fine Arts at Washington University in St. Louis, where he considered a career in architecture or engineering. While designing exhibitions for the Chicago World's Fair of 1893 and working at the Grand Opera House (Chicago), he began focusing on theatrical design and construction. He began his collaboration with Frank Gates in 1894 and together they founded the scenic studio Gates and Morange in New York. Most of the designs produced by Gates and Morange were credited to the firm, but in 1935 Edward A. Morange received credit for the set for one production himself. He died May 20, 1955 in Torrington, Connecticut at age 90.

Scenic Designs:
1935: *For Valor*

James Morcom

James Stewart Morcom was born in Covington, Kentucky in 1906 and studied at the Grand Central School of Art and the John Murray Anderson-Robert Milton School of the Theatre. He has spent the majority of his career in New York City at Radio City Music Hall where he was an assistant to Clarke Robinson in the late 1930s, Resident Costume Designer from 1947 to 1950, and Art Director from 1950 until his retirement in 1973. Additional credits include *Five Kings* for Orson Welles' Mercury Theatre Group, and productions for the Federal Theatre

Project, the New York Ballet, Ballet Caravan and Jones Beach Theatre.

Scenic Designs:
1938: *Case History* **1941:** *Native Son* **1942:** *Native Son*

Dickson Morgan

Dickson Morgan designed sets, directed, and produced plays on Broadway between 1923 and 1926. He moved to Hollywood in the 1930s to head the Mary Pickford Dramatic Academy located at the El Capitan Theatre. He subsequently directed and produced numerous plays on the West Coast, including *Waterloo Bridge* at the Music Box Theatre in Hollywood, and *Mimie Scheller, Loyalties, Lysistrata, Shanghai Gesture, Curtain Call* and *Never Trouble Trouble.* He was also a dialogue coach and associate director for films produced by Universal Studios and Columbia Pictures.

Scenic Designs:
1923: *Peter Weston* **1924:** *Road Together, The; Topsy and Eva* **1925:** *Valley of Content, The* **1926:** *Down Stream*

James Morgan

James Morgan designed scenery on Broadway for the first time in 1989 and received a Drama Desk Award nomination for his efforts. He is an active designer in regional theatres, off-off and off-Broadway, and has been resident designer for the York Theatre Company in New York City, the American Stage Company in New Jersey and the Caldwell Theater Company in Florida. He designed the premiere of *The Fan* for the Blackstone Theatre in Chicago and the national tour of *On the 20th Century.*

Scenic Designs:
1989: *Sweeney Todd*

Roger Morgan

Roger Morgan was born on December 19, 1938 in New Kensington, Pennsylvania and graduated from the Carnegie Mellon University Department of Drama in 1961. He has designed over two hundred productions on and off-Broadway and in regional theatres and received both the Tony and the Drama Desk

Awards for *The Crucifer of Blood.* He worked for three years as assistant theatre designer to Jo Mielziner, assisting with the Vivian Beaumont Theatre at Lincoln Center and the Power Center for the Performing Arts at the University of Michigan. As principal owner of the firm Roger Morgan Studios, Inc. he has had several theatre projects honored with regional and national awards, including both the Indiana Repertory Theatre and the Circle Theatre in Indianapolis, the Playhouse Square in Cleveland, and the Grand Opera House in Wilmington, North Carolina. He is co-author of *Space for Dance* and a founding member of Ensemble Studio Theatre in New York City.

Scenic Designs:
1972: *Dude*

Lighting Designs:
1966: *Under the Weather* **1968:** *Sudden and Accidental Reeducation of Horse Johnson, The* **1970:** *Wilson in the Promise Land* **1971:** *Unlikely Heroes* **1972:** *Elizabeth I; Ring Round the Bathtub* **1974:** *Saturday Sunday Monday* **1977:** *Dracula* **1978:** *Crucifer of Blood, The; First Monday in October; Gorey Stories* **1979:** *Gilda Radner Live from N.Y.; I Remember Mama* **1980:** *Nuts* **1981:** *It Had to Be You* **1982:** *Agnes of God; Almost An Eagle* **1985:** *Octette Bridge Club, The* **1987:** *Mort Sahl on Broadway!*

Christopher Morley

Christopher Morley became an associate artist with the Royal Shakespeare Company in 1966 and designed many productions while in residence there. In 1974 he formed Christopher Morley Associates. He has since designed further productions for the Royal Shakespeare Company, the Birmingham Rep and in London's West End. Opera designs include productions for the English National Opera, the Royal Opera, the English Music Theatre and the Royal Danish Opera.

Scenic Designs:
1971: *Abelard and Heloise*

Carter Morningstar

Carter Morningstar, scenic designer for theatre and television, was born in Lanstown, Pennsylvania and studied at the Philadelphia Academy of Fine Arts and in Europe. He began professional life as a graphic artist and illustrator, but after service in the Navy during World War II he moved to New York and became a scenic designer. He only rarely designed costumes and lighting. Carter Morningstar died in February 1964 at the age of 53.

Scenic Designs:
1960: *Beg, Borrow, Or Steal*

Lighting Designs:
1960: *Beg, Borrow, Or Steal*

Costume Designs:
1960: *Beg, Borrow, Or Steal*

Selma Morosco

Selma Morosco designed scenery on Broadway in 1924.

Scenic Designs:
1924: *Artistic Temperament*

Billy Morris

Billy Morris designed a Broadway set in 1976.

Scenic Designs:
1976: *Debbie Reynolds Show*

Charles T. Morrison

Charles T. Morrison designed one set in 1964 on Broadway.

Scenic Designs:
1964: *Conversation At Midnight*

Paul Morrison

Paul Morrison, a scenic, lighting and costume designer, was born in Altoona, Pennsylvania on July 9, 1906. He graduated from Lafayette College where he also taught. He began his theatre career as an actor and stage manager and first designed costumes in New York in 1939 for *Thunder Rock*. Beginning in 1941 he specialized in scenery and lighting and had numerous shows to his credit on Broadway and in other locations. Mr. Morrison served as Executive Director of the Neighborhood Playhouse beginning in 1963. He died in New York City on December 29, 1980.

Scenic Designs:
1941: *Walk into My Parlor* 1942: *Hedda Gabler* 1943: *I'll Take the High Road* 1944: *Love on Leave; Mrs. January and Mr. X; That Old Devil* 1946: *John Gabriel Borkman; What Every Woman Knows* 1948: *Young and the Fair, The* 1949: *Closing Door, The* 1950: *Affairs of State; Arms and the Man* 1951: *Billy Budd; Faithfully Yours; Twilight Walk* 1952: *Four Saints in Three Acts; Golden Boy* 1953: *On Borrowed Time* 1954: *Abie's Irish Rose; Confidential Clerk, The; Tender Trap, The* 1955: *Joyce Grenfell Requests the Pleasure* 1956: *Loud Red Patrick, The; Sixth Finger in a Five Finger Glove* 1958: *Make a Million; Maybe Tuesday; Visit, The* 1959: *Masquerade; Nervous Set, The* 1960: *Rape of the Belt* 1962: *Cantilevered Terrace* 1963: *Too True to Be Good* 1973: *Jockey Club Stakes, The*

Lighting Designs:
1941: *Walk into My Parlor* 1942: *Hedda Gabler* 1943: *I'll Take the High Road* 1944: *Mrs. January and Mr. X; That Old Devil* 1946: *John Gabriel Borkman; What Every Woman Knows* 1948: *Young and the Fair, The* 1949: *Closing Door, The* 1950: *Affairs of State; Arms and the Man* 1951: *Billy Budd; Faithfully Yours; Twilight Walk* 1952: *Four Saints in Three Acts; Golden Boy* 1953: *On Borrowed Time* 1954: *Abie's Irish Rose; Confidential Clerk, The; Tender Trap, The* 1955: *Bus Stop; Joyce Grenfell Requests the Pleasure; Once Upon a Tailor; Tiger At the Gate* 1956: *Candide; Cranks; Loud Red Patrick, The; Separate Tables; Sixth Finger in a Five Finger Glove; Tamburlaine the Great* 1957: *Sin of Pat Muldoon, The; Ziegfeld Follies* 1958: *Make a Million; Maybe Tuesday* 1959: *Flowering Cherry; Happy Town; Kataki; Masquerade; Much Ado About Nothing; Nervous Set, The* 1960: *Duel of Angels; Invitation to a March; Rape of the Belt; Thurber Carnival, A* 1961: *Complaisant Lover, The; Man for All Seasons, A* 1962: *Cantilevered Terrace* 1963: *Student Gypsy, or The Prince of Liederkrantz; Too True to Be Good* 1964: *Sponono* 1968: *Price, The* 1973: *Jockey Club Stakes, The*

Costume Designs:
1939: *Thunder Rock* 1940: *Night Music* 1941: *Walk into My Parlor* 1943: *Apology* 1946: *John Gabriel Borkman* 1947: *All My Sons* 1950: *Arms and the Man* 1952: *Four Saints*

in *Three Acts*; *Golden Boy* 1953: *On Borrowed Time* 1954: *Abie's Irish Rose*; *Confidential Clerk, The* 1955: *Bus Stop*; *Once Upon
a Tailor* 1956: *Loud Red Patrick, The* 1962:
Cantilevered Terrace

Winn Morton

Winn Morton was born on December 12, 1928 in
Lancaster, Texas into a family of artists which
included a scenic artist who specialized in opera
house drops. He studied at the Parsons School of
Design, the Ringling School of Art in Sarasota,
Florida, and with Woodman Thompson. He began designing costumes in high school with a
production of *The Gondoliers* and has designed
numerous costumes (and occasionally settings)
since then on and off-Broadway. Inspired by the
movie musicals of the 1940s and 1950s, Winn
Morton has won numerous awards for his creations.

Scenic Designs:
1968: *New Faces of 1968*

Costume Designs:
1967: *Spofford* 1968: *Avanti!*; *Education of
H.Y.M.A.N. K.A.P.L.A.N., The*; *New Faces of
1968* 1969: *Teaspoon Every Four Hours, A*
1971: *How the Other Half Loves* 1980: *Blackstone!*

Motley

Motley is the trade name of three scenery and
costume designers from Britain. The trio con-
sisted of two sisters, Margaret Harris and (Audrey) Sophia Harris, who worked mainly in
London, and Elizabeth Montgomery, who represented them in the United States. They
first worked together to design a production of
Romeo and Juliet for the Oxford University Dramatic Society in 1932, and from then until the
early 1970s designed countless plays and operas
in England and the United States. The three
met in art school and entered a contest at the
Old Vic's annual costume ball. They won half
the prizes and a job offer from the judge, John
Gielgud. Elizabeth Montgomery, who was responsible for most of the Broadway designs, was
born on February 15, 1904 in Kidlington, Ox-
fordshire, England, and studied at the Westminster School of Art. Sophia Harris Devine was

born in 1901 and died in 1966. Margaret Harris, who resides in London and has had a long
term relationship with Riverside Studios, was
born in 1904. In 1987 she was head of the design
course at Almeda Theatre in London. Motley's
first Broadway design was *Romeo and Juliet* for
Laurence Olivier and Vivian Leigh. Winners of
numerous awards, their Tonys include *The First
Gentlemen* (1958) and *Becket* (1961) and many
additional nominations. Their name is taken
from a line of Jacques in *As You Like It*, in
which he says "Motley's the only wear." In 1981
a 5,500 item collection of the 300 productions
designed by Motley between 1932 and 1976 was
acquired by the University of Illinois at Urbana-
Champaign.

Scenic Designs:
1940: *Romeo and Juliet* 1942: *Three Sisters,
The* 1943: *Lovers and Friends*; *Richard III*
1944: *Bell for Adano, A*; *Cherry Orchard, The*
1945: *Hope for the Best*; *Skydrift*; *Tempest,
The*; *You Touched Me* 1946: *Dancer, The*; *He
Who Gets Slapped*; *Second Best Boy* 1947: *Importance of Being Earnest, The* 1950: *Happy
As Larry* 1957: *Country Wife* 1959: *Requiem
for a Nun* 1961: *Complaisant Lover, The*; *Man
for All Seasons, A*; *Ross*

Lighting Designs:
1959: *Requiem for a Nun*

Costume Designs:
1934: *Richard of Bordeaux* 1940: *Romeo and
Juliet* 1941: *Doctor's Dilemma* 1942: *Three
Sisters, The* 1943: *Lovers and Friends* 1944:
Bell for Adano, A; *Cherry Orchard, The*; *High-
land Fling, A*; *Sadie Thompson* 1945: *Carib
Song*; *Pygmalion*; *Skydrift*; *Tempest, The*; *You
Touched Me* 1946: *Dancer, The*; *He Who Gets
Slapped*; *Second Best Boy* 1947: *Importance
of Being Earnest, The* 1948: *Anne of 1000
Days* 1949: *Miss Liberty*; *South Pacific* 1950:
Happy As Larry; *Innocents, The*; *Liar, The*; *Pe-
ter Pan* 1951: *Grand Tour, The*; *Paint Your
Wagon* 1952: *Candida*; *To Be Continued* 1953:
Can-Can; *Mid-summer* 1954: *Immoralist, The*;
Mademoiselle Colombe; *Peter Pan* 1955: *Hon-
eys, The*; *Island of Goats*; *Young and Beauti-
ful, The* 1956: *Long Day's Journey Into Night*;
Middle of the Night; *Most Happy Fella, The*
1957: *Country Wife*; *First Gentleman, The*;
Look Homeward, Angel; *Shinbone Alley* 1958:
Cold Wind and the Warm, The; *Jane Eyre*; *Love
Me Little* 1959: *Majority of One, A*; *Requiem*

for a Nun; Rivalry, The 1960: *Becket* 1961:
Kwamina; Man for All Seasons, A; Ross 1963:
*110 Degrees in the Shade; Lorenzo; Mother
Courage and Her Children; Tovarich* 1964: *Ben
Franklin in Paris* 1965: *Baker Street; Devils,
The* 1966: *Don't Drink the Water*

Joseph Mullen

Joseph Mullen, interior designer and arts philanthropist, designed scenery and costumes on
Broadway during the 1920s. His designs also
include John Gay's opera *Polly* in 1926. In the
1920s he designed sets, mainly for Gilbert Miller
productions before turning to interior design.
He was president in the 1940s of the organization which became the American Institute of Interior Designers. Joseph Mullen died at age 73
in 1974.

Scenic Designs:
1924: *Way of the World, The* 1925: *Wild Birds*
1926: *Bad Habits of 1926; Right to Kill, The*
1927: *Garden of Eden, The* 1930: *Gala Night;
Petticoat Influence* 1931: *Paging Danger*

Costume Designs:
1924: *Man Who Ate the Popomack, The; Way
of the World, The* 1926: *Bad Habits of 1926;
Right to Kill, The* 1927: *Garden of Eden, The;
Lady in Love, A*

Stephen Mullin

Stephen Mullin designed one set in 1964 on
Broadway. He reviewed *The Image of the Architect* by Andrew Saint for the March 1983 issue
of *The New Statesman*.

Scenic Designs:
1964: *Cambridge Circus*

Leon Munier

Leon Munier designed one set in 1967 on Broad-
way. He also designed the set for the off-
Broadway production of *Torch Song Trilogy* at
Actors Playhouse.

Scenic Designs:
1967: *Ninety-day Mistress, The*

Tom Munn

Tom Munn was born on March 24, 1944 in
New Britain, Connecticut and received a B.F.A.
from Boston University in 1967, where he studied with Raymond Sovey and Horace Armistead.
He also credits Dore Schary, author of the book
for his first Broadway production, *Brightower*,
with further "education". His professional debut was *The Heiress* at the Theatre-by-the-Sea
in Portsmouth, New Hampshire. Since 1976 he
has been design consultant and Resident Lighting Designer for the San Francisco Opera. Tom
Munn received an Emmy Award for daytime
programming for *La Gioconda* in 1979, a production of the San Francisco Opera.

Scenic Designs:
1970: *Brightower*

C. Murawski

C. Murawski began a career in theatre at age
17 as stage manager for the Starlight Theatre in
Kansas City, Missouri. Television productions
include Barbra Streisand specials, Alan King
productions and the Kraft Music Hall productions of *Death of a Salesman* and *The Pueblo*.
Productions off-Broadway include *A View from
the Bridge, Canterbury Tales* and *Fortune in
Men's Eyes*.

Scenic Designs:
1975: *Shenandoah*

Jane Musky

Jane Musky designs primarily for film and has
been production designer for *When Harry Met
Sally, Young Guns, Raising Arizona* and *Blood
Simple*, among others. She was born in New Jersey on May 27, 1954 and received a B.F.A. at
Boston University. Off-Broadway she designed
Marathon 1984 at the Ensemble Studio Theatre
and *Hackers* at the Manhattan Punchline Theatre. In 1981 she was production designer of
the Second Company of the Williamstown Theatre Festival, and in 1982 was assistant designer
on the Mainstage. Her designs have been influenced by travel throughout Europe and work
at Harker's Studio, London. She was assistant
designer and scenic artist for productions designed by David Hockney, Ralph Koltai and Julia Oman at the English National Opera, Glyndebourne Opera and Pinewood Studios.

Scenic Designs:
1985: *News, The*

Pieter Myer

Pieter Myer was active on Broadway between 1919 and 1922 as a scenery and costume designer. He was president in 1922 of Armstrong & Myer, Inc., 200 West 10th Street in New York City, where he worked in collaboration with costume designer Dorothy Armstrong.

Scenic Designs:
1922: *Greenwich Village Follies* 1921: *Right Girl, The*

Costume Designs:
1919: *Greenwich Village Follies* 1921: *Tangerine*

John Napier

Born in London in 1944, John Napier studied at the Hornsey College of Art before training as a designer of sets and costumes at the Central School of Arts and Crafts. After working at the Leicester Phoenix as Head of Design, he joined the Open Space Theatre as Resident Designer and subsequently became associate designer for the Royal Shakespeare Company. He has designed extensively in London's West End and for both the Royal Shakespeare Company and the National Theatre. His Broadway debut was *Equus* in 1974, and in 1982 he received a Tony Award for Outstanding Costume Design for *Cats*. Mr. Napier has also designed sets and costumes around the world for television, film and opera. He is married to costume and fashion designer Andreane Neofitou. Recent credits include scenery for the London and 1991 Broadway productions of *Miss Saigon*.

Scenic Designs:
1974: *Equus* 1976: *Equus* 1981: *Life and Adventures of Nicholas Nickleby*, 1982: *Cats* 1987: *Les Miserables; Starlight Express*

Costume Designs:
1974: *Equus* 1976: *Equus* 1981: *Life and Adventures of Nicholas Nickleby*, 1982: *Cats* 1986: *Life and Adventures of Nicholas Nickleby, The* 1987: *Starlight Express*

Geoffrey Nares

Geoffrey Nares, actor and designer, was born in London on June 10, 1917. From his debut in 1934 through the end of the 1930s he acted in many plays, mainly in London. He also designed plays such as *Girl Unknown, Candida* and *George and Margaret*, which subsequently played on Broadway. He died at age 25 on August 20, 1942.

Scenic Designs:
1937: *George and Margaret*

Curt Nations

Curt Nations designed one set in 1959 on Broadway.

Scenic Designs:
1959: *Happy Town*

Caspar Neher

Caspar Neher designed many plays for Bertolt Brecht including *Eduard II, Baal* and *In Dickicht der Stadte*. A German designer, he was born in Augsburg in 1897 and studied at the Munich School of Applied Arts and the Munich Academy of Arts. From 1934 to 1944 he worked at the Deutsches Theatre in Berlin. In 1948 he designed *Antizione* for Brecht in Switzerland and then returned to Germany to design *Herr Puntila* and *Sein Knecht Malti*. He also designed for the Salzburg Festival and the Vienna Opera. Credits at the Metropolitan Opera include *Wozzeck*. Caspar Neher died in Vienna on June 30, 1962.

Scenic Designs:
1933: *Threepenny Opera, The*

Andreane Neofitou

Andreane Neofitou, a British fashion and costume designer, has designed for the Royal Shakespeare Company in collaboration with her husband, John Napier. She designed *Hedda Gabbler, Once in a Lifetime, Peter Pan* and others for the Royal Shakespeare Company. She also designed costumes for Gemma Craven and Liz Robertson for *Song & Dance*. Her designs for film include *Rosencrantz and Guildenstern Are Dead*, directed by playwright Tom Stoppard. Recent theatre credits include costume design (in collaboration with Suzy Benzinger) for the London and New York productions of *Miss Saigon*.

Scenic Designs:
1986: *Life and Adventures of Nicholas Nickleby, The*

Costume Designs:
1987: *Les Miserables*

Neppel and Brousseau

Neppel and Brousseau collaborated on the scenic design for a Broadway production in 1929. Hermann Neppel was a sculptor born in Munich in 1882 who created tombstones, busts and decorative sculpture. His partner, James Brousseau, also operated Brousseau Scenic Construction Company at 428 11th Avenue in New York City in 1927. In 1932, James Brousseau was employed by Cleon Throckmorton, Inc.

Scenic Designs:
1929: *White Flame*

Newby and Alexander

Newby and Alexander collaborated on scenery for a production on Broadway in 1921. George Newby was a painter who lived at 641 East 222nd Street in New York City in 1932. No information was available on Alexander.

Scenic Designs:
1921: *Sun-kist*

Gertrude Newell

Gertrude Newell, born and raised in St. Johnsbury, Vermont, studied painting in Italy with Frazatti and in Allegheri's studio. She began professional life as an interior decorator. The design of a door for Grace George's production of *Major Barbara* led her to scenic, lighting and ultimately costume design. She also produced plays in New York and London.

Scenic Designs:
1915: *Earth, The* **1916:** *Pendennis*

Lighting Designs:
1916: *Pendennis*

Costume Designs:
1916: *Pendennis* **1917:** *Claim, The; Hamilton; Peter Ibbetson* **1920:** *Little Old New York* **1921:** *Fair Circassian, The* **1928:** *Age of Innocence, The*

J. Nievinsky

J. Nievinsky designed a set in 1948 on Broadway. A Russian designer, his work influenced Boris Aronson. Among many credits he designed sets for a commedia dell'arte version of *Turnadot*, directed by E. Vachtangov in the 1920s.

Scenic Designs:
1948: *Golem, The*

Jacques Noël

Jacques Noël, a French designer, designed scenery and costumes for a play in 1960. He is primarily a scenic designer who often works with Jacques Baratier. His Paris debut was in 1947 at the Théâtre de Babylone for *Le Marchand D'Étoiles* and was followed by numerous other productions for a variety of theatres. In 1963 he designed the film *Dragées au Poivre*. In 1982 he designed *Il Turco in Italia*, directed by Jean-Louis Thamin for the Aix-En-Provence Festival in France.

Scenic Designs:
1960: *Good Soup, The*

Costume Designs:
1960: *Good Soup, The*

"None"

Scenic design was the first of the theatrical design areas to develop, with a heritage stretching from the Greek tragedies to the court masques designed by Inigo Jones and the great nineteenth century scenic painters. Yet even as late as the early twentieth century and during the beginning of the movement referred to as the "New American Stagecraft," hundreds of playbills omitted designers names. Scenic designers were admitted to the union with jurisdiction over theatrical productions beginning in the mid 1920s. They subsequently received credit on the title page of the playbill as one of their contract features. However, prior to the 1940s, designers continued to be overlooked. The citation "None" in the index of this book means that no individual or studio received mention and that there were no acknowledgments in a playbill as to acquisition of furniture or stage properties.

Olle Nordmark

Olle (Olof E.) Nordmark designed and executed works in the old Nordic "murals" style in churches in New York City and in Sweden. An exhibit of his paintings was held at the Delphic Studio in 1934 in New York City. He was born in Dalecarlia, Sweden on May 21, 1890. From 1928 to 1944 he worked for the United States Indian Services teaching art.

Scenic Designs:
1927: *Rang Tang*

Costume Designs:
1927: *Rang Tang*

Christopher Nowak

Christopher Nowak was born August 15, 1950 in San Marcos, Texas. In 1972 he received a Bachelor's degree in Environmental Design at Texas A&M University and in 1975 an M.F.A. from the Yale University School of Drama, where he studied with Ming Cho Lee. He assisted Ben Edwards for a number of years and has designed on and off-Broadway and in regional theatres. Currently he concentrates on film and has been art director for films such as *Parenthood*, *Coming To America*, *Sweet Liberty*, *The Dream Team*, *Hanky Panky* and *Fort Apache, The Bronx*.

Scenic Designs:
1977: *Gemini* 1982: *Pump Boys and Dinettes*

Timothy O'Brien

Timothy O'Brien, a designer of sets who mainly works in London, was born in Shillong, Assam, India on March 8, 1929. After study at Wellington College, Cambridge and Yale Universities, his first professional design was the sets and costumes for *The Bald Primadonna and the New Tenant* in 1956 in London. From 1955 to 1966 he was head of design for ABC-TV, while continuing to design numerous plays, ballets and operas. He has been an associate artist with the Royal Shakespeare Company and since 1961 has designed in partnership with Tazeena Firth. He has designed exhibitions for Madame Tussaud's in London and Amsterdam, was art director for the film *Night Must Fall*, and occasionally designs costumes. Honors include the Gold Medal for set design at the 1975 Prague Quadriennale (shared with Tazeena Firth, Ralph Koltai and John Bury) and a Tony nomination for costumes for *Evita*.

Scenic Designs:
1964: *Poor Bitos* 1979: *Bedroom Farce; Evita* 1982: *Doll's Life, A*

Costume Designs:
1979: *Bedroom Farce; Evita*

Donald Oenslager

Donald Oenslager is known mainly as a scenic designer and a long-time teacher of design at Yale University, where he influenced a generation of designers. He was born in Harrisburg, Pennsylvania on May 7, 1902 and graduated from Harvard in 1923. His first sets on Broadway were seen in 1925, the same year he began teaching at Yale, and were followed by nearly two hundred additional designs for plays and operas. He wrote *Scenery Then and Now* and *Part of a Lifetime* and consulted on the design of many theatre spaces. He won a Tony Award for his set design for *A Majority of One* in 1956. He occasionally designed costumes and lighting for productions along with sets. Donald Oenslager died on June 11, 1975 at the age of 73.

Scenic Designs:
1925: *Bit of Love, A; Morals; Sooner Or Later* 1927: *Good News; Pinwheel* 1928: *Anna; New Moon, The* 1929: *Follow Through; Heads Up; Stepping Out* 1930: *Girl Crazy; Overture* 1931: *America's Sweetheart; East Wind; Free for All; Rock Me, Juliet; You Said It* 1932: *Adam Had Two Sons; Thousand Summers, A; Whistling in the Dark* 1933: *Forsaking All Others; Keeper of the Keys; Uncle Tom's Cabin* 1934: *Anything Goes; Dance with Your Gods; Divided By Three; Gold Eagle Guy; Lady from the Sea, The* 1935: *First Lady; Something Gay; Sweet Mystery of Life; Tapestry in Gray* 1936: *200 Were Chosen; Johnny Johnson; Matrimony RFD; Red, Hot and Blue; Russet Mantle; Stage Door; Sweet River; Ten Million Ghosts; Timber House; You Can't Take It with You* 1937: *Doll's House, A; Edna His Wife; I'd Rather Be Right; Miss Quis; Robin Landing* 1938: *Circle, The; Fabulous Invalid; Good, The; I Am My Youth; Spring Meeting; Spring Thaw; Woman's a Fool To Be Clever, A* 1939: *American Way, The; From Vienna; I Know What I Like; Man Who Came to Dinner, The; Margin for Error; Off to Buffalo; Skylark* 1940: *Beverly Hills; My Dear*

Children; My Sister Eileen; Old Foolishness, The; Retreat to Pleasure; Young Couple Wanted **1941:** *Claudia; Doctor's Dilemma; Lady Who Came to Stay, The; Mr. Bib; Pie in the Sky; Spring Again; Theatre* **1942:** *Flowers of Virtue, The* **1943:** *Hairpin Harmony* **1945:** *Pygmalion* **1946:** *Born Yesterday; Fatal Weakness; Land's End; Loco; On Whitman Avenue; Park Avenue; Present Laughter; Three to Make Ready; Years Ago* **1947:** *Angel in the Wings; Eagle Has Two Heads, The; Eastward in Eden; How I Wonder; Lovely Me; Message for Margaret; Portrait in Black* **1948:** *Goodbye, My Fancy; Leading Lady, The; Life with Mother; Men We Marry, The; Town House* **1949:** *At War with the Army; Father, The; Rat Race, The; Smile of the World, The; Velvet Glove, The* **1950:** *Liar, The; Live Wire, The* **1951:** *Constant Wife, The; Second Threshold; Small Hours, The* **1952:** *Candida; Paris '90; To Be Continued* **1953:** *Escapade; Horses in Midstream; Prescott Proposals, The; Sabrina Fair* **1954:** *Dear Charles* **1955:** *Janus; Roomful of Roses, A; Wooden Dish, The* **1956:** *Major Barbara* **1957:** *Four Winds; Nature's Way; Shadow of My Enemy, A* **1958:** *Girls in 509, The; Man in the Dog Suit, The; Marriage-Go-Round, The; Pleasure of His Company, The* **1959:** *Highest Tree, The; Majority of One, A* **1960:** *Dear Liar* **1961:** *Blood, Sweat and Stanley Poole; Call on Kuprin, A; Far Country, A; First Love* **1962:** *Venus At Large* **1963:** *Case of Libel, A; Irregular Verb to Love, The* **1964:** *One By One* **1967:** *Love in E-Flat; Spofford* **1968:** *Avanti!* **1969:** *Wrong Way Light Bulb, The* **1974:** *Good News*

Lighting Designs:

1946: *Fatal Weakness; On Whitman Avenue; Park Avenue* **1947:** *Angel in the Wings; Eastward in Eden; How I Wonder; Lovely Me; Portrait in Black* **1948:** *Goodbye, My Fancy; Leading Lady, The; Men We Marry, The; Town House* **1949:** *Father, The; Rat Race, The; Smile of the World, The* **1950:** *Live Wire, The* **1951:** *Second Threshold* **1953:** *Escapade; Horses in Midstream; Sabrina Fair* **1954:** *Dear Charles* **1955:** *Janus; Roomful of Roses, A; Wooden Dish, The* **1956:** *Major Barbara* **1957:** *Four Winds; Nature's Way; Shadow of My Enemy, A* **1958:** *Girls in 509, The; Man in the Dog Suit, The; Marriage-Go-Round, The; Pleasure of His Company, The* **1959:** *Highest Tree, The; Majority of One, A* **1961:** *Blood, Sweat and Stanley*

Poole; Call on Kuprin, A; Far Country, A; First Love **1962:** *Venus At Large* **1963:** *Case of Libel, A; Irregular Verb to Love, The* **1964:** *One By One* **1967:** *Love in E-Flat; Spofford* **1968:** *Avanti!* **1969:** *Wrong Way Light Bulb, The*

Costume Designs:

1925: *Sooner Or Later* **1927:** *Grand Street Follies; Pinwheel* **1933:** *Uncle Tom's Cabin* **1934:** *Dance with Your Gods; Gold Eagle Guy; Lady from the Sea, The* **1935:** *Tapestry in Gray* **1936:** *Sweet River* **1937:** *Doll's House, A* **1938:** *Good, The; I Am My Youth* **1941:** *Lady Who Came to Stay, The* **1947:** *Land's End* **1947:** *Eastward in Eden* **1948:** *Life with Mother* **1953:** *Escapade; Horses in Midstream* **1957:** *Four Winds; Shadow of My Enemy, A*

Robert O'Hearn

Robert O'Hearn, a designer of settings, costumes and lights for the opera, ballet and theatre, is best known for his opera sets. He was born on July 19, 1921 in Elkhart, Indiana and studied at Indiana University and the Art Students League. He designed his first play in 1948 for the Brattle Theatre Company in Cambridge, Massachusetts, where he subsequently designed sixty productions. His first opera was *Falstaff* with Sarah Caldwell in 1951, and since that time he has designed for every major opera company in the United States and several in Austria and Germany. His debut at the Metropolitan Opera, was *L'Elisir d'Amore* (1960) and was followed by many more including his most recent, *Porgy and Bess* (1985). He credits Robert Messel as an influential figure in his career. His designs have been widely exhibited and he has taught at Lester Polakov's Studio and Forum of Stage Design. In 1987 he was appointed Professor and Chair of Design at the Indiana University School of Music.

Scenic Designs:

1950: *Relapse, The* **1953:** *Date with April, A* **1955:** *Festival* **1956:** *Apple Cart, The; Child of Fortune* **1964:** *Abraham Cochrane*

Lighting Designs:

1955: *Festival* **1956:** *Apple Cart, The; Child of Fortune* **1964:** *Abraham Cochrane*

Costume Designs:

1950: *Relapse, The*

Alexander Okun

Alexander Okun emigrated to the United States from the Soviet Union where he was Resident Designer for the Moscow Art Theatre. He taught for ten years at the Moscow Art Theatre Academic Institute and at Boston University after moving the to U.S. He has designed on, off, and off-off-Broadway for productions including *Tales of Tinseltown*. Regional theatre credits include *Three Sisters* at the Arena Stage, *La Voie Humane* and *Facade* for the Boston Shakespeare Company, and *The Cherry Orchard* at Williams College.

Scenic Designs:
1987: *Roza*

Power O'Malley

Power O'Malley was born in County Waterford, Ireland in 1870 and studied at the National Academy of Design, as well as with Henri Shirlaw. His paintings are in the collections of the Fort Worth Museum of Art, the Library of Congress and the Phillips Memorial Gallery among others. He received several prizes for his paintings, etchings and illustrations. Power O'Malley died on July 3, 1946 in New York City.

Scenic Designs:
1932: *Well of the Saints, The*

Julia Trevelyan Oman

Julia Trevelyan Oman, a British designer of sets and costumes for television, film, and stage, was born in Kensington, England on July 11, 1930. She attended the Royal College of Art and is married to designer Roy Strong. Her first professional design of sets and costumes, *Brief Lives*, played in both London and New York. She has also designed operas and exhibitions, and has created film and television designs in collaboration with her husband.

Scenic Designs:
1967: *Brief Lives* **1974:** *Brief Lives*

Lighting Designs:
1974: *Brief Lives*

Costume Designs:
1967: *Brief Lives* **1974:** *Brief Lives*

Horton O'Neil

Horton O'Neil designed one set in 1940 on Broadway.

Scenic Designs:
1940: *Flying Gerardos, The*

Alice O'Neil

Alice O'Neil (a.k.a.   AVON, Av O'Neil) designed numerous costumes and a single setting on Broadway between 1916 and 1924. She appeared as "Ethel Dante" in musical comedies before devoting her talents to design. She was a staff designer for the Schneider Anderson Costume Company for ten years beginning in 1916. Between 1927 and 1930 she designed films at Fox Studios and for United Artists. In the film industry she collaborated with Stephanie Wachner. Alice O'Neil died in Nottingham, England on March 30, 1954 at age 92.

Scenic Designs:
1922: *Greenwich Village Follies*

Costume Designs:
1916: *Miss Springtime; Ziegfeld Follies: 1916*
1919: *Aphrodite; Rose of China, The; Royal Vagabond, The; Ziegfeld Midnight Frolic* **1920:** *Sally; Ziegfeld Follies: 1920; Ziegfeld Girls: 1920* **1921:** *George White's Scandals; Love Letter, The; Music Box Revue; O'Brien Girl, The; Ziegfeld's 9 O'clock Frolic* **1922:** *Greenwich Village Follies; Ziegfeld Follies: 1922* **1923:** *Kid Boots; Ziegfeld Follies: 1923* **1924:** *Grab Bag, The; Sitting Pretty*

Hector Orezzoli

A native of Argentina, Hector Orezzoli attended the University of Buenos Aires before studying design at the University of Belgrano. He has designed sets and costumes for many productions in Europe and South America. His collaborations with Claudio Segovia have resulted in the production of several music spectaculars, including a version of *Flamenco Puro* in Seville in 1980, a second version in Paris in 1984, and a Broadway production in 1986. *Tango Argentino* resulted from his continuing collaboration with Mr. Segovia and was honored with a Tony nomination for costume design.

Scenic Designs:
1985: *Tango Argentino* 1986: *Flamenco Puro*
1989: *Black and Blue*

Lighting Designs:
1986: *Flamenco Puro*

Costume Designs:
1985: *Tango Argentino* 1986: *Flamenco Puro*
1989: *Black and Blue*

A. A. Ostrander

Albert A. Ostrander designed sets, lights and costumes for the theatre and fashion shows during his career. He initially worked as technical director for Norman Bel Geddes before designing shows. He staged several *Fashions of the Times* productions in the late 1940s and also designed for three years for the Ringling Brothers and Barnum & Bailey Circus. A.A. Ostrander died in New York on September 29, 1964 at age 61.

Scenic Designs:
1939: *Where There's a Will* 1940: *Case of Youth, A* 1943: *All for All* 1944: *Sleep No More* 1946: *Duchess Misbehaves, The*

Lighting Designs:
1944: *Sleep No More*

Costume Designs:
1944: *Sleep No More*

Samuel Ostrovsky

Sam Ostrovsky was born on May 5, 1886 in Russia and studied painting in Kiev, Paris and Chicago. He exhibited at the Salon d'Automne, Salon des Tuileries, and Sale des Índépendants in Paris. He also created illustrations for *Esquire* magazine.

Scenic Designs:
1923: *Anathema; Inspector General, The*

Teo Otto

Teo Otto was born in Remscheid, Germany and studied in Paris and Weimar. He was set designer for the Berlin State Theatre in the early 1930s. In 1933 he moved to Switzerland and designed for the Zurich City Stage until the end of World War II, when he returned to Frankfurt and designed for theatre and opera. His designs were seen in operas and plays throughout Europe and in New York. He also painted. Mr. Otto died on June 9, 1964 at age 64.

Scenic Designs:
1958: *Visit, The*

Costume Designs:
1958: *Visit, The*

Paul Ouzounoff

Paul Ouzounoff (a.k.a. Paul Rover) was born in Russia and worked as a seaman, rising to the rank of pilot before devoting his talents to scene painting and design. He spent twelve years on the staff of the Moscow Art Theatre as a scene painter. He moved permanently to the United States in 1923 and worked at Triangle Studios, again as a scene painter. In 1922 he contributed designs for scenery and costumes to a Broadway show. He died at age 64 on October 24, 1942 in New York City.

Scenic Designs:
1922: *Revue Russe* 1926: *Scarlet Letter, The*

Costume Designs:
1922: *Revue Russe*

Robert Rowe Paddock

Robert Rowe Paddock was born on August 12, 1914 in Mansfield, Ohio. He studied at the Cleveland School of Art and received a B.S. in art and education at Case Western Reserve University. He has designed and worked as technical director in summer and stock theatres throughout the United States including the Ivoryton (Connecticut) Playhouse, the Hilltop Lodge, and the Pocono Playhouse during the 1930s and 1940s. From 1951 to 1957 he designed for CBS-TV, creating sets for productions from *Douglas Edwards and The News* and *The Garry Moore Show* to features and series. He also designed special events, including the Inaugural Anniversary Party for John F. Kennedy and New York's "Salute to President Johnson" in Madison Square Garden.

Scenic Designs:
1946: *Burlesque* 1947: *Alice in Wonderland and Through the Looking Glass*

Ginafranco Padovani

Ginafranco Padovani, an Italian designer of operas, plays and television, was born on June 20, 1928 in Venice. He studied in Milan at the Accad di Belle Arti Brera and first designed at the Teatro Stabile di Genova in Italy. He has designed for all the major Italian opera companies, and in 1968 designed sets and costumes for a Broadway play.

Scenic Designs:
1968: *Venetian Twins, The*

Costume Designs:
1968: *Venetian Twins, The*

Reginald Pale

Reginald Pale was known primarily as a director. In 1923 he contributed costume and scenic designs to Broadway productions which he also directed.

Scenic Designs:
1923: *King Lear; Morphia*

Costume Designs:
1923: *King Lear*

Clifford Palmer

Clifford Palmer designed one set in 1917 on Broadway.

Scenic Designs:
1917: *Country Cousin, The*

Eric Pape

Eric Pape was born in San Francisco and studied painting in Paris with individual artists and at the École des Beaux Arts. He taught in Boston before opening his own school in New York, the Eric Pape School of Art, where he was director and chief instructor from 1888 to 1918. His studio was located at 200 West 57th Street in New York City in the 1930s. In addition to exhibiting paintings in Europe and the United States, he designed sets for numerous plays, including *Canterbury Pilgrims*, a command performance for President Taft in 1909, and *Trilby* in 1895. He died in 1938 at age 68.

Scenic Designs:
1924: *Flame of Love*

Costume Designs:
1927: *Julius Caesar* 1930: *Milestones*

Gerald Parker

Gerald Parker designed the set for a 1961 Broadway play starring George C. Scott.

Scenic Designs:
1961: *General Seeger*

Gower Parks

Gower Parks designed sets in 1946 for two Shakespearean plays performed on Broadway.

Scenic Designs:
1946: *Henry IV, Part II; Henry IV, Part I*

Russell Patterson

Russell Patterson designed scenery and costumes on Broadway in the 1930s. He was known mainly as a cartoonist and illustrator who did much to popularize the "flapper" in the 1920s. He was born in Omaha, Nebraska on December 26, 1894. He studied painting with Monet and at the Art Institute of Chicago, McGill Univeristy in Canada and the Academy of Fine Arts. He served as Vice President of the Society of Illustrators and was co-founder of the National Cartoonists Society. During the 1930s he designed scenery and costumes for Broadway and films, later turning his talents solely to illustrations for magazines and advertisements. He also designed Christmas Toy Windows for Macy's, hotel lobbies, restaurants, and the Women's Army Corps (WAC) Uniforms in World War II. Russell Patterson died at age 82 on March 17, 1977.

Scenic Designs:
1932: *Ballyhoo of 1932* 1933: *Hold Your Horses* 1934: *Fools Rush in* 1935: *George White's Scandals*

Costume Designs:
1931: *Gang's All Here, The* 1932: *Ballyhoo of 1932* 1933: *Hold Your Horses* 1934: *Fools Rush in; Ziegfeld Follies: 1934*

Herbert Paus

Born in 1880 in Minneapolis, Minnesota, the illustrator Herbert Paus studied at the Art Students League with George Bridgman. He designed covers for many magazines, such as *The Saturday Evening Post, Popular Science, Redbook* and *Collier's* and created book illustrations and posters for Liberty Loan drives and advertisers. He also designed scenery, notably *The Betrothal* by Maurice Maeterlinck in 1913. He died on June 1, 1946.

Scenic Designs:
1918: *Betrothal, The*

Miss Peacock

Miss Ada Peacock was costume designer on Broadway for a show in 1926 and costume and scenic designer for another in 1929. She was also active in London and designed costumes for *One Dam Thing After Another* in 1927 in collaboration with Aubrey Hammond, Doris Zinkeisen, and Kitty Shannon, and *The Girl Friend*, also in 1927. In 1928 she designed *This Year of Grace!* with Oliver Messel, G. E. Calthrop and Doris Zinkeisen, and in 1929 designed costumes for *Wake up and Dream* with Oliver Messel, Louis Curti, Maraud Michael Guiness and Norman Wilkinson.

Scenic Designs:
1929: *Wake Up and Dream*

Costume Designs:
1926: *Happy-Go-Lucky* 1929: *Wake Up and Dream*

Esther Peck

Esther Peck was active on Broadway primarily as a costume designer but occasionally as a scenic designer between 1916 and 1927. She designed numerous sets and costumes for the Neighborhood Playhouse. Known in private life as Mrs. David Peck, she resided at 48 East 89th Street in 1915 and at 2095 Creston Avenue, New York City in the early 1930s.

Scenic Designs:
1926: *Burmese Pwe, A* 1927: *Ritornele*

Costume Designs:
1915: *Jephthah's Daughter* 1916: *La Boite a Joujoux; Petrouchka* 1926: *Burmese Pwe, A* 1927: *Grand Street Follies; Ritornele*

Ernest Peixotto

Ernest Clifford Peixotto was born on October 5, 1869 in San Francisco. He was a painter and author who specialized in travel books about California, the American Southwest and Europe. He

studied in California and at the Academie Julien in Paris with Benjamin Constant and Jules Le Febvre. He painted murals, among them "Le Mort d'Arthur" at the Cleveland Public Library in 1911, and public rooms in New York, Paris and California. During World War I he was an official artist with the American Expeditionary Force in France, creating illustrations now in the collections of the National Gallery in Washington, D.C. In 1921 he was made a Chevalier of the Legion of Honor in France, becoming an officer in 1924. He died in New York City on December 6, 1940.

Scenic Designs:
1922: *Fools Errand*

Clifford F. Pember

Clifford F. Pember designed numerous sets between 1917 and 1947. He was among a group of designers who was inducted into United Scenic Artists in 1923. Until that time U.S.A. was generally regarded as the union of scenic painters. Clifford Pember, Woodman Thompson, Robert Edmond Jones, Lee Simonson and Joseph Urban were among those who joined the union, thereafter receiving fees on an approved scale, legal contracts, and credit in playbills placed above the cast list. Clifford Pember also worked as a decorator. He was active in London during the 1920s, creating scenery and costume designs for plays such as *Lawful, Larceny, Polly Preferred, The Punch Bowl, The Odd Spot, Tricks, R.S.V.P., Loose Ends, C.O.D., The Cave Man* and *The Last Enemy*.

Scenic Designs:
1917: *'Ception Shoals; Hamilton; Happiness; Pipes of Pan, The; Wooing of Eve, The* 1918: *Doll's House, A; Getting Together; Girl Behind the Gun, The; Kiss Burglar, The; Ladies First; Oh, Lady! Lady!; Sick-a-Bed; Someone in the House; Toot-Toot!* 1919: *Clarence; Five O'Clock; Kiss Burglar, The; On the Hiring Line* 1920: *Bab; Footloose; His Chinese Wife; Sophie* 1921: *Circle, The; Get Together; Pot-Luck; Sonny Boy; White Peacock, The* 1922: *Blue Kitten, The; Daffy Dill; East of Suez; Faithful Heart, The; Fool, The; Lawful Larceny* 1923: *Anything Might Happen; Camel's Back, The; Guilty One, The; Hurricane; Lady, The* 1924: *Dancing Mothers; Gypsy Jim* 1947: *Under the Counter*

Peters and Kennel

Peters and Kennel collaborated on the scenic design for a Broadway production in 1918. Rollo Peters, an actor and set designer, worked for the Washington Square Players and the Theatre Guild and also designed under his own name. Louis Kennel has Broadway credits as a costume and lighting designer, but his major activity during fifty years in the theatre was scenic design. His primary business was Louis Kennel Scenic Studios, in North Bergen, New Jersey. He also collaborated with Robert C. Entwistle through "Kennel and Entwistle" from 1919 to 1931, and with Rollo Peters through "Peters and Entwistle" in 1918.

Scenic Designs:
1918: *Army with Banners, The*

Rollo Peters

Rollo Peters, known as an actor and set designer, was born Charles Rollo Peters III in Paris on September 25, 1892. He studied in California and Europe and initially followed his father into the art world as a portrait painter. While seeking roles he stayed busy designing and building scenery on Broadway for the Washington Square Players and the Theatre Guild. His designs were included in an exhibition of the New American Stagecraft in 1919 at the Bourgeois Galleries, New York City. His first appearance as an actor occurred in 1918 with *Salome* and included several seasons as a leading man for Jane Cowl. Although his acting career was successful, he continued to design occasionally. He died on January 21, 1967, age 74.

Scenic Designs:
1917: *Grasshopper*; *Little Man, The*; *Madame Sand* 1918: *Josephine* 1919: *Bonds of Interest, The*; *John Ferguson*; *One Night in Rome*; *Palmy Days* 1920: *Mixed Marriage*; *Prince and the Pauper, The*; *Youth* 1922: *Dolly Jordan* 1923: *Pelleas and Melisande*; *Romeo and Juliet* 1924: *Anthony and Cleopatra* 1925: *Depths, The*; *Taming of the Shrew, The* 1927: *Out of the Sea* 1928: *Diversion* 1931: *Pillars of Society, The*; *Streets of New York, Or Poverty Is No Crime*

Costume Designs:
1917: *Grasshopper*; *Lady of the Camellias, The*; *Madame Sand* 1918: *Josephine* 1919: *Bonds*

of Interest, The*; *John Ferguson*; *Moliere* 1920: *Prince and the Pauper, The* 1922: *Dolly Jordan* 1923: *Pelleas and Melisande* 1924: *Anthony and Cleopatra* 1925: *Taming of the Shrew, The* 1931: *Streets of New York, Or Poverty Is No Crime*

Mogens Petri

Mogens Petri designed one set in 1932 on Broadway.

Scenic Designs:
1932: *Black Souls*

Olga Petrova

Olga Petrova, an actress who wrote and starred in her own plays, was born Muriel Harding in Liverpool, England in 1886 and studied in Paris, London and Brussels. Her stage debut was in London in 1906 and was followed by appearances throughout Great Britain and in New York, initially in vaudeville. She appeared in silent movies under contract with Paramount Pictures beginning in 1914, including *The Vampire*, *Black Butterfly*, *The Orchid Lady*, *Law of the Land*, *The Soul of Magdalen*, *Patience Sparhawk*, *The Silence Sellers*, and *The Panther Woman*. Her autobiography, *Butter with My Bread*, was published in 1942. She died on November 30, 1977 at age 93 in Clearwater, Florida.

Scenic Designs:
1921: *White Peacock, The* 1923: *Hurricane*

Victor J. Petry

Victor J. Petry was born in Philadelphia in 1863 and studied at the Academy of Fine Arts in Philadelphia and the École des Beaux Arts in Paris. He was an interior designer with a studio on Fifth Avenue in New York City who also designed sets. His specialization in theatrical scenery was with interiors. He began professional life as a newspaper illustrator, later designing jewelry and stationery. After arriving in New York he worked with W. & J. Sloan and Elsie de Wolfe before opening his own business. Victor Petry died in July 1924.

Scenic Designs:
1920: *Call the Doctor*; *Cornered*; *One*

George Phillips

George Phillips designed lights on Broadway in 1937 for one show.

Scenic Designs:
1937: *Professor Mamlock*

Rufus Phillips

Rufus Phillips designed one Broadway set in 1937.

Scenic Designs:
1937: *Lady Has a Heart, The*

Wendell K. Phillips

Wendell K. Phillips, an actor and director, was born on November 27, 1907 in Bladinsville, Illinois. He graduated from the University of Wisconsin and also attended the Goodman School of Theatre. He studied acting with Lee Strasberg and Michael Chekhov. He began acting in New York City in the early 1930s as a member of the famed Group Theatre, and began directing in the late 1930s. He received a prize as Best Supporting Actor for *Abe Lincoln in Illinois*. He has worked steadily ever since, adding television and film to his credits in the 1950s and 1960s and forming StageGroup in San Francisco in the late 1970s. He has occasionally also designed lights and sets, mainly fir stock companies.

Scenic Designs:
1933: *Black Diamond*

Lois Phipps

Lois Phipps designed two sets in 1915 in collaboration with other designers. She often worked with scene designer Warren Dahler.

Scenic Designs:
1915: *Glittering Gate, The; Tethered Sheep*

Joseph Physioc

Joseph Allen Physioc was born in Richmond, Virginia and began designing scenery in small theatres before moving to New York and becoming a scenic painter for the Metropolitan Opera. He was a painter as well as a scenic designer and in the 1930s exhibited widely. Known for a traditional realistic style, he did not readily accept the design trend known as the New American Stagecraft. Many of his designs on Broadway occurred before 1915 and included productions for Richard Mansfield such as *Richard III* (1896), *Courted into Court* (1896), *Beau Brummell* (1900), *The Climbers* (1901), *The Lion and the Mouse* (1905), *The Traveling Salesman* (1908), *Within the Law* (1912), *Peg 'o My Heart* (1912) and *Arms and the Man* (1892). He was married to actress and soprano Jessica Eskridge Thomas and together they produced musicals as vehicles for her. He also constructed and painted scenery for other designers through Joseph Physioc Studios and, towards the end of his career, through the Central Park Three Arts Theatre. Also known as Joseph Fisiac and Joseph Physive, he died in Columbia, South Carolina on August 3, 1951 at age 86.

Scenic Designs:
1915: *Abe and Mawruss; Fair and Warmer; Under Fire* **1916:** *Merry Wives of Windsor, The; Our Little Wife* **1917:** *Brat, The; Daybreak; Doing Our Bit; Losing Eloise; Merry Wives of Windsor, The* **1918:** *Crowded Hour, The; Lightinin'; Madonna of the Future; Roads of Destiny; Watch Your Neighbor; Where Poppies Bloom* **1920:** *Girl with the Carmine Lips, The; Jimmie; Tickle Me* **1921:** *Wait Till We're Married* **1922:** *Lady Bug; Seventh Heaven* **1923:** *Within Four Walls* **1924:** *Across the Street; Artistic Temperament; Gift, The; Sweeney Todd* **1925:** *Cousin Sonia; His Queen; Love's Call* **1926:** *90 Horse Power; Henry's Harem; Man from Toronto, The; Matinee Girl, The; Night Duel, The* **1927:** *Dracula* **1929:** *Philadelphia* **1931:** *Dracula*

Joseph Physioc Studios

Joseph Allen Physioc constructed his own designs and painted scenery for other designers through his scenic studio. Joseph Physioc Studio was located in 1919 at 447 1st Avenue, New York City and moved to 416 W. 26th Street in 1927. For additional information, see "Joseph Physioc".

Scenic Designs:
1916: *Rich Man, Poor Man* **1917:** *Why Marry* **1918:** *Why Marry?* **1919:** *Tumble in* **1920:** *Blue Flame, The; Bonehead, The; Scrambled Wives* **1922:** *Serpent's Tooth, A; Torch Bearers,*

The **1923:** *Not So Fast* **1925:** *Four Flusher, The* **1926:** *Autumn Fire; Friend Indeed, A* **1928:** *Lawyer's Dilemma, The*

Robin Pidcock

Robin Pidcock, a British designer of sets and costumes, has designed numerous shows for the Glasgow Citizens' Theatre since 1965, when he was named head of the design department. *The Critic, The Wild Duck* and *Mrs. Warren's Profession* are only a few of his many credits there. Additional designs include sets and costumes for *Rodelinde* at Sadler's Wells, and productions for the Nottingham Playhouse and the New Shakespeare Company.

Scenic Designs:
1968: *Day in the Death of Joe Egg, A*

Costume Designs:
1968: *Day in the Death of Joe Egg, A*

Colin Pigott

Colin Pigott, a British scenic designer, debuted on Broadway in 1986. He studied at the Kingston School of Art and received a B.A. in interior desgin. An active designer of television specials, commercials and feature films, he worked for BBC-TV from 1963 to 1967. He received a Bursary from the Royal Society of Art in 1963 for television and film set design.

Scenic Designs:
1986: *Jerome Kern Goes to Hollywood*

John Piper

John Egerton Christmas Piper, a British designer and artist, also wrote and illustrated books. He was born in Epsom, Surrey, England on December 13, 1903 and studied at Epsom College, the Royal College of Art (with Sir William Richardson) and at the Slade School of Art. He began exhibiting in 1925 and during World War II recorded bomb damage in paintings for the British government. A retrospective of his art, "50 Years of Work," was held at the Museum of Modern Art, Oxford in 1979. His works are in the permanent collections of the Tate Gallery, the Guggenheim Museum and the Victoria and Albert Museum among others. In addition he has designed many operas and ballets, notably *The Quest* for Sadler's Wells Ballet in 1943 for Frederick Ashton, and the operas of Benjamin Britten.

Scenic Designs:
1946: *Oedipus* **1948:** *Oedipus Rex; Rape of Lucretia, The* **1956:** *Cranks*

William Pitkin

William Pitkin was born in Omaha, Nebraska on July 15, 1925. A scenic designer, he also occasionally contributed costume designs to productions. After attending colleges in the United States and serving in the Army Air Force, he studied in Paris with Christian Bérard at the École Paul Colin. He designed settings in summer stock beginning in 1947 and was a staff designer for Raymond Loewy Associates in 1953. His first New York production was *The Threepenny Opera* starring Lotte Lenya at the Theatre de Lys in 1954. He also designed for opera and extensively for ballet. Mr. Pitkin won an Emmy Award in 1978 for the costumes for *Romeo and Juliet* on PBS. He died on May 10, 1990.

Scenic Designs:
1957: *Cave Dwellers, The; Moon for the Misbegotten, A; Potting Shed, The* **1960:** *Invitation to a March* **1961:** *Conquering Hero, The* **1962:** *Beauty Part, The; Seidman and Son; Something About a Soldier* **1965:** *Impossible Years, The* **1968:** *Guide, The* **1970:** *Chinese, The/ Dr. Fish*

Lighting Designs:
1962: *Beauty Part, The; Seidman and Son*

Costume Designs:
1956: *Child of Fortune* **1962:** *Seidman and Son; Something About a Soldier* **1968:** *Guide, The*

Joseph B. Platt

Best remembered as the set designer for *Gone With The Wind*, Joseph Brereton Platt was an industrial and interior designer. He was born on March 26, 1895 in Plainfield, New Jersey and studied at the Parsons School of Design. After service in World War I he worked as a mural painter, magazine illustrator, and interior designer and in 1933 became head of design for Marshall Field and Company in Chicago. In

1936 he formed his own company and designed for various businesses, creating (among other things) the Whitman Sampler Box and cosmetic packages for Elizabeth Arden. He also designed sets for movies and plays and was a member of United Scenic Artists, The Society of Industrial Designers and the Art Directors Club of America. He taught at the Parsons School of Design from 1933 to 1952 and died on February 6, 1968 in Wayne, Pennsylvania.

Scenic Designs:
1944: *In Bed We Cry*; *Suds in Your Eye*

Livingston Platt

Livingston Platt was born in Plattsburg, New York in 1874 and went to Europe to develop his skills as a painter. While in Paris he became acquainted with many actors and managers who introduced him to theatre and its possibilities. He first designed for a small theatre in Bruges, Belgium, which led to designs for several opera productions. He returned to the United States in 1911 and became head of design at the Toy Theatre in Boston, where in 1914 he designed four productions for Margaret Anglin. He preferred to be called a "stage decorator" and designed numerous settings in New York, many of them before 1915, occasionally contributing costume designs to these same productions.

Scenic Designs:
1915: *Beverly's Balance* **1917:** *Billeted* **1918:** *East Is West*; *Electra* **1919:** *Abraham Lincoln*; *First is Last*; *Lusmore*; *Shakuntala* **1920:** *Bad Man, The*; *Thy Name Is Woman* **1921:** *Bluebeard's Eighth Wife*; *Children's Tragedy, The*; *Eyvind of the Hills*; *Launcelot and Elaine*; *Mary Stuart*; *Two Blocks Away*; *White Villa, The* **1922:** *Banco*; *Ever Green Lady, The*; *First 50 Years, The*; *It Is the Law*; *Lady Christilinda, The*; *Madame Pierre* **1923:** *Floriani's Wife*; *In Love with Love*; *Robert E. Lee* **1924:** *Catskill Dutch*; *Cock O' the Roost*; *Far Cry, The*; *Goose Hangs High, The*; *No Other Girl*; *Outsider, The*; *Outward Bound*; *Tantrum, The*; *Youngest, The* **1925:** *Aloma of the South Seas*; *Backslapper, The*; *Dark Angel, The*; *Holka Polka*; *It All Depends*; *Oh! Mama*; *Pierrot the Prodigal*; *School for Scandal, The*; *She Had to Know*; *Stolen Fruit*; *Stronger Than Love*; *Two Married Men* **1926:** *Creaking Chair, The*; *Daisy Mayme*; *Devils*; *Great Gatsby, The*; *Kitty's Kisses*; *Puppy Love*; *Slaves All*; *Sport of Kings, The*; *Witch, The* **1927:** *A La Carte*; *Baby Mine*; *Behold the Bridegroom*; *Dark, The*; *Electra*; *House of Shadows*; *L'Aiglon*; *Lally*; *Legend of Leonora, The*; *Puppets of Passion*; *Savage Under the Skin*; *Storm Center*; *Strawberry Blonde, The*; *Venus* **1928:** *Carry On*; *Distant Drum, A*; *Elmer Gantry*; *Free Soul, A*; *Great Power, The*; *In Love with Love*; *Lady Dedlock*; *Outsider, The*; *Pleasure Man*; *Queen's Husband, The*; *Say When*; *Tomorrow...* **1929:** *Abraham Lincoln*; *First Mrs. Fraser, The*; *Flight*; *Maggie the Magnificent*; *Merry Andrew*; *Precious*; *Strong Man's House, A*; *Thunder in the Air* **1930:** *Greeks Have a Word for It, The*; *Launcelot and Elaine* **1931:** *Berlin*; *Church Mouse, A*; *Guest Room, The* **1932:** *Alice Sit By the Fire/ The Old Lady Shows*; *Dinner At Eight*; *Domino*; *Lilly Turner*; *Mademoiselle*; *Man Who Reclaimed His Head, The*; *Round-Up, The*; *Stork Is Dead, The*; *We Are No Longer Children* **1933:** *£25.00 an Hour*; *For Services Rendered*; *Hangman's Whip*; *Her Tin Soldier*; *Party, A*; *Saturday Night, A*; *Three and One*

Lighting Designs:
1932: *When Ladies Meet*

Costume Designs:
1918: *Electra*; *Freedom* **1919:** *Abraham Lincoln*; *First is Last*; *Lusmore*; *Shakuntala* **1921:** *Eyvind of the Hills*; *Mary Stuart* **1922:** *Banco*; *First 50 Years, The* **1925:** *Aloma of the South Seas*; *Holka Polka*; *Stronger Than Love* **1926:** *Creaking Chair, The*; *Sport of Kings, The* **1927:** *Electra*; *L'Aiglon* **1928:** *Elmer Gantry* **1930:** *Launcelot and Elaine* **1931:** *Guest Room, The* **1933:** *Pursuit of Happiness, The*

Sue Plummer

Susan Jennifer Plummer, a British designer of scenery and costumes, was born on January 20, 1943 in London. She studied at St. Martin's School of Art and has designed for opera as well as theatre. In 1972 she designed *Rigoletto* for the Welsh National Opera.

Scenic Designs:
1985: *Home Front*

Willy Pogany

Willy Pogany was born on August 23, 1882 in Szeged, Hungary and studied in Budapest, Munich and Paris. His career in the visual arts was

illustrious and varied. He began as a caricaturist, settled in New York in 1914, created murals (including the one for the Ziegfeld Theatre),
wrote and illustrated books and magazines, designed buildings, painted portraits and designed
sets and costumes. He remains well- recognized
as an illustrator by bibliophiles and book collec-
tors. At the height of his theatrical career he
was regarded as an authority on the color effects created by lighting. He designed the sets
for numerous Broadway plays between 1914 and
1930, costumes for a few, and also designed costumes and scenery for the Fokine and Adolph
Bloom ballets. He founded Willy Pogany Associates and collaborated with Joseph Teichner
in Pogany-Teichner Studios. His career also included work in films as an art director. Mr.
Pogany died on July 30, 1955 at age 72.

Scenic Designs:
1921: *As Ye Mould; Great Broxopp, The* **1924:**
Little Angel, The; Madame Pompadour **1925:**
Earl Carroll's Vanities; Florida Girl; The ...
1926: *2 Girls Wanted; Jeweled Tree, The;*
Queen High **1928:** *Houseboat on the Styx* **1929:**
Divided Honors; Hawk Island **1930:** *Sari*

Costume Designs:
1921: *Get Together* **1924:** *Little Angel, The*
1925: *The ...* **1930:** *Sari*

Willy Pogany Associates

Willy Pogany Associates, 152 West 46th Street,
New York City, was credited with the scenic design of a Broadway production in 1928. For additional information, see "Willy Pogany".

Scenic Designs:
1928: *Kidding Kidders*

Pogany-Teichner Studios

Scenic designers Willy Pogany and Joseph Teichner were associated with Pogany-Teichner
Studios where they constructed and painted
scenery. In 1925 the studio received credit for
the scenic design of a Broadway production. For
additional information see the entries under each
of their names.

Scenic Designs:
1925: *When You Smile*

H.R. Poindexter

H.R. Poindexter was a scenic and lighting designer who worked principally on the West
Coast. He was production supervisor and lighting designer for the American Ballet Theatre,
the Martha Graham Company, and the Dallas
Civic Opera Company. He was technical supervisor at the Mark Taper Forum in Los Angeles
from 1969 to 1974, and at the time of his death
on September 24, 1977 was technical supervisor
for the Ahmanson Theatre. He received a Tony
Award for *Paul Sills' Story Theatre* in 1971 and
a Los Angeles Drama Critics' Award for *Metamorphoses*, one of many lighting designs created
for the Mark Taper Forum. He also created
scenery and lighting for many national tours.
Two productions he designed, *Paul Robeson* and
Vincent Price in Diversions and Delights, were
on tour prior to their Broadway openings when
he died in 1977 at age 41.

Scenic Designs:
1974: *Henry Fonda As Clarence Darrow* **1975:**
Henry Fonda As Clarence Darrow **1976:** *Belle
of Amherst, The; Night of the Iguana, The*
1978: *Paul Robeson; Vincent Price in Diversions and Delights*

Lighting Designs:
1970: *Ovid's Metamorphoses; Paul Sills' Story
Theatre* **1971:** *Abelard and Heloise* **1972:**
*Evening with Richard Nixon, An; Funny Thing
Happened on the Way to the Forum, A* **1974:**
Henry Fonda As Clarence Darrow **1975:** *Henry
Fonda As Clarence Darrow; Private Lives* **1976:**
*Belle of Amherst, The; Music Is; Night of the
Iguana, The* **1978:** *Vincent Price in Diversions
and Delights*

Paul Poiret

Paul Poiret was born on April 20, 1879 in Paris
and began his career selling sketches to fashion
designers. While working for Doucet in 1896
he discovered his passion for the theatre. He
reigned between 1904 and 1924 as the fashion
designer who banned the corset (although he
hobbled legs with narrow skirts). He designed
often for the theatre in New York and Paris and
for the ballet, concentrating on costumes but occasionally also contributing scenic designs. Like
most of the Parisian art community at that time
he was a great friend of Diaghilev. The same

extravagance which brought him fame led to his decline, as he was unable to adjust to the changes created by World War I. He died in poverty in Paris on April 28, 1944.

Scenic Designs:

1920: *Afgar* 1925: *Naughty Cinderella*

Costume Designs:

1920: *Afgar* 1922: *Bunch and Judy, The* 1923: *Cinders*; *Little Miss Bluebeard* 1925: *Naughty Cinderella*

Lester Polakov

Lester Polakov was born in Chicago in 1916 and studied painting in New York with George Grosz, stagecraft with Milton Smith at Columbia University, and drafting with Emeline Roche. He began his career designing sets in summer stock. His New York debut was a 1935 production of *White Trash* at Columbia University, and in 1938 he designed scenery for *The Mother*, making his Broadway debut. He assisted Harry Horner on many productions and credits him as his mentor. After service in the Army Air Corps in World War II he resumed designing and had several exhibitions. In 1958 Polakov established the Lester Polakov Studio of Stage Design, now known as the "Studio and Forum of Stage Design," where he employs some of the best-known designers of sets, lights and costumes to teach design. In addition to teaching and overseeing the operation of this school he continues to design sets and costumes for stage and film.

Scenic Designs:

1938: *Mother, The* 1946: *Call Me Mister* 1950: *Golden State, The; Member of the Wedding, The* 1952: *Mrs. McThing* 1953: *Emperor's Clothes, The* 1954: *Winner, The* 1955: *Skin of Our Teeth, The* 1961: *Great Day in the Morning* 1980: *Charlotte*

Lighting Designs:

1950: *Golden State, The* 1953: *Emperor's Clothes, The* 1961: *Great Day in the Morning*

Costume Designs:

1940: *Reunion in New York* 1941: *Crazy with the Heat* 1947: *Crime and Punishment* 1950: *Member of the Wedding, The*

Helen Pond

Helen Pond was born on June 26, 1924 in Cleve-

land, Ohio and is the daughter of Ralph Herbert and Charlotte Waters Pond. She studied at Ohio State and Columbia Universities. She began designing at the Chagrin Falls Summer Theatre in Ohio with *Papa is All* and made her New York debut in 1955 with *The House of Connelly*. Since then she has created numerous scenic and lighting designs throughout the United States, including productions for the Paper Mill Playhouse and the Cape Playhouse, Dennis, Massachusetts for twenty-plus seasons. Opera designs include numerous credits as principal designer for the Opera Company of Boston since 1970 and additional productions for the New York City Opera. She often works in collaboration with Herbert Senn.

Scenic Designs:

1963: *Double Dublin* 1964: *Roar Like a Dove*; *What Makes Sammy Run?* 1968: *Noel Coward's Sweet Potato* 1973: *No Sex Please, We're British* 1981: *Macbeth* 1983: *Show Boat* 1986: *Oh Coward!*

Lighting Designs:

1963: *Double Dublin* 1964: *Roar Like a Dove*; *What Makes Sammy Run?*

Mike Porter

Mike Porter, a British painter, designed sets for one play on Broadway in 1980. An exhibition of his work, "Paintings on Wood and Papers," was held at Keattle's Yard in Cambridge, England in June 1980.

Scenic Designs:

1980: *Censored Scenes from King Kong*

David Potts

David Potts, son of Edward and Joanne Potts, was born on July 29, 1949 in Cleveland, Ohio. He received a B.A. from Purdue University and a M.F.A. from Brandeis University where he debuted with *Boys in the Band*. He has numerous credits for set designs in regional and off-Broadway theatres and has been resident designer at Circle Repertory Theatre since 1981. He was Assistant Professor of Design at the State University of New York at Purchase from 1985 to 1988, and design consultant for the Berkshire Theatre Festival from 1978 to 1987. The setting for *Full Hookup* at Circle Rep was nominated for a Drama Desk Award, and his art direction for *Fifth of July* on the PBS series *Theatre in America* was nominated for an ACE award. David Potts designed the national tours of *I Never Sang For My Father* and *Sleuth*.

Scenic Designs:
1985: *As Is* 1987: *Musical Comedy Murders, The* 1989: *Born Yesterday*

Anthony Powell

Anthony Powell, a designer of sets and costumes, was born in Manchester, England and studied at the Central School of Arts and Crafts in London and at Trinity College. His lyrical, creative sets and costumes have been seen in England and Europe of operas, plays and ballets, and occasionally also in the United States. A prolific designer of films, his credits include *Death on the Nile, Papillion, Nicholas and Alexandra* and *Tess of the D'Ubervilles.* Anthony Powell's scenery and costumes for *The School for Scandal* were nominated for Tony Awards in 1963, with the costumes receiving an award.

Scenic Designs:
1963: *School for Scandal, The* 1975: *Private Lives*

Costume Designs:
1963: *School for Scandal, The* 1990: *Lettice & Lovage*

John Pratt

John Pratt mainly designed costumes on Broadway but also created scenery and lights on for Broadway productions between 1938 and 1955. A naturalized United States citizen, he was born in Saskatchewan, Canada and graduated from the University of Chicago. His credits designing for dance were numerous and include costumes for Agnes De Mille, Ruth Page, Miriam Winslow and his wife, Kathryn Dunham. He worked with the Federal Theatre Project and usually designed both sets and costumes for productions. Mr. Pratt died at age 74 on March 26, 1986.

Scenic Designs:
1955: *Kathryn Dunham and Her Company*

Lighting Designs:
1946: *Bal Negre*

Costume Designs:
1938: *Swing Mikado, The* 1946: *Bal Negre* 1948: *Look Ma, I'm Dancin'* 1950: *Kathryn Dunham and Her Company* 1955: *Kathryn Dunham and Her Company*

Mary Purvis

Mary Purvis designed scenery on Broadway in 1952 for one production.

Scenic Designs:
1952: *Women of Twilight*

Isaac Rabinovitch

Isaac Rabinovitch designed sets and costumes for two plays on Broadway in 1925. He studied at the Kiev Art School and began designing sets and costumes in the late teens in Russia for the Moscow Art Theatre.

Scenic Designs:
1925: *Carmencita and the Soldiers*; *Lysistrata*

Costume Designs:
1925: *Carmencita and the Soldiers*; *Lysistrata*

Saul Radomsky

Saul Radomsky was born in South Africa and educated in England, where his lighting design activity has been centered. He has designed lights for *Small Craft Warnings, Gaslight, The Club, Loot, York Cycle of Mystery Plays* and many others in the West End. Saul Radomsky has also designed lighting for productions at the Royal Shakespeare Company, the Hampstead Theatre Club, the Oxford Playhouse Company, Cambridge and Company and other regional theatres in the United Kingdom.

Scenic Designs:
1981: *Moony Shapiro Song Book, The*

Phil Raiguel

Phil Raiguel designed sets for three plays in the 1940s on Broadway.

Scenic Designs:
1943: *Barber Had Two Sons, The; Slightly Married* 1949: *Mr. Adam*

O. L. Raineri

Orestes L. Raineri designed sets for plays in the 1930s on Broadway. He worked mainly as a scenic artist, lived at 2551 Cruger Avenue in New York City in 1932, and was associated with Gates and Morange Scenic Studio.

Scenic Designs:
1931: *Singing Rabbi, The* **1937:** *Bough Breaks, The*

Karl Ramet

Karl Ramet designed sets for one Broadway show in 1932. Five paintings in oils and watercolors by Karl Ramet were included in an exhibition of painting and designs at the E.B. Dunkel Scenic Studios. He became a member of the forerunner of United Scenic Artists in 1916. The majority of his career, until his retirement in the 1970s, was spent as a scenic painter. He was born in 1891, and celebrated his 100th birthday in April 1991 when a special party was held in his honor by United Scenic Artists in New York City.

Scenic Designs:
1932: *Housewarming*

Roger Ramsdell

Roger Ramsdell designed scenery for a Broadway production in 1950.

Scenic Designs:
1950: *Daphne Laureola*

Robert Randolph

Robert Randolph, a scenic designer, was born on March 9, 1926 in Centerville, Iowa, and received both B.F.A. and M.A. degrees at the University of Iowa. Before designing professionally he worked as an architect and industrial designer and taught at Iowa State University. He designed on Broadway for the first time in 1954, creating both sets and costumes for *The Saint of Bleecker Street*. Since that time he has designed numerous shows, concentrating his efforts on scenery but occasionally designing costumes and lights as well. His designs have been nominated for Tony Awards for *Golden Rainbow* and *Applause*, and he has also designed settings for the Tony Award ceremonies.

Scenic Designs:
1954: *Saint of Bleecker Street, The* **1960:** *Bye, Bye, Birdie* **1961:** *How to Succeed in Business Without Really Trying* **1962:** *Bravo Giovanni; Calculated Risk; Little Me* **1963:** *Sophie* **1964:** *Any Wednesday; Foxy; Funny Girl; Something More!* **1965:** *Anya; Minor Miracle; Skyscraper; Xmas in Las Vegas* **1966:** *It's a Bird...It's a Plane...It's Superman; Sweet Charity; Walking Happy* **1967:** *Henry, Sweet Henry; How to Be a Jewish Mother; Sherry!* **1968:** *Golden Rainbow* **1969:** *Angela; Teaspoon Every Four Hours, A* **1970:** *Applause* **1971:** *70, Girls, 70; Ari* **1973:** *Good Evening; No Hard Feelings* **1974:** *Gypsy; Words and Music* **1975:** *Norman Conquests, The; We Interrupt This Program* **1976:** *Porgy and Bess* **1982:** *Seven Brides for Seven Brothers* **1986:** *Sweet Charity*

Lighting Designs:
1961: *How to Succeed in Business Without Really Trying* **1962:** *Bravo Giovanni; Little Me* **1963:** *Sophie* **1964:** *Foxy; Funny Girl; Something More!* **1965:** *Skyscraper; Xmas in Las Vegas* **1966:** *It's a Bird...It's a Plane...It's Superman; Sweet Charity; Walking Happy* **1967:** *Henry, Sweet Henry; Sherry!* **1968:** *Golden Rainbow* **1969:** *Angela* **1971:** *70, Girls, 70* **1973:** *Good Evening; No Hard Feelings* **1974:** *Gypsy* **1975:** *Norman Conquests, The* **1986:** *Sweet Charity*

Costume Designs:
1954: *Saint of Bleecker Street, The* **1955:** *Desperate Hours, The* **1973:** *Good Evening* **1974:** *Words and Music*

Mark Ravitz

Mark Ravitz was born on August 18, 1948 in New York City and received a B.F.A. at New York University in 1970. Since he was seven he has been drawing and painting. He attended the Music and Art High School in New York City. Designs for special events include: the Playboy *Bunny of the Year* show in 1970 (which marked his professional debut); Liberty Weekend, the official opening of the Statue of Liberty; and industrial promotions. He has designed sets for numerous music tours, clubs, and theatre productions such as "The Diamond Dogs Tour," "The Serious Moonlight Tour," and "The Glass Spider Tour," all for David Bowie. He also designed the national tour of *Tommy, The Rock*

Opera, the *Kiss* world premiere and national tour, the Billy Idol tour, and the Aquacade at the Louisiana World Exposition in New Orleans in 1984. Mark Ravitz is married to Jo Beth Ravitz and they have one son, Miles.

Scenic Designs:
1982: *Rock 'n Roll! The First 5,000 years*

Ray Recht

Ray Recht was born on August 9, 1947 in Staten Island, New York. He received a B.F.A. in 1969 at Carnegie Mellon University and an M.F.A. in 1972 from the Yale University School of Drama. Ming Cho Lee and Tony Walton have been influential in his career. He began designing in regional theatres with *One Flew Over the Cuckoo's Nest* at Baltimore's Center Stage. His New York debut was *Medal of Honor Rag* at Theatre de Lys. He has also designed for film and television, notably as set designer for *Another World* on NBC-TV, and in regional theatres, including *The Real Thing* at the Pittsburgh Public Theatre. Ray Recht was art director for the 1982 film *Amityville II: The Possession*.

Scenic Designs:
1983: *Slab Boys* **1984:** *Babe, The*

Max Ree

Max Ree spent most of his career as an art director for films. He was born in Copenhagen, Denmark and trained as an architect at the Royal Academy of Copenhagen. He met Max Reinhardt and worked with him in Berlin before coming to the United States and contributing designs of sets and costumes to musical revues and Broadway shows. In 1925 he went to work for Metro Goldwyn Mayer designing costumes, serving as costume designer and art director for many films including Max Reinhardt's adaptation of *A Midsummer Night's Dream* in 1935. He also designed for television. Mr. Ree died in California at age 64 on March 7, 1953.

Scenic Designs:
1924: *Earl Carroll's Vanities*

Costume Designs:
1924: *Music Box Revue*

Larry Reehling

Lawrence C. Reehling (a.k.a. Lawrence Clair) designed sets for numerous productions in summer stock on Cape Cod and for opera companies in St. Louis, Santa Fe, and Minneapolis. He designed the films *Funny Girl* and *Hello, Dolly* among others and also designed for television, including *Today* and *The Tonight Show*. He was born in Hanover, Pennsylvania and received degrees from Carnegie Mellon University and the Yale University School of Drama. He died at age 45 on September 5, 1986 in Lancaster, Pennsylvania.

Scenic Designs:
1968: *Happiness Is Just a Little Thing Called a Rolls Royce*

Anton Refreiger

Anton Refreiger was born in Moscow on March 2, 1905 and studied sculpture in Paris. After coming to the United States in 1921 he continued his study at the Rhode Island School of Design. He became an American citizen in 1930 and was best known as a mural painter. His paintings are in the permanent collections of museums including the Metropolitan Museum of Art. One of his murals, comissioned for the Rincon Annex Post Office in San Francisco in 1941, was threatened with destruction by the House Un-American Activities Committee in 1953 because it included a Soviet flag. He lived and worked from his home in Woodstock, New York. Anton Refreiger died in Moscow in October 1979 at age 75.

Scenic Designs:
1937: *Pepper Mill, The*

Adina Reich

Adina Reich designed sets and costumes for a play in 1980.

Scenic Designs:
1980: *Wish Me Mazel-Tov*

Costume Designs:
1980: *Wish Me Mazel-Tov*

Marvin Reiss

Marvin Reiss was born on August 29, 1923 in St. Louis and received a B.F.A. at the Art Institute of Chicago. He began his career designing for summer stock theatres in Oconomowoc, Wisconsin, Fitchburg, Massachusetts, and Westport, Connecticut. He is art director and original designer for the television series *All My Children*. He was also art director for the soap opera *The Doctors*. Well known as a scene designer, he has created scenic and lighting designs for many Broadway shows and has occasionally contributed costume designs as well. His New York debut was *An Evening with Mike Nichols and Elaine May* off-Broadway. Mr. Reiss worked for many years as a chargeman in New York City shops.

Scenic Designs:
1954: *Home Is the Hero* **1958:** *Back to Methuselah; Party with Betty Comden and Adolph Green; Third Best Sport* **1959:** *Requiem for a Nun* **1960:** *Thurber Carnival, A* **1961:** *New Faces of '62* **1963:** *Love and Kisses* **1968:** *Portrait of a Queen*

Lighting Designs:
1954: *Home Is the Hero* **1958:** *Back to Methuselah; Party with Betty Comden and Adolph Green* **1961:** *New Faces of '62* **1963:** *Love and Kisses* **1968:** *Portrait of a Queen*

Costume Designs:
1954: *Home Is the Hero* **1959:** *Highest Tree, The*

Frank Rembach

Frank Rembach designed sets and lights for a 1966 Broadway production. He has designed in South Africa for Krishna Shah and also in London.

Scenic Designs:
1966: *Wait a Minim!*

Lighting Designs:
1966: *Wait a Minim!*

Nicholas Remisoff

Nicholas Remisoff (a.k.a. Nikolai Vladimirovich Remisoff, "Re-Mi") contributed designs for scenery and costumes to musical revues in the 1920s. He was born in Petrograd, Russia on May 7, 1887 and studied with Kardovsky at the Imperial Academy of Fine Arts. He worked professionally as an illustrator for the Russian

Weekly *Novy Satirikon*, also serving as its editor until its demise. His paintings were exhibited along with those by Alexander Benois and Léon Bakst through the "World of Art." In 1920 he moved to Paris and worked for the impressario Balieff, designing sets and costumes. Balieff brought him to New York with *Chauve-Souris* in 1922. He spent many years in Hollywood as a set and production designer for films including *Ocean's Eleven, Guest in the House, The Strange Woman, Dishonored Lady* and *When I Grow Up*.

Scenic Designs:
1922: *Chauve Souris* **1925:** *Chauve Souris* **1927:** *Chauve Souris* **1929:** *Chauve Souris*

Costume Designs:
1922: *Chauve Souris*

Roy Requa

Roy Requa was active on Broadway in the 1920s as a scenic and costume designer.

Scenic Designs:
1925: *Edgar Allan Poe* **1926:** *Hush Money*

Costume Designs:
1925: *Edgar Allan Poe*

John Retsek

John Retsek designed a set in 1971 for a Broadway production.

Scenic Designs:
1971: *No Place to be Somebody*

James Reynolds

James Reynolds, an author, artist and illustrator as well as a designer of sets and costumes, was born in Warrenton, Virginia. Of Irish descent, he wrote *Ghosts in Irish Houses* and later *Ghosts in American Houses*, demonstrating a flair for wit and the supernatural. He designed numerous plays on Broadway, contributing both sets and costumes to many before turning his attention to travelling so he might write about his adventures and paint. He died in Bellagio, Italy, from injuries suffered in a traffic accident, on July 21, 1957 at age 65.

Scenic Designs:
1919: *Tents of the Arabs, The* **1920:** *What's in a Name* **1921:** *Greenwich Village Follies;*

Ziegfeld Follies: 1921 **1922:** *Greenwich Village Follies* **1923:** *Sancho Panza* **1924:** *Greenwich Village Follies* **1925:** *Bird Cage, The; Last Night of Don Juan, The/ The Pilgrimage; Last of Mrs. Cheyney, The; Sunny; These Charming People; Vagabond King, The* **1926:** *Criss Cross; Oh, Please; On Approval* **1927:** *Bally Hoo; Lucky; Royal Family, The; White Eagle* **1928:** *Furies, The* **1929:** *Trip to Scarborough, A* **1934:** *Come of Age; O'Flynn, The; Thumbs Up; Within the Gates*

Costume Designs:
1919: *Tents of the Arabs, The* **1920:** *What's in a Name* **1921:** *Ziegfeld Follies: 1921* **1923:** *Sancho Panza; Ziegfeld Follies: 1923* **1924:** *Dear Sir; Greenwich Village Follies; Music Box Revue* **1925:** *Dearest Enemy; Puzzles of 1925; Sunny; Vagabond King, The* **1926:** *Criss Cross; Oh, Please* **1927:** *Command to Love, The; Immortal Isabella?; Royal Family, The* **1928:** *Chee-Chee* **1929:** *Fifty Million Frenchmen* **1930:** *Sweet and Low* **1931:** *Woman Denied, A* **1933:** *Hangman's Whip* **1934:** *Life Begins At 8:40; O'Flynn, The; Within the Gates* **1935:** *Jumbo; On to Fortune* **1936:** *Daughters of Atreus* **1943:** *Vagabond King, The*

Adams T. Rice

Adams T. Rice designed lights for one production in 1920 and the set for another in 1923. He also wrote *Pinocchio, A Fantastic Comedy In Eight Scences*, published by Samuel French in 1931. He was appointed technical director of the Children's Theatre in the 1930s after working for the Detroit Civic Theatre, the Washington Square Players, the Theatre Guild, and for his own company, the Detroit Players.

Scenic Designs:
1923: *Enchanted Cottage, The*

Lighting Designs:
1920: *Youth*

Peter Rice

Peter Rice, a British designer of both sets and costumes, was born on September 13, 1928 in Simla, India and studied at the Royal College of Art. His first design assignment was *Sex and Seraphim* in London in 1951. He designs regularly in England for the theatre, ballet and

opera, and occasionally in New York. He has numerous credits for productions at the Greenwich Theatre, the Aldeburgh Theatre and at Covent Garden, Glyndebourne, and Sadler's Wells.

Scenic Designs:
1972: *Ambassador*

Costume Designs:
1965: *Pickwick* **1972:** *Ambassador*

Clive A. Rickabaugh

Clive A. Rickabaugh designed sets for two plays in the mid-1930s on Broadway.

Scenic Designs:
1933: *It Pays to Sin* **1938:** *Swing Mikado, The*

Charles Ricketts

Charles Ricketts, a distinguished designer, artist and author, was born in Geneva, Switzerland on October 2, 1866, and studied in France. After founding and running the Vale Press from 1896 to 1904 he began designing sets and costumes for plays and operas in Europe and occasionally in the United States. He was instrumental in developing the course of modern scene design, using realism creatively to support a production's intent. His sculpture and designs are often displayed in major British museums. Charles Ricketts died on October 31, 1931 at age 65.

Scenic Designs:
1947: *Mikado, The* **1948:** *Gondoliers, The* **1951:** *Mikado, The*

Costume Designs:
1947: *Mikado, The* **1948:** *Gondoliers, The* **1951:** *Mikado, The* **1955:** *Mikado, The*

Kevin Rigdon

Kevin Rigdon, a lighting and set designer, was born on February 17, 1956 and raised in Highland Park, Illinois. He studied at Drake University and was an intern at The Guthrie Theatre during the 1975-76 season. He was resident scenic and lighting designer for the Steppenwolf Company in Chicago from 1976 to 1982, the Goodman Theatre from 1982 to 1983, and for Mordine and Company Dance Company from

1983 to 1984. He has designed for the Virginia Museum Theatre, the Williamstown Theatre Festival and other regional theatres. Honors include Joseph Jefferson Awards in Chicago for *Balm in Gilead* (1981), for *Tooth of Crime* (1982) and for *Moby Dick* (1983). He also received the American Theatre Design Award for lighting in 1985 and in 1990, and the American Theatre Wing Award (formerly the Maharam) for the scenic design of *The Grapes of Wrath*. His first Broadway play, *Glengarry Glen Ross*, started at the Goodman and transferred to Broadway. Other designs in New York include *The Shawl*, *Prairie du Chien*, *Clara* and *I Can't Remember Anything* at the Mitzi Newhouse Theatre with the director Gregory Mosher, who has helped shape his design style.

Scenic Designs:
1986: *Caretaker, The* 1990: *Grapes of Wrath, The*

Lighting Designs:
1984: *Glengarry Glen Ross* 1986: *Caretaker, The* 1988: *Our Town* 1989: *Ghetto* 1990: *Grapes of Wrath, The*

Otis M. Riggs, Jr.

Otis M. Riggs, Jr. began his career as a set designer in Hollywood, California in the early 1930s designing for Walter Wanger Productions. After World War II he moved to New York where he designed for television. He was art director for *Another World* and *Lovers and Friends* on NBC-TV and an assistant art director for films. He won three Emmys for art direction, one for the musical version of *Our Town* and two for *Another World* in 1973 and in 1976. He died at age 63 on May 4, 1977 in Yonkers, New York.

Scenic Designs:
1953: *Trip to Bountiful, The*

Albert Rights

Albert Rights supervised the setting for a Broadway production in 1930.

Scenic Designs:
1930: *Lysistrata*

James Riley

James Riley designed one set in 1976 on Broadway. Additional productions include *Dancing in the End Zone* in the 1983-84 season at the Coconut Grove Playhouse in Miami.

Scenic Designs:
1976: *So Long, 174th Street*

William Ritman

William Ritman was well known as a set designer with dozens of Broadway shows to his credit during his twenty-five year theatre career, including *Morning's at 7*, *Who's Afraid of Virginia Woolf?* and *Happy Days*. He also designed lights and occasionally costumes for productions for which he designed the settings. A native of Chicago, he graduated from the Goodman School of Theatre and designed professionally for the first time in 1959, contributing sets and lights to the revival of *On the Town*. Prior to designing for the theatre he was active in television. He was producer of the Rebekah Harkness Dance Festival at the New York Shakespeare Festival for eight years, and also taught design at Yale and Buffalo Univerisities. Mr. Ritman died on May 6, 1984 at age 56.

Scenic Designs:
1962: *Who's Afraid of Virginia Woolf?* 1963: *Riot Act, The* 1964: *Absence of a Cello*; *Tiny Alice* 1965: *Entertaining Mr. Sloane* 1966: *Delicate Balance, A*; *Malcolm* 1967: *Birthday Party, The*; *Come Live with Me*; *Everything in the Garden*; *Johnny No-trump*; *Promise, The* 1968: *Loot*; *Playwrights Repertory–One Acts*; *We Bombed in New Haven* 1969: *Gingham Dog, The*; *Mundy Scheme, The*; *Penny Wars, The*; *Play It Again, Sam* 1972: *Evening with Richard Nixon, An*; *Last of Mrs. Lincoln, The*; *Moonchildren*; *Sign in Sidney Brustein's Window, The*; *Six Rms Riv Vu* 1974: *Find Your Way Home*; *God's Favorite*; *My Fat Friend*; *Noel Coward in Two Keys* 1975: *P.S. Your Cat Is Dead* 1976: *California Suite*; *Eccentricities of a Nightingale, The*; *Who's Afraid of Virginia Woolf?*; *Zalmen Or the Madness of God* 1977: *Chapter Two* 1978: *Death Trap*; *Tribute* 1979: *Last Licks*; *Once a Catholic* 1980: *Mornings At Seven*; *Onward Victoria*; *Roast, The* 1981: *Lolita*; *Supporting Cast, The* 1983: *Corn Is Green, The*

Lighting Designs:

1962: *Who's Afraid of Virginia Woolf?* **1964:** *Absence of a Cello* **1965:** *Entertaining Mr. Sloane* **1967:** *Come Live with Me; Johnny Notrump* **1968:** *Loot; Playwrights Repertory-One Acts* **1969:** *Mundy Scheme, The* **1970:** *Sleuth* **1972:** *Last of Mrs. Lincoln, The* **1974:** *Noel Coward in Two Keys* **1975:** *P.S. Your Cat Is Dead* **1976:** *Who's Afraid of Virginia Woolf?*

Costume Designs:

1962: *Who's Afraid of Virginia Woolf?* **1964:** *Tiny Alice* **1965:** *Entertaining Mr. Sloane* **1967:** *Birthday Party, The; Everything in the Garden; Johnny No-trump* **1968:** *Playwrights Repertory-One Acts*

William Riva

William Riva, known primarily as a set designer, also contributed costumes to two Broadway plays in the early 1950s. In 1955 he was active in forming the Stamford Playhouse in Stamford, Connecticut.

Scenic Designs:

1950: *Telephone, The and The Medium* **1951:** *Razzle Dazzle*

Lighting Designs:

1950: *Telephone, The and The Medium* **1951:** *Razzle Dazzle*

Costume Designs:

1950: *Telephone, The and The Medium* **1951:** *Razzle Dazzle*

R.M.

See Robert Milton

R.N. Robbins

Robert Nelson Robbins was the creative partner and Mitchell Cirker the business manager of Cirker and Robbins Scenic Studio. This studio produced designs for numerous Broadway shows between 1919 and 1944 and also built or painted dozens more for other designers. Robert Robbins also designed sets under his own name in the 1920s and 1930s. Additional information is available under the entry "Cirker and Robbins" in this book.

Scenic Designs:

1927: *Seventh Heart, The; Synthetic Sin* **1928:** *Box Seats; Courage; Gentlemen of the Press; Gods of the Lightening; Night Hostess; Poppa; Ringside* **1929:** *Buckaroo* **1932:** *Heigh-Ho, Everybody*

Erling Roberts

Erling Roberts designed one set in 1951 on Broadway.

Scenic Designs:

1951: *Jotham Valley*

Sarah Roberts

Sarah Roberts studied in South Africa and the United Kingdom. She designed scenery and costumes for the Market Theatre in Johannesburg including *Born in the R.S.A., Sophiatown, Have You Seen Zandile?* and *Strike the Woman, Strike the Rock!* Her designs have been seen in the *Woza Africa!* Fesitval at Lincoln Center, at the Zurich, Berlin and Edinburgh Fesitvals, and in Basel and Frankfurt.

Scenic Designs:

1988: *Sarafina!*

Costume Designs:

1988: *Sarafina!*

Clarke Robinson

Clarke Robinson, who created designs for many productions between 1921 and 1941, was born in Bradford, Pennsylvania on November 26, 1894. He studied voice in Europe and debuted at the age of fifteen singing in opera, light opera and vaudeville. He designed scenery at the Roxy, Rialto and Capitol theatres, and for the Music Box Revues. He replaced Robert Edmund Jones as art director at Radio City Music Hall and was replaced by his assistant, James Morcom, after six months. He also appeared on radio shows and created television shows. Between World War I and World War II he wrote novels and biographies, designed sets and occasionally lights and costumes, raised horses and became an authority on turf. He died on January 18, 1962 at age 67.

Scenic Designs:

1921: *Music Box Revue* **1922:** *Music Box Revue* **1923:** *Music Box Revue* **1924:** *Music Box Revue* **1925:** *Dearest Enemy; Greenwich Village Follies; Gypsy Fires; Just Beyond; Young Blood* **1926:** *No Trespassing; Peggy Ann* **1927:** *Delmar's Revels; Enchantment; Patience; Revery; Rufus LeMaire's Affairs* **1928:** *Jarnegan; Rain Or Shine* **1929:** *Fioretta; Ghost Parade, The; Murray Anderson's Almanac; Woof, Woof* **1930:** *Nine-Fifteen Revue* **1933:** *Roberta* **1934:** *Keep Moving; Say When* **1935:** *Earl Carroll's Sketch Book* **1936:** *Broadway Sho-Window; Granite; Mainly for Lovers* **1937:** *Call Me Ziggy* **1941:** *Viva O'Brien*

Lighting Designs:

1927: *Delmar's Revels; New Yorkers, The* **1931:** *Billy Rose's Crazy Quilt*

Costume Designs:

1925: *Just Beyond* **1927:** *Patience; Revery*

Emeline Roche

The daughter of a clergyman, Emeline Clarke Roche was born in Brooklyn, New York and lives in New York City. Both a scenic and costume designer, she studied with Norman Bel Geddes before making her Broadway debut in 1940 as costume designer for *The Male Animal*. Emeline Roche worked with Aline Bernstein as an assistant for scenery and costumes, beginning with sets for *The Grand Hotel*. She worked in summer theatre in Newport, Rhode Island from 1935 to 1941 and toured as stage manager with Ruth Draper. Later she designed the backgrounds for the weekly *Kate Smith Show* on NBC-TV, and served as costume director of the New York City Center, designing costumes for over thirty shows. At City Center she designed the costumes for a production of *Anna Christie*, which she considers her greatest personal success. Ms. Roche has also been active with United Scenic Artists.

Scenic Designs:

1938: *Eye on the Sparrow* **1942:** *Papa Is All* **1947:** *Volpone* **1952:** *Anna Christie*

Costume Designs:

1940: *Male Animal, The* **1942:** *Mr. Sycamore; Papa Is All* **1944:** *Jacobowsky and the Colonel; Pick-Up Girl* **1945:** *Deep Are the Roots; State*

of the Union **1946:** *Flamingo Road; Loco* **1947:** *Love Goes to Press* **1948:** *Goodbye, My Fancy; Red Gloves* **1949:** *Gayden* **1950:** *Devil's Disciple, The* **1952:** *Anna Christie*

Norman Rock

Norman Rock graduated from San Diego Stage College, studied at the Yale University School of Drama, and received an M.A. from Stanford University in 1950. He served in the Naval Reserve during World War II and spent most of his professional career in California. His Broadway debut occurred in 1936 and was followed by an additional production in 1938. He also designed numerous productions for the Hollywood Bowl, the Theater of Etienne Decroux, the American Mime Theater, and for television. Norman Rock died at age 77 in Sonoma, California on November 14, 1985.

Scenic Designs:

1936: *Reflected Glory* **1938:** *Soliloquy*

Edward Roelker

Edward Roelker contributed scenic designs to a 1920 Broadway production. He worked as a carpenter in the teens and twenties and resided at 368 West 50th Street. In the 1920s he lived at 245 West 50th Street.

Scenic Designs:

1920: *Good Times*

John Root

John Root was born in Chicago in 1904 and met his wife, actress Margaret Mullin, during the run of one of his more than fifty Broadway shows, *Red Harvest*. He also designed television, notably *The Armstrong Circle Theatre, The Perry Como Show* for several years, and commercials. Prior to working in New York he designed for the Red Barn Theatre, Locust Valley, Long Island. In the early 1960s he changed careers and formed his own company, John Root, Inc. Real Estate, in Lumberville, Pennsylvania. John Root died on March 13, 1990 at age 85 in Doylestown, Pennsylvania.

Scenic Designs:

1934: *Piper Paid* **1935:** *Ceiling Zero; Crime Marches On; Cross Ruff; Hell Freezes Over;*

*If This Be Treason; Substitute for Murder;
There's Wisdom in Women* **1936:** *Seen But
Not Heard; So Proudly We Hail* **1937:** *Angel
Island; Chalked Out; Now You've Done It; One
Thing After Another; Red Harvest; Sun Kissed*
1938: *All That Glitters; Brown Danube; Great-
est Show on Earth, The; Kiss the Boys Good-
bye; Run Sheep Run* **1939:** *Pastoral; Ring Two;
Sea Dogs* **1940:** *George Washington Slept Here;
Glamour Preferred; Lady in Waiting; Out from
Under* **1941:** *Cuckoos on the Hearth* **1942:** *Cat
Screams, The; Janie; Jason* **1943:** *Counterat-
tack; Get Away Old Man; Kiss and Tell; Nine
Girls; Pillar to Post* **1944:** *Doctors Disagree;
Harvey; Highland Fling, A; Snafu* **1945:** *Boy
Who Lived Twice, A* **1947:** *It Takes Two; Tent-
ing Tonight* **1949:** *Love Me Long; Mrs. Gibbon's
Boys* **1950:** *Mr. Barry's Etchings* **1951:** *Not
for Children*

Lighting Designs:
1949: *Mrs. Gibbon's Boys* **1951:** *Not for Children*

Jean Rosenthal

Jean Rosenthal is usually recognized as one of
the pioneers of lighting design. She emerged
as a specialist in lighting at a time when the
lighting of a production was handled by a set
designer or an electrician, and in the course of
her career made lighting designers crucial members of production teams. Born Eugenia Rosenthal on March 16, 1912 in New York City, she
was the daughter of two doctors who were Ro-
manian immigrants. After studying acting and
dance at the Neighborhood Playhouse from 1929
to 1930 she became a technical assistant to faculty member Martha Graham, the beginning of
a life long association between them. She studied at Yale with Stanley McCandless and joined
the Federal Theatre Project in 1935, where she
launched her professional career. After working with Orson Welles' Mercury Theatre, she
formed Theatre Production Service in 1940 and
Jean Rosenthal Associates in 1958, for consulting on major theatre and architectural projects.
During her career she designed over two hundred
Broadway shows for Martha Graham, the New
York City Ballet, and the Metropolitan Opera.
Among her major contributions were the elimi-
nation of stage shadows by using rich floods of
upstage lighting, revising the use of light plots,

and controlling angles and mass of illumination
to create contrasts without shadows. She died
at age 57 on May 1, 1969 after a long battle
with cancer, ten days after attending the opening of Martha Graham's *Archaic Hours.* She
received the Outer Critics Circle Award for contributions to stage design in 1968-69 and the
Henrietta Lord Memorial Award from the Yale
School of Drama in 1932. In 1972 her book *The
Magic of Light* was published, the result of a
collaboration begun much earlier between Jean
Rosenthal and Lael Wertenbaker.

Scenic Designs:
1961: *Conquering Hero, The* **1963:** *Beast in
Me, The; On An Open Roof*

Lighting Designs:
1938: *Danton's Death* **1942:** *Rosalinda* **1943:**
Richard III **1947:** *Telephone, The and The
Medium* **1948:** *Joy to the World; Sundown
Beach* **1949:** *Caesar and Cleopatra* **1952:** *Cli-
mate of Eden, The* **1954:** *House of Flowers;
Ondine; Quadrille; Saint of Bleecker Street, The*
1956: *Great Sebastian, The* **1957:** *Dark At the
Top of the Stairs, The; Hole in the Head, A; Ja-
maica; West Side Story* **1958:** *Disenchanted,
The; Winesburg, Ohio* **1959:** *Destry Rides
Again; Redhead; Saratoga; Sound of Music, The;
Take Me Along* **1960:** *Becket; Caligula; Dear
Liar; Taste of Honey, A; West Side Story* **1961:**
*Conquering Hero, The; Daughter of Silence;
Gay Life, The; Gift of Time, A; Night of the
Iguana, The* **1962:** *Funny Thing Happened on
the Way to the Forum, A; Lord Pengo* **1963:**
*Ballad of the Sad Cafe, The; Barefoot in the
Park; Beast in Me, The; Jennie; On An Open
Roof* **1964:** *Chinese Prime Minister, The; Fid-
dler on the Roof; Hamlet; Hello, Dolly; Luv;
Poor Bitos* **1965:** *Baker Street; Odd Couple,
The* **1966:** *Apple Tree, The; Cabaret; I Do!
I Do!; Ivanov; Show Boat; Star Spangled Girl,
The; Time for Singing, A* **1967:** *Hello, Dolly;
Illya Darling* **1968:** *Exercise, The; Happy Time,
The; Plaza Suite; Weekend* **1969:** *Dear World*
1980: *West Side Story*

Herman Rosse

Herman Rosse was born in the Hague, studied
at the South Kensington College of Art in London and received a degree in architecture from
Stanford University. He created over two hundred sets during his career and taught at both

the Art Institute of Chicago and the University of California. He designed relatively few films but received an Oscar for art direction of *King of Jazz*. He also designed many sets for the Chicago Opera Company and the Paper Mill Playhouse. The author of *Masks and Dreams*, written in collaboration with Kenneth MacGowan, he is also remembered as the designer of the medallions for the Antoinette Perry (Tony) Award. Herman Rosse died on April 13, 1965 at age 78.

Scenic Designs:
1922: *Ziegfeld Follies: 1922* **1923:** *Little Miss Bluebeard; Swan, The* **1924:** *Greenwich Village Follies* **1925:** *Stork, The* **1928:** *Americana; Hello, Daddy* **1930:** *King Lear* **1931:** *Merchant of Venice, The* **1932:** *Great Magoo*

Costume Designs:
1925: *Chauve Souris*

Rossoni

Rossoni designed a set in 1938 on Broadway.

Scenic Designs:
1938: *Pasquale Never New*

Karen Roston

Karen Roston is a native of New York City. After receiving a B.A. at Antioch College she studied with Jane Greenwood at Lester Polakov's Studio and Forum of Stage Design. Her professional debut was as costume designer for *The School for Wives* in Dayton, Ohio. The recipient of an Emmy Award for *Saturday Night Live*, she designed her first Broadway show with Franne Lee, who has been influential in her career. She has designed over one hundred-seventy episodes of NBC-TV's *Saturday Night Live* and television specials for Steve Martin, David Letterman, Bob and Ray, and Robert Klein among others. Her films include *Muppets Take Manhattan, Gilda Live* and *Mondo Video*. Karen Roston is married to Peter Bochan and they have a daughter, Toby.

Scenic Designs:
1986: *Into The Light*

Costume Designs:
1979: *Gilda Radner Live from N.Y.* **1989:** *Sid Caesar and Company*

Wolfgang Roth

Wolfgang Roth came to the United States in 1938 from Berlin. Born in the German capital on February 10, 1910, he studied at Berlin's Academy of Art and worked with the Piscator Theatre and Bertolt Brecht. He designed numerous sets and occasionally costumes as well. His designs for opera were seen in major houses around the world including the Metropolitan Opera and the New York City Opera. He also designed for television and film, painted, illustrated and worked as an architect. Wolfgang Roth died on November 11, 1988 in New York City.

Scenic Designs:
1943: *First Million, The* **1945:** *Too Hot for Maneuvers* **1946:** *Pound on Demand* **1947:** *Yellow Jack* **1948:** *Oh, Mr. Meadowbrook* **1950:** *Now I Lay Me Down to Sleep* **1951:** *Twentieth Century* **1953:** *Porgy and Bess* **1958:** *Portofino* **1960:** *Deadly Game, The* **1979:** *Strider*

Lighting Designs:
1960: *Deadly Game, The*

Costume Designs:
1946: *Pound on Demand* **1947:** *Yellow Jack* **1960:** *Deadly Game, The*

Paul Rover

See Paul Ousounoff

Steve Rubin

Steve Rubin was born in Portland, Oregon in 1942 and studied at the University of Utah and at Yale, where he also taught design for two years. He prefers to do both sets and costumes for productions but has also designed numerous sets for additional productions. He has designed for the Indiana Repertory Theatre, the San Diego Shakespeare Festival, the Old Globe, and the Pennsylvania Ballet. He has also held the position of resident designer with several companies. Recent credits include *The Snow Ball*, a co-production by Hartford Stage and San Diego Shakespeare Festival.

Scenic Designs:
1975: *Ah, Wilderness* **1979:** *Devour the Snow; On Golden Pond* **1980:** *Horowitz and Mrs.*

Washington **1981:** *Survivor, The* **1988:** *Romance/Romance*

Costume Designs:
1979: *On Golden Pond*

Kevin Rupnik

Kevin Rupnik designed a set on Broadway in 1982. He also designed *Greater Tuna* at the Hartford Stage Company, which later transferred to Circle in the Square Downtown in New York. He was born on February 28, 1956 in Warren, Ohio and received a B.F.A. at Carnegie Mellon University and an M.F.A. at the Yale University School of Drama in 1981. His initial professional productions were for the Pittsburgh Civic Light Opera. Awards include the Los Angeles Drama Logue Award for the scenic design of *Greater Tuna*. He was assistant art director for *One Life to Live* on ABC-TV from 1983 to 1984.

Scenic Designs:
1982: *Ghosts*

James Spencer Russell

James Spencer Russell was born on April 7, 1915 in Monticello, Indiana. He studied at the University of New Mexico with Raymond Johnson. He also studied with Donald Oenslager at Yale University and has both B.F.A. and M.F.A. degrees. A painter, he has exhibited at the American Federation of Arts, the Rhode Island School of Design and Small Environments.

Scenic Designs:
1949: *Happiest Years, The*

Anthony Sabatino

Anthony Sabatino has a B.A. degree from the University of Houston and an M.F.A. from Brandeis University, where he studied with Howard Bay. He was born in Galveston, Texas on October 30, 1944. He has spent twenty years in Hollywood as a production designer and primarily designs for television. In 1989 he received an Emmy Award for excellence in design. He was art director in 1983 for the television special *Richard Pryor...Here and Now.*

Scenic Designs:
1977: *Toller Cranston's Ice Show*

Loudon Sainthill

Loudon Sainthill, a painter and designer, was born in Hobart, Tasmania, Australia in 1919 and in early 1950 moved to London where he did most of his design work, both sets and costumes. In London his paintings were widely exhibited. His first major success in the theatre was *The Tempest* for the Royal Shakespeare Company in Stratford-upon-Avon in 1951, and was followed by many designs in London's West End and for ballet companies. In the United States he designed between 1955 and 1969, winning a Tony for *Canterbury Tales* and a nomination for *The Right Honorable Gentleman*. He died on June 9, 1969 in London at age 50.

Scenic Designs:
1955: *Tiger At the Gate* **1956:** *Romeo and Juliet* **1965:** *Half a Sixpence; Right Honorable Gentleman, The*

Costume Designs:
1955: *Tiger At the Gate* **1956:** *Romeo and Juliet* **1965:** *Half a Sixpence; Right Honorable Gentleman, The* **1969:** *Canterbury Tales*

James D. Sandefur

James D. Sandefur was born on February 26, 1958 in St. Louis. He received a B.F.A. in 1981 from Southern Methodist University and a M.F.A. from the Yale School of Drama in 1985, where he was a Donald Oenslager Scholar. His early experience in theatre was as an actor. As a designer, he believes that having performed aids his understanding of actors' and dancers' needs. James Sandefur also states that his background in various skilled areas such as scenic painting, properties, and construction in regional theatres also helps him realize designs. He includes Ming Cho Lee and William and Jean Eckart as mentors. In 1987 he received the American Theatre Wing Design Award for *Fences*.

Scenic Designs:
1987: *Fences*

Bruno Santini

Bruno Santini, a native of Switzerland, studied at the Wimbledon School of Theatre Design with Richard Negri and assisted several designers (including Barry Kaye) early in his career. He has designed sets for the National Theatre (including *Single Spies*), for the Lyric Studio (Hammersmith), the Scottish Opera, English Music Theatre, D'Oyly Carte, Welsh National Opera and many others. He has collaborated with director Simon Callow in the United Kingdom on productions including *Shirley Valentine*, which subsequently moved to Broadway. He is also production designer for Simon Callow's 1991 film version of Carson McCullers' novel *Ballad of the Sad Cafe*.

Scenic Designs:
1989: *Shirley Valentine*

Costume Designs:
1989: *Shirley Valentine*

Tony Sarg

An artist and puppeteer, Tony Sarg originated the large balloons now universally associated with Macy's Thanksgiving Day Parade. Born on April 24, 1882 in Guatemala and educated in Europe, he began professional life as an illustrator in London where he became fascinated with Holden, the great English puppet master. He subsequently established his own puppet theatre at the Old Curiosity Shop. He came to the United States in 1915 and became a citizen in 1921, working mainly as an illustrator for magazines and newspapers such as *The New York Times, Saturday Evening Post* and *Colliers*. In the late 1920s he formed the Tony Sarg Company (later the Tony Sarg Marionette Workshop), which produced marionette shows, window displays, and animated cartoons. He also illustrated children's books and designed furnishings. Tony Sarg died on March 7, 1942 in New York City.

Scenic Designs:
1917: *Morris Dance, The*

William Noel Saulter

William Noel Saulter designed two sets in the mid-1940s on Broadway.

Scenic Designs:
1945: *Make Yourself At Home* **1946:** *Haven, The*

Steele Savage

Steele Savage designed scenery and costumes for a play on Broadway in 1934. He was born in Detroit, Michigan in 1900 and studied at the Detroit School of Fine Arts, the Chicago Art Institute and the Slade School in London. He is primarily a magazine and book illustrator. For four years he lived and painted in the West Indies. He has illustrated a number of books for children including M. Komroff's *Bible Dictionary for Boys and Girls*.

Scenic Designs:
1934: *Caviar*

Costume Designs:
1934: *Caviar*

Carol Sax

Mr. Carol Sax established several theatres including the Vagabond Theatre in Baltimore in 1918 and the Romany Theatre in Lexington, Kentucky. He produced plays in Paris with a company of American actors for the 1929-30 season and was managing producer of the Manchester Repertory Company in England. He was also on the faculty at the Universities of Kentucky and Iowa as a professor of Art. Mr. Sax died at age 76 on September 28, 1961.

Scenic Designs:
1928: *Lady Dedlock*

Schaffner and Sweet

Walter Schaffner and Chandos Sweet ran a scenic studio at 449 First Avenue in New York City in the 1920s. They produced their own designs and constructed and painted scenery for other designers. Chandos Sweet moved to New York from his native Kansas City, Missouri in 1910. He was a stage manager and theatrical manager for producers including Charles Frohman, Arthur Hopkins and Henry W. Savage. Chandos Sweet died at age 77 in Queens, New York on February 29, 1960. Walter Schaffner was a scenic painter and landscape artist who worked for the Shuberts in addition to his association with Sweet. Walter Schaffner also designed under his own name and additional information is available under the heading "Walter Schaffner."

Scenic Designs:
1925: *Easy Terms* **1926:** *New York Exchange* **1927:** *We All Do* **1928:** *This Thing Called Love* **1929:** *Kibitzer*

Walter Schaffner

Walter Schaffner studied at the National Academy of Design and was a landscape painter in addition to being a scenic painter and designer. He was associated with Chandos Sweet in the scenic studio Schaffner and Sweet in the 1920s. His designs were no doubt more extensive than those credited to him because he also worked for the Shuberts and other producers. He died on September 30, 1934 in Montrose, New York.

Scenic Designs:
1924: *Bye, Bye, Barbara* **1925:** *China Rose*; *Oh! Oh! Nurse*

Douglas Schmidt

Douglas Schmidt has designed sets for numerous shows both on and off-Broadway and in regional theatres around the United States. Born on October 4, 1942 in Cincinnati, he studied at Boston University with Horace Armistead and Raymond Sovey and with Lester Polakov at the Studio and Forum of Stage Design. His theatre experience includes directing and stage management and occasionally costume design. He began designing with *The Thirteen Clocks* by James Thurber at High Mowing School in Wilton, New Hampshire in 1960 and in summer stock. Design activity in regional theatres includes Cincinnati Playhouse in the Park, Center Stage in Baltimore, the Old Globe, the Ahmanson Theatre, the Mark Taper Forum and The Guthrie Theatre. He has designed numerous sets for operas at the Tanglewood Festival and the Juilliard School. Often honored for outstanding scenic design, Mr. Schmidt received a Maharam Award for *Enemies* in 1973, and Drama Desk Awards for *Veronica's Room* and *Over Here!*. He has also designed sets for television and José Limon. *Nick and Nora*, with settings by Douglas W. Schmidt, is scheduled for the 1990-91 Broadway season.

Scenic Designs:
1970: *Paris Is Out* **1972:** *Country Girl, The*; *Grease*; *Love Suicide At Schofield Barracks, The* **1973:** *Measure for Measure*; *Streetcar Named Desire, A*; *Veronica's Room* **1974:** *American Millionaire, An*; *Fame*; *Over Here*; *Who's Who in Hell* **1975:** *Angel Street* **1976:** *Herzl*; *Robber Bridegroom, The* **1977:** *Threepenny Opera, The* **1978:** *Runaways*; *Stages* **1979:** *Most*

Happy Fella, The; *Peter Allen "Up in One"*; *Romantic Comedy*; *They're Playing Our Song* **1981:** *Frankenstein* **1983:** *Porgy and Bess* **1985:** *Dancing in the End Zone* **1986:** *Smile*

Lighting Designs:
1972: *Country Girl, The*

Costume Designs:
1972: *Love Suicide At Schofield Barracks, The* **1976:** *Let My People Come*

M. Schmidt

Minna M. Schmidt was known primarily as a costume designer. She designed one set in 1948 for Broadway.

Scenic Designs:
1948: *David's Crown*

William Schroder

William Schroder is a designer of sets and costumes who has been active on Broadway since the mid-1970s. He has also designed for many regional theatres and in Europe. He wrote the children's book *Pea Soup and Sea Serpents*.

Scenic Designs:
1976: *Your Arms Too Short to Box with God* **1979:** *But Never Jam Today* **1980:** *Your Arms Too Short to Box with God* **1982:** *Your Arms Too Short to Box with God*

Costume Designs:
1976: *Your Arms Too Short to Box with God* **1979:** *But Never Jam Today* **1980:** *Horowitz and Mrs. Washington*; *Your Arms Too Short to Box with God* **1982:** *Your Arms Too Short to Box with God*

Edwin J. Schruers

In 1938 Edwin J. Schruers designed a set on Broadway.

Scenic Designs:
1938: *On the Rocks*

Karen Schultz

Karen Schultz was born in Wisconsin in 1951. She received a B.A. at the University of Wisconsin-Madison in 1974 under John Ezell and a M.F.A. at Yale in 1977 under Ming Cho

Lee. She began designing for the Madison Civic Theatre with *Scenes from American Life* and since then has designed dance, music videos, television commericals and scenery for films including *The Last Day of Frank and Jesse James*, *Mr. and Mrs. Bridge*, *Slaves of New York* and and an NBC-TV Movie of the Week. Recent off-Broadway designs include *Only Kidding* for West Side Arts. She is married to the set designer David Gropman.

Scenic Designs:
1978: *Inspector General, The*

Ernest Schütte

Ernest Heinrich Conrad Schütte designed one set on Broadway in 1928. A painter and an architect, he was born on April 5, 1890 in Berlin.

Scenic Designs:
1928: *Redemption*

Tom Schwinn

Tom Schwinn was born on November 20, 1947 in Sendai, Japan and received a B.A. at Wichita State University, where he began designing in the experimental theatre. He also has an an M.F.A. from the University of Iowa. He has been a visiting artist at the University of Delaware and has designed sets for industrial promotions, for regional theatres including the Long Wharf, and for off-Broadway theatres including the Manhattan Theatre Club. Herman Sichter and William Ritman have been instrumental in his career. Designs for television include *New Music Awards* and *A Tribute to Roy Orbison* (on the Showtime Network) which was nominated for an ACE Award. His wife, Helene Beba Shamash, is a costume designer.

Scenic Designs:
1980: *Nuts*

Mr. Scotson-Clark

Mr. George Frederick Scotson-Clark, a British artist and author, was born February 9, 1872 in Brighton, Sussex, England. He studied painting at the Slade School in London and came to the United States in 1891, where he worked as a commercial artist specializing in posters. He then moved back to England and after several years in London illustrating magazines returned to the United States to paint portraits and landscapes, while continuing to create advertising illustrations. Between 1918 and 1921 he was art director for *Century Magazine*. After service in World War I with the New York National Guard he became a U.S. citizen. Mr. Scotson-Clark died on December 20, 1927 in Connecticut.

Scenic Designs:
1916: *Beau Brummell*

Costume Designs:
1916: *Beau Brummell*

Ashmead Scott

Ashmead Eldridge Scott designed one Broadway set in 1922. He was associated with Stagecraft Studio, 17 East 39th Street, New York City in the 1920s. He also appeared in *The Mask of Hamlet* in 1921.

Scenic Designs:
1922: *Cat and the Canary, The*

J. Hutchinson Scott

J. Hutchinson Scott designed sets and costumes for two plays in the late 1960s. A British designer of sets and costumes, he was born in Northumberland, England in 1924. He studied at the Edward VII Art School, Durham University and the People's Theatre in Newcastle-Upon-Tyne. His first London production was *The Circle of Chalk* in 1945. At various times he served as resident set designer for the Oxford Playhouse and the Bristol Old Vic. He was a founding member of the Crest Theatre in Toronto. Mr. Scott died in September 1977 at age 53.

Scenic Designs:
1965: *Boeing-Boeing* 1966: *Help Stamp Out Marriage* 1967: *There's a Girl in My Soup* 1968: *Flip Side, The*

Costume Designs:
1965: *Boeing-Boeing* 1968: *Flip Side, The*

Arthur Segal

Arthur Segal designed sets on Broadway between 1926 and 1934. He was born on July 13, 1875 in Jassy, Romania and studied at the Berlin Academy (with Professors Schmidt-Reute and Hoelzel) and in Paris and Italy. Known primarily as a painter, he began exhibiting in Berlin in 1904 and helped found the Neue Secession (Salon der Refusierten). His paintings are in major collections around the world, including The Petit Palais in Geneva, The Tate Gallery in London, The Leo Baeck Institute in New York City, and The Museum of Modern Art in Zurich. Arthur Segal died in London in 1944.

Scenic Designs:
1926: *Broadway* **1933:** *Both Your Houses*; *First Apple, The*; *Her Man Max*; *Three-Cornered Moon* **1934:** *But Not for Love*; *Sky's the Limit, The*

George Segare

George Segare designed a set on Broadway in 1932.

Scenic Designs:
1932: *Laughing Past, The*

Richard Seger

Richard Seger studied at the Art Institute of Chicago and the Royal Poinciana Playhouse in Palm Beach, California where he had a scholarship to work and study theatre. He was born in Hinsdale, Illinois on May 3, 1937 and began designing for community theatres in Chicago, where he made his debut as a set designer with *The Importance of Being Earnest*. His New York productions include *Day of Absence and Happy Ending* and *The World of Günter Grass* as well as his shows on Broadway. He has also designed many productions for theatres on the West Coast, where he lives and paints. His many awards include Drama Logues for *Little Foxes, Hotel Paradiso, End of the World With Symposium to Follow* and *5th of July* at A.C.T., and *The Country Wife, Rashomon, Pygmalion, Tartuffe, Anthony and Cleopatra*, and *The Night of the Iguana* at the Old Globe. For the past two years he has devoted his talents to painting large figurative works in oil.

Scenic Designs:
1969: *Butterflies Are Free* **1976:** *Something's Afoot*

Claudio Segovia

Claudio Segovia was born in Buenos Aires, where he studied scenery and painting at the Academia Naçional de Artes Visuales. He has designed sets and costumes for plays and operas around the world since 1965. In addition he creates productions using popular music and folk traditions such as *Flamenco Puro*, performed for the first time in Seville, Spain and in a second edition in 1984 in Paris. Mr. Segovia often collaborates as a director, creator and set and costume designer with Hector Orezzoli. Their scenic designs for *Black and Blue* were nominated for a Tony Award in 1989.

Scenic Designs:
1985: *Tango Argentino* **1986:** *Flamenco Puro* **1989:** *Black and Blue*

Lighting Designs:
1986: *Flamenco Puro*

Costume Designs:
1985: *Tango Argentino* **1986:** *Flamenco Puro* **1989:** *Black and Blue*

Roderick Seidenberg

Roderick Seidenberg graduated from Columbia University with a degree in architecture. He was a member of the New York architectural firm Sugarman & Berger and designed the New Yorker Hotel and the Garment Center Building. In 1927 he also designed scenery for a Broadway play. In the late 1930s he left New York and moved to Bucks County, Pennsylvania where he wrote, painted and continued to work as an architect, specializing in restoring and rebuilding old houses. His books include *Post-Historic Man* and *Anatomy of the Future*. He died in Doylestown, Pennsylvania at age 83 on August 27, 1973.

Scenic Designs:
1927: *Prisoner, The*

Richard Harrison Senie

Richard Harrison Senie designed scenery for one play on Broadway in 1951. He worked as a scenic designer in New York, creating scenery for the Theatre Guild and the Balinese Dancers among other companies. He also designed for television.

Scenic Designs:
1951: *Saint Joan*

Herbert Senn

(Charles) Herbert Senn was born on October 9, 1924 in Ilion, New York and studied at Columbia University with his mentor Woodman Thompson. He began designing while in high school and made his debut in London's West End with *The Boys From Syracuse* at the Drury Lane Theatre in November 1963. He often designs in collaboration with Helen Pond, concentrating on sets but occasionally designing lights. The team has designed extensive productions off-Broadway, for numerous summer seasons at the Cape Play House, Dennis, Massachusetts, and for operas and ballets throughout the United States.

Scenic Designs:
1963: *Double Dublin* 1964: *Roar Like a Dove*; *What Makes Sammy Run?* 1968: *Noel Coward's Sweet Potato* 1973: *No Sex Please, We're British* 1975: *Musical Jubilee, A* 1981: *Macbeth* 1983: *Show Boat* 1986: *Oh Coward!*

Lighting Designs:
1963: *Double Dublin* 1964: *Roar Like a Dove*; *What Makes Sammy Run?*

James Shannon

James Shannon designed one set in 1932 on Broadway. A painter, he resided at 240 West 17th Street, New York City in 1918.

Scenic Designs:
1932: *Marriage of Cana, The*

Irene Sharaff

During an illustrious career Irene Sharaff designed costumes for twenty-two ballets in New York, London, Tokyo, Milan, Copenhagen and San Francisco; thirty movies, seventeen of which were musicals; two television specials, and sixty-one productions on Broadway, thirty-three of which were musicals. For her efforts she has been rewarded with a Donaldson Award, the Antoinette Perry Award for *The King And I* in 1951 and five Academy Awards (out of sixteen nominations). Originally from Boston, she studied at the Art Students League, the New York School of Fine and Applied Arts and in Paris at the Grande Chaumière. Miss Sharaff was introduced to Aline Bernstein in 1928 and became her assistant for costumes, sets and properties at the Civic Repertory Theatre. It was her designs for the scenery and costumes of *Alice In Wonderland* at the Civic in 1932 which launched her own career. Shortly afterward she debuted on Broadway with the costume designs for *As Thousands Cheer*. The revivals of *The King and I* in 1981 using her original designs and *Jerome Robbins' Broadway* in 1988 were the culmination of a Broadway career which spanned five decades for one of the premier costume designers of the twentieth century. Irene Sharaff resides in New York City.

Scenic Designs:
1932: *Alice in Wonderland* 1935: *Crime and Punishment*; *Rosmersholm* 1939: *American Way, The*

Costume Designs:
1929: *On the High Road*; *Seagull, The* 1930: *Green Cockatoo, The*; *Lady from Alfaqueque, The*; *Siegfried* 1932: *Alice in Wonderland* 1933: *As Thousands Cheer* 1934: *Great Waltz, The*; *Life Begins At 8:40*; *Union Pacific* 1935: *Great Waltz, The*; *Jubilee*; *Parade*; *Rosmersholm* 1936: *Idiot's Delight*; *On Your Toes*; *White Horse Inn* 1937: *I'd Rather Be Right*; *Virginia* 1938: *Boys from Syracuse, The* 1939: *American Way, The*; *From Vienna*; *Streets of Paris* 1940: *All in Fun*; *Boys and Girls Together* 1941: *Banjo Eyes*; *Lady in the Dark*; *Land Is Bright, The*; *Mr. Bib*; *Sunny River* 1942: *By Jupiter*; *Count Me in*; *Star and Garter* 1943: *Lady in the Dark* 1945: *Billion Dollar Baby*; *Hamlet* 1946: *Would-Be Gentleman, The* 1948: *Magdalena* 1949: *Montserrat* 1950: *Dance Me a Song*; *Michael Todd's Peep Show* 1951: *King and I, The*; *Tree Grows in Brooklyn, A* 1952: *Of Thee I Sing* 1953: *Me and Juliet* 1954: *By the Beautiful Sea*; *On Your Toes* 1956: *Candide*; *Happy Hunting*; *Shangri-La* 1957: *Small War on Murray Hill*; *West Side Story* 1958: *Flower Drum Song* 1959: *Juno* 1960: *Do Re Mi*; *West Side Story* 1963: *Girl Who Came to Supper, The*; *Jennie* 1964: *Funny Girl* 1966: *Sweet Charity* 1967: *Hallelujah, Baby!* 1973: *Irene* 1977: *King and I, The* 1980: *West Side Story* 1985: *King and I, The*

Redington Sharpe

Redington Sharpe, a set designer born Robert Redington Sharpe, studied at the Art Institute in Cleveland before moving to New York at the age of seventeen to study with and assist Norman Bel Geddes. In 1924 he became Art Director of the Pasadena Community Playhouse in California, where he designed numerous sets and occasionally costumes. He also designed in Los Angeles and Europe before making his Broadway debut in 1936 with the set designs for *Tobacco Road*. He died on May 14, 1934 at the age of 29.

Scenic Designs:
1915: *Major Barbara; Two Virtues, The* **1928:** *Major Barbara* **1929:** *Claire Adams* **1930:** *Joseph* **1933:** *Saint Wench; Tobacco Road* **1937:** *Tobacco Road* **1942:** *Tobacco Road* **1943:** *Tobacco Road*

Costume Designs:
1928: *Major Barbara*

Bob Shaw

Bob Shaw has designed scenery on Broadway throughout the 1980s and has extensive credits at the Public Theatre, including *Tacky Stuff* in 1988. He was born in Philadelphia on January 1, 1957 and received a B.F.A. at the Pratt Institute in 1978. He collaborated with his mentor Wilford Leach, principal director of the New York Shakespeare Festival, on twelve productions including his New York debut, *The Mandrake*. Awards include Drama Desk nominations for *The Pirates of Penzance, The Mystery of Edwin Drood* and *Hamlet*, and an Outer Critics Circle Award for *The Mystery of Edwin Drood*.

Scenic Designs:
1981: *Pirates of Penzance, The* **1984:** *Human Comedy, The* **1985:** *Mystery of Edwin Drood, The* **1987:** *Coastal Disturbances*

William Sheafe

William Sheafe, Jr. designed both scenery and lighting on Broadway during the teens. In collaboration with George H. Skelton he ran a design business, Sheafe & Skelton at 1547 Broadway in New York City in 1919. He resided at 64 West 9th Street in 1922.

Scenic Designs:
1916: *Six Who Passed While the Lentils Boiled*

Lighting Designs:
1919: *Phantom Legion, The*

Paul Shelving

Paul Shelving, a British designer and artist, was born in Rowley Regis, Staffordshire, England and studied art in London. He designed sets and costumes for the first time at the Court Theatre in 1914 for *The Cockyolly Bird*. After World War I he became resident designer for the Birmingham Repertory Theatre Company, designing numerous shows there over the next several years. He also created many sets and costumes at the Malvern Festival during the 1930s, in addition to numerous credits in London. He usually designed sets and costumes for the same production. Mr. Shelving died at age 79 in June 1968.

Scenic Designs:
1927: *Yellow Sands*

Costume Designs:
1927: *Yellow Sands*

George Sheringham

George Sheringham, a British painter and designer, was born in London on November 13, 1885 and studied art at the Slade School and in Paris. He began designing sets and costumes in 1924 in London with *Midsummer Madness* and often worked in collaboration with Sir Nigel Playfair. He first designed in New York in 1931. His paintings were exhibited throughout Europe and are in the collections of the South Kensington Museum, the Musée de Luxembourg, the Manchester Whitworth Gallery and the Ottawa Gallery. Honors include the Paris Grand Prix for theatre design and architectural decoration in 1925 and an award from the Royal Society of Arts in 1936. He died on November 11, 1937 at age 53.

Scenic Designs:
1948: *Patience; Pirates of Penzance, The*

Costume Designs:
1931: *Unknown Warrier, The; Venetian, The* **1948:** *H.M.S. Pinafore; Patience; Pirates of Penzance, The* **1951:** *Trial By Jury/ H.M.S. Pinafore* **1955:** *H.M.S. Pinafore; Pirates of Penzance, The; Trial By Jury*

Loren Sherman

Loren Sherman was born on January 21, 1955 in Chicago. He has designed numerous off-Broadway productions including the Playwright

Horizons premieres of *Romance Language, The Dining Room, Baby with the Bathwater* and *The Nice and the Nasty*. He designed *Coriolanus, Coming of Age in Soho, The Marriage of Bette and Boo, Richard III* and *Wenceslaus Square* among others for the New York Shakespeare Festival. He has also designed for the Roundabout, Circle Rep, INTAR, Juilliard, and the Young Playwrights Festival, and in regional theatres throughout the United States. In 1985 he won an Obie Award for sustained excellence in set design. He acknowledges Robert Keil at the University of Chicago High School, Henry May at the University of California at Berkeley, and Ming Cho Lee at the Yale University School of Drama as mentors. He also designed sets for *Shogun* on Broadway in 1991.

Scenic Designs:
1986: *Shakespeare on Broadway for the Schools* **1987:** *Sleight of Hand*

Paul Sheriff

Paul Sheriff, an art director, was born Paul Shouvalov in Moscow on November 13, 1903. When he became a British citizen in 1930 he took his professional name. His grandfather was the Czar's Ambassador to London in the 1880s. He studied at Oxford and worked as an architect and mining engineer before studying film design with Lazare Meerson and working in the British film industry in the late 1930s. He was highly regarded in England for his set designs for films which included *Henry V, The Millionairess, The Grass is Greener, Dark Journey* and *Moulin Rouge*, for which he received an Academy Award for Art Direction in 1952. He occasionally also designed costumes and in 1948 designed a Broadway show. Paul Sheriff died at age 57 on September 28, 1965.

Scenic Designs:
1947: *Crime and Punishment* **1948:** *Macbeth*

Costume Designs:
1948: *Macbeth*

Walter Sherwood

Walter Sherwood designed sets for three plays in the mid-1920s on Broadway. A painter, he resided at 1344 St. Nicholas Avenue in New York City in 1918.

Scenic Designs:
1925: *Night Hawk* **1926:** *Blonde Sinner, The*; *Night Hawk*

Everett Shinn

Everett Shinn, born on November 6, 1873 in Woodstown, New Jersey, was best known as a mural painter, illustrator and set designer. He studied at the Pennsylvania Academy of Fine Arts before moving to New York, where he worked as an illustrator for various newspapers and magazines. A member of "The Eight" (also known as the "Ashcan School"), he painted many street scenes in addition to clowns, dancers and actors. He also painted the murals in the Belasco Theatre in New York. Mr. Shinn, who died at age 79 on May 1, 1953, was elected to the National Institute of Arts and Letters in 1951 in recognition of his artistic contributions during a career spanning fifty years.

Scenic Designs:
1917: *In for the Night*

Costume Designs:
1930: *Roadside*

John Shipley

John Shipley designed sets in 1980 for a Broadway play.

Scenic Designs:
1980: *Quick Change*

Hassard Short

(Hubert) Hassard Short was born in Edlington, Lincolnshire, England on October 15, 1877 and made his acting debut at the Drury Lane Theatre in 1895. He came to the United States in 1901 and continued acting but became interested in directing and producing. In 1920 he directed *Honeydew*, the first of more than fifty hit musicals. He installed his own lighting system at the Music Box Theatre for *Honeydew* and often designed lights and occasionally scenery for plays he also directed. He produced many popular musicals such as *Roberta, Show Boat, Music Box Revues, The Great Waltz* and *As Thousands Cheer*. An innovative director, he used colored lights and other effects and is considered by many to be the first to replace footlights with lights hung from the ceiling over the audience and directed toward the stage. Hassard Short died in Nice, France on October 9, 1956.

Scenic Designs:
1924: *Hassard Short's Ritz Revue*

Lighting Designs:
1920: *Honey Girl* 1933: *Roberta* 1934: *Great Waltz, The* 1937: *Frederika* 1939: *American Way, The; From Vienna* 1941: *Banjo Eyes; Lady in the Dark* 1943: *Carmen Jones; Lady in the Dark* 1944: *Mexican Hayride; Seven Lively Arts* 1947: *Music in My Heart* 1948: *Make Mine Manhattan* 1950: *Michael Todd's Peep Show*

Costume Designs:
1920: *Honey Girl*

Vassily Shoukhoeff

Vassily Shoukhoeff (a.k.a. Vasilii Ivanovich Shukhaev) collaborated on the scenery and costume designs for a musical revue in 1925 which had originated in London. He was born on January 12, 1887 in Moscow and died May 14, 1973 in Tbilisi, U.S.S.R. He studied at the Academy of Arts in St. Petersburg and became a member of the World of Art Society in 1917. He exhibited frequently and emigrated to western Europe in 1922 living mainly in Paris. He also painted portraits, illustrated books, created murals, and designed the interior of La Maisonnette Russe in Paris. He moved to Leningrad in 1935 and was Professor of Drawing at the Academy of Arts in Tbilisi beginning in 1947.

Scenic Designs:
1925: *Chauve Souris*

Costume Designs:
1925: *Chauve Souris*

James Shute

James L. Shute designed sets for two shows in the mid-1920s. A playwright, he wrote *Trapped* in 1928 with F.G. Johnson and *Fools for Scandal* with Nancy Hamilton and Rosemary Casey in 1938.

Scenic Designs:
1926: *Trumpet Shall Sound, The* 1927: *Granite*

Stanley Simmons

Stanley Simmons was born in New Orleans and took drawing classes there as a child. After moving to New York he studied for a time at the Art Students League, but gave up drawing to devote himself to dancing. As a dancer he performed in several Broadway shows, including *Out of this World* in 1950 and with various dance companies. He studied with Louis Chalif, Anatole Vilzak and Madame Alexander among others. His first major assignment as a designer was *On Your Toes* in summer stock, but it was Agnes De Mille who pushed him into design. She choreographed a piece for him and gave him a ballet to design as incentive. Karinska constructed the costumes and encouraged him further. He now designs costumes regularly for dance companies in the United States, Europe and Canada, including the Joffrey Ballet and the Eliot Feld Ballet. Recent dance designs include Baryshnikov's *The Spectre of the Rose*. He concentrates on costumes and only rarely designs scenery.

Scenic Designs:
1956: *Waiting for Godot*

Costume Designs:
1955: *Almost Crazy* 1956: *Waiting for Godot* 1957: *Waiting for Godot* 1961: *Come Blow Your Horn* 1966: *Show Boat* 1967: *There's a Girl in My Soup* 1969: *Come Summer* 1975: *Rogers and Hart* 1976: *So Long, 174th Street* 1977: *King and I, The* 1980: *Brigadoon; Music Man, The* 1985: *King and I, The*

Victor Simoff

Victor Simoff designed scenery for two plays on Broadway in 1923.

Scenic Designs:
1923: *Lower Depths, The; Tsar Fyodor Ivanovitch*

Lee Simonson

Lee Simonson, a designer of sets, costumes and occasionally lights, was born on June 26, 1888 in New York City and was graduated from Harvard in 1909. He designed scenery for the Washington Square Players from 1917 until drafted into the service a year later. After World War I he helped found the Theatre Guild and served as one of its directors from 1919 to 1940. He debuted on Broadway with the Theatre Guild's production of *The Faithful.* He designed sets and costumes for numerous plays and operas and also taught design. In 1947 he designed Wagner's *Ring Cycle* for the Metropolitan Opera, one of his many designs there. He wrote several books about scene design, including *The Art of Scenic Design, The Stage is Set* and an autobiography, *Part of a Lifetime* published in 1943. This talented, prolific designer died at age 78 on January 23, 1967. His second wife was the costume designer Carolyn Hancock.

Scenic Designs:

1919: *Faithful, The; Moliere* **1920:** *Cat Bird, The; Heartbreak House; Jane Clegg; Martinique; Mirage, The; Power of Darkness, The; Treasure, The* **1921:** *Don Juan; Liliom; Mr. Pim Passes; Tangerine* **1922:** *Back to Methuselah; From Morn Till Midnight; He Who Gets Slapped; Lucky One, The; R.U.R.; Tidings Brought to Mary, The; World We Live In, The* **1923:** *Adding Machine, The; As You Like It; Failures, The; Peer Gynt; Spring Cleaning* **1924:** *Carnival; Fata Morgana; Man and the Masses; Mongrel, The; Sweet Little Devil* **1925:** *Arms and the Man; Glass Slipper, The* **1926:** *Goat Song; Juarez and Maximillian* **1927:** *Mr. Pim Passes By; Road to Rome, The* **1928:** *Marco Millions; Road to Rome, The; Volpone* **1929:** *Camel Through the Needle's Eye; Carnival; Damn Your Honor; Dynamo* **1930:** *Apple Cart, The; Elizabeth the Queen; Hotel Universe; Marco Millions; Roar China; Volpone* **1931:** *Lean Harvest; Miracle At Verdun* **1932:** *Collision; Good Earth, The; Red Planet* **1933:** *American Dream; Mask and the Face, The; Masks and Faces; School for Husbands* **1934:** *Days Without End; Jigsaw; Rain from Heaven; Sleeping Clergyman, A; They Shall Not Die* **1935:** *Parade; Simpleton of the Unexpected Isles* **1936:** *Call It a Day; End of Summer; Idiot's Delight; Prelude to Exile* **1937:** *Amphitryon 38; Madame Bovary; Masque of Kings, The; Virginia* **1938:** *Lorelei; Wine of Choice* **1944:** *Streets Are Guarded, The* **1945:** *Foxhole in the Parlor* **1946:** *Joan of Lorraine*

Lighting Designs:

1924: *Carnival* **1933:** *American Dream* **1946:** *Joan of Lorraine*

Costume Designs:

1919: *Faithful, The* **1920:** *Jane Clegg; Martinique; Power of Darkness, The; Treasure,*

The **1921:** *Don Juan; Liliom* **1922:** *Back to Methuselah; He Who Gets Slapped; R.U.R.; Tidings Brought to Mary, The* **1923:** *Adding Machine, The; As You Like It; Failures, The; Peer Gynt* **1924:** *Fata Morgana; Man and the Masses* **1925:** *Arms and the Man; Glass Slipper, The* **1926:** *Goat Song; Juarez and Maximillian* **1927:** *Road to Rome, The* **1928:** *Marco Millions; Road to Rome, The; Volpone* **1929:** *Camel Through the Needle's Eye; Damn Your Honor; Dynamo* **1930:** *Apple Cart, The; Elizabeth the Queen; Marco Millions; Roar China; Volpone* **1932:** *Collision* **1933:** *School for Husbands* **1934:** *Sleeping Clergyman, A* **1935:** *Parade; Simpleton of the Unexpected Isles* **1936:** *Prelude to Exile* **1937:** *Madame Bovary; Masque of Kings, The* **1945:** *Foxhole in the Parlor* **1946:** *Joan of Lorraine*

Thomas R. Skelton

Thomas R. Skelton entered the field of lighting design as an apprentice electrician under Jean Rosenthal while on a scholarship at the American Dance Festival. Interestingly he later influenced the career of lighting designer Jennifer Tipton under similar circumstances. He was born in Bridgetown, Maine on September 24, 1927 and received a B.F.A. at Middlebury College. His New York debut was *The Enchanted* in 1958, soon followed by an extensive list on and off-Broadway and throughout the United States. He has been associated with major dance companies such as the Joffrey Ballet, New York City Ballet, Paul Taylor, and José Limon and is co-founder and associate artistic director of the Ohio Ballet. Primarily a lighting designer, he has occasionally designed sets. Recent productions include *Papa*, starring George Peppard as Ernest Hemingway, and *Songs Without Words, Printemps, Cotillion, Clowns* and *Nutcracker* for the Joffrey Ballet. During the course of his career Thomas Skelton has been instrumental in making lighting designers indispensable members of production teams and fostering the talents of new generations of lighting designers.

Scenic Designs:

1962: *Tiao Ch'in, or The Beautiful Bait*

Lighting Designs:

1963: *Oh Dad, Poor Dad, Mamma's Hung You...* **1964:** *Wiener Blut (Vienna Life); Zizi* **1968:** *Jimmy Shine; Mike Downstairs*

1969: *Coco; Come Summer; Does a Tiger Wear a Necktie?; Indians; Partiot for Me, A* **1970:** *Henry V; Lovely Ladies, Kind Gentlemen; Purlie* **1972:** *Lincoln Mask, The; Purlie; Secret Afairs of Mildred Wild, The; Selling of the President, The* **1973:** *Gigi; Status Quo Vadis; Waltz of the Toreadors, The* **1974:** *Absurd Person Singular; Where's Charley?* **1975:** *All God's Chillun Got Wings; Death of a Salesman; First Breeze of Summer, The; Glass Menagerie, The; Musical Jubilee, A; Shenandoah* **1976:** *Days in the Trees; Guys and Dolls; Kings; Lady from the Sea, The; Legend; Matter of Gravity, A* **1977:** *Caesar and Cleopatra; King and I, The; Romeo and Juliet* **1978:** *Kingfisher, The; November People, The* **1979:** *Oklahoma!; Peter Pan; Richard III* **1980:** *Brigadoon; Camelot; Filumena* **1981:** *Camelot; Can-Can; West Side Waltz, The* **1982:** *Seven Brides for Seven Brothers* **1983:** *Dance a Little Closer; Mame; Peg; Show Boat* **1984:** *Death of a Salesman* **1985:** *Iceman Cometh, The* **1986:** *Lillian* **1989:** *Few Good Men, A*

J. Blanding Sloan

J. Blanding Sloan was a set designer active on Broadway between 1918 and 1923. Earlier he had designed sets for the Little Theatre in Chicago for fellow scenic designers Ellen Von Volkenburg and Maurice Browne. His designs were included in an exhibition of the New American Stagecraft at the Bourgeois Galleries in New York City in 1919. He was a member of the Wits and Fingers Scenic Studio in the 1920s and worked with marionette units of the Federal Theatre Project. He was born in Corsicana, Texas on September 19, 1886 and studied at the Chicago Academy of Fine Arts with B.J.O. Nordfeldt and George Senseney.

Scenic Designs:
1918: *Jonathan Makes a Wish* **1922:** *Greenwich Village Follies* **1923:** *Uptown West*

Bruce Smith

Bruce Smith, a leading British scenic artist, collaborated with R. McCleery on the scene design for a production on Broadway in 1915. He was active during the late nineteenth and early twentieth centuries. The production was brought to New York "intact from the Theatre Royal,

Drury Lane, London." As was common at the time, Bruce Smith designed Act I, scene, 2 Act II, scenes, 5, 6, Act III, scenes, 2, 4, 5, 6, 7 and R. McCleery designed the remaining scenes. He also designed the pantomines *Jack and the Beanstalk* in 1899 and *Babes in the Wood* in 1907 at the Drury Lane Theatre in London, working again with R. McCleery and also with Harry Brooke, Harry Emden, and E. Nichols. He received dozens of credits for scenic design and mechanical effects for productons in London between 1890 and 1929. Bruce Smith was born in 1855 and died at age 87 on November 8, 1942. In 1985 a biography, *"Sensation" Smith of Drury Lane* by Dennis Castle, his grandson, was published by Charles Skilton Ltd., London.

Scenic Designs:
1915: *Stolen Orders*

Ernest Allen Smith

Ernest Allen Smith was born in Erie, Pennsylvania on May 9 1943. After receiving a B.A. in General Arts and Sciences at Pennsylvania State University and an M.A. in Directing and History at Hunter College, he studied design at Columbia and marketing and finance at New York University. Mr. Smith is principally a scene designer who also does lighting and costumes. He has assisted many New York designers including Charles Elson, Patton Campbell and David Hayes. His designs have been seen in operas, films, industrials and regional theatres. Recent sets include *Camelot* at the American Musical Theatre and a showcase production of *The Good Life* in New York City. The Con-Ed Industrial Show on "The Life of Thomas Edison" featured costumes by Ernest Allen Smith.

Scenic Designs:
1980: *Musical Chairs*

Costume Designs:
1977: *Gemini*

Oliver Smith

Oliver Lemuel Smith was born in Wawpawn, Wisconsin on February 13, 1918 and graduated from the Pennsylvania State University in 1939. Known primarily as a scenic designer, he first designed professionally for the Ballet Russe de Monte Carlo performance at the Metropolitan

Opera in 1941, making his debut on Broadway the following year with the scenic design for *Rosalinda*. Since that time he has designed sets for over four hundred productions for ballet, opera, theatre and film, and occasionally contributed costume designs to those productions. The recipient of Tony Awards for scenic design for *My Fair Lady*, *West Side Story*, *The Sound of Music*, *Becket*, *Camelot*, *Hello, Dolly* and *Baker Street*, he received many other nominations. He was also nominated for an Academy Award for *Guys and Dolls* and has produced many of the shows he has designed. From 1945 to 1981 he was co-director of the American Ballet Theatre with Lucia Chase, returning as Artistic Co-Director in 1989 following the departure of Mikhail Baryshnikov.

Scenic Designs:

1942: *Rosalinda* **1944:** *On the Town*; *Perfect Marriage, The*; *Rhapsody* **1945:** *Billion Dollar Baby* **1946:** *Beggar's Holliday* **1947:** *Brigadoon*; *High Button Shoes*; *Topaz* **1948:** *Look Ma, I'm Dancin'* **1949:** *Along Fifth Avenue*; *Gentlemen Prefer Blondes*; *Miss Liberty*; *Miss Liberty* **1950:** *Bless You All* **1951:** *Paint Your Wagon* **1952:** *Pal Joey* **1953:** *Carnival in Flanders*; *In the Summer House* **1954:** *Burning Glass, The*; *On Your Toes* **1955:** *Will Success Spoil Rock Hunter?* **1956:** *Auntie Mame*; *Candide*; *Mr. Wonderful*; *My Fair Lady* **1957:** *Clearing in the Woods, A*; *Eugenia*; *Jamaica*; *Nude with Violin*; *Time Remembered*; *Visit to a Small Planet, A*; *West Side Story* **1958:** *Flower Drum Song*; *Present Laughter*; *Say, Darling*; *Winesburg, Ohio* **1959:** *Cheri*; *Destry Rides Again*; *Five Finger Exercise*; *Goodbye Charlie*; *Juno*; *Sound of Music, The*; *Take Me Along* **1960:** *Becket*; *Camelot*; *Taste of Honey, A*; *Under the Yum-Yum Tree*; *Unsinkable Molly Brown, The*; *West Side Story* **1961:** *Daughter of Silence*; *Gay Life, The*; *Mary, Mary*; *Night of the Iguana, The*; *Sail Away*; *Show Girl* **1962:** *Come On Strong*; *Lord Pengo*; *Romulus*; *Tiger Tiger Burning Bright* **1963:** *110 Degrees in the Shade*; *Barefoot in the Park*; *Children from Their Games*; *Girl Who Came to Supper, The*; *Natural Affection* **1964:** *Bajour*; *Beeckman Place*; *Ben Franklin in Paris*; *Chinese Prime Minister, The*; *Dylan*; *Hello, Dolly*; *I Was Dancing*; *Luv*; *Poor Richard*; *Slow Dance on the Killing Ground* **1965:** *Baker Street*; *Cactus Flower*; *Kelly*; *Odd Couple, The*; *On a Clear Day You Can See Forever*; *Very Rich Woman, A* **1966:** *Best Laid Plans, The*; *I Do! I Do!*; *Show Boat*; *Star Spangled Girl, The* **1967:** *Hello, Dolly*; *How Now Dow Jones*; *Illya Darling*; *Song of the Grasshopper* **1968:** *Darling of the Day*; *Exercise, The*; *Plaza Suite*; *Weekend* **1969:** *But, Seriously*; *Come Summer*; *Dear World*; *Indians*; *Jimmy*; *Last of the Red Hot Lovers*; *Partiot for Me, A* **1970:** *Lovely Ladies, Kind Gentlemen* **1971:** *Four in a Garden* **1972:** *Little Black Book, The*; *Lost in the Stars* **1973:** *Gigi*; *Tricks*; *Women, The* **1974:** *All Over Town* **1975:** *Don't Call Back*; *Hello, Dolly (Starring Pearl Bailey)*; *Royal Family, The* **1976:** *Heiress, The*; *My Fair Lady* **1978:** *Do You Turn Somersaults*; *First Monday in October*; *Hello, Dolly* **1979:** *Carmelina* **1980:** *Clothes for a Summer Hotel*; *Lunch Hour*; *Mixed Couples*; *West Side Story* **1981:** *My Fair Lady*; *Talent for Murder, A* **1982:** *84 Charing Cross Road*

Lighting Designs:
1963: *Children from Their Games*

Costume Designs:
1955: *Will Success Spoil Rock Hunter?* **1959:** *Five Finger Exercise* **1961:** *Daughter of Silence*; *Sail Away*

Russell Smith

Russell (Rusty) Smith is from Winder, Georgia and is married to the actress Anne Allgood. He has designed productions at the Yale University School of Drama, in regional theatres, for films and summer stock. Productions include the national tour of *One Mo' Time* and *Guys and Dolls* at the StageWest Theatre. He was assistant production designer for the film *Sticky Fingers*.

Scenic Designs:
1985: *Blood Knot*

M. Solotaroff

M. Solotaroff designed one set in 1935 for a Broadway production.

Scenic Designs:
1935: *Recruits*

Sergi Soudeikine

Sergi Soudeikine (a.k.a.   Sergei Yurievich Soudeikine) was born in Tiflis, Russia on March

19, 1882 and studied at the Moscow Fine Arts School, the Imperial Academy in St. Petersburg and the Grande Chaumière in Paris. He began his career designing stage sets in Moscow in 1905 for Maeterlinck's *The Death of Tintagiles* and soon became one of Russia's foremost designers. At the onset of the Russian Revolution he settled in Paris. His designs were first seen in New York in 1922 when the impresario Balieff brought *Chauve Souris* to New York. His success led him to many more opportunities in the theatre and opera designing sets and occasionally costumes. He became a member of the stage production staff at Radio City Music Hall in New York in 1934 and worked there for many years. In addition he ran a decorative arts studio in Stony Point, New York. Married to the operatic soprano Jeanne Palmer, Mr. Soudeikine died on August 12, 1946 in Nyack, New York.

Scenic Designs:

1922: *Chauve Souris; Revue Russe* **1925:** *Chauve Souris* **1926:** *Chief Thing, The* **1927:** *Chauve Souris* **1929:** *Chauve Souris* **1934:** *Chinese Nightingale, The; New Faces* **1935:** *Porgy and Bess* **1936:** *Forbidden Melody* **1943:** *Chauve Souris: 1943*

Costume Designs:

1922: *Chauve Souris; Revue Russe* **1926:** *Chief Thing, The* **1927:** *Chauve Souris* **1929:** *Chauve Souris* **1934:** *Chinese Nightingale, The; New Faces* **1943:** *Chauve Souris: 1943*

Raymond Sovey

Raymond Sovey was a prolific scenic designer who followed the common practice of his time of creating costumes for productions he was engaged to design. Born in 1897 in Torrington, Connecticut, he studied at Columbia University and taught art in Baltimore before beginning his association with the theatre. He began as an actor, appearing on Broadway in 1919 before designing his first production in 1920. The following forty years were busy ones for him, filled with designs for numerous plays. Mr. Sovey died at age 72 on June 25, 1966. He received Tony Award nominations for his scenic designs for *The Great Sebastians* and for his costume designs for *All the Way Home*.

Scenic Designs:

1920: *George Washington; Mirage, The* **1921:** *Iphigenia in Aulis* **1923:** *Icebound; Jolly Roger,*

The; Saint Joan; White Desert; You and I **1924:** *Cheaper to Marry; Dear Sir; Mask and the Face, The; Nancy Ann; New Toys* **1925:** *Butter and Egg Man, The; Harvest; Puppets; Something to Brag About* **1926:** *Adorable Liar, The; Gentlemen Prefer Blondes; Glory Hallelujah; Ladder, The; Proud Woman, A; Ramblers, The* **1927:** *Brother's Karamazov, The; Coquette; Letter, The; Mikado, The; Wild Man of Borneo, The* **1928:** *Animal Crackers; Command Performance, The; Front Page, The; Goin' Home; Hotbed; Little Accident; She's My Baby; Three Cheers; Tonight At 12; Wings Over Europe* **1929:** *Meteor; Other Men's Wives; Scarlet Pages; Strictly Dishonorable; Top Speed* **1930:** *Art and Mrs. Bottle; As Good As New; Inspector General, The; Strike Up the Band; That's the Woman; Twelfth Night; Vinegar Tree, The; Waterloo Bridge* **1931:** *After All; Cloudy with Showers; Counsellor-At-Law; Fast Service; Green Grow the Lilacs; Left Bank, The; Way of the World, The; Wiser They Are, The; Wonder Boy* **1932:** *Black Sheep; Counsellor-at-Law; Here Today; Hey, Nonny Nonny; Honeymoon; I Loved You Wednesday; Men Must Fight; She Loves Me Not; Wild Waves* **1933:** *Blue Widow, The; Conquest; Doctor Monica; Her Master's Voice; Lone Valley; She Loves Me; Shooting Star* **1934:** *Distaff Side, The; Oliver! Oliver!; Portrait of Gilbert; Post Road; Ragged Army; Wooden Slipper, The* **1935:** *Bright Star; Distant Shore, The; Dominant Sex, The; Eldest, The; Fly Away Home; Libel; Life's Too Short; May Wine; Most of the Game; Petrified Forest, The* **1936:** *Alice Takat; Promise, The; Star Spangled; Sweet Aloes; Tovarich* **1937:** *Amazing Dr. Clitterhouse; And Now Good-Bye; Babes in Arms; French Without Tears; Loves of Women; Yes, My Darling Daughter* **1938:** *Dance Night; If I Were You; Knights of Song; Once Is Enough; Oscar Wilde; Our Town* **1939:** *Miss Swan Expects; Woman Brown, The* **1940:** *Delicate Story; Grey Farm; Jupiter Laughs; Ladies in Retirement* **1941:** *Arsenic and Old Lace; Boudoir; Happy Days, The; Letters to Lucerne; Ring Aroung Elizabeth; Village Green; Walrus and the Carpenter, The; Your Loving Son* **1942:** *Broken Journey; Counsellor-at-Law; Damask Cheek, The; Flare Path; Guest in the House; Strip for Action* **1943:** *Another Love Story; Murder Without Crime; Outrageous Fortune; Tomorrow the World; Vagabond King, The*

1944: *Feathers in a Gale*; *For Keeps*; *Jackpot*; *Lower North*; *Over Twenty-One*; *Sleep, My Pretty One*; *Soldier's Wife* 1945: *And Be My Love*; *Hasty Heart, The*; *Mermaids Singing*; *Place of Our Own, A*; *Rich Full Life, The*; *Ryan Girl, The*; *State of the Union*; *Therese* 1946: *Antigone*; *Apple of His Eye*; *Temper the Wind*; *This, Too, Shall Pass*; *Wonderful Journey* 1947: *For Love Or Money*; *Heiress, The*; *I Gotta Get Out*; *Love Goes to Press*; *Parlor Story* 1948: *Edward, My Son*; *Grandma's Diary*; *Hallams, The*; *Harvest of Years* 1949: *Traitor, The* 1950: *Cocktail Party*; *Ring 'Round the Moon* 1951: *Four Twelves Are 48*; *Gigi*; *Gramercy Ghost*; *Remains to Be Seen* 1952: *One Bright Day* 1954: *Living Room, The*; *Witness for the Prosecution* 1956: *Great Sebastian, The*; *Reluctant Debutant, The* 1957: *Under Milkwood* 1958: *Patate*

Lighting Designs:
1948: *Edward, My Son*; *Grandma's Diary* 1950: *Cocktail Party*; *Ring 'Round the Moon* 1954: *Living Room, The* 1955: *Chalk Garden, The* 1959: *Look After Lulu*

Costume Designs:
1920: *George Washington* 1921: *Macbeth* 1923: *Saint Joan* 1924: *Flame of Love* 1927: *Coquette*; *Mikado, The* 1928: *Command Performance, The*; *Jealous Moon, The*; *La Gringa*; *She's My Baby* 1930: *As Good As New*; *Second Little Show, The*; *Twelfth Night* 1931: *Third Little Show, The*; *Way of the World, The* 1932: *Here Today*; *Hey, Nonny Nonny*; *Wild Waves* 1933: *Her Master's Voice* 1934: *Portrait of Gilbert*; *Ragged Army* 1935: *Distant Shore, The* 1936: *Tovarich* 1938: *Oscar Wilde* 1939: *Woman Brown, The* 1940: *Grey Farm*; *Jupiter Laughs* 1942: *Damask Cheek, The* 1944: *Lower North* 1945: *Hasty Heart, The*; *Therese* 1951: *Gramercy Ghost* 1954: *Living Room, The*; *Witness for the Prosecution* 1960: *All the Way Home*

Bill Stabile

Bill Stabile began his career in theatre in Ohio with the Kenley Players. He moved to the East Coast in the early 1970s to paint floats for Macy's Thanksgiving Day Parade but quickly became involved with experimental theatres. He has designed sets for numerous productions at La Mama E.T.C., Circle Rep and Spookhouse. He has also collaborated often with Tom O'Horgan, including *Lily* at the New York State Opera and *The Architect and the Emperor of Assyria*.

Scenic Designs:
1981: *I Won't Dance* 1982: *Torch Song Trilogy*

Paul Staheli

Paul Staheli designed one set on Broadway in 1969. He has been art director for numerous films, including *Revenge of the Ninja, The Boogens, Earthbound, Hangar 18* and *In Search of the Historical Jesus*.

Scenic Designs:
1969: *Three Sisters, The*

George S. Steele

George S. Steele designed one set on Broadway in 1936. An architect, he worked at 420 Madison Avneue in 1932 and resided in Shrewsbury, New Jersey.

Scenic Designs:
1936: *Fresh Fields*

Douglas Stein

Douglas Stein graduated from the Yale University School of Drama in 1982 and has since become an active designer in regional theatres. A native of Harrisburg, Pennsylvania, he has designed for the Manhattan Theatre Club, Arena Stage, and the Goodman Theatre. Recent credits include *Our Town* at Lincoln Center and *The Skin of Our Teeth* for The Guthrie Theatre. He teaches at New York and Princeton Universities and is on the board of Theater Communications Group. He received an Obie Award for *Through the Leaves*.

Scenic Designs:
1988: *Our Town* 1989: *Largely New York*

Charles Stepanek

Charles (Karel) Stepanek designed a Broadway set in 1931. An actor, he was born in Brno,

Czechoslovakia on October 29, 1899 and debuted on stage in his hometown in 1920. Occasionally he contributed ideas for designs of productions in which he also performed. He appeared for several seasons in Berlin with major companies, one of which toured the United States in the early 1930s. In 1940 he moved to London, initially working as a political commentator for the BBC before resuming his acting career in 1941. He also appeared in New York in 1951 as Baron Prus in *The Makropoulos Secret*.

Scenic Designs:
1931: *If Love Were All*

Ernest Stern

Ernest (a.k.a. Ernst) Stern was born in 1876 in Bucharest, Romania and trained in Munich at the Academy of Arts. In 1906 he joined Max Reinhardt's theatre as art director and created designs of sets and costumes for numerous plays during the following years. In 1911 his designs were first seen in London and in 1912 a production of *Sumurum*, with sets and costumes by Ernest Stern, came to New York from Berlin. His designs in London, included *Kismet* and *Bitter-Sweet* in 1925. Between 1943 and 1945 he designed for Sir Donald Wolfit. He also designed films both in London and Hollywood, mainly for Ernst Lubitsch. His book of reminiscences, *My Life, My Stage*, was published in London in 1951. Ernest Stern died in 1954.

Scenic Designs:
1927: *Danton's Tod* **1929:** *Bitter Sweet* **1936:** *White Horse Inn* **1937:** *Young Madame Conti* **1947:** *As You Like It*; *King Lear*

Costume Designs:
1927: *Danton's Tod* **1929:** *Bitter Sweet* **1947:** *As You Like It*; *King Lear*

Dale Stetson

Dale Stetson debuted on Broadway with the set for *The New Yorkers*, designed from sketches by Peter Arno, who wrote the musical extravaganza in 1927. While he specialized in scenic design he also designed costumes. Also a mural painter, he created a large painting of the East River for the opening of the East River Savings Bank on Cortlandt Street in New York City in 1935.

Scenic Designs:
1927: *New Yorkers, The* **1930:** *New Yorkers, The* **1931:** *Here Goes the Bride*; *Three Times the Hour* **1932:** *Christopher Comes Across*; *Fatal Alibi, The*

Costume Designs:
1932: *Christopher Comes Across*

Florine Stettheimer

Florine Stettheimer was a portrait painter and set designer who lived and worked at the Beaux Arts Studio, the legendary arts salon run by Florine and her sisters at 80 West 40th Street in New York City. She was born on August 19, 1871 and studied at the Art Students League. She began painting portraits with studies of her family. Her paintings are in the collections of the Museum of Modern Art and at Columbia University. Her designs for *Four Saints in Three Acts* were remarkable since few established artists of the time also designed for the theatre. Although the practice is now more common, Florine Stettheimer was the first established mainstream artist to design for the Broadway theatre. She died on May 12, 1944 in New York City.

Scenic Designs:
1934: *Four Saints in Three Acts*

Frank W. Stevens

Frank W. Stevens designed sets for two Broadway productions in the early 1940s. He was associated with Joseph Teichner Studios, Inc. at 152 West 46th Street in New York City in 1931 and was a company director.

Scenic Designs:
1942: *Keep 'Em Laughing*; *Laugh, Town, Laugh*

John Wright Stevens

John Wright Stevens has designed sets for film, television, operas, industrial promotions and theatre. He has designed for the New York Shakespeare Festival at Lincoln Center and for Early Music Dramas presented by the Waverly Consort. He also designed the set for *Without Willie* off-Broadway in 1983. His film work includes *The Lathe of Heaven*, *La Voix Humaine*, and art direction for the 1989 film *Rooftops*.

He received a B.A. at Catholic University and an M.F.A. from the Yale University School of Drama.

Scenic Designs:
1981: *Animals; One Act Play Festival, The*

Frank Stout

Frank Stout, who designed a set on Broadway in 1915, was director of scenic art at the Carnegie Institute of Technology. He also painted still lifes and landscapes. He died on April 10, 1955 at age 79 in Sharon, Connecticut.

Scenic Designs:
1915: *Maker of Dreams, The*

Frederick Stover

Although primarily a designer for film and television, Frederick Stover designed sets and lights on Broadway during the 1940s. He was one of the first students in the graduate program at Yale University where he studied with Donald Oenslager. He was an active designer on the West Coast and was chief designer of the Los Angeles unit of the Federal Theatre Project.

Scenic Designs:
1940: *Meet the People* **1945:** *Hamlet* **1947:** *Man and Superman* **1949:** *Browning Version, The and A Harlequinade*

Lighting Designs:
1949: *Harlequinade, A and The Browning Version*

C. Strahlendorff

C. Strahlendorff designed scenery on Broadway in 1915.

Scenic Designs:
1918: *Passing Show of 1918, The*

Tony Straiges

Tony Straiges was born in Minersville, Pennsylvania on October 31, 1942. While living in Washington, D.C. he became involved with theatre through the American Light Opera Company and the American Puppet Theatre. After serving in the army he studied briefly at Carnegie Mellon and worked as a design assistant in San Francisco. He subsequently studied with Eldon Elder at Brooklyn College and with Ming Cho Lee at the Yale School of Drama and credits both men as mentors.. The technical director Peter Feller has also influenced his career. Tony Straiges has designed in major regional theatres in the United States and off- Broadway. He is the recipient of a Maharam and a Tony Award for *Sunday in the Park with George*, a Phoebe Award, a Boston Critics Award, a Drama Desk Award and an Outer Critics Circle Award in New York City.

Scenic Designs:
1978: *History of the American Film, A*; *Timbuktu* **1979:** *Richard III* **1980:** *Harold and Maude* **1981:** *Copperfield* **1984:** *Sunday in the Park with George* **1986:** *Long Day's Journey into Night* **1987:** *Into The Woods* **1988:** *Rumors* **1989:** *Artist Descending a Staircase*; *Dangerous Games*

Anthony W. Street

Anthony W. Street (a.k.a. A.W. Street) designed scenery on Broadway during the 1930s.

Scenic Designs:
1930: *International Review, The* **1932:** *Zombie* **1934:** *Furnished Rooms* **1935:** *Satellite*

Walter Street

Walter Street designed a Broadway show in 1934. He resided with his wife Annie at 1851 7th Avenue in New York City in 1932.

Scenic Designs:
1934: *Late Wisdom*

Oscar Strnad

Oscar Strnad, an Austrian architect and designer was associated with Max Reinhardt at the Kunstgewerbe Schule in Vienna. He built the Schloss Theatre in the park at Reinhardt's Castle in Leopoldskron near Salzburg. He also rebuilt the Salzburg Festspielhaus and "Fausttown" in the Salzburg Felsenreitschule. He designed *Don Juan* at Théâtre des Champs-Élysées in Paris in 1928. Both Robert Edmond Jones and Jo Mielziner studied his theories of

architecture and design. Professor Strnad died
at age 56 on September 3, 1935 in Vienna.

Scenic Designs:
1927: *Midsummer Night's Dream, A* **1928:** *Peripherie*

Austin Strong

Austin Strong, the playwright who wrote the
hit comedy *Seventh Heaven*, was born in San
Francisco in 1881 and raised in New Zealand
and Samoa. He attended Wellington College
in Australia and studied in France and Italy
as a landscape architect. The grand-stepson of
Robert Louis Stevenson, he began writing soon
after settling in London and his first play, *The
Exile*, was produced in 1903. He wrote several hit plays, among them *A Good Little Devil,
Three Wise Fools* and *A Play Without A Name*
(for which he also designed the set.) He contributed to the *New York Times, Saturday Review of Literature, The Atlantic Monthly* and
other publications and served for several years
on the Pulitzer Prize Drama jury, resigning in
1934 due to restrictions placed on the jury. He
died on September 17, 1952 in Nantucket, Massachusetts.

Scenic Designs:
1928: *Play Without Name, A*

Stroppa of Milan

Stroppa of Milan designed one set in 1923.
Stroppa is credited with scenery for the London
productions of *Thais* at the Drury Lane Theatre
in 1920, and for *Ghosts* and *Cosi Sia* at the New
Oxford Theatre in 1923.

Scenic Designs:
1923: *Laugh, Clown, Laugh*

Zenobius Strzelecki

Zenobius Strzelecki, a Polish theatrical designer,
created scenery for a production on Broadway in
1967. The production originated at the Jewish
State Theatre of Poland with Ida Kaminska as
Artistic Director. He was born in Burgstadt,
Germany on October 23, 1915 and studied at
the Warsaw Academy of Fine Arts and the State
Theatrical Insistute with L. Schiller. An active

scenic designer in Poland, he wrote *Polska plas-
tyka teatralna (Polish Theatrical Plastic Art)*, a
history of stage design in Poland, published in
1966, *Kierunki scenografii wsyólczesnez (Trends
in Modern Polish Scenery)* in 1979 and *Kon-
wencje scenograficzne (Contemporary Scenography)* in 1973.

Scenic Designs:
1967: *Mother Courage*

Ed Sullivan

Edward Vincent Sullivan, known to television
audiences for the *Ed Sullivan Show* which ran
Sunday nights on CBS-TV for twenty-three
years, was involved in many aspects of show
business. He was born on September 28, 1902 in
New York City. He worked for a series of newspapers, settling at *The Evening Graphic* in 1927
where he became Broadway columnist in 1929.
He produced vaudeville shows and emceed radio shows, organized benefits during World War
II and wrote film scripts. In 1947 he was hired
to emcee *Toast of the Town* which became the
Ed Sullivan Show. An early advocate for hiring black performers on television, he practiced
his own philosophy, providing audiences with an
extraordinary performance by Marian Anderson
in 1952 among others. As a young sportswriter
he had helped publicize a basketball game between the original Celtics and Bob Douglas' Renaissance team at the Armory. He later produced vaudeville and legitimate productions and
in 1948 with Noble Sissle directed and designed
Harlem Calvacade, the first Broadway production with a black cast. Ed Sullivan died on October 13, 1974 at age 72.

Scenic Designs:
1942: *Harlem Cavalcade*

Ed Sundquist

Ed Sundquist was an easel painter, scenic
painter and designer. He designed and painted
sets in New York, San Francisco, and Pittsburgh. As proprietor of the Ed Sundquist Studio
he designed additional productions and painted
sets for other designers. Known for his marine
paintings, he died on October 11, 1961 at age 80
in Taconic, Connecticut.

Scenic Designs:
1915: *Ware Case, The* **1916:** *Her Soldier Boy*
1917: *De Luxe Annie* **1918:** *Cure for Curables,*
A **1930:** *Brown Buddies* **1935:** *Weather Permitting* **1938:** *Wild Duck, The*

Ed Sundquist Studio

Scenic painter and designer Ed Sundquist also operated a scenic studio which was active in the teens. For additional information, see "Ed Sundquist".

Scenic Designs:
1917: *Fugitive, The; Imaginary Invalid, The*

Josef Svoboda

Josef Svoboda is an internationally renowned Czechoslovakian scenographer. He was born on May 10, 1920 in Caslav, Czechoslovakia and trained as an architect in Prague. Since 1948 he has been the head designer at the National Theatre, Prague and has designed sets and costumes throughout the world for operas, ballets, plays and films. He is an advocate of a blend of contemporary technology and traditional scenic design techniques and uses both projections and mirror effects. He has designed over five hundred productions during his career and influenced the designs of countless designers and productions. His British debut was *The Storm* in 1966 at the National Theatre. His designs have been seen only rarely in the United States, but include a notable *Carmen* at the Metropolitan Opera in the 1970s. Josef Svoboda has been honored with numerous prizes and honorary degrees.

Scenic Designs:
1974: *Jumpers*

Lyall Swete

Lyall Swete, a British actor, playwright and producer, was born in Wrington, Somerset, England on July 25, 1865 and studied at Trinity College at Stratford-upon-Avon. He debuted as an actor in 1887 in Margate, England in *The Road to Ruin*, and made his first appearance in London in 1900 in *Henry V*. He produced *Chu-Chin-Chow* in New York in 1917, subsequently appearing and producing other plays including

Clair de Lune, for which he also designed the settings. He died on February 19, 1930.

Scenic Designs:
1921: *Clair De Lune*

Richard Sylbert

Richard Sylbert, known primarily as a production designer for movies, was born in Brooklyn, New York in April 1928. He attended the Tyler School of Fine Arts and Temple University, hoping to be a painter. His mentor was William Cameron Menzies, perhaps the greatest American film designer, with whom he was associated for two months just prior to Menzies' death. He began his design career with NBC-TV in 1952. His list of film credits reads like a list of the best recent films and includes *Carnal Knowledge, Tequilla Sunrise, Fat City, Baby Doll, Dick Tracy, Face in the Crowd, The Graduate, The Manchurian Candidate, Splendor in the Grass, Rosemary's Baby, Cotton Club,* and *Bonfire of the Vanities.* He was nominated for Academy awards for *Shampoo, Chinatown* and *Reds* and received Oscars for art direction for *Who's Afraid of Virginia Woolf?* and *Dick Tracy.* In addition, he also designed the set for the long running television show, *Cheers.*

Scenic Designs:
1957: *Egghead, The* **1971:** *Prisoner of 2nd Avenue, The*

Vic Symonds

Vic Symonds, a British designer, has often worked in collaboration with Alan Pickford during the past twenty-five years. He was production designer with Pickford for *The Jewel in the Crown* shown on *Masterpiece Theatre* on PBS in 1984. The production won the Royal Television Society Design Award for 1983-84. Vic Symonds has designed other television films including *Bedroom Farce, Occupations* and the feature film *The Long Good Friday.*

Scenic Designs:
1962: *Rattle of a Simple Man* **1963:** *Rattle of a Simple Man*

Sointu Syrjala

Sointu Syrjala, born in Toronto on December 30, 1904, grew up in Fitchburg, Massachusetts. He attended the Worcester Museum School, the National Academy of Design and the Boston Museum School of Fine Arts. He designed scenery for the theatre and television beginning with *Precedent* in the early 1930s. Earlier he had performed in the chorus in several musicals before becoming an assistant to Jo Mielziner and Willy Pogany. With Ben Hecht he put on pageants to aid Israel, including *We Will Never Die* in 1943 and *Salute to Israel* in 1970. During 1968 he designed the restoration of Ford's Theatre in Washington, D.C. Mr. Syrjala also designed regularly for television beginning in 1951. For CBS-TV his credits included *The Guiding Light* and *Secret Storm*. He retired in 1972 due to failing eyesight and died at age 74 in April 1979.

Scenic Designs:

1928: *Heavy Traffic* **1931:** *Devil in the Mind; Precedent* **1933:** *Armourette; Far-Away Horses* **1934:** *Milky Way, The; Stevedore* **1935:** *Blind Alley; Remember the Day* **1936:** *Double Dummy; Stark Mad; Swing Your Lady* **1937:** *Pins and Needles* **1938:** *Pins and Needles* **1951:** *Fourposter, The*

Costume Designs:

1936: *Swing Your Lady* **1937:** *Pins and Needles*

Samuel L. Tabor

Samuel L. Tabor designed a set in 1934 on Broadway. In 1918 he worked as a cap maker and resided at 632 East 11th Street, New York City.

Scenic Designs:

1934: *Late Wisdom*

Alan Tagg

Alan Tagg trained for a career in theatre at the Old Vic Theatre School. He was born in Sutton-in-Ashfield, England and has been designing in London since 1952. He has designed numerous productions in the West End, for the Royal Court Theatre, the Royal Shakespeare Company, the National Theatre, and in Chichester as well as in New York, Europe and Australia. Alan Tagg also designs exhibitions.

Scenic Designs:

1957: *Look Back in Anger* **1958:** *Entertainer, The* **1965:** *All in Good Time* **1967:** *Black Comedy* **1974:** *London Assurance* **1978:** *Kingfisher,*

The **1979:** *Whose Life Is It Anyway?* **1980:** *Who's Life Is It Anyway?* **1986:** *Corpse!* **1990:** *Lettice & Lovage*

Costume Designs:

1967: *Black Comedy*

Herman Patrick Tappé

Herman Patrick Tappé had a varied career in New York. He was a successful women's dress designer and proprietor of shops on East 50th and West 57th streets in New York City, and also headed the millinery manufacturers Chez Tappé LaMode, Inc. He designed scenery and costumes for productions on Broadway spanning four decades, specializing in costumes. In addition John and Herman Tappé operated a saloon, "Tappé Brothers," in 1919 at 383 West 125th Street. Herman Tappé died at age 78 on September 20, 1954.

Scenic Designs:

1917: *Polly with a Past*

Costume Designs:

1921: *Good Morning, Dearie* **1927:** *Ivory Door, The* **1930:** *Uncle Vanya* **1940:** *International Incident, An*

Tarazona Brothers

Tarazona Brothers received credit for one set in 1917. Enrique Tarazona and Luis Crispo were proprieters of Acme Scenery & Decorating Company, supplying "High Grade European Art on Guaranteed Fire Proof Material" at 1547 Broadway, New York City in 1916.

Scenic Designs:

1917: *Land of Joy, The*

James A. Taylor

James A. Taylor designed a set in 1965 on Broadway. He has extensive credits for ABC-TV and CBS-TV, including the daytime programs *The Nurses* and *As the World Turns* as well as special news events. He has designed off-Broadway, for stock companies, the St. Paul Civic Opera, Theatre Under The Stars in Atlanta, Georgia and for the Papermill Playhouse, among others.

Scenic Designs:

1965: *Glass Menagerie, The*

Morris Taylor

Morris Taylor designed a set in 1982 on Broadway.

Scenic Designs:
1982: *Cleavage*

Robert U. Taylor

Robert U. Taylor was born in 1941 in Lexington, Pennsylvania. He studied at the University of Pennsylvania, the Pennsylvania Academy of Fine Arts and the Yale University School of Drama. He has taught at Hunter College and Princeton. Since his Broadway debut he has designed for many of the foremost regional theatres, including the Goodman, McCarter and Guthrie theatres, among others. He received a Drama Desk and Marharam Award for *Beggars' Opera* in 1972. As design coordinator he designed many productions for the Colonnades Theatre Lab in the 1970s including *A Month in the Country*. He has also worked with the Chelsea Theatre Group and more recently for the off-off-Broadway Greek Theatre. He has devoted increasing attention to art direction of television commercials. Recent accounts have included Anacin, Canada Dry, Charmin, Nyquil and Scott Paper.

Scenic Designs:
1971: *Unlikely Heroes* 1973: *Beggar's Opera, The*; *Raisin* 1974: *Lamppost Reunion* 1975: *Boccaccio* 1977: *Happy End*

Charles Teichner

Charles Teichner designed scenery for Broadway plays between 1928 and 1930 under his own name and through his scenic studio. He worked primarily as a scenic artist and resided with his wife Martha at 735 Mace Avenue, New York City in 1933.

Scenic Designs:
1930: *Dora Mobridge*

Charles Teichner Studios

Charles Teichner designed scenery both under his name and through his studio. For additional information see "Charles Teichner."

Scenic Designs:
1928: *Parisiana*

Joseph Teichner

Joseph Teichner was active on Broadway during the 1920s under his own name and through his studio, Joseph Teichner Scenic Studios. He was born in Gyoma, Hungary on February 18, 1888 and studied painting with J. Carlson. Joseph Teichner received credit for productions under various spellings of his name, including Josef Tichenor and Joseph Tickner.

Scenic Designs:
1925: *Earl Carroll's Vanities*; *Florida Girl* 1927: *Babbling Brooks*; *Bottom of the Cup, The*; *Junk*; *What Do We Know?*

Joseph Teichner Studio

Joseph Teichner operated a scenic studio at 314 Eleventh Avenue in the 1920s. In the early 1930s, in association with Armin and Bertha Teichner and Frank W. Stevens, Joseph Teichner Studios was located at 152 West 46th Street. In addition to theatrical work the firm also worked as decorators. For additional information, see "Joseph Teichner" and "Pogany-Teichner Studios."

Scenic Designs:
1927: *Africana* 1929: *Earl Carroll's Sketch Book* 1932: *Girls in Uniform*; *Tell Her the Truth* 1933: *Man Bites Dog* 1934: *Caviar*

Rouben Ter-Arutunian

Rouben Ter-Arutunian, a scenic and costume designer, was born on July 24, 1920 in Tiflis, Russia. He studied concert piano in Berlin and art in both Berlin and Paris. His first design was for *The Bartered Bride* in Dresden in 1941, followed by costumes for the Berlin State Opera Ballet. In 1951 he moved to the United States, becoming a citizen in 1957. His extensive designs include scenery, costumes and occasionally lights for ballets, operas and theatres in the United States and around the world. He has been staff designer for the three major television networks and has also designed variety shows and specials. Mr. Ter-Arutunian received an Emmy Award for Art Direction in 1957 for *Twelfth Night*, an Outer Critics Circle Award for *Who Was that Lady I Saw You With?* in 1958, and a Tony Award for Costume Design for *Redhead* in 1959.

Scenic Designs:

1957: *New Girl in Town* 1958: *Maria Golovin*; *Who Was That Lady I Saw You With?* 1959: *Redhead* 1960: *Advise and Consent* 1961: *Donnybrook!* 1962: *Passage to India, A* 1963: *Arturo Ui*; *Hot Spot* 1964: *Deputy, The*; *Milk Train Doesn't Stop Here Anymore, The* 1965: *Devils, The* 1966: *Ivanov* 1968: *Exit the King*; *I'm Solomon* 1969: *Dozens, The* 1971: *All Over* 1975: *Goodtime Charley* 1976: *Days in the Trees*; *Lady from the Sea, The* 1980: *Goodbye Fidel*; *Lady from Dubuque, The*

Lighting Designs:

1957: *New Girl in Town* 1963: *Arturo Ui*

Costume Designs:

1957: *New Girl in Town* 1959: *Redhead* 1961: *Donnybrook!* 1962: *Passage to India, A* 1963: *Arturo Ui*; *Hot Spot* 1964: *Milk Train Doesn't Stop Here Anymore, The* 1966: *Ivanov* 1969: *Dozens, The* 1971: *All Over* 1976: *Days in the Trees*; *Lady from the Sea, The*

Max Teuber

Max Teuber designed lights in 1929 and scenery in 1933 on Broadway. A theatrical producer he resided at 203 West 103rd Street, New York City in 1925.

Scenic Designs:

1933: *Murder At the Vanities*

Lighting Designs:

1929: *Earl Carroll's Sketch Book*

Clara Fargo Thomas

Mrs. Clara Fargo Thomas was a set designer for two plays in the 1920s on Broadway. A commercial artist, she resided at 114 East 19th Street, New York City in 1933.

Scenic Designs:

1924: *Second Mrs. Tanqueray, The* 1928: *High Road, The*

Woodman Thompson

Woodman Thompson was a scenic designer who also created costumes. He began his theatrical career in 1918 and worked steadily in the theatre until his death on August 30, 1955 at the age of 66. He was a member of the faculty at Carnegie

Tech when the undergraduate theatre program was established, but left for New York City in 1921, a move that would prove permanent. He was resident designer for the Theatre Guild, the Actor's Theatre, and the Equity Theatre and taught design both privately and at Columbia University. A member of United Scenic Artists from 1923, he served his fellow designers as President, Vice President and Treasurer at various times.

Scenic Designs:

1922: *Malvaloca*; *Rivals, The*; *Why Not?* 1923: *Business Widow, The*; *Chastening, The*; *Neighbors*; *Queen Victoria*; *Roger Bloomer*; *Sweet Nell of Old Drury* 1924: *Admiral, The*; *Beggar on Horseback*; *Candida*; *Close Harmony*; *Expressing Willie*; *Firebrand, The*; *Habitual Husband, The*; *Hedda Gabler*; *Macbeth*; *Marjorie*; *Minick*; *New Englander, The*; *What Price Glory?* 1925: *Beggar on Horseback*; *Candida*; *Cocoanuts, The* 1926: *Desert Song, The*; *God Loves Us*; *Hedda Gabler*; *Importance of Being Earnest, The*; *Iolanthe*; *Pirates of Penzance, The*; *Shelf, The*; *White Wings* 1927: *Iolanthe*; *Pirates of Penzance, The* 1928: *Merchant of Venice, The*; *These Few Ashes* 1929: *Primer for Lovers, A* 1930: *Merchant of Venice, The*; *Midnight*; *This One Man* 1932: *Dangerous Corner*; *Warrior's Husband, The* 1933: *Dangerous Corner* 1934: *Lady Jane* 1935: *Bishop Misbehaves, The*; *Tomorrow's a Holiday* 1936: *Plumes in the Dust* 1937: *Candida*; *Ghost of Yankee Doodle, The* 1942: *Candida* 1946: *Candida*; *Hear the Trumpet*; *Magnificent Yankee*

Lighting Designs:

1946: *Hear the Trumpet*

Costume Designs:

1922: *Malvaloca* 1923: *Neighbors*; *Queen Victoria*; *Sweet Nell of Old Drury* 1924: *Beggar on Horseback*; *Firebrand, The*; *Hedda Gabler* 1925: *Beggar on Horseback*; *Candida* 1926: *Iolanthe*; *Pirates of Penzance, The*; *Shelf, The* 1928: *Merchant of Venice, The* 1930: *Merchant of Venice, The* 1932: *Warrior's Husband, The* 1936: *Plumes in the Dust* 1937: *Candida* 1942: *Candida* 1946: *Hear the Trumpet*; *Magnificent Yankee*

Brian Thomson

Brian Thomson designed lighting for a Broadway production in 1979.

Scenic Designs:
1975: *Rocky Horror Show, The*

Mary C. Thornton

Mary C. Thornton was born in Hamilton, Ontario, Canada in 1916. Her parents had come to Canada from Ascoli Piceno, Italy and Mary studied in Ontario and in Italy. She apprenticed with ceramics and fabrics artisans. After considering a career as an opera singer, she became wardrobe mistress for the Hamilton Opera Company. In 1986 she was scenic and costume designer and consultant for a production of the Famous People Players, whose artistic director is her daughter, Diana Dupuy. She has been associated with the company since its inception in 1974.

Scenic Designs:
1986: *Little Like Magic, A*

Costume Designs:
1986: *Little Like Magic, A*

Cleon Throckmorton

Cleon Throckmorton was supposed to play a part in the premiere of Eugene O'Neill's play *The Emperor Jones* at the Provincetown Players, but ended up designing the setting. "Throck" was born October 18, 1897 in Atlantic City, New Jersey. After earning a degree in engineering he studied design at the Carnegie Institute of Technology and George Washington University. He designed hundreds of plays during his career, and although his name is not as well known as his contemporary Robert Edmond Jones, he was instrumental in advancing the art and profession of scenic design. During the Depression he also produced melodramas in Hoboken, New Jersey, as well as plays at the Old Rialto and The Lyric Theatre in New York City, and the Millpond Playhouse in Roslyn, Long Island. He was associated with many theatre groups including the Provincetown Players, the Theatre Guild, the Neighborhood Playhouse and the Civic Repertory Theatre. Cleon Throckmorton died on October 23, 1965 at age 68 in Atlantic City, New Jersey.

Scenic Designs:
1921: *Hand of the Potter, The; Verge, The*
1922: *God of Vengeance, The; Greenwich Village Follies; Hairy Ape, The; Mr. Faust; Old Soak, The; Pigeon, The; Red Geranium, The;* Six Characters in Search of An Author 1923: *Children of the Moon; Potters, The; We've Got to Have Money* 1924: *All God's Chillun Got Wings; Crime in the Whistler Room, The; Emperor Jones, The; Fashion; George Dandin, Or the Husband Confounded; S.S. Glencairn; Six Characters in Search of An Author; Spook Sonata, The; Tantrum, The* 1925: *Adam Solitaire; Blue Peter, The; Devil to Pay, The; Emperor Jones, The/ The Dreamy Kid; Houses of Sand; Lovely Lady; Man Who Never Did, The; Man's Man, A; O, Nightingale; Odd Man Out; Outside Looking in; Rosmersholm; Ruint; Triumph of the Egg, The; Weak Sisters; Wisecrackers, The* 1926: *Beyond Evil; Beyond the Horizon; Bride of the Lamb; Dream Play, The; East Lynne; Emperor Jones, The; In Abraham's Bosom; Makropoulos Secret, The; Sandalwood; Saturday Night* 1927: *Burlesque; Earth; Good Hope, The; In Abraham's Bosom; Inheritors; Ivory Door, The; Jacob Slovak; King Can Do No Wrong, The; Lovely Lady; Menace; Paradise; Porgy; Rapid Transit; Stairs, The; Triple Crossed; Triumphant Bachelor, The; Wall Street* 1928: *Congai; Hot Pan; Killers; Napoleon; On Call; Patience; Rope; Scarlet Fox, The; These Modern Women* 1929: *Fiesta; Getting Even; Inspector Kennedy; Man's Estate; Porgy; Unsophisticates, The* 1930: *Old Rascal, The; Penny Arcade; Stepping Sisters; Torch Song* 1931: *Brass Ankle; Bride the Sun Shines On, The; Did I Say No?; Doctor X; Gray Shadow; Hobo; House of Connelly, The; How Money; Just to Remind You; Lady Beyond the Moon; Louder, Please; Regular Guy, A; Sentinels; She Means Business; Six Characters in Search of An Author; Springtime for Henry; Two Seconds; Widow in Green, A* 1932: *Another Language; Back Fire; Bulls, Bears, and Asses; Chyrasalis; Criminal At Large; Dark Hours, The; Hired Husband; Monkey; Moon in the Yellow River, The; Other One, The; Page Pygmalion; Rendezvous; Take a Chance; Truth About Blayds, The* 1933: *Alien Corn; Another Language; Comic Artist, The; Eight Bells; Give Us This Day; Is Life Worth Living?; Peace on Earth; Run, Little Chillun; Springtime for Henry; Threepenny Opera, The* 1934: *Gods We Make, The; Lord Bless the Bishop, The; Ode to Liberty; Sing and Whistle* 1935: *Bitter Oleander; Creeping Fire; Noah; Prisoners of War* 1936: *Bitter Stream; I Want*

a Policeman; In Heaven and Earth; Jefferson Davis; Lights O'London, The; Searching for the Sun; Woman of Destiny, A **1937:** *Curtain Call; Love in My Fashion; Without Warning* **1941:** *Ghost for Sale* **1942:** *Nathan the Wise*

Costume Designs:
1930: *Torch Song*

Cleon Throckmorton Studios

Cleon Throckmorton Scenic Studio, also known as Cleon Throckmorton, Incorporated, was located at 102 West 3rd Street. It was operated by Cleon Throckmorton in association with Oscar Liebetrau, Bernard Reiss, and Ralph Colin. For additional information, see "Cleon Throckmorton" and "Oscar Liebetrau".

Scenic Designs:
1926: *Silver Cord, The* **1933:** *Birthright*

Jane Thurn

Jane Thurn has designed numerous off-Broadway productions at the Manhattan Theatre Club, the Vineyard Theatre, and others. She designed the set for *Silent Dancing*, the PBS documentary on the Joffrey Ballet, and was art director for the New York unit of the film *Honky Tonk Freeway*. She has an M.F.A. in scenic design from Carnegie-Mellon University and has also designed television commercials.

Scenic Designs:
1981: *Scenes and Revelations*

Jan Tichacek

Jan Tichacek designed one set in 1938. An artist named Stephen Tichacek resided at 541 East 83rd Street, New York City in 1932.

Scenic Designs:
1938: *Danton's Death*

Martin Tilley

A British designer who specializes in scenery, Martin Tilley received his training at the Leicester Phoenix Theatre. His designs are seen in theatres around England. Other designs include the tour of *Suez* starring Roy Dotrice and the opera *Cosi Fan Tutti* at the 1978 Oxford

Festival. He has designed several productions for the King's Head in London, including *Kingdom Come* and *Catchpenny Twist*. In 1980 he designed on Broadway for the first time.

Scenic Designs:
1980: *Fearless Frank* **1983:** *Edmund Kean*

Costume Designs:
1983: *Edmund Kean*

James F. Tilton

James F. Tilton began designing while in the United States Army Special Services Division (1959-1962) as Resident Designer at the Frankfurt, West Germany Playhouse. After his discharge in 1963 he became principal designer for the APA Repertory. From 1963 to 1971 he designed numerous plays for APA, including the first production at the Phoenix Theatre, *Scapin*. He has designed for many regional theatres, industrial shows, and for other New York theatres. In 1970 he designed his first film, *Dear Dead Delilah*. He concentrates on the design of scenery and lights and only rarely designs costumes. James Tilton was born in Rochelle, Illinois on July 30, 1937 and received a B.A. at the University of Iowa in 1959.

Scenic Designs:
1965: *You Can't Take It with You* **1966:** *Right You Are...; School for Scandal, The; We, Comrades Three* **1967:** *Pantagleize; Show-Off, The; War and Peace; Wild Duck, The; You Can't Take It with You* **1968:** *Cherry Orchard, The; Cocktail Party, The; Misanthrope, The; Pantagleize; Show-Off, The* **1969:** *Cock-a-doodle Dandy; Hamlet; Private Lives* **1970:** *Harvey* **1971:** *Grass Harp, The; Oh! Calcutta!; School for Wives, The* **1975:** *Seascape* **1976:** *Comedians; Oh! Calcutta!* **1977:** *Vieux Carre* **1981:** *Twice Around the Park* **1983:** *You Can't Take It with You*

Lighting Designs:
1965: *You Can't Take It with You* **1967:** *Pantagleize; Show-Off, The* **1968:** *Cherry Orchard, The; Cocktail Party, The; Exit the King; Misanthrope, The; Pantagleize; Show-Off, The* **1969:** *Cock-a-doodle Dandy; Hamlet; Private Lives* **1970:** *Harvey* **1971:** *Grass Harp, The; School for Wives, The* **1975:** *Seascape* **1977:** *Vieux Carre* **1983:** *You Can't Take It with You*

Hal Tiné

Hal Tiné has designed over one hundred productions in regional theatres such as Syracuse Stage, The Guthrie Theatre, Studio Arena, Long Wharf Theatre and Actors Theatre of Louisville. He was born in Cambridge, Massachusetts on July 7, 1943 and received a B.F.A. in Theatre Design from Carnegie-Mellon University in 1967, after which he spent a season as a design intern at The Guthrie Theatre. Career influences include Tyrone Guthrie, Peter Wexler and Ming Cho Lee. He began designing in the mid-1960s at the Carnegie Museum Concert Hall in Pittsburgh. From 1986 to 1990 he was a principal designer and project manager for Peter Wexler, Inc., a design and programming firm in New York City. Major projects for Wexler, Inc. included *World War II Exhibit*, a proposal for a touring exhibit for the National Archives, and *The Search for Life* and *American Anthem* at the Smithsonian Institution in Washington, D.C. In 1990-91 he was an Adjunct Assistant Professor of Design at the State University of New York, Purchase.

Scenic Designs:
1977: *Trip Back Down, The* **1985:** *Jerry's Girls*

Ben Tipton

Ben Tipton designed scenery for a 1949 Broadway production.

Scenic Designs:
1949: *Ken Murray's Blackout of 1949*

Carl Toms

Carl Toms, a British designer of sets and costumes, was born on May 29, 1929 in Kirkby-in-Ashfield, England and studied at the Mansfield College of Art, the Royal College of Art and the Old Vic School. His mentors were Margaret Harris (Motley) and Oliver Messel, whom he assisted for six years. His stage creations have been seen extensively in theatre, opera and films since his debut, *The Apollo de Bellac*, at the Royal Court in 1957. When the Young Vic Company was established he was appointed Head of Design and Associate Director. He has worked often in London's West End and at the National Theatre. In 1967 he received the Order of the British Empire (O.B.E.) and won both a Tony Award and Drama Desk Award for his set for *Sherlock Holmes*, originally produced by the Royal Shakespeare Company. He also received the Laurence Olivier Award in 1981 for *The Provoked Life* at the National Theatre and a 1984 Drama Logue Award in Hollywood. In 1987 he became a Fellow of the Royal Society of Arts.

Scenic Designs:
1970: *Sleuth* **1972:** *Vivat! Vivat Regina!*
1974: *Scapino; Sherlock Holmes; Travesties*
1975: *Habeas Corpus* **1979:** *Night and Day*

Costume Designs:
1970: *Sleuth* **1972:** *Vivat! Vivat Regina!*
1974: *Scapino; Sherlock Holmes; Travesties*
1975: *Habeas Corpus* **1979:** *Night and Day*

James Trittipo

James Trittipo was known mainly as a set designer and art director for television. He was born in Ohio and graduated from the Carnegie Institute of Technology. He began designing for television in its early days, for both live variety shows and dramatic productions. The recipient of three Emmys for his designs for *Hollywood Palace*, which he designed for eight years, he also worked in theatre on the West Coast. As a set designer his work was often seen on Broadway and included *On the Town*, which he designed just prior to his death in 1971 at the age of 43.

Scenic Designs:
1962: *Captains and the Kings, The* **1970:** *Ovid's Metamorphoses* **1971:** *On the Town* **1972:** *Funny Thing Happened on the Way to the Forum, A*

Lighting Designs:
1962: *Captains and the Kings, The*

Costume Designs:
1962: *Captains and the Kings, The*

Princess Troubetsky

Princess Troubetsky (a.k.a. Amelie Rives) was born in Richmond, Virginia on August 23, 1863, the daughter of Sadie McMurdo Rives and Colonel Alfred Landon Rives. Raised in Alabama, she studied art in Paris. When her first marriage ended in divorce in 1895, Oscar Wilde introduced her to Prince Pierre Troubetsky (Troubetzkoy), a Russian artist who became her second husband. She was a successful romantic fiction writer and playwright. Several of her plays were produced including four on Broadway: *Prince and the Pauper* (1920), *Love-in-a-Mist* (1926), *Allegiance* (1918) and *Fear Market* (1916), for which she also designed the set. She died at age 81 on June 15, 1945 in Charlottesville, Virginia.

Scenic Designs:
1916: *Fear Market, The*

Dean Tschetter

Dean Tschetter, who designed a production on Broadway in 1983, has also been Art Director for *Another World* on NBC-TV. He began designing in regional theatres and for opera and ballet after serving an apprenticeship at the National Opera in Munich, Germany. His designs have been honored with nominations for a Bay Area Critics Award in San Francisco for *The Passion of Dracula* and a nomination for a Maharam Award for *Goose and Tom-Tom* by David Rabe at the Public Theatre. He was art director for the 1989 film *Fright Night, Part 2.*

Scenic Designs:
1983: *Breakfast with Les and Bess*

Richard Walton Tully

Playwright Richard Walton Tully was born in Nevada City, California on May 7, 1877. He studied at the University of California, winning the Junior Farce Contest in 1899 with his first play and graduating with a Bachelor of Law degree. His plays, including *The Bird of Paradise, Omar the Tentmaker, The Poor Little Rich Girl* and others, were Broadway successes. He produced many of his own plays and also designed some of them. His plays were especially popular in the teens but his later works met with little success. Richard Walton Tully died on January 31, 1945 at age 67 in New York City.

Scenic Designs:
1916: *Flame, The* 1917: *Masquerader, The*
1918: *Keep Her Smiling*

Barney Turner

In 1937 Barney Turner designed for scenery for one play on Broadway.

Scenic Designs:
1937: *Cat and the Canary, The*

Ultz

David Ultz, a British designer of scenery and costumes, has many credits in London's West End and designs regularly for the Royal Shakespeare Company. He attended the Central School of Speech and Drama in London (where he studied with Ralph Koltai) and Sadler's Wells Design School. He also studied with Margaret Harris (Motley) and Hayden Griffen. After college he assisted Hayden Griffen at the Exeter Repertory for two years, followed by design for the Citizens Theatre of Glasgow. He subsequently returned to London where his innovative designs soon attracted attention. He has designed many productions, including *The Twin Rivals* and *Our Friends of the North* at Cambridge Arts Theatre, *Our Friends of the North* at The Pit/Barbican Centre, and scenery and costumes for *A Comedy of Errors* at Stratford-upon-Avon. He has also designed for the National Arts Center in Ottawa, Canada among many other theatres and locations.

Scenic Designs:
1982: *Good*

Unitt and Wickes

The scenic studio Unitt and Wickes was operated at 152 West 46th Street, New York City during the teens and twenties by Edward G. Unitt and Joseph Wickes. The studio received design credit for many productions before 1915 in New York City and Boston, including *Macbeth* at the Shubert Theatre in Boston in 1910 and *The Blue Bird* in New York City in 1913. Edward G. Unitt and Joseph Wickes were active designers who received individual credit for many productions. Additional information is available under their entries.

Scenic Designs:
1915: *Girl Who Smiles, The* 1916: *Hush!*; *Passing Show of 1916, The*; *Pride of the Race, The* 1917: *His Little Widows*; *Lassoo, The*; *Misalliance*; *Romance and Arabella* 1919: *Little Whopper, The*; *Too Many Husbands* 1920: *Americans in France, The*; *Cave Girl, The*; *Crooked Gamblers*; *Genius and the Crowd*; *Honey Girl*; *Just Suppose*; *Tavern, The* 1921: *Green Goddess, The*; *Intimate Strangers, The*; *O'Brien Girl, The*; *Tavern, The*; *Toto*

Edward G. Unitt

Edward G. Unitt, a scenic painter, maintained a studio at the Lyceum Theatre of Daniel and Charles Frohman, for whom he designed many shows. He designed many productions prior to 1915: *Aristocracy* (1892), *Under the Red Robe* (1896), *The Little Minister* (1897), *The Conquerors* and *The Liars* (1898), *Barbara Frietchie* (1899), *Hamlet* and *David Harum* (1900), *Captain Jinks of the Horse Marines, If I Were King* and *Quality Street* (1901), *The Girl with Green Eyes* (1902), *The Red Mill* (1906), and *A Grand Army Man* (1907). He was also involved in Morosco-Wagner, Co. Inc., amusements, in 1915 with Oliver Morosco and Charles Wagner.

Scenic Designs:

1923: *Cymbeline*

Gretl Urban

Gretl Urban Thurlow, daughter of Joseph Urban, worked with her father in films including *When Knighthood Was in Flower* (1922), *Enemies of Women* (1923), and *Zander the Great* and *Never the Twain Shall Meet* (1925). She also designed scenery for Broadway plays in 1925 and 1935.

Scenic Designs:

1925: *Louie the 14th* **1935:** *Season Changes, The*

Joseph Urban

Joseph Urban was born in Vienna in 1872 and studied both architecture and stage design. He is credited with introducing many Continental stagecraft techniques to the United States. After working in Vienna for several years, he came to Boston in 1910 to design an opera. The success of the production led to an opportunity to design at the Metropolitan Opera. He designed scenery and costumes for many revues presented by Florenz Ziegfeld and also designed the Ziegfeld Theatre. He was art director for numerous films between 1920 and 1931. Productions in London included scenery for *Snow Flakes, Giselle* and *Macbeth* in 1920, and revivals of *Snow Flakes* in 1924 and 1927. Joseph Urban died in 1933.

Scenic Designs:

1915: *Ziegfeld Follies: 1915; Ziegfeld Midnight Frolic* **1916:** *Century Girl, The; FloraBella;*

Macbeth; Miss Springtime; Pom-Pom; Ziegfeld Follies: 1916 **1917:** *Jack O'Lantern; Miss 1917; Nju; Riviera Girl, The; Ziegfeld Follies: 1917* **1918:** *By Pigeon Post; Canary, The; Glorianna; Head Over Heels; Invisible Foe, The; Nothing But Lies; Rainbow Girl, The; Ziegfeld Follies: 1918* **1919:** *Apple Blossoms; Hitchy Koo 1919; Rose of China, The; Smilin' Through; Young Man's Fancy, A; Ziegfeld Midnight Frolic* **1920:** *Sally; Ziegfeld Follies: 1920* **1921:** *Love Letter, The; Merry Widow, The; Ziegfeld Follies: 1921; Ziegfeld Midnight Follies; Ziegfeld's 9 O'clock Frolic* **1922:** *Sally, Irene and Mary; Yankee Princess, The; Ziegfeld Follies: 1922* **1923:** *Ziegfeld Follies: 1923* **1924:** *Moonlight; Ziegfeld Follies: 1924* **1925:** *Antonia; Human Nature; Song of the Flame; Tale of the Wolf, A* **1926:** *No Foolin'; Wild Rose, The* **1927:** *Golden Dawn; Rio Rita; Show Boat; Yours Truly; Ziegfeld Follies: 1927* **1928:** *Rosalie; Three Musketeers, The; Treasure Girl; Whoopee; Yours Truly* **1929:** *Midnite Frolics; Show Girl; Sons O' Guns* **1930:** *Flying High; Princess Charming; Ripples; Simple Simon; Smiles* **1931:** *George White's Scandals; Good Fairy, The; Simple Simon; Ziegfeld Follies: 1931* **1932:** *Good Fairy, A; Hot-Cha!; Music in the Air; Show Boat* **1933:** *Melody* **1948:** *Sally* **1938:** *Bridal Crown*

Costume Designs:

1925: *Tale of the Wolf, A*

Brian Vahey

Brian Vahey was born on May 31, 1956 in Dublin, Ireland and earned a diploma at the Dunlaoghaire School of Arts where he studied animation and sculpture. He has served as resident designer, assistant and tutor at Riverside Studios, assisting Miss Margaret Harris (Motley) with whom he studied in 1982. He has held a Cincellin Fellowship at Bristol Univeristy and served as assistant designer at the Abbey Theatre, where he has contributed designs for scenery and costumes to many productions. He made his debut in 1982 at the Abbey Theatre with *Mr. Joyce is Leaving Paris*. He has been production designer at R.T.E. Television in Ireland and designed the film *The Walk of Life*. Major influences include Margaret Harris and John Dexter. He worked with Dexter at the Buxton Opera Festival in 1985 and designed *The Cocktail Party* for him in London in 1986.

Scenic Designs:
1984: *Moon for the Misbegotten, A*

Costume Designs:
1984: *Moon for the Misbegotten, A*

Vail Studios

Vail Scenic Construction Company was founded in 1910 by George M. Vail who served as president until 1950, when it became Chester Rakeman Scenic Studios. The company built sets for *Ziegfeld Follies, George White's Scandals, Kiss Me, Kate, Bloomer Girl, Mr. Pickwick*, and many more. Vail Studios also supplied settings to CBS-TV. George Vail died at age 81 in November 1952.

Scenic Designs:
1934: *House of Ramsen*

E. Van Ackerman

In 1927 Earl Van Ackerman created sets for a Broadway play. He also painted the sets for *Made for Each Other* in 1939, which were constructed by Nolan Brothers. In the early 1920s he operated Beaux Arts Scenic Studios with George W. Korb in Newark, New Jersey, where he also resided.

Scenic Designs:
1924: *Green Beetle, The* 1927: *Tia Juana*

Edwin H. Vandernoot

Edwin H. Vandernoot designed scenery for one play in 1940 on Broadway.

Scenic Designs:
1940: *What D' You Call It/ According to Law/ etc.*

Robert Van Rosen

Robert Van Rosen, a surrealist painter, often lectured on art and theatre in major museums in the greater New York area. He occasionally contributed designs to plays. He worked as an industrial designer in the 1940s and 1950s designing packaging and consulting on packaging. The author of *Comeback* (1949), a book about his recovery from a stroke, he died at age 62 on November 16, 1966.

Scenic Designs:
1926: *Princess Turandot* 1931: *Bloody Laughter* 1932: *Wolves* 1938: *Empress of Destiny*

Costume Designs:
1926: *Princess Turandot* 1938: *Empress of Destiny*

Ellen Van Volkenburg

Ellen Van Volkenburg founded the Little Theatre of Chicago in 1912 with her husband Maurice Browne. The theatre operated at the Fine Arts Building on Michigan Avenue and was active for three years. She was born in Battle Creek, Michigan and attended the University of Michigan. An actress and producer, she toured the United States, and performed in New York and London. In 1931 she directed, designed and acted in a Broadway production.

Scenic Designs:
1931: *Venetian, The*

Adrian Vaux

Adrian Vaux designs extensively in England and Israel. He was resident designer for the Mermaid Theatre from 1964 to 1970 and created sets for *Treasure Island, Fanny's First Play, The Imaginary Invalid* and *The Philanderer* among others. From 1971 to 1980 he was resident designer at the Leicester Haymarket. He has also been resident designer at the Old Vic and has extensive credits in the West End. At the Haifa Municipal Theatre in Israel he designed *Soul of a Jew, Magda, Ghetto* and *The Jerusalem Syndrome*. He debuted on Broadway in 1989.

Scenic Designs:
1989: *Ghetto*

Kaj Velden

Kaj Velden, a scenic and interior designer, designed a Broadway play in 1944. His wife, Mrs. Inge Jesperson Velden was a fashion designer who worked for Christian Dior in Paris.

Scenic Designs:
1944: *Take a Bow*

Vertès

Marcel Vertès was born in Budapest, Hungary in 1895 and spent most of his life in France as a painter and illustrator, gaining an international reputation. He participated in a 1920 exhibition of paintings and began theatrical design with the support of Ferenc Molnar. His first designs were seen in Paris in 1933 and for many years he designed sets and costumes for plays, operas and ballets in Paris and New York. He also designed eight hundred circus costumes for Ringling Brothers & Barnum and Bailey Circus. Marcel Vertès, the recipient of Oscars for both sets and costumes for *Moulin Rouge*, died at age 66 on October 31, 1961 in Paris.

Scenic Designs:
1955: *Seventh Heaven*

Costume Designs:
1955: *Seventh Heaven*

Sheldon K. Viele

Sheldon Knickerbocker Viele designed sets and occasionally costumes for many plays in the 1920s on Broadway. He was originally from Buffalo, New York and in 1927 was instrumental in founding the Studio Theatre in that city. A graduate of Yale, he served in World War I in France in the Camouflage Corps. For two years Mr. Viele, who also was a painter, was technical director of the Theatre Guild. He died on September 23, 1934 at the age of 42.

Scenic Designs:
1920: *Enter Madame; Miss Lulu Betat* **1921:** *Ambush; Cloister, The; John Hawthorne; We Girls* **1922:** *Fashions for Men; Plot Thickens, The; Shadow, The* **1923:** *Helen of Troy, New York; Meet the Wife; Rita Coventry; Shadow, The* **1924:** *Easy Mail, The; Fake, The; Lollipops; Rising Sun, The; Show-Off, The* **1925:** *Craig's Wife; Enchanted April, The; Jane, Our Stranger; One of the Family; Servant in the House, The* **1927:** *Sidewalks of New York; Wasp's Nest, The* **1928:** *Three Cheers*

Costume Designs:
1921: *Cloister, The; John Hawthorne*

August Vimnera

August Vimnera designed sets for several plays on Broadway in the 1920s. The playbill for *Earl Carroll Vanities* (1926) referred to him as "A. Vimnera of Paris."

Scenic Designs:
1925: *Small Timer, The; Tell Me More* **1926:** *Earl Carroll's Vanities* **1927:** *Footlights; Hearts and Trumps; Kiss Me; Mulberry Bush, The; Tales of Rigo* **1928:** *Breaks, The; Forbidden Roads; Girl Trouble; Intruder, The; Red Dust; Silver Box, The* **1929:** *Red Dust*

August Vimnera Studio

August Vimnera received credit for scenic design on Broadway both under his own name and through August Vimnera Studio.

Scenic Designs:
1928: *Diamond Lil*

H.A. Vincent

Harold Aiken Vincent collaborated on the scenery for a Broadway play in 1915. He was born in Boston on February 14, 1864 and died on September 27, 1931. A self-taught painter, he exhibited widely and won several prizes for his marine paintings. In 1918 he resided at 904 Ogden Avenue and in 1932 at 10 West 61st Street in New York City.

Scenic Designs:
1915: *You Never Can Tell*

Fred Voelpel

Fred Voelpel was born in Peoria, Illinois and attended the University of Illinois and Yale, where he studied with Donald Oenslager and Frank Poole Bevan. He has been designing costumes and sets since 1943 when he debuted at both Peoria Players Little Theatre and Peoria Central High School. He has been designing professionally since 1956 for television and the theatre. In 1959 he debuted in New York with the costume designs for *On the Town*. Additional costume credits include *Seascape* and *The Effect of Gamma Rays on Man-in-the-Moon Marigolds*. He has won two New York Critic's Circle Awards for set design, an Obie Award for *The Effect of Gamma Rays on Man-in-the-Moon Marigolds*, a Variety Poll Award, an Esquire Dubious Achievement Award for *Oh, Calcutta*, and a Miami (Florida) L.O.R.T. Award for *Seascape*.

He has been a master teacher of design at New York University's Tisch School of the Arts since 1964, and from 1966 to 1988 designed for the National Theatre for the Deaf. He has been Resident Designer for the National Playwrights' Conference since 1965 and on the faculty of the National Theatre Institute since its founding in 1970. From 1964 to 1987 he designed sets and costumes for Paul Green's *The Lost Colony*, the nation's longest running outdoor drama, located at Manteo, North Carolina.

Scenic Designs:
1960: *From A to Z; Vintage '60* **1961:** *Young Abe Lincoln* **1969:** *Home Fires/ Cop Out* **1970:** *Sganarelle* **1971:** *And Miss Reardon Drinks a Little* **1972:** *Hurry, Harry* **1975:** *Very Good, Eddie* **1981:** *Einstein and the Polar Bear*

Lighting Designs:
1960: *From A to Z* **1961:** *Young Abe Lincoln*

Costume Designs:
1960: *From A to Z* **1961:** *Young Abe Lincoln* **1963:** *Sophie* **1964:** *Absence of a Cello; Murderer Among Us, A; Sign in Sidney Brustein's Window, The* **1965:** *Drat! the Cat!; Peterpat* **1969:** *Home Fires/ Cop Out* **1970:** *Sganarelle; Songs from Milkwood; Two By Two* **1971:** *Oh! Calcutta!* **1975:** *Seascape* **1981:** *Bring Back Birdie*

Elfi Von Kantzow

Elfi Von Kantzow designed scenery and costumes for Broadway shows in the early 1950s.

Scenic Designs:
1952: *Brass Ring, The; Jane*

Costume Designs:
1950: *Edwina Black* **1952:** *Brass Ring, The; Jane*

Carl Vose

Carl Vose designed sets and costumes for two shows on Broadway in the late 1920s. In 1928 he wrote *Radio Fundamentals, Volume 1: Sources of Electromotive* with A.G. Zimmerman. He received a B.S. in Electrical Engineering. He was a member of the Radio Engineering Department, General Electric Company and also worked at one time as an electrician for Western Electric Company.

Scenic Designs:
1927: *Arabian, The* **1928:** *Sakura* **1985:** *Strange Interlude*

Costume Designs:
1927: *Arabian, The* **1928:** *Sakura*

James Wade

James Wade designed sets and costumes on Broadway in 1955. The same James Wade perhaps also designed scenery for a 1921 production.

Scenic Designs:
1921: *Dear Me* **1955:** *Princess Ida*

Costume Designs:
1955: *Princess Ida*

Robin Wagner

Robin Samuel Wagner was born on August 31, 1933 in San Francisco. After attending the California School of Fine Arts he began designing in San Francisco for the Golden Gate Opera Workshop in 1953. His first New York production was *And the Wind Blows* at St. Mark's Playhouse in 1959. Since then he has designed many productions, including some of Broadway's most popular musicals of the last twenty years: *A Chorus Line, Dream Girls,* and *Hair.* He has also designed off-Broadway and for opera, ballet, and film. He received the Tony Award, a Drama Desk and Outer Critic's Cirle Award for *On the Twentieth Century,* a Drama Desk Award for *Lenny,* Maharam Awards for *Seesaw, Dreamgirls* and *Chorus Line,* and a Lumen Award for a Rolling Stones tour of the United States.

Scenic Designs:
1967: *Trial of Lee Harvey Oswald, The* **1968:** *Cuban Thing, The; Great White Hope, The; Hair; Lovers and Other Strangers; Promises, Promises* **1969:** *My Daughter, Your Son; Watering Place, The* **1970:** *Engagement Baby, The; Gantry* **1971:** *Jesus Christ Superstar; Lenny* **1972:** *Inner City; Lysistrata; Sugar* **1973:** *Full Circle; Seesaw* **1974:** *Fifth Dimension, The; Mack and Mabel* **1975:** *Chorus Line, A* **1977:** *Hair* **1978:** *Ballroom; On the Twentieth Century* **1979:** *Comin' Uptown* **1980:** *42nd Street* **1981:** *Dreamgirls* **1983:** *Merlin* **1985:** *Song & Dance* **1987:** *Dreamgirls; Teddy and Alice* **1988:** *Chess* **1989:** *City of Angels; Jerome Robbins' Broadway*

John Wain

John Wain collaborated on the designs for a 1977 Broadway production.

Scenic Designs:
1977: *Ipi Tombi*

Walter Walden

Walter Walden conceived costume, lighting and particularly scenic designs for Broadway productions in the 1920s and 1930s.

Scenic Designs:
1928: *Dark Mirror, The* 1929: *Subway, The; Vegetable, The* 1930: *At the Bottom; Life Line, The; Seagull, The* 1932: *Lost Boy* 1934: *Jayhawker* 1937: *Swing It* 1938: *Prologue to Glory*

Lighting Designs:
1928: *Dark Mirror, The*

Costume Designs:
1930: *At the Bottom; Troyka*

Jane Wallack

Jane Wallack designed sets for a 1919 Broadway production.

Scenic Designs:
1919: *Exchange of Wives, An*

William Oden Waller

William Oden Waller, known as W. Odenwaller, William Oldenwald and by other variations on his name, was active on Broadway between 1921 and 1940. In 1924 the W. Oden Waller Scenic Studio was located at 530 West 47th Street and he resided in Woodcliff, New Jersey. In 1932 he resided at 1813 2nd Avenue, New York City with Charles Odenwald, a decorator, Karl Odenwald, a painter, and Max Odenwald, an electrician.

Scenic Designs:
1921: *Dover Road* 1922: *Lights Out* 1923: *Nervous Wreck, The; Red Light Annie; Square Peg, A* 1924: *In His Arms* 1925: *Paid; Sea Woman, The* 1926: *Chicago; George White's Scandals; Loose Ends* 1927: *Manhattan Mary; Spider, The; Take the Air* 1928: *George White's Scandals; He Understood Women; Song Writer, The; Spider, The* 1929: *George White's Scandals; June Moon* 1930: *Suspense* 1931: *Social Register, The* 1933: *June Moon* 1935:
Rain; Seven Keys to Baldpate 1936: *Bright Honor; County Chairman, The; Dear Old Darling* 1937: *Fulton of Oak Falls* 1940: *Boys and Girls Together; Return of the Vagabond*

Thomas A. Walsh

Thomas A. Walsh was born on September 20, 1955 in Burbank, California and attended Hollywood High School and the California Institute of the Arts. His father, Arthur Walsh, was a Metro-Goldyn-Meyer contract actor and a night-club comedian. He has worked as a scenic artist, union stagehand, assistant designer (to Sally Jacobs at the Mark Taper Forum), and carpenter as well as a designer. His credits also include television, interior design, theatres and the film *The Handmaid's Tale*. He credits Sally Jacobs, Tony Walton and Edward Burbridge as major influences . He is married to costume designer Merrily Murray-Walsh.

Scenic Designs:
1979: *Zoot Suit* 1980: *Children of a Lesser God* 1983: *Brothers*

Tony Walton

Tony Walton, a scenic and costume designer, was born in Walton-on-Thames, Surrey, England on October 24, 1934, and studied at Radley College, the City of Oxford School of Technology, Art and Commerce and at the Slade School of Fine Arts. Prior to designing for the theatre he worked as a commercial artist and illustrator. His theatrical designs have often been seen in both England and the United States, beginning with the 1955-56 season for Peter Haddon's Company at the Wimbledon Theatre. His designs for film include the costumes for *Mary Poppins* and *Murder on the Orient Express, All That Jazz, The Wiz* and *The Boy Friend*. A prolific and creative designer, Mr. Walton has won many awards and nominations for set design in both theatre and film, including Tony Awards for *Lend Me a Tenor* and *Jerome Robbins' Broadway*. A 1989 exhibit at the American Museum of the Moving Image, "Tony Walton: Designing for Stage and Screen," featured his designs.

Scenic Designs:
1961: *Once There Was a Russian* 1962: *Funny Thing Happened on the Way to the Forum, A*

bf1964; *Golden Boy* 1966: *Apple Tree, The* 1972: *Pippin* 1973: *Good Doctor, The; Shelter; Uncle Vanya* 1975: *Bette Midler's Clams on the Half Shell Revue; Chicago* 1977: *Act, The* 1980: *Day in Hollywood, A/A Night in the Ukraine* 1981: *Sophisticated Ladies; Woman of the Year* 1982: *Little Me* 1984: *Hurlyburly; Real Thing, The; Whoopi Goldberg* 1985: *I'm Not Rappaport; Leader of the Pack* 1986: *House of Blue Leaves, The; Social Security* 1987: *Front Page, The* 1989: *Grand Hotel, The Musical; Lend Me A Tenor*

Costume Designs:
1961: *Once There Was a Russian* 1962: *Funny Thing Happened on the Way to the Forum, A* 1963: *Rehearsal, The* 1964: *Golden Boy* 1966: *Apple Tree, The* 1973: *Good Doctor, The; Shelter; Uncle Vanya* 1975: *Bette Midler's Clams on the Half Shell Revue* 1976: *1600 Pennsylvania Avenue* 1982: *Little Me* 1984: *Whoopi Goldberg*

Ward and Harvey Studios

Ward and Harvey Studios, comprised of designers Herbert Ward and Walter Harvey, received credit for the scenic design of Broadway productions from 1921 to 1932.

Scenic Designs:
1927: *Oh, Ernest; Talk About Girls; White Lights* 1928: *Atlas and Eva; Divorce a La Carte; Present Arms* 1929: *Booster, The; Crooks Convention, The; Lady Fingers; Silver Swan, The* 1930: *Bad Girl; Lew Leslie's Blackbirds; So Was Napoleon* 1931: *Old Man Murphy* 1932: *Surgeon, The*

Lighting Designs:
1930: *Vanderbilt Revue, The*

Herbert Ward

Herbert Ward designed scenery for Broadway plays from 1921 to 1934 and through Ward and Harvey Studios.

Scenic Designs:
1921: *George White's Scandals* 1922: *George White's Scandals* 1923: *Adrienne; Nifties of 1923* 1927: *Bye, Bye, Bonnie; Caste* 1930: *First Night* 1931: *Papavert; Unexpected Husband* 1932: *Through the Years; Trick for Trick* 1933: *It Happened Tomorrow* 1934: *All the King's Horses; Ship Comes In, A*

Leon R. Warren

Leon R. Warren designed a set in 1932 for a Broadway show. In 1932 he was also associated with Warren Bros., Inc., dress manufacturers, at 463 Seventh Avenue New York City.

Scenic Designs:
1932: *Incubator*

William Warren

William Warren, an actor and company manager, died at age 73 on February 28, 1941. He spent sixteen years as head carpenter at the Metropolitan Opera House, beginning in 1925. He toured with the production of *Uncle Tom's Cabin* at the turn of the century, performed often in Boston, and played a role in *Dr. Clyde*. His father, the actor William Warren, Sr., was a long time member of the company at the Walnut Street Theatre in Philadelphia in the latter half of the nineteenth century.

Scenic Designs:
1933: *Thoroughbred*

Perry Watkins

Perry Watkins worked as a flower seller, journalist and insurance salesman before taking a trip to New York City and discovering scene design. He broke the color barrier by becoming the first black member of United Scenic Artists in the late 1930s. He designed several productions for the Harlem unit of the Federal Theatre Project, including *S.S. Glencairn, Androcles and the Lion, Horse Play* and others. He worked as a producer, beginning with *Beggars' Holiday* in 1946 and *Moon of Mah'no'men* in 1947, working through Production Associates with Thomas Ward Lanyan and Dale Wasserman. He was also a director and art director for films and was preparing to go to Africa to make a film at the time of his death. Mr. Watkins died in Newburgh, New York at age 67 on August 14, 1974.

Scenic Designs:
1937: *Moon of the Caribees, Etc.* 1938: *Haiti; Pinocchio* 1939: *Mamba's Daughter's* 1940: *Big White Fog; Mamba's Daughter's* 1942: *Heart of a City; Three Men on a Horse; You'll See the Stars* 1943: *Bright Lights of 1943; Manhattan Nocturne; Run, Little Chillun*

1944: *Take It As It Comes* **1945:** *Blue Holiday* **1949:** *Forward the Heart* **1954:** *Integration Show Case, The* **1956:** *Harbour Lights*

Lighting Designs:
1940: *Big White Fog* **1945:** *Blue Holiday* **1949:** *Forward the Heart*

Costume Designs:
1935: *Three Men on a Horse* **1938:** *Androcles and the Lion* **1939:** *Mamba's Daughter's* **1940:** *Mamba's Daughter's* **1942:** *Three Men on a Horse* **1943:** *Bright Lights of 1943*; *Run, Little Chillun* **1945:** *Blue Holiday*

Lee Watson

Leland Hale Watson worked steadily after his professional debut at the Provincetown Playhouse in 1950. He was principally a lighting designer who worked in theatre, ballet, opera and television. Born on February 18, 1926 in Charleston, Illinois, he received an M.F.A. at Yale in 1951 after service in World War II and work as a radio engineer. His interest in the theatre began in high school. Occasionally Mr. Watson also designed scenery for plays and more rarely costumes. He served as lighting director for CBS-TV from 1951 to 1955 and taught design in many universities and at Lester Polakov's Studio and Forum of Stage Design. He also wrote articles about lighting design and two books, beginning with *Theatrical Lighting Practice* in 1955. *Lighting Design Handbook*, one of the few comprehensive books about lighting design, was published posthumously in 1990. His awards included an Obie for *Machinal* in 1957. Lee Watson died on December 10, 1989.

Scenic Designs:
1958: *Next President, The-A Musical Salamagundi* **1960:** *Lovely Night, A* **1961:** *Importance of Being Oscar, The*

Lighting Designs:
1955: *Diary of Anne Frank, The*; *View from the Bridge, A* **1956:** *Girls of Summer*; *Harbour Lights*; *Protective Custody* **1957:** *Cave Dwellers, The*; *Mask and Gown*; *Miss Isobel*; *Moon for the Misbegotten, A* **1958:** *Next President, The-A Musical Salamagundi*; *Night Circus, The*; *Portofino* **1959:** *Legend of Lizzie* **1960:** *Lovely Night, A* **1961:** *Do You Know the Milky Way?*; *Importance of Being Oscar, The* **1962:** *Moby Dick*

Costume Designs:
1958: *Next President, The-A Musical Salamagundi* **1961:** *Importance of Being Oscar, The*

Rollo Wayne

Rollo Wayne, the designer of the first revolving stage set used in the United States, was born in Louisville, Kentucky on March 5, 1899. He studied at Harvard University and with George Pierce Baker at Workshop 47. The first revolving stage set was used for a production of *H.M.S. Pinafore* produced by the Shuberts in 1926. He worked for the Shuberts for twelve years and also for Florenz Ziegfeld, Lew Leslie and Max Gordon. He died at age 55 on March 18, 1954 in Louisville.

Scenic Designs:
1916: *Such Is Life* **1921:** *Chocolate Soldier, The* **1922:** *Springtime of Youth* **1924:** *Parasites*; *Top-Hole* **1925:** *Crooked Friday, The*; *Man Or Devil*; *Man with a Load of Mischief, The*; *Offence, The* **1926:** *H.M.S. Pinafore* **1927:** *Murray Will*; *Ruddigore*; *Such Is Life* **1928:** *Common Sin, The*; *Exceeding Small*; *Gang Way*; *Great Necker, The*; *Lady for a Night, A*; *Sign of the Leopard*; *So Am I*; *White Lilacs*; *Within the Law* **1929:** *Babes in Toyland*; *Cape Cod Follies*; *Congratulations*; *Death Takes a Holiday*; *First Law, The*; *Jonesy*; *Nigger Rich*; *Rope's End*; *Security*; *Stripped*; *Young Sinners* **1930:** *Babes in Toyland*; *Bird in Hand*; *Chocolate Soldier, The*; *Count of Luxembourg, The*; *His Majesty's Car*; *Infinite Shoeblack, The*; *Insult*; *Ladies All*; *Lady Clara*; *Last Enemy, The*; *Man in Possession, The*; *Nine Till Six*; *On the Spot*; *Prince of Pilsen, The*; *Purity*; *Serenade, The*; *Topaz*; *Truth Game, The*; *Up Pops the Devil* **1931:** *Constant Sinner, The*; *Death Takes a Holiday*; *Everybody's Welcome*; *Good Companions, The*; *Marriage for Three*; *Melo*; *Modern Virgin, A*; *Silent Witness, The*; *Topaz*; *Young Sinners* **1932:** *Autumn Crocus*; *Best Years*; *Blessed Event*; *Boy Friend, The*; *Happy Landing*; *If Booth Had Missed*; *Peacock*; *Perfect Marriage, The*; *Silent House, The* **1933:** *Best Sellers*; *Double Door*; *Going Gay*; *Young Sinners* **1934:** *First Episode*; *Spring Freshet* **1935:** *If a Body*; *Journey By Night, A* **1936:** *In Heaven and Earth*; *Kick Back, The* **1937:** *Trial of Dr. Beck, The*

William Weaver

William Weaver received an award for outstanding period design from *Stage Magazine* in the mid-1930s. He was active as a costume and scenic designer for twenty years, designing on Broadway, for the Metropolitan Opera Company, and for the 1933 *Showboat Revue*, which was performed aboard the steamers of the Hudson River Day Line. Mr. Weaver, originally from Asheville, North Carolina, died on August 14, 1937.

Scenic Designs:
1920: *Passing Show of 1921, The* 1921: *Rose Girl, The* 1924: *Princess April* 1925: *Bringing Up Father*

Costume Designs:
1923: *Music Box Revue* 1924: *Bye, Bye, Barbara*; *Princess April* 1926: *George White's Scandals* 1927: *Much Ado About Nothing* 1930: *Rivals, The* 1936: *Broadway Sho-Window* 1937: *Frederika*

Virginia Dancy Webb

Virginia Dancy Webb was born in New York City on April 8, 1940 and has a B.A. from Vassar and an M.F.A. from Yale. She often works in collaboration with her husband, Elmon Webb. She has designed for the Mark Taper Forum, Syracuse Stage, Pittsburgh Public Theatre, Long Wharf Theatre and off-Broadway. She was staff artist for CBS-TV from 1975 to 1978 and has taught at Vassar and Marymount Colleges.

Scenic Designs:
1974: *National Health, The*

Ben Webster

Ben Webster designed scenery and costumes for a Broadway play in 1925.

Scenic Designs:
1925: *Merchants of Glory*

Costume Designs:
1925: *Merchants of Glory*

Gustav A. Weidhaas

Gustav A. Weidhaas designed sets and special effects for *George White's Scandals* throughout the 1920s. He also worked for other producers of plays, musicals and variety shows such as Billy Rose, Florenz Ziegfeld, David Belasco and Charles Frohman, specializing in "illusions". His wife was the costume designer Frances Feist and they had one son, Ted Weidhaas, also a theatrical designer. Gustav Weidhaas was the head of Weidhaas Studios, 536 West 29th Street. He died at age 62 in Bronxville, New York on August 21, 1938.

Scenic Designs:
1923: *George White's Scandals* 1924: *George White's Scandals* 1925: *George White's Scandals* 1926: *George White's Scandals* 1928: *George White's Scandals* 1929: *George White's Scandals*

Ted Weidhaas

Ted Weidhaas was born into a family of theatrical designers. His mother, Frances Feist, was a costume designer active on Broadway in the 1930s who also designed eight productions at the Cotton Club. His father, Gustaav Weidhaas, created scenic designs and effects on Broadway and for other theatres during the teens and twenties. Ted Weidhaas designed the contour curtain for Radio City Music Hall and also created masks and murals as well as scenic designs.

Scenic Designs:
1929: *George White's Scandals*; *Ned Wayburn's Gambols* 1934: *Thumbs Up*

Michael Weight

Michael Weight was born in Somerset West, Cape Colony, South Africa on May 31, 1906. He studied at the University of Cape Town and the Slade School of Art after moving to England. His debut as a set designer was *Dandy Dick* at the Hammersmith Lyric Theatre in 1930, followed by many productions throughout the United Kingdom and in London from the 1930s to the 1950s. He designed the *Sherlock Holmes Exhibition* for the Festival of Britain in 1951, and also designed films and television plays.

Scenic Designs:
1956: *Separate Tables*

Max Weldy

Max Weldy first designed costumes for the Folies Bergére. He had his own business in Paris in the 1920s and early 1930s (Weldy, Paris) where he executed costume designs for use in Paris and New York. In the late 1930s he moved to London where John Ringling saw his designs and invited him to work for Ringling Brothers Circus. He remained with the circus until the 1960s. His credits on Broadway include many costume designs and a single scenic design in 1931.

Scenic Designs:
1931: *Laugh Parade, The*

Costume Designs:
1926: *Gay Paree*; *Katja* 1927: *Artists and Models* 1931: *Laugh Parade, The*; *Of Thee I Sing* 1932: *Face the Music* 1933: *Of Thee I Sing* 1942: *Heart of a City*

Orson Welles

Orson Welles is remembered as the "boy wonder" who took Hollywood by storm with the film classic *Citizen Kane*, and who scared thousands of Americans with a radio broadcast about a Martian invasion of Earth, *War of the Worlds*. He was born George Orson Welles on May 6, 1915 in Kenosha, Wisconsin and began performing at the age of two. He spent most of his life at the center of various controversies. In 1937, while working with the Federal Theatre Project, he designed and directed a production of *Dr. Faustus* notable for its austerity. Mr. Welles died at the age of 70 on October 10, 1985.

Scenic Designs:
1937: *Dr. Faustus* 1938: *Cradle Will Rock, The*

Costume Designs:
1937: *Dr. Faustus*

John Wenger

John Wenger was born in Elizabeth, Odessa, Russia on June 16, 1891. He studied at the Imperial Art School in Odessa and the National Academy of Design. After moving to the United States in 1903 he found work as a jewelry designer and scenic artist. He designed settings for the Boston Opera Company, the Metropolitan Opera, and the Greenwich Village Theatre

and was art director for the Rivoli, Capital and Roxy movie theatres. His film designs included *Paramount on Parade* in 1929. He was the first designer to use gauze backdrops and lateral moving scenery, for *Good Boy* in 1928. This innovative designer and watercolorist died on August 24, 1976 in Manhattan at age 89. His designs and paintings are in the permanent collections of the Museum of the City of New York, the Metropolitan Museum of Art, and The Museum of Modern Art.

Scenic Designs:
1921: *Poppy God, The* 1922: *George White's Scandals* 1924: *Great Music*; *Round the Town*; *Ziegfeld Follies: 1924* 1925: *Bridge of Distances*; *Master of the Inn, The*; *Monkey Talks, The*; *Tip Toes* 1926: *No Foolin'*; *Oh, Kay* 1927: *Funny Face*; *Hit the Deck*; *Piggy*; *Spring Song* 1928: *Good Boy*; *Here's Howe*; *Oh, Kay*; *Ups-A-Daisy* 1929: *Spring Is Here* 1933: *Pardon My English* 1946: *Walk Hard*

Lighting Designs:
1946: *Walk Hard*

Lou Wertheim

Lou Wertheim, who designed sets on Broadway in 1919 and 1930, was credited in the *Messin' Around* playbill as the former manager of Willy Pogany Studios. Louis and Hyman Wertheim produced ladies hats at 49 West 37th Street in New York City in the 1920s and 1930s.

Scenic Designs:
1929: *Messin' 'Round* 1930: *With Privileges*

Roland West

Roland West was a film director who began acting in plays and vaudeville in his native Cleveland, Ohio. He began writing some of his own sketches prior to joining the Lowe circuit as a producer of short acts and skits. His first film was the silent *Lost Souls*, which he directed and co-produced. Later films included several starring Norma Talmadge. The first talkie he directed was *Alibi* with Chester Morris in 1928. He died on March 31, 1952 in Santa Monica, California at age 65.

Scenic Designs:
1918: *Unknown Purple, The*

Lighting Designs:
1918: *Unknown Purple, The*

Peter Wexler

Peter Wexler received a B.S. in design in 1958 from the University of Michigan, where he majored in photography and painting. He attended graduate school at Yale University. Born on October 31, 1936, in New York City, he began designing with sets, costumes and lights for the New York Shakespeare Festival's production of *Anthony and Cleopatra* in 1959. Since then he has amassed extensive credits for plays, operas, television and films throughout the United States. In the early 1970s he began producing and programming, after many years of designing theatrical events. Beginning with the Promenades and Rug Concerts at the New York Philharmonic, his company has produced, programmed, and directed museum exhibitions, concerts, public spaces and media events for major symphony orchestras, opera companies, museums, government agencies and the private sector. His models and drawings have been widely collected and exhibited. Peter Wexler has been married to Emmy award winning costume designer Constance Ross Wexler since 1962.

Scenic Designs:
1966: *Joyful Noise, A* **1968:** *Happy Time, The* **1970:** *Minnie's Boys* **1971:** *Trial of the Catonsville Nine, The* **1978:** *Broadway Musical, A*

Lighting Designs:
1966: *Joyful Noise, A*

James Whale

James Whale was born on July 22, 1896 in Dudley, Staffordshire, England and spent his career as an actor, designer and film director. He started work as a cartoonist for *The Bystander* but began acting while a prisoner of war in Germany in 1917-18. After the war he performed and designed for the Birmingham Repertory Company, followed by ten years of theatre performances and designs throughout England. He moved to New York City in 1929 where he directed and produced plays before going to Hollywood. His films include *Frankenstein, The Invisible Man, The Road Back,* and *Show Boat.* He died on May 29, 1957 in Hollywood, California.

Scenic Designs:
1929: *Hundred Years Old, A*; *Journey's End*

Gary James Wheeler

Gary James Wheeler designed a set in 1973 on Broadway.

Scenic Designs:
1973: *River Niger, The*

Rex Whistler

Rex Whistler, a theatrical designer, etcher and painter, was born in London on June 24, 1905. He studied at the Architectural Association, the Slade School of Art and in Rome. His first designs were seen at Covent Garden in 1934. He was known for his murals and book illustrations. He fought with the British forces during World War II and died at Normandy, France on July 27, 1944.

Scenic Designs:
1929: *Wake Up and Dream* **1935:** *Victoria Regina* **1936:** *Victoria Regina* **1938:** *Victoria Regina* **1947:** *Love for Love*

Costume Designs:
1929: *Wake Up and Dream* **1935:** *Victoria Regina* **1936:** *Victoria Regina* **1938:** *Victoria Regina*

John Biddle Whitelaw

John Biddle Whitelaw was active on Broadway in the mid-1930s. He was born in Chicago and served in the army during and after World War II. Also known as an artist, he died on August 6, 1948 in New York City.

Scenic Designs:
1934: *Bridal Quilt* **1935:** *Reprise*

Vantile Whitfield

Vantile Whitfield was born on September 8, 1930 in Washington, D.C. and received a B.A. at Howard University and a M.A. at the University of California. In his varied career as an administrator and designer he has held positions such as art director for Ad Graphics in Hollywood, general manager of the American Theatre of Being, and set designer for Universal Studios. He has also served as program director, Expansion Arts, at the National Endowment for the Arts in Washington, D.C.

Scenic Designs:
1965: *Amen Corner, The*

Lighting Designs:
1965: *Amen Corner, The*

Costume Designs:
1965: *Amen Corner, The*

Richard Whorf

Richard Whorf was born in Winthrop, Massachusetts on June 4, 1906 and worked in the theatre as an actor, director and designer. He first appeared on stage in 1921 in Boston. He had an active career as an actor and director for theatre and film and ocasionally also designed costumes. He began designing in the early 1940s and in 1949 played the role of Richard III in the play *Richard III* and also designed the costumes and scenery. He also directed numerous television programs, including episodes of *Gunsmoke*, *Alfred Hitchcock* and *The Beverly Hillbillies*. In 1954 he received both a Donaldson Award and a Tony Award for his costume design for *Ondine*. Richard Whorf died in 1966.

Scenic Designs:
1940: *Fledgling*; *Old Acquaintance*; *There Shall Be No Night* **1944:** *But Not Goodbye* **1949:** *Richard III* **1957:** *Genius and the Goddess, The*

Lighting Designs:
1957: *Genius and the Goddess, The*

Costume Designs:
1949: *Richard III* **1954:** *Ondine*

Joseph E. Wickes

Joseph E. Wickes was active on Broadway between 1922 and 1931. He designed productions both under his own name and through Joseph Wickes Studio. Joseph Wickes died on January 20, 1950.

Scenic Designs:
1922: *Marjolaine* **1923:** *Rise of Rosie O'Reilly, The* **1924:** *Harem, The*; *Ladies of the Evening*; *Tiger Cats* **1925:** *Dove, The* **1926:** *Fanny*; *Home Towners, The*; *Lilly Sue*; *Lulu Belle*; *What Never Dies*; *Yellow* **1927:** *Hidden*; *Merry Malones* **1928:** *Bachelor Father, The*; *Big Fight, The*; *Billie*; *Minna* **1929:** *It's a Wise Child* **1930:** *Dancing Partner*; *Tonight Or Never*

Joseph Wickes Studio

Joseph Wickes operated a scenic studio at 241 West 62nd Street, New York City which was active in the 1920s and 1930s. For additional information see "Joseph Wickes".

Scenic Designs:
1922: *Secrets*; *Texas Nightingale, The* **1925:** *Accused*; *American Born*; *Canary Dutch*; *Tangletoes* **1927:** *Baby Cyclone* **1930:** *Rhapsody, The* **1931:** *Friendship*

Clement Wilenchick

Clement Wilenchick was born in New York City on October 28, 1900. He studied art in Cardiff, Wales and in Paris at the L'Ecole des Beaux Arts, after which he returned to the United States to paint. His first involvement in the theatre was as an actor at the Neighborhood Playhouse and the Provincetown Playhouse. He also performed in Europe while continuing to paint and exhibit. He returned to New York City in 1931 and performed with the Group Theatre as an artist-actor and in several plays on Broadway, supplying sets and costume designs for one play. As "Crane Whiley" and "Clem Wilenchick" he appeared in a few films in 1938 and 1939, among them *The Lazy Warning* and *Charlie McCarthy, Detective*. He died on February 28, 1957 in Los Angeles.

Scenic Designs:
1928: *Dr. Knock*

Costume Designs:
1928: *Dr. Knock*

Thomas Wilfred

Thomas Wilfred invented the Clavilus, an organ with keys connected to projectors behind a translucent screen. He became known for his "lumina" compositions which he performed throughout the United States, first demonstrated at the Neighborhood Playhouse in 1922. In 1930 he founded the Art Institute of Light. He was born on June 18, 1889 in West Nyack, New York. He also made a variety of light machines for theatrical productions and designed and installed lighting systems at the University of Washington Playhouse and the Center Theatre at the University of Georgia. In 1930 he contributed designs for sets and costumes to a

Broadway production. His work is in the collections of the Cleveland Museum of Art, the Museum of Modern Art and the Metropolitan Museum of Art.

Scenic Designs:
1930: *Vikings, The*

Costume Designs:
1930: *Vikings, The*

Wilhelm

C. Wilhelm (a.k.a. William John Charles Pitcher) was born in Northfleet, Kent, England on March 21, 1858. During the last quarter of the 19th century he designed sets and costumes for pantomimes in Drury Lane in London, later working at the Empire Theatre designing sets, costumes and creating ballets. A watercolor painter, he contributed designs to revues on Broadway in the early 1920s. Wilhelm died at age 67 in 1925.

Scenic Designs:
1923: *Stepping Stones* 1924: *Stepping Stones*

Costume Designs:
1922: *Better Times* 1923: *Stepping Stones* 1924: *Stepping Stones*

Norman Wilkinson

The distinguished British designer Norman Wilkinson was born in 1882 and studied at the Birmingham School of Art. He worked with Charles Frohman, D'Oyly Carte and Harley Granville-Barker. He was a governor of the Shakespeare Memorial Theatre and designed a *A Midsummer Night's Dream* in 1932 for that theatre. He is known in the United States primarily as the designer of *Androcles and the Lion* in 1915, which included *The Man Who Married a Dumb Wife* as a curtain raiser. The designs for the curtain raiser by Robert Edmond Jones are generally regarded as the beginning of both the "New American Stagecraft" and the modern era on Broadway. Norman Wilkinson died in 1934.

Scenic Designs:
1915: *Androcles and the Lion*; *Doctor's Dilemma, The*; *Midsummer Night's Dream, A* 1929: *Wake Up and Dream*

Costume Designs:
1929: *Wake Up and Dream*

Clement M. Williams

Clement M. Williams designed settings for two plays in the mid-1930s. An architect, he resided at 405 East 54th Street, New York City in 1932.

Scenic Designs:
1934: *Come What May* 1936: *Puritan, The*

Robert T. Williams

Robert T. Williams designed sets for Broadway in the 1960s and early 1970s. For one production he also designed lights.

Scenic Designs:
1964: *Girl Could Get Lucky, A* 1965: *Glass Menagerie, The* 1967: *Warm Body, A* 1970: *Charley's Aunt*

Lighting Designs:
1967: *Warm Body, A*

Hugh Willoughby

Hugh Willoughby was born in Croyden, England on October 15, 1891 and first designed costumes for a musical revue in The Hague, Netherlands. He went on to design costumes for many shows throughout Europe and occasionally contributed sets as well. He designed costumes and scenery on Broadway in the 1920s and 1930s. Hugh Willoughby died at age 82 on April 4, 1939.

Scenic Designs:
1926: *Castles in the Air* 1928: *Earl Carroll's Vanities* 1929: *Earl Carroll's Sketch Book* 1930: *Earl Carroll's Vanities* 1931: *Earl Carroll's Vanities* 1934: *Saluta* 1937: *Tide Rising* 1938: *Where Do We Go from Here?*

Costume Designs:
1925: *Mercenary Mary* 1927: *Judy; Piggy*

E. Carlton Winckler

The lighting designer E. Carlton Winckler was born on January 20, 1908 in Jersey City, New Jersey. For twenty years he worked with John Murray Anderson, who encouraged his interest in lighting design while they created "units" for Paramount Movie Theatres. He worked for producer Billy Rose for nearly thirty years while also designing lights throughout the United

States for theatre and films. He designed numerous shows for which he did not receive program credit, working at a time when the profession of lighting design was only beginning to emerge. He was also actively designing during the period when United Scenic Artists and IATSE Local One struggled over jurisdiction of theatrical lighting design. He designed the lights for Walt Disney's *Fantasia*, pioneering new techniques in film lighting. In 1943 he became involved in television, working in New York and on the West Coast, and in 1951 he became General Manager of the Program Department for CBS-TV where he remained until retirement in 1973. He then joined Imero Fiorentino Associates as senior production consultant and director of the Education Division. In 1977 the Society of Motion Picture and Television Engineers honored him with their Progress Award Gold Medal for contributions to television development.

Scenic Designs:
1927: *Lace Petticoat*

Lighting Designs:
1929: *Murray Anderson's Almanac* **1940:** *Earl Carroll's Vanities; Lousiana Purchase* **1941:** *Ah, Wilderness; Clash By Night; Hope for a Harvest; Liberty Jones; Sunny River* **1942:** *New Faces of 1943; R.U.R.* **1943:** *Counterattack* **1944:** *Seven Lively Arts* **1945:** *Assassin, The; Concert Varieties; Hamlet* **1946:** *Duchess Misbehaves, The; If the Shoe Fits* **1948:** *Light Up the Sky*

Ferry Windberger

Ferry Windberger designed one Broadway set in 1964. He was also known as Franz V. Reiner.

Scenic Designs:
1964: *Wiener Blut (Vienna Life)*

Nancy Winters

Nancy Winters designed a Broadway set in 1984. In 1986 she designed the set for *Africanis Instructus*, directed by Richard Foreman, with whom she often works. She has also designed *The Golem* and *Don Juan* at the Delacorte and *Egyptology* at the New York Shakespeare Festival. Nancy Winters is also a landscape painter.

Scenic Designs:
1984: *Three Musketeers, The*

Ed Wittstein

Ed Wittstein was born in Mt. Vernon, New York on April 7, 1929 and received a B.S. at New York University. He also studied at the Parsons School of Design, Cooper Union, and Erwin Piscator's Dramatic Workshop in New York City, where he first designed in 1947. He has designed sets for numerous plays and in addition often designs costumes and/or lights. He has also designed sets and costumes for operas, ballets and television. Designs include the long-running off-Broadway play *The Fantasticks, The Adams Chronicles* on television, and the films *Endless Love* and *Fame*. He received an Obie Award in 1966 for *Sergeant Musgrave's Dance* and a Maharam Award in 1974 for *Ulysses in Nighttown*.

Scenic Designs:
1961: *Kean* **1963:** *Enter Laughing; Rainy Day in Newark, A* **1964:** *White House, The* **1965:** *And Things That Go Bump in the Night; Yearling, The* **1967:** *Natural Look, The; You Know I Can't Hear You When the Water's* **1968:** *Before You Go; Man in the Glass Booth, The* **1969:** *Celebration* **1970:** *Blood Red Roses* **1972:** *Ring Round the Bathtub; Tough to Get Help* **1974:** *Ulysses in Nighttown*

Lighting Designs:
1963: *Enter Laughing; Rainy Day in Newark, A* **1969:** *Celebration*

Costume Designs:
1961: *Kean* **1962:** *Bravo Giovanni* **1963:** *Enter Laughing; Rainy Day in Newark, A* **1964:** *White House, The* **1965:** *Yearling, The* **1969:** *Celebration*

Peter Wolf

Peter Wolf debuted on Broadway as a set designer in 1947 and as a lighting designer in 1950. After forsaking acting as a career, he studied at the Grand Central School of Art and the Yale School of Drama. He then worked as an assistant for several New York-based scenic designers and at the New York City Center with Maurice Evans. A position supplying scenery for summer musicals in Dallas led to considerable travel and eventual relocation to Texas. His firm, Peter Wolf Concepts (formerly Peter Wolf Associates), began as a major scenic studio and has become a firm which designs and builds commercial buildings, industrial promotions, restaurants, exhibits, etc. He has credits for settings for hundreds of plays, musicals and operas throughout the United States.

Scenic Designs:
1947: *Sweethearts* 1948: *Linden Tree, The* 1950: *Devil's Disciple, The* 1977: *King and I, The* 1979: *Peter Pan* 1980: *Blackstone!*; *Music Man, The* 1983: *Mame* 1984: *Wiz, The* 1985: *King and I, The*

Lighting Designs:
1950: *Devil's Disciple, The*

Sir Donald Wolfit

Sir Donald Wolfit, a British actor, was born in Newark-on-Trent, Nottinghamshire, England on April 20, 1902. He was one of the last of the actor-managers and earned his reputation as a Shakespearean actor at the Old Vic and Stratford-upon-Avon. In 1937 he formed his own company and toured around the world. During World War II he entertained the troops, resuming the presentation of plays in a repertory format at the end of the war. In 1955 he published his autobiography, *First Interval.* Knighted in 1957, Sir Donald Wolfit died in February 1968 at the age of 65.

Scenic Designs:
1947: *Hamlet*; *Merchant of Venice, The*

Costume Designs:
1947: *Hamlet*

Patricia Woodbridge

Patricia Woodbridge designs mainly for film and television but tries to design one or two productions each year for the theatre, her first love. She was born on August 9, 1946 in Philadelphia and received a B.A. from Bennington College and an M.F.A. at New York University's Tisch School of the Arts, where she teaches part-time. Her first design as a professional was *The Wonderful Ice Cream Suit* for the Puerto Rico travelling theatre. She has designed for many regional theatres including Arena Stage, the Goodman Theatre, the Philadelphia Drama Guild and the Cincinnati Playhouse. Productions off-Broadway include *Faith, Hope and Charity, How I Got that Story* and *Dispatches* at

theatres such as the New York Shakespeare Festival, Manhattan Theatre Club and Intar. She was art director for the film *Cadillac Man* and counts Ben Edwards, Tony Walton and Ming Cho Lee, (all of whom she has assisted) as influential in her career. She won the Helen Hayes Award for the set design for *Isn't It Romantic?* at Arena Stage.

Scenic Designs:
1976: *Runner Stumbles, The*

Jack Woodson

Jack Woodson designed a Broadway set in 1954.

Scenic Designs:
1954: *Hayride*

Reginald Woolley

Reginald Woolley designed scenery and costumes on Broadway in 1954. The 1951 *London City Directory* lists Reginald Woolley as a member of Williams and Woolley, Theatrical Managers, 33 Great Windmill Street. *Playing With Punch* by Frank Baker, published in 1944, was illustrated by Reginald Woolley and Douglas Campbell.

Scenic Designs:
1954: *Boyfriend, The*

Costume Designs:
1954: *Boyfriend, The*

Michael Wright

Michael Wright designed a Broadway set in 1947.

Scenic Designs:
1947: *Winslow Boy, The*

Russell Wright

Russell Wright, an industrial designer, was born on April 3, 1905 in Lebanon, Ohio. Exhibiting an artistic talent as a young boy, he took classes at the Cincinnati Art Academy before going to New York to study at the Art Students League. While in college at Princeton he directed plays and designed sets, which led to an offer from Norman Bel Geddes to travel to Paris. He left school and began work as a theatrical designer assisting designers and creating sets for the The-atre Guild, the Neighborhood Playhouse and the Group Theatre. A workshop where he produced theatrical properties grew into a small factory as his talent and originality for custom-made furniture and decorative accessories became known. He gave up a career in theatre to design functional, modernist home furnishings.

Scenic Designs:
1925: *Exiles; Grand Street Follies*

Costume Designs:
1925: *Exiles; Grand Street Follies*

John E. Wulp

John E. Wulp began working as a paint boy in his teens and then designed for the Boston Summer Theatre. He attended Yale University prior to military service. He is a Broadway pro-ducer *(Dracula, The Crucifier of Blood* among others), a playwright *(The Saintliners of Mar-jery Kempe* among others) and a designer. He is also a painter and editor (the magazine *Readers' Digest)*, teacher (set design at Carnegie Mel-lon University) and a director. He has served on the Board of Directors of Playwrights Hori-zons and the Eglevsky Ballet. Honors include an Obie Award for directing *Red Eye of Love* and a Tony nomination for the set design of *Crucifer of Blood*, which was also honored with Drama Desk, Outer Critics' Circle and Los An-geles Critics Awards.

Scenic Designs:
1978: *Crucifer of Blood, The* 1979: *Bosoms and Neglect*

Stuart Wurtzel

Stuart Wurtzel was raised in Hillside, New Jer-sey. After receiving an M.F.A. from Carnegie-Mellon University he joined Bill Ball at the Pittsburgh Playhouse and travelled with him to the American Conservatory Theatre as an as-sistant designer. He designed forty productions for ACT once it settled in San Francisco. He has designed at the Alliance Theatre, Cincin-nati's Playhouse in the Park and off-Broadway, including productions for the Dodger Theatre at the Brooklyn Academy of Music. His first film was *Hester Street* and was followed by many more as production designer, such as *Hair, Si-mon, Hannah and Her Sisters, The Purple Rose*

of *Cairo, Brighton Beach Memoirs, An Innocent Man, The Old Gringo, Staying Together* and *Three Men and a Little Lady.* He is married to production designer Patrizia Von Brandenstein, with whom he began working at ACT.

Scenic Designs:
1969: *Flea in Her Ear, A; Tiny Alice* 1974: *Sizwe Banzi is Dead; Summer Brave* 1977: *Un-expected Guests* 1981: *Wally's Cafe*

John Wyckham

John Wyckham Suckling was born on May 18, 1926 in Solihull, Warwickshire, England. He first worked in theatre as a stage manager in the early 1950s and began his career as a lighting de-signer in 1955. He has extensive credits for light-ing in the West End, for the Royal Shakespeare Company, and Sadler's Wells, among others. He is senior partner in John Wyckham Associates, theatre consultants, and was a founding mem-ber of the Society of Theatre Consultants. He has also consulted on the design and renovation of many theatres in the United Kingdom.

Scenic Designs:
1965: *Beyond the Fringe*

Lighting Designs:
1963: *Oliver!* 1965: *Beyond the Fringe; Oliver!*

Alexander Wyckoff

Alexander Wyckoff was active on Broadway in the 1920s and 1930s. He was on the faculty of Carnegie Technical Institute in the 1920s where he taught scene design and scene painting with Woodman Thompson. One of his many students was the lighting designer Abe Feder. He also founded a school in Edgewater, New Jersey as-sociated with the summer season at the Ogun-quit (Maine) Playhouse to train stagecraft in-structors. He wrote *Early American Dress* with Edward Warwick and Henry C. Pitz.

Scenic Designs:
1925: *Cain; White Gold* 1932: *Anatomist, The; When the Bough Breaks*

Costume Designs:
1925: *Cain*

Michael Yeargan

Michael Yeargan was born in Dallas, Texas on February 13, 1946 and studied at Stetson University, the University of Madrid and Yale University, where he received an M.F.A. in 1972. An elementary school teacher, Miss Frances Parr, first interested him in set design, which remains his primary interest. His first professional designs were seen in the Yale Repertory Theatre production of *Happy End* and his New York debut came in 1974. He has frequently collaborated on productions with the director Andrei Serban, an association that began at Yale and continues around the world with productions of plays and operas (another of his interests). Mr. Yeargan occasionally designs sets and costumes for productions to achieve an integration of style and effect.

Scenic Designs:
1974: *Bad Habits* **1975:** *Ritz, The* **1980:** *Lesson from Aloes, A* **1981:** *It Had to Be You* **1985:** *Hay Fever* **1988:** *Ah, Wilderness!*

Costume Designs:
1974: *Bad Habits* **1976:** *Me Jack, You Jill* **1977:** *Something Old, Something New*

Nicholas Yellenti

Nicholas Yellenti, who was active on Broadway from 1923 to 1963, usually designed settings but also designed lights for one production. He also constructed sets for other designers.

Scenic Designs:
1923: *Breaking Point, The* **1924:** *Bluffing Bluffers; Flossie* **1925:** *Easy Come, Easy Go; Family Upstairs, The; Mud Turtle, The; Solid Ivory; Twelve Miles Out* **1926:** *Ashes of Love; Bells, The; Black Boy; Donovan Affair, The; Gertie; If I Was Rich; Just Life; Kongo; She Couldn't Say No; They All Want Something; This Woman Business; We Americans* **1927:** *Bless You, Sister; Fog Bound; Fog; Her First Affairs; Jazz Singer, The; Lady in Love, A; Mystery Shop, The; Nightstick; Restless Women; Set a Thief; Shannons of Broadway, The; Skin Deep; Take My Advice; Tenth Avenue* **1928:** *Adventure; Behavior of Mrs. Crane, The; Brothers; Get Me in the Movies; Golden Age, The; Happy Husband, The; Man with Red Hair, A; Mirrors; Mystery Man, The; Quicksand; Tin*

Pan Alley; War Song, The **1929:** *House Unguarded; Ladies Don't Lie; Scotland Yard; Veneer* **1930:** *Love, Honor and Betray; Made in France; Schoolgirl; Sweet Chariot* **1931:** *Her Supporting Cast; In the Best of Families; In Times Square* **1932:** *Absent Feather; Web, The* **1933:** *Curtain Rises, The; Family Upstairs, The* **1934:** *American–Very Early; Baby Pompadour; Theodora, the Queen; When in Rome* **1935:** *Good Men and True; Ragged Edge, The; Woman of the Soil, A* **1936:** *Around the Corner; Arrest That Woman; Love on the Dole* **1937:** *Behind Red Lights; Places Please; Something for Nothing* **1938:** *Bright Rebel; Censored* **1939:** *Aries Is Rising* **1948:** *Vigil, The* **1963:** *Golden Age, The*

Lighting Designs:
1948: *Vigil, The*

Alison Yerxa

Alison Yerxa won an American Theatre Wing Design Award (formerly the Maharam Award) for special theatrical effects in 1989 for *The Warrior Ant*. She was born on February 2, 1952 in Woodland, California the daughter of Charles and Virginia Yerxa, a fourth generation northern California farming family. She received a B.A. in Art from the University of California at Santa Cruz. Her first design was *Prelude to a Death in Venice*. She has also worked in visual special effects for motion pictures.

Scenic Designs:
1988: *Gospel at Colonus, The*

Robert Yodice

Robert Yodice (Iodice) was resident designer at Juilliard from 1973 to 1977. He is a painter as well as a set designer and received an Obie Award in 1978 for Joseph Papp's *Museum*. He also designed *Alice at the Palace* for the New York Shakespeare Festival. Related expereince includes positions as technical director for various theatres and service on the staffs of Ride and Show Engineering, Stage Engineering International and The Great American Market. Born in New York City, he studied painting with Robert Rabinowitz in addition to earning B.F.A. and M.F.A. degrees. He began his career as an assistant to Ming Cho Lee and Wolfgang Roth and has also been an assistant professor and resident designer at the University of California.

Scenic Designs:
1973: *Beggar's Opera, The*

Akita Yoshimura

Akita "Leo" Yoshimura has an M.F.A. from the Yale University School of Drama. He also studied painting at the Art Institute of Chicago and the American Academy of Art in Chicago. Additional credits include designs for television (with two Emmy nominations for *Saturday Night Live*) and regional theatres, such as the Dallas Theatre Center, the Public Theatre and the Hartman Theatre. His career began with Paul Sills at the Second City Repertory.

Scenic Designs:
1979: *Gilda Radner Live from N.Y.*

Young Brothers

Young Brothers received credit for a 1915 Broadway production. John H. Young (1858-1944) and Louis C. Young (1864-1915) were partners in Young Brothers and worked primarily as scene painters. The business was located at 536 West 29th Street, New York City and was active between 1900 and 1920. John and Louis Young resided in Pelham, New York.

Scenic Designs:
1915: *Two is Company*

John Young

John H. Young was born in Grand Rapids, Michigan in 1858 and worked as a scenic designer and painter in Chicago and New York City. He moved to Chicago after attending school in Michigan to be a scenic painter. He moved to New York at the turn of the century and designed shows for major producers such as Florenz Ziegfield, Earl Carroll and George White. His brother Louis C. Young (1864-1915) was also a scenic painter. A specialist in mechanical displays, he amassed a large library of photographs for use in creating authentic scenes. He died in North Pelham, New York on January 5, 1944 at age 86.

Scenic Designs:
1916: *Robinson Crusoe, Jr.* **1917:** *Doing Our Bit* **1921:** *In the Night Watch*

Leonard Young

Leonard Young designed sets and costumes and served as assistant director for a Broadway show in 1921.

Scenic Designs:
1921: *Biff! Biff! Bang!*

Costume Designs:
1921: *Biff! Biff! Bang!*

Roland Young

Roland Young's career as an actor began in the United States with the Washington Square Players. He was born in London on November 11, 1887 and performed in the West End before coming to America. He was a star of stage and screen and was nominated for an Academy Award for Best Supporting Actor in 1937 for *Topper*, one of numerous films including *Ruggles of Red Gap* and *The Man Who Could Work Miracles* in which he appeared. He also was a successful actor in New York City in plays such as *Beggar on Horseback*, *The Queen's Husband*, *Good Gracious Annabelle*, *A Touch of Brimstone* and *Rollo's Wild Oats*, for which he also designed the settings. He was a caricaturist and author of the verse collection *Not for Children*. Married to the actress Dorothy Patience May, Roland Young died on June 7, 1953 at age 65.

Scenic Designs:
1920: *Rollo's Wild Oat*

Sylvia Younin

Sylvia Younin, a native New Yorker, designed a set on Broadway in 1967. She received a B.A. from Brooklyn College and an M.A. from Columbia University. In addition to writing Yiddish short stories she translates books from Yiddish into English.

Scenic Designs:
1967: *Sing, Israel, Sing*

Victor Zanoff

Victor Zanoff designed one Broadway set in 1937.

Scenic Designs:
1937: *Swing It*

Franco Zeffirelli

Franco Zeffirelli originally planned to become an actor or join the family textile import business. Born on February 12, 1923 in Florence, Italy, he attended the University of Architecture in Florence. He began acting in 1945 but soon turned to design and gradually began directing. He designed films for Luchino Visconti, Vittorio de Sica and Michelangelo Antonioni. He has designed operas at La Scala and the Metropolitan Opera, most recently *Turandot* and *La Boheme*. Notable film work as director and designer include *Romeo and Juliet, Brother Sun, Sister Moon, The Taming of The Shrew, Otello* and *Hamlet*. He was nominated for an Academy Award for direction for *Romeo and Juliet* in 1968. Additional New York credits include directing *Filumena* in 1980. He is author of *Zeffirelli by Zeffirelli* (1986).

Scenic Designs:
1963: *Lady of the Camellias, The* **1974:** *Saturday Sunday Monday*

Frank J. Zimmerer

Frank J. Zimmerer was born in Nebraska City, Nebraska in 1882 and studied at the Art Institute of Chicago, the Glasgow School of Art, and in Paris. During the teens he was active in New York, creating sets for Broadway plays, and painting. He served in administrative positions at the Kansas City Art Institute and Northwest Missouri Normal before relocating to California in the mid-1920s to work as a commercial artist and exhibit his paintings.

Scenic Designs:
1916: *Birthday of the Infanta, The; Golden Doom, The; King Arimenes and the Unknown Warrior; Petrouchka; Trimplet, The* **1918:** *Jonathan Makes a Wish; Seventeen* **1919:** *Night in Avignon, A*

Costume Designs:
1916: *Golden Doom, The; King Arimenes and the Unknown Warrior* **1919:** *Night in Avignon, A*

Frank Zimmerman

Frank Zimmerman was the son of one of New York's most influential theatrical managers, J.

Fred Zimmerman. He graduated from the University of Pennsylvania in 1903 and spent six years as business manager of the Garrick Theatre. In 1913 he began working in management for Zimmerman Vaudeville enterprises.   Mr. Zimmerman died, a suicide, on July 12, 1927.

Scenic Designs:
1916: *Gods of the Mountain, The* **1919:** *Book of Job; Golden Doom, The; Laughter of the Gods; Stingy*

Costume Designs:
1916: *Gods of the Mountain, The* **1919:** *Book of Job; Golden Doom, The; Laughter of the Gods; Stingy*

Doris Zinkeisen

Doris Zinkeisen was born in Gareloch, Scotland and began designing sets and costumes for plays in 1923. She designed mainly in England for the theatre and the ballet, beginning in 1923 with sets and costumes for *The Insect Play*. An artist as well as a designer, her pictures were exhibited in London, Liverpool and Paris. Miss Zinkeisen wrote *Designing for the Stage*, published in 1938.

Scenic Designs:
1929: *Wake Up and Dream*

Costume Designs:
1928: *This Year of Grace* **1929:** *Wake Up and Dream* **1934:** *Great Waltz, The*

Appendix 1:
The Tony Awards

The Antoinette Perry or Tony Award is given at the end of each season for an outstanding contribution to Broadway in several categories including scenic design. Under the auspices of the American Theatre Wing, nominees and winners are selected by members of the governing boards of professional organizations, opening night press lists, the board of directors of the American Theatre Wing, and members of the League of New York Theatres and Producers. (Winners are printed in boldface.)

1948 . . . . **Horace Armistead:** *The Medium*

1949 . . . . **Jo Mielziner:** *Sleepy Hollow/ Summer and Smoke/ Anne of the Thousand Days/ Death of a Salesman/ South Pacific*

1950 . . . . **Jo Mielziner:** *The Innocents*

1951 . . . . **Boris Aronson:** *The Rose Tattoo/ The Country Girl/ Season in the Sun*

1952 . . . . **Jo Mielziner:** *The King and I*

1953 . . . . **Raoul Pene du Bois:** *Wonderful Town*

1954 . . . . **Peter Larkin:** *Ondine* and *The Teahouse of the August Moon*

1955 . . . . **Oliver Messel:** *House of Flowers*

1956 . . . . **Peter Larkin:** *Inherit the Wind/ No Time for Sergeants*
Boris Aronson: *The Diary of Anne Frank/ Bus Stop/ Once Upon A Tailor/ A View from the Bridge*
Ben Edwards: *The Ponder Heart/ Someone Waiting / The Honeys*
Jo Mielziner: *Cat on a Hot Tin Roof/ The Lark/ Middle of the Night/ Pipe Dream*
Raymond Sovey: *The Great Sebastians*

1957 . . . . **Oliver Smith:** *My Fair Lady/ A Clearing in the Woods/ Candide/ Auntie Mame/ Eugenia/A Visit To A Small Planet*
Boris Aronson: *A Hole In The Head/ Small War On Murray Hill*
Ben Edwards: *The Waltz Of The Toreaders*
George Jenkins: *The Happiest Millionaire/ Too Late The Phalarope*
Donald Oenslager: *Major Barbara*

1958 . . . . **Oliver Smith:** *West Side Story*

1959 . . . . **Donald Oenslager:** *A Majority of One*
Boris Aronson, J.B. Ballou: *The Legend of Lizzie*
Ben Edwards: *Jane Eyre*
Oliver Messel: *Rashomon*
Ted Otto: *The Visit*

1960 . . . . (Dramatic)
  Howard Bay: *Toys in the Attic*
  Will Steven Armstrong: *Caligula*
  David Hays: *The Tenth Man*
  George Jenkins: *The Miracle Worker*
  Jo Mielziner: *The Best Man*
  (Musical)
  Oliver Smith: *The Sound of Music*
  Cecil Beaton: *Saratoga*
  William and Jean Eckart: *Fiorello*
  Peter Larkin: *Greenwillow*
  Jo Mielziner: *Gypsy*

1961 . . . . (Dramatic)
  Oliver Smith: *Becket*
  Roger Furse: *Duel of the Angels*
  David Hays: *All the Way Home*
  Jo Mielziner: *The Devil's Advocate*
  Rouben Ter-Arutunian: *Advise and Consent*
  (Musical)
  Oliver Smith: *Camelot*
  George Jenkins: *13 Daughters*
  Robert Randolph: *Bye, Bye Birdie*

1962 . . . . **Will Steven Armstrong:** *Carnival*
  Rouben Ter-Arutunian: *A Passage to India*
  David Hays: *No Strings*
  Oliver Smith: *The Gay Life*

1963 . . . . **Sean Kenny:** *Oliver!*
  Will Steven Armstrong: *Tchin-Tchin*
  Anthony Powell: *The School for Scandal*
  Franco Zeffirelli: *The Lady of the Camellias*

1964 . . . . **Oliver Smith:** *Hello, Dolly!*
  Raoul Pene Du Bois: *The Student Gypsy*
  Ben Edwards: *The Ballad of the Sad Cafe*
  David Hays: *Marco Millions*

1965 . . . . **Oliver Smith:** *Baker Street, Luv* and *The Odd Couple*
  Boris Aronson: *Fiddler on the Roof* and *Incident at Vichy*
  Sean Kenny: *The Roar of the Greasepaint - The Smell of the Crowd*
  Beni Montresor: *Do I Hear A Waltz?*

1966 . . . . **Howard Bay:** *Man of La Mancha*
  William and Jean Eckart: *Mame*
  David Hays: *Drat! The Cat!*
  Robert Randolph: *Anya, Skyscraper* and *Sweet Charity*

1967 . . . . **Boris Aronson:** *Cabaret*
  John Bury: *The Homecoming*
  Oliver Smith: *I Do! I Do!*
  Alan Tagg: *Black Comedy*

1968 . . . . **Desmond Heeley:** *Rosencrantz and Guildenstern are Dead*
  Boris Aronson: *The Price*
  Robert Randolph: *Golden Rainbow*

Peter Wexler: *The Happy Time*

1969 . . . . **Boris Aronson:** *Zorba*
Derek Cousins: *Canterbury Tales*
Jo Mielziner: *1776*
Oliver Smith: *Dear World*

1970 . . . . **Jo Mielziner:** *Child's Play*
Howard Bay: *Cry for Us All*
Ming Cho Lee: *Billy*
Robert Randolph: *Applause*

1971 . . . . **Boris Aronson:** *Company*
John Bury: *The Rothschilds*
Sally Jacobs: *A Midsummer Night's Dream*
Jo Mielziner: *Father's Day*

1972 . . . . **Boris Aronson:** *Follies*
John Bury: *Old Times*
Kert Lundell: *Ain't Supposed to Die a Natural Death*
Robin Wagner: *Jesus Christ Superstar*

1973 . . . . **Tony Walton:** *Pippin*
Boris Aronson: *A Little Night Music*
David Jenkins: *The Changing Room*
Santo Loquasto: *That Championship Season*

1974 . . . . **Franne and Eugene Lee:** *Candide*
John Conklin: *The Au Pair Man*
Santo Loquasto: *What the Wine Sellers Buy*
Oliver Smith: *Gigi*
Ed Wittstein: *Ulysses in Nighttown*

1975 . . . . **Carl Toms:** *Sherlock Holmes*
Scott Johnson: *Dance With Me*
Tanya Moiseiwitsch: *The Misanthrope*
William Ritman: *God's Favorite*
Rouben Ter-Arutunian: *Goodtime Charley*
Robert Wagner: *Mack and Mabel*

1976 . . . . **Boris Aronson:** *Pacific Overtures*
Ben Edwards: *A Matter of Gravity*
David Mitchell: *Trelawny of the "Wells"*
Tony Walton: *Chicago*

1977 . . . . **David Mitchell:** (Tie) *Annie*
Santo Loquasto: (Tie) *American Buffalo*
Santo Loquasto: *Threepenny Opera*
Robert Randolph: *Porgy and Bess*

1978 . . . . **Robin Wagner:** *On The Twentieth Century*
Zack Brown: *The Importance of Being Ernest*
Edward Gorey: *Dracula*
David Mitchell: *Working*

1979 . . . . **Eugene Lee:** *Sweeney Todd*
Karl Eigsti: *Knockout*

David Jenkins: *The Elephant Man*
John Wulp: *The Crucifier of Blood*

1980 . . . . **John Lee Beatty:** (Tie) *Tally's Folly*
David Mitchell: (Tie) *Barnum*
Timothy O'Brien and Tazeena Firth: *Evita*
Tony Walton: *A Day in Hollywood/A Night in Ukraine*

1981 . . . . **John Bury:** *Amadeus*
John Lee Beatty: *Fifth of July*
Santo Loquasto: *The Suicide*
David Mitchell: *Can-Can*

1982 . . . . **John Napier and Dermot Hayes:** *The Life and Adventures of Nicholas Nickleby*
Ben Edwards: *Medea*
Lawrence Miller: *Nine*
Robin Wagner: *Dreamgirls*

1983 . . . . **Ming Cho Lee:** *K-2*
John Gunter: *All's Well That Ends Well*
David Mitchell: *Foxfire*
John Napier: *Cats*

1984 . . . . **Tony Straiges:** *Sunday in the Park with George*
Clarke Dunham: *End of the World*
Peter Larkin: *The Rink*
Tony Walton: *The Real Thing*

1985 . . . . **Heidi Landesman:** *Big River*
Clarke Dunham: *Grind*
Ralph Koltai: *Much Ado About Nothing*
Voytek and Michael Levine: *Strange Interlude*

1986 . . . . **Tony Walton:** *The House of Blue Leaves*
Ben Edwards: *The Iceman Cometh*
David Mitchell: *The Boys in Winter*
Beni Montresor: *The Marriage of Figaro*

1987 . . . . **John Napier:** *Les Miserables*
Bob Crowley: *Les Liasons Dangereuses*
Martin Johns: *Me and My Girl*
Tony Walton: *The Front Page*

1988 . . . . **Maria Bjornson:** *The Phantom of the Opera*
Eiko Ishioka: *M. Butterfly*
Tony Straiges: *Into the Woods*
Tony Walton: *Anything Goes*

1989 . . . . **Santo Loquasto:** *Cafe Crown*
Thomas Lynch: *The Heidi Chronicles*
Claudio Segovia and Hector Orezzoli: *Black and Blue*
Tony Walton: *Lend Me a Tenor*

1990 . . . . **Robin Wagner:** *City of Angels*
Alexandra Byrne: *Some Americans Abroad*
Kevin Rigdon: *The Grapes of Wrath*
Tony Walton: *The Grand Hotel*

Appendix 2:
The Maharam Awards

The Maharam Awards (a.k.a. Marharam Awards) were presented each fall to recognize distinguished design on, off and off-off Broadway. Each award included a cash stipend and a citation, and was given as part of a yearly design seminar. These awards were sponsored by the Joseph Maharam Foundation from 1964 when they began until 1986. Beginning in 1986 the awards were under the auspices of the American Theatre Wing and known as the American Theatre Wing Design Awards. Winners of the Maharam Awards were selected by members of the professional theatre.

1964-65 .... Boris Aronson: *Fiddler on the Roof*
Ming Cho Lee: *Electra*

1965-66 .... Howard Bay: *Man of La Mancha*

1966-67 .... Boris Aronson: *Cabaret*

1967-68 .... Peter Wexler: *The Happy Time*
Ming Cho Lee: *Ergo*

1968-69 .... Jo Mielziner: *1776*
Julian Beck: *Frankenstein*

1969-70 .... Boris Aronson: *Company*
Jo Mielziner: *Child's Play*

1970-71 .... Peter Larkin: *Les Blancs*
Boris Aronson: *Follies*

1971-72 .... Kurt Lundell: *Ain't Supposed To Die a Natural Death*
Robert U. Taylor: *Beggars Opera*

1972-73 .... Douglas W. Schmidt: *Enemies*
Robin Wagner: *Seesaw*

1973-74 .... Franne and Eugene Lee: *Candide*
Ed Wittstein: *Ulysses in Nighttown*

1974-75 .... Robin Wagner: *A Chorus Line*
Robert Wilson: *Letter for Queen Victoria*

1975-76 .... Boris Aronson: *Pacific Overtures*
John Lee Beatty: *Knock Knock*

1976-77 .... Douglas W. Schmidt: *Agamemnon*
Santo Loquasto: *American Buffalo*

1977-78 .... Edward Gorey and Lynn Pecktal: *Dracula*
John Lee Beatty: *A Life In The Theatre*

1978-79 .... David Jenkins: *The Elephant Man*
Karl Eigsti: *Knockout*
Michael H. Yeargan: *The Umbrellas of Cherbourg*

1979-80 . . . . **David Mitchell:** *Barnum*
          Julie Taymor: *The Haggadah*
          Stuart Wurtzel: *The Sorrows of Stephen*

1980-81 . . . . **John Lee Beatty:** *Fifth of July*
          Manuel Lutgenhorst and Douglas E. Ball: *Request Concert*

1981-82 . . . . **David Chapman:** *The First*
          Edward T. Gianfrancesco: *Big Apple Messenger* and *The Little Shop of Horrors*

1982-83 . . . . **Ming Cho Lee and Leslie Taylor:** *K2*
          Julie Archer, Linda Hartinian, Greg Mehrten, Bryan St. John Schofield,
            L. B. Dallas, Craig Miller, Stephanie Rudolph, Craig Jones
            and David Hardy: *Cold Harbor, Company* and *Haff*

1983-84 . . . . **Tony Straiges and Bran Ferren:** *Sunday in the Park with George*
          Bill Stable: *Spookhouse*

1984-85 . . . . **Heidi Landesman:** *Big River*
          Charles Ludlam: *The Mystery of Irma Vep*
          Angus Moss: *Nosferatu*

Appendix 3:
The American Theatre
Wing Design Awards

The American Theatre Wing Design Awards were first given in 1986. The American Theatre Wing took responsibility for this award program from the Joseph Maharam Foundation which had awarded a cash stipend and citation in recognition of distinguished design on, off and off-off Broadway beginning in 1964. Awards are given in costume, lighting, scenery, sustained contribution and noteworthy unusual effects. Winners are selected by members of the professional theatre and the awards are presented as part of a yearly seminar on theatrical design.

1986 .... Tony Walton: *The House of Blue Leaves*
1987 .... Robert Israel: *The Hunger Artist*
                   James D. Sandefur: *Fences*
1988 .... John Lee Beatty: *Burn This*
1989 .... Jerome Sirlin: *1000 Airplanes on the Roof*
1990 .... Kevin Rigdon: *The Grapes of Wrath*

Appendix 4:
The Donaldson Awards

The Donaldson Awards were given annually in July in honor of W.H. Donaldson, founder of *The Bill Board*, beginning with the 1943-44 season and ending with the 1954-55 season. The winners were selected by a poll of theatre people. Two awards were given in the scenery category, one for a musical and one for a straight play.

1943-44 . . . . **Stewart Chaney:** *The Voice of the Turtle* (Play)
                Howard Bay: *Carmen Jones* (Musical)

1944-45 . . . . **George Jenkins:** *I Remember Mama* (Play)
                Howard Bay: *Up in Central Park* (Musical)

1945-46 . . . . **Jo Mielziner:** *Dream Girl* (Play)
                Robert Edmond Jones: *Lute Song* (Musical)

1946-47 . . . . **Cecil Beaton:** *Lady Windermere's Fan* (Play)
                Oliver Smith: *Brigadoon* (Musical)

1947-48 . . . . **Jo Mielziner:** *A Streetcar Named Desire* (Play)
                Oliver Smith: *High Button Shoes* (Musical)

1948-49 . . . . **Jo Mielziner:** *Death of a Salesman* (Play)
                Lemuel Ayers: *Kiss Me, Kate* (Musical)

1949-50 . . . . **Jo Mielziner:** *The Innocents* (Play)
                Oliver Smith: *Gentlemen Prefer Blondes* (Musical)

1950-51 . . . . **Frederick Fox:** *Darkness at Noon* (Play)
                Jo Mielziner: *The King and I* (Musical)

1951-52 . . . . **Cecil Beaton:** *The Grass Harp* (Play)
                Oliver Smith: *Pal Joey* (Muscial)

1952-53 . . . . **Lemuel Ayers:** *Camino Real* (Play)
                Raoul Pène du Bois: *Wonderful Town* (Musical)

1953-54 . . . . **Peter Larkin:** *Teahouse of the August Moon* (Play)
                William and Jean Eckart: *The Golden Apple* (Muscial)

1954-55 . . . . **Peter Larkin:** *Inherit the Wind* (Play)
                Oliver Messel: *House of Flowers* (Musical)

Aline Bernstein. *Grand Street Follies*, 1929.

Norman Bel Geddes. *The Miracle*, 1924.

William and Jean Eckart. *Fiorello,* The Marino Club, Act I, Scene 2; Act I, Scene 10; Act II, Scene 7, 1959.

Ben Edwards. *Purlie*. Act I, Scene 1, 1959.

Desmond Heeley. *The Circle*, 1989.

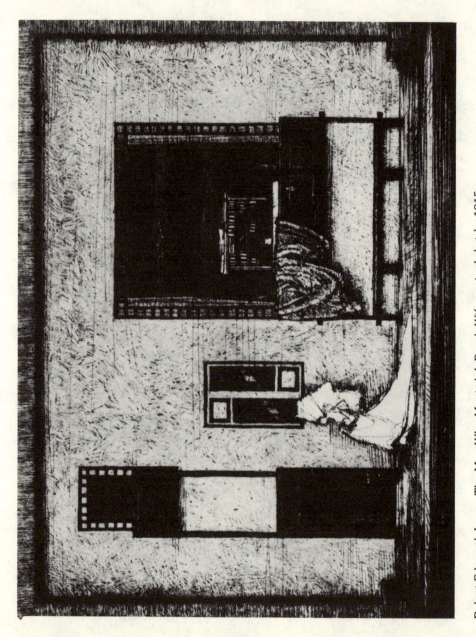

Robert Edmond Jones. *The Man Who Married A Dumb Wife*, revised sketch, 1915.

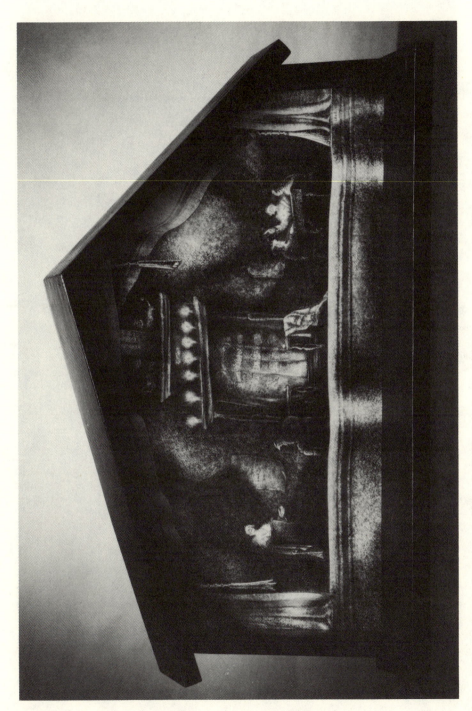

Samuel Leve. *The Dybbuck*. Act I, Scene 1, 1982.

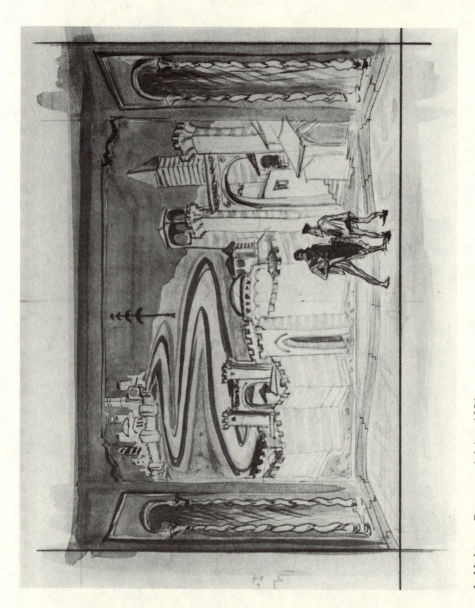

Jo Mielziner. *Romeo and Juliet*, 1931.

Douglas Schmidt. *Frankenstein.* Act I, Scene 1, The Graveyard, 1981.

Douglas Schmidt. *Frankenstein*. Act I, Scene 3, Victor's Laboratory, 1981.

Douglas Schmidt. *Frankenstein*. Act II, Scene 4, Elizabeth's Boudoir, 1981.

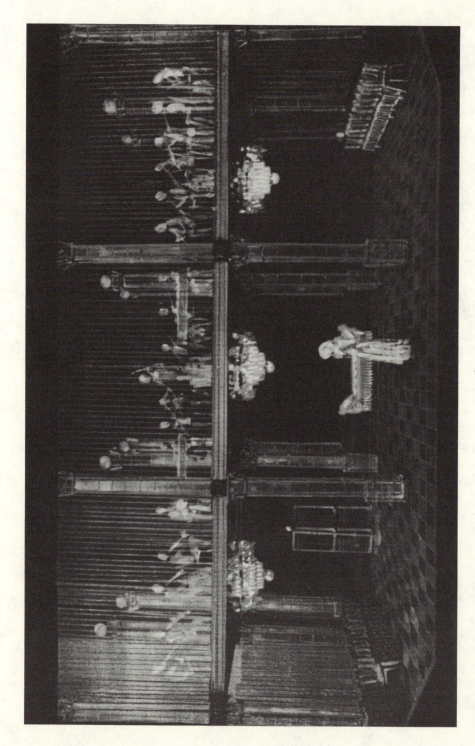

Tony Walton. *Grand Hotel*, 1989.

Selected Bibliography

Appia, Adolphe. *Music and the Art of the Theatre.* Coral Gables, Fla.: University of Miami Press, 1962.

Aronson, Arnold. *American Set Design.* New York: Theatre Communications Group, 1985.

Bay, Howard. *Stage Design.* New York: Drama Book Specialists, 1974.

Beaumont, Cyril W. and Browse, Lillian (eds.). *Leslie Hurry, Settings and Costumes for Sadler's Wells Ballets.* London: for the Shenval Press by Faber and Faber, 1946.

Binnie, Eric. *The Theatrical Designs of Charles Ricketts.* Ann Arbor: University of Michigan Research Press, 1985.

Boll, André. *Du decor de Theatre.* Paris: E. Chiron, 1926

Bowit, John E. *Russian Stage Design.* Jackson, Miss.: Mississippi Museum of Art, 1982.

Breitman, Ellen. *Art and the Stage.* Cleveland, Ohio: Cleveland Art Museum in cooperation with Indiana University Press, 1981

Castle, Charles. *Oliver Messel.* New York: Thames and Hudson, 1986.

Cheney, Sheldon. *Stage Decoration.* New York: The John Day Company, 1928.

Cheney, Sheldon. *The New Movement in the Theatre.* Westport, Conn.: Greenwood Press, 1971.

Cogniat, Raymond. *Les Décorateurs de Théâtre.* Paris: Librairie Théâtrale, 1955.

Craig, Edward Gordon. *Craig on Theatre.* London: Methuen, 1983.

Craig, Edward Gordon. *Towards a New Theatre.* New York: Benjamin Blom, 1969.

DeShong, Andrew. *The Theatrical Designs of George Grosz.* Ann Arbor: University of Michigan Research Press, 1982.

Diaghilev and Russian Stage Designers. Washington: The Foundation, 1972.

Elder, Eldon. *Designs for the Theatre.* New York: Drama Book Specialists, 1978.

Fuerst, Walter Rene and Samuel J. Hume. *Twentieth Century Stage Decoration.* Vol. 1, text. Vol. 2 ill. New York: Dover Publications, 1929.

Goodwin, John. *British Theatre Design.* New York: St. Martin's Press, 1989.

Gorelik, Mordecai. *New Theatres for Old.* New York: Samuel French, 1940.

Hainaux, Rene. *Stage Design Throughout the World Since 1935.* New York: Theatre Arts Books, 1964.

Hainaux, Rene. *Stage Design Throughout the World Since 1960.* New York: Theatre Arts Books, 1972.

Hainaux, Rene. *Stage Design Throughout the World: 1970-1975.* New York: Theatre Arts Books, 1976.

Hay, Richard L. *A Space for Magic.* Ashland, Oreg: Oregon Shakespearean Fesival, 1979.

Hodgman, Ann. *A Day in the Life of a Theater Set Designer.* Mahwah, N.J.: Troll Associates, 1988.

Holt, Michael. *Stage Design and Properties.* New York: Schirmer Books, 1989.

International Federation for Theatre Research. *Innovations in Stage and Theatre Design.* New York: American Society for Theatre Research, 1972.

International Theatre Institute of the United States, Inc. *Contemporary Stage Design U.S.A.* Middletown, Conn.: Wesleyan University Press, 1974.

International Theatre Institute. *Stage Design Throughout the World Since 1935.* London: G.G. Harrap, 1956.

International Theatre Institute. *Stage Design Throughout the World Since 1950.* Middletown, Conn.: Wesleyan University Press, 1964.

Jenkins, David Fraser, et al. *John Piper.* London: Tate Gallery of Art, 1983. (Catalogue of exhibition at the Tate Gallery).

Jones, Robert Edmond. *The Dramatic Imagination.* New York: Theatre Arts Books, 1941.

Jones, Robert Edmond. *Drawings for the Theatre.* New York: Theatre Art Books, 1978.

Komisarjevsky, Theodore, and Lee Simonson. *Settings and Costumes for the Modern Stage.* New York: Benjamin Blom, 1966.

Lacy, Robin Thurlow. *A Biographical Dictionary of Scenographers, 500 B.C. to 1900 A.D.* New York: Greenwood Press, 1990.

Larson, Orville K. *Scene design for Stage and Screen.* East Lansing, Mich.: Michigan State University Press, 1961.

MacGown, Kenneth, and Robert Edmond Jones. *Continental Stagecraft.* New York: Benjamin Blom, 1964.

Marion Koogler McNay Art Museum. *Robert Edmond Jones and the American Theatre.* San Antonio, Tex.: Marion Koogler McNay Art Museum, 1986.

Melvill, Harald. *Designing and Painting Scenery for the Theatre.* London: Art Trade Press, 1963.

Mielziner, Jo. *Designing for the Theatre.* New York: Atheneum, 1965.

Minnelli, Vincente. *Vincente Minnelli from Stage to Screen.* Palm Springs: The Museum, 1983.

Oenslager, Donald. *Stage Design: Four Centuries of Scenic Invention.* New York: Viking Press, 1975.

Oenslager, Donald. *Scenery Then and Now.* New York: Russell and Russell, 1966.

Oenslager, Donald. *The Theatre of Donald Oenslager.* Middletown, Conn.: Wesleyan University Press, 1978.

Ptackova, Vera. *Josef Svoboda.* Praha: Divadelni Ustav, 1984.

Pecktal, Lynn. *Designing and Painting for the Theatre.* New York: Holt, Reinhart, and Winston, 1975.

Rischbieter, Henning (ed.) *Art and the Stage in the 20th Century.* Greenwich, Conn.: Greenwood Press, 1969.

Rich, Frank. *The Theatre Art of Boris Aronson.* New York: Knopf, 1967.

Rischbieter, Henning. *Art and the Stage in the 20th Century.* Greenwich, Conn.: New York Graphic Society, 1968.

Rowell, Kenneth. *Stage Design.* London: Studio Vista, 1968.

Sainthill, Loudon. *Loudon Sainthill.* London: Hutchinson, 1973.

Sayler, Oliver Martin. *Max Reinhardt and His Theatre.* New York: Benjamin Blom, 1968.

Schouvaloff, Alexander. *Set and Costume Designs for Ballet and Theatre.* (Catalogue of the Thyssen-Bornemisza Collection). London, 1987

Sheringham, George and Laver, James (eds.) *Design in the Theatre.* London: The Studio, Ltd., 1927.

Simonson, Lee. *The Stage is Set.* New York: Theatre Arts Books, 1932.

Simonson, Lee. *The Designer in the Theatre.* New York, 1934.

Simonson, Lee. *The Art of Scenic Design.* New York: Reinhold, 1950.

Smith, Ronn. *American Set Design 2.* New York: Theatre Communications Group, 1991.

Strzelecki, Zenobiusz. *Wspo Czesna Scenografia Polska.* Warszawa: Arkady. 1983-1984.

Welker, David Harold. *Theatrical Set Design, The Basic Techniques.* Boston: Allyn and Bacon, 1969.

Willett, John. *Caspar Neher, Brecht's Designer.* London, New York: Methuen, 1986.

Index of Plays

The plays in this index can be found listed under the scenic designer's name in the main portion of the text.

About the Author

BOBBI OWEN is Associate Professor of Dramatic Art, University of North Carolina at Chapel Hill. She is the author of the parallel volumes *Costume Design on Broadway* (Greenwood, 1987) and *Lighting Design on Broadway* (Greenwood, 1991), and she has contributed articles on design and designers to *Notable Women in the American Theatre* (Greenwood, 1989) and the forthcoming *Cambridge Guide to American Theatre*.